# Table of Contents

SECOND EDITION

# Java Web Services:
# Up and Running

*Martin Kalin*

O'REILLY®

mbridge · Farnham · Köln · Sebastopol · Tokyo

Java Web Services: Up and Running, Second Edition

by Martin Kalin

Printed in the United States of America.

Published by O'Reilly Media, Inc., 1005 Gravenstein Highway North, Sebastopol, CA 95472.

O'Reilly books may be purchased for educational, business, or sales promotional use. Online editions are also available for most titles (*http://my.safaribooksonline.com*). For more information, contact our corporate/institutional sales department: 800-998-9938 or *corporate@oreilly.com*.

| | |
|---|---|
| **Editor:** Meghan Blanchette | **Indexer:** Judith McConville |
| **Production Editor:** Rachel Steely | **Cover Designer:** Randy Comer |
| **Copyeditor:** Rachel Leach | **Interior Designer:** David Futato |
| **Proofreader:** BIM Indexing and Proofreading Services | **Illustrator:** Rebecca Demarest |

September 2013: Second Edition

**Revision History for the Second Edition:**

2013-08-23: First release

See *http://oreilly.com/catalog/errata.csp?isbn=9781449365110* for release details.

ISBN: 978-1-449-36511-0

[LSI]

# Preface

Welcome to the second edition of *Java Web Services: Up and Running*. This edition, like the first, is for programmers interested in developing web services and clients against such services. This edition, again like the first, emphasizes code. My aim is to make web services and their clients come alive through focused but realistic programming examples in Java but, of course, in other languages as well: web services are designed to be language-neutral, a point best illustrated through the interaction of services and clients written in different languages. Indeed, the client of a well-designed web service can remain agnostic about the service's implementation details, including the language in which the service is written. To ease the task of compiling and publishing services, the ZIP file with the code samples includes an Ant script that compiles, packages, and deploys web services. The major client examples include either Ant scripts for compiling and running the clients or executable JAR files with all of the dependencies included therein. The code examples are available at *https://github.com/mkalin/jwsur2*.

## What's Changed in the Second Edition?

In the four years or so since the first edition, there has been continuity as well as change. Web services remain a popular and arguably even dominant approach toward *distributed software systems*—that is, systems that require the interaction of software on physically distinct devices. The Web itself is a prime example of a distributed system, and the current trend is to blur the distinction between traditional, HTML-centric *websites* and modern *web services*, which typically deliver XML or JSON payloads instead of HTML ones. Web services are an appealing way to create distributed systems because these services can piggyback on existing infrastructure such as HTTP(S) transport, web servers, database systems, modern programming languages of various stripes, widespread software libraries for JSON and XML processing, security providers, and so on. Indeed, web services are a lightweight and flexible way to integrate divergent software systems and to make the functionality of such systems readily accessible.

Java remains a major player in web services, and Java support for these services, in the form of standard and third-party software libraries and utilities, continues to improve. Yet two important and related shifts in emphasis have occurred since this book was first published:

- The consumers or clients of web services are increasingly written in JavaScript, particularly in the jQuery dialect, and these clients naturally prefer response payloads in JSON (JavaScript Object Notation) rather than in XML because a JSON document is the text representation of a native JavaScript object. A JavaScript client that receives, for example, an array of products as a JSON rather than an XML document can process the array with the usual JavaScript programming constructs. By contrast, a JavaScript client that receives an XML payload would face a challenge common across programming languages: the challenge of parsing an XML document to extract its informational content before moving on to specific application logic. Modern web services and web service frameworks acknowledge the growing popularity of JSON by treating JSON and XML formats as equals. In some frameworks, such as Rails, JSON even gets the nod over XML.

- REST-style services are increasingly popular among familiar sites such as eBay, Facebook, LinkedIn, Tumblr, and Twitter. Amazon, a web service pioneer, continues to support REST-style and SOAP-based versions of its services. The services from newer players tend to be REST-style for an obvious reason: REST-style services are relatively low fuss and their APIs are correspondingly simple. SOAP-based services still are delivered mostly over HTTP(S), although Java and DotNet continue to explore the use of other protocols, especially TCP, for transport. The first edition of this book underscored that SOAP-based services over HTTP can be seen as a special case of REST-style services; the second edition pursues the same theme.

The two changes in web services are reflected in how the second edition is organized. Chapter 1 begins with an overview of web services, including the link between such services and Service-Oriented Architecture (SOA), and the chapter includes a code-based contrast of SOA and the competing Distributed Object Architecture (DOA). The discussion then turns to REST: what the acronym means, why HTTP can be treated as an API and not just a transport, and how the RESTful mindset continues to impact the design and implementation of modern web services. The first chapter includes sample HTTP clients in Java, clients that can be targeted at either websites or web services. The first chapter ends with a RESTful service implemented as a JSP script with support from two backend POJO classes; the service is published with the Tomcat web server. The first chapter goes into the details of installing and running Tomcat; the second chapter does the same for the Jetty web server. The aforementioned Ant script is also clarified so that the sample web services can be packaged and deployed automatically.

Although this edition of the book starts with REST-style services, SOAP-based services are treated thoroughly. Chapter 4 covers SOAP-based services at the *application level,* a level in which the SOAP remains transparent; Chapter 5 explores the *handler* and the *transport* levels at which the SOAP is exposed for inspection and manipulation. Starting with REST-style services helps to explain the advantages that come with SOAP-based services, in particular the benefit of having the XML remain mostly under the hood. Issues such as security cut across the REST/SOAP boundary, and Chapter 6 is dedicated to practical web security, from wire-level security through users/roles security up to WS-Security.

# Web Service APIs and Publication Options

In the first edition, the JAX-WS APIs and their Metro implementation were dominant. In this edition, the two are important but less dominant. For REST-style services, the book has examples based on the following APIs:

HttpServlet

> The HttpServlet is well designed for REST-style services because the API is so close to the HTTP metal. Servlet instances encapsulate callbacks such as doPost, doGet, doPut, and doDelete, which cover the familiar CRUD operations: *create* (POST), *read* (GET), *update* (PUT), and *delete* (DELETE). There are symbolic versions of HTTP status codes to signal the outcome of an HTTP request, support for MIME types, utilities to access HTTP headers and bodies, and so on. JSP and other Java-based scripts execute as servlet instances and, therefore, fall under the servlet umbrella. The HttpServlet is grizzled but hardly obsolete. Servlets are still an excellent way to deliver REST-style services.

*JAX-RS*

> This is a relatively recent and increasingly popular API for delivering REST-style services. The API centers on annotations such as @GET and @POST to route HTTP requests to particular Java methods. There is likewise a convenient @Path annotation to identify the particular resource targeted in a request. JAX-RS can be configured to automatically generate XML and JSON responses. This API, like the Restlet API described next, has a contemporary look and feel. At the implementation level, JAX-RS represents a layering atop servlets. The same options for publishing servlet-based services are available for their JAX-RS cousins.

*Restlet*

> This API is similar in style to JAX-RS, although the claim is likely to upset proponents of both. The Restlet API also centers on annotations for routing HTTP requests to designated Java methods and for generating payloads. Restlet encourages interplay with other APIs. It is possible, for example, to use JAX-RS annotations in a Restlet-based service. Restlet offers an easy-to-use publisher for development and testing. Restlet services, like their JAX-RS counterparts, represent an

implementation level on top of servlets. Programmers should be able to move easily between the JAX-RS and Restlet APIs.

*JAX-WS* @WebServiceProvider

This is a deliberately XML-centric and low-level API that could be used for either SOAP-based or REST-style services. However, JAX-WS has the @WebService annotation precisely for SOAP-based services; hence, the most obvious use of the @WebServiceProvider annotation is for XML-based REST-style services. This API is well suited for services that require granular control over XML generation and processing.

For SOAP-based services, most of the examples use the reference implementation of JAX-WS, which is Metro. However, this edition now covers Axis2 as well. Axis2 implements JAX-WS but has additional features.

## The Publication Options

Each of these APIs, whether for REST-style or SOAP-based services, honors the separation-of-concerns principle with respect to publishing a web service. The web service is one concern; its publication is quite another concern. Services developed with any of these APIs can be published with a standalone web server such as Tomcat, a Java Application Server (JAS) such as GlassFish, or even with a simple command-line utility such as the standard Endpoint publisher. To underscore the separation-of-concerns principle and to emphasize the production-grade options, my examples are published in the following ways:

*Standalone web servers*

The two obvious choices in Java are Tomcat and Jetty, although other choices are available. The aforementioned Ant script automatically compiles and packages web services, REST-style and SOAP-based alike, for publication. Although the Ant script is tailored for Tomcat publication, a generated WAR file can be deployed, as is, to Jetty, Tomcat, or one of the many JASes. Tomcat and Jetty provide the usual services such as wire-level and users/roles security, logging/debugging, and administration that one expects from a production-grade web server.

*Java Application Servers*

The reference implementation is still GlassFish, which is part of the community-based Metro project. GlassFish can be used to publish either *servlet-based* services, which are the type that Tomcat and Jetty can publish, or *EJB-based* services, which are @Stateless Session Enterprise JavaBeans. TomEE, which is essentially Tomcat7 with OpenEJB extensions, is an emphatically lightweight publisher of both servlet-based and EJB-based services. Under TomEE, even an EJB-based service can be deployed as a standard WAR (Web ARchive) file. TomEE includes an implementation of JAX-RS.

*Command-line publishers*

Examples are the standard `Endpoint` utility class and the Restlet `Component` class. These publishers are useful for development, testing, and even low-volume production.

Java in general draws strength from the many options that the language and the runtime offer; this strength carries over to web services as well. There are many ways to program web services and web service clients in Java, and there are various attractive options for publishing such services. There is no need to claim any particular way in web services as the best way. My aim is to examine and clarify the choices so that in the end, the API, implementation, and method of publication can be determined by what is best suited for the service.

# Chapter-by-Chapter Overview

The second edition has seven chapters. The following list offers a summary of each chapter.

*Chapter 1, Web Services Quickstart*

This chapter begins the code-driven tour of web services with an overview of the differences—and the similarities—between REST and SOAP. Why are web services of any use? This question is addressed with examples: one example focuses on using web services to automate access to the data and functionality available on the Web; the other example focuses on web services as a way to integrate diverse software systems. The theme of *interoperability* is pursued throughout the book with examples. Chapter 1 includes a short history of web services, with emphasis on how the SOA approach to distributed systems differs significantly from the DOA approach that predates yet continues to compete with web services. The chapter then focuses on how HTTP itself is at the center of the RESTful way to web-based, distributed software systems. XML and JSON are introduced as document-exchange formats of special interest in RESTful services. The chapter includes code examples: a pair of Java HTTP clients used to illustrate key features of HTTP; and a first RESTful service, which consists of a JSP script and two backend POJO classes. The *curl* utility is used to make sample client calls, including failed ones, against the first service. The chapter covers practical matters such as installing the Tomcat web server and using the provided Ant script to compile, package, and deploy a web service.

*Chapter 2, RESTful Web Services: The Service Side*

This chapter introduces various APIs and implementations available for programming and delivering RESTful web services in Java. The `HttpServlet`, JAX-RS, Restlet, and JAX-WS `@WebServiceProvider` APIs are explored through full code examples. The chapter clarifies various ways of generating XML and JSON payloads, using both standard Java classes and different third-party ones. The code examples adhere to RESTful principles such as honoring the intended meaning of each CRUD verb; using intuitive URIs to name resources; relying upon MIME data types to describe resource representations; and taking full advantage of those HTTP status codes that report on the outcome of an HTTP request against a RESTful service. Chapter 2, along with later chapters, looks at options for publishing RESTful services. The options include standalone web servers such as Tomcat and Jetty together with command-line publishers such as `Endpoint`, `HttpServer`, and Restlet `Compo nent`. The chapter goes into the technical details of multithreading and thread synchronization in services deployed with a web server such as Tomcat or Jetty. The installation and management of Jetty are also covered. Chapter 2 also takes a first look at the powerful JAX-B (Java API for XML-Binding) and JAX-P (Java API for XML-Processing) utilities, which are especially important in the Chapter 3 coverage of the client side in RESTful services.

*Chapter 3, RESTful Web Services: The Client Side*

This chapter shifts focus from the service to the client side of RESTful services. There are sample clients written with the weathered but still trusty `URLConnec tion` class and also clients written using REST-specific APIs. (JAX-RS, Restlet, and JAX-WS provide both service-side and client-side APIs.) As evidence of interoperability, the chapter offers jQuery and Perl clients against Java services and Java clients against commercial services whose implementation language is officially unknown. The code samples explore various possibilities for dealing with XML and JSON payloads, in particular the standard JAX-B packages and third-party contributions such as `XStream`. These utilities are especially useful in transforming XML documents into native Java objects, which obviates the need for explicit parsing. Most RESTful services now furnish a grammar, in the form of an XML Schema or equivalent, for the service; core Java has utilities such as *xjc* that convert an XML Schema into Java classes. Chapter 3 has clients against real-world RESTful services at Twitter, Amazon, and the Chicago Transit Authority. This chapter pays special attention to the growing importance of JavaScript clients, which are highlighted in several examples using jQuery. Finally, the chapter shows how distinct web services can be orchestrated to form a single, composite service.

*Chapter 4, SOAP-Based Web Services*

This chapter turns from REST-style to SOAP-based services, in particular to the JAX-WS API and its central annotation `@WebService`. The chapter opens by converting a REST-style service from earlier chapters to a SOAP-based service. The emphasis in this chapter is on the application level, a level in which the XML in SOAP-based messaging remains transparent. Indeed, a chief attraction of SOAP-based services is that neither the services nor their clients require any attention to the underlying XML: service operations are, in Java, `public` methods preferably annotated with `@WebMethod`, and remote clients invoke the operations straightforwardly. The data types of arguments and return values include all of the primitive types and their wrappers, the `String` and `Calendar` types, various other standard types, arrays of any acceptable type, and programmer-defined classes whose properties reduce ultimately to any of these. The chapter explains in detail the programmer-friendly *wsimport* utility, which generates client-side support code from the web service contract, the WSDL (Web Service Description Language) document. The structure, purpose, and various uses of the WSDL are clarified through coding examples. The role of XML Schema or equivalent in a WSDL document is given particular emphasis. The chapter includes two Java clients against the Amazon E-Commerce service together with C# and Perl clients against a Java service. These examples underscore that SOAP-based services, like their REST-style cousins, are language-neutral. The clients against the SOAP-based version of the Amazon E-Commerce service introduce but do not explore the handler level of SOAP-based services; these examples also provide a first look at security issues.

*Chapter 5, SOAP Handlers and Faults*

This chapter examines the handler and transport levels in SOAP messaging, levels at which the XML in a SOAP message comes to the fore for inspection and manipulation. The chapter begins with a look at the SOAP message architecture, which distinguishes among a message *sender*; an *intermediary* that should confine its activity to the SOAP header rather than the SOAP body or attachments in a message; and an ultimate *receiver*, which should have access to the entire SOAP message. The distinct parts of SOAP messages, the raw XML and any attachments, are accessible to SOAP handlers, which come in two flavors: *message handlers* have access to the entire SOAP message (header, body, and attachments), whereas *logical handlers* have access only to the payload in the body. WS-Security and related extensions of SOAP beyond the *basic profile* may use such access to inject or inspect security elements in SOAP headers. Handlers are akin to `Filter` instances in websites, although handlers are inherently bidirectional and can occur on either the client or the service side. The chapter covers both individual handlers and handler chains, in this case a chain consisting of a message and a logical handler. The handler chain example mimics the user authentication at work in Amazon's web services. The chapter likewise examines the related topic of SOAP *faults*, special error messages that can be generated at either the application or the handler level. The chapter also looks at how SOAP messages can transport arbitrary binary data as attachments. A final topic is the transport level, usually HTTP; this level is especially useful in the users/roles security examined in Chapter 6.

*Chapter 6, Web Services Security*

This chapter covers security, a topic that cuts across the REST/SOAP boundary, at three levels: wire-level security of the type that HTTPS provides, users/roles security, and WS-Security in SOAP-based messaging. The chapter begins with wire-level security and its constituent services of *peer authentication*, *message confidentiality*, and *message integrity*. The clarification of these terms requires, in turn, an examination of concepts such as *symmetric* and *asymmetric* encryption/ decryption, *public key security, cryptographic hash function,* and *cryptographic suite.* HTTPS is examined in detail through coding examples: two HTTPS clients against the Google site and a lightweight HTTPS server built with the HttpsServer class that comes with the core Java JDK. There is also a sample HTTPS client against a RESTful service. These and other coding examples clarify additional security artifacts such as the *keystore* and the *truststore, digital certificates,* and *certificate authority.* There is a section to explain how a web server such as Tomcat can be set up to handle and even to enforce HTTPS connections. Chapter 6 also covers *container-managed* users/roles security, again with coding examples that involve a production-grade web server such as Tomcat. The two-phased user authentication and roles authorization process is studied in detail and includes examples of HTTP BASIC and DIGEST authentication. The chapter ends with a code example focused on WS-Security and its end-to-end approach to security.

*Chapter 7, Web Services and Java Application Servers*

This chapter introduces the Java Application Server as an alternative to the standalone web server for deploying REST-style and SOAP-based services. The JAS as a service publisher also brings the option of deploying a web service as an EJB, in particular a web service as a @Stateless Session EJB. The chapter begins with a list of the popular JASes and then clarifies the core components and attendant functionalities of a JAS. There is a review of how sample services from previous chapters —from HttpServlet examples through JAX-RS, Restlet, @WebServiceProvider, and @WebService examples—can be ported to a JAS. In all cases, almost no change is required. Chapter 7 also motivates the option of a JAS, in particular the benefits that come with deploying a service in the thread-safe EJB container. A typical JAS is not only a publisher but also a development, testing, and management environment. This chapter has a further coding example of how web services and websites can interact, and the excellent JPA (Java Persistence API) is introduced with two coding examples that persist data in different databases: HSQLDB and Java Derby. The chapter introduces two JASes through code examples: GlassFish, which is the reference implementation, and TomEE, which is an emphatically lightweight option among JASes. Various sidebars explain installation and management details. The chapter ends with a review and a recommendation that programmers embrace the many excellent choices of API and implementation that Java offers in the area of web services.

# Tools and IDEs

Java programmers have a wide choice of productivity tools. Among the build tools are Ant, Maven, and Meister; among the many testing tools are EasyMock, JMockit, JUnit, Mockito, and TestNG. Java likewise offers choices among IDEs, including Eclipse,

IntelliJ IDEA, and NetBeans. In a production environment, tools and IDEs are the way to go as they hide the grimy details that slow the journey from initial design through deployment and maintenance. In a learning environment, a build tool makes sense because it facilitates experimentation. My Ant script is meant to serve this purpose: it allows a web service, with all of the dependencies, to be compiled, built, and deployed with a single command:

```
% ant deploy -Dwar.name=myFirstService
```

Chapter 1 goes into the setup details, which are minimal.

With respect to IDEs, this second edition is, like the first, neutral. The very grimy details that are an obstacle in a production environment are critical in a learning environment. For that reason, my code examples include all of the import statements so that dependencies are clear. Package/directory structure is explained whenever third-party libraries are used. The code listings usually have numbered statements and expressions for ease of reference and explanation. The examples themselves are designed to highlight the challenges inherent in any serious programming, but these examples also focus on patterned approaches to meeting the challenges. Web services and their clients are, in the end, code—and this book focuses on code.

# Conventions Used in This Book

The following typographical conventions are used in this book:

*Italic*
    Indicates new terms, URLs, filenames, file extensions, and emphasis.

`Constant width`
    Used for program listings as well as within paragraphs to refer to program elements such as variable or method names, data types, environment variables, statements, and keywords.

*Sidebars*
    The book uses sidebars (see "This Is a Sidebar" on page xv) to focus on particular topics. Sidebars often contain practical information about installing and running applications such as a standalone web server or a Java Application Server.

---

### This Is a Sidebar

A topic of special interest.

---

# Using Code Examples

This book is here to help you get your job done. In general, if this book includes code examples, you may use the code in your programs and documentation. You do not need to contact us for permission unless you're reproducing a significant portion of the code. For example, writing a program that uses several chunks of code from this book does not require permission. Selling or distributing a CD-ROM of examples from O'Reilly books does require permission. Answering a question by citing this book and quoting example code does not require permission. Incorporating a significant amount of example code from this book into your product's documentation does require permission.

We appreciate, but do not require, attribution. An attribution usually includes the title, author, publisher, and ISBN. For example: "*Java Web Services: Up and Running*, Second Edition, by Martin Kalin. Copyright 2013 Martin Kalin, 978-1-449-36511-0."

If you feel your use of code examples falls outside fair use or the permission given above, feel free to contact us at *permissions@oreilly.com*.

# Safari® Books Online

 *Safari Books Online* is an on-demand digital library that delivers expert content in both book and video form from the world's leading authors in technology and business.

Technology professionals, software developers, web designers, and business and creative professionals use Safari Books Online as their primary resource for research, problem solving, learning, and certification training.

Safari Books Online offers a range of product mixes and pricing programs for organizations, government agencies, and individuals. Subscribers have access to thousands of books, training videos, and prepublication manuscripts in one fully searchable database from publishers like O'Reilly Media, Prentice Hall Professional, Addison-Wesley Professional, Microsoft Press, Sams, Que, Peachpit Press, Focal Press, Cisco Press, John Wiley & Sons, Syngress, Morgan Kaufmann, IBM Redbooks, Packt, Adobe Press, FT Press, Apress, Manning, New Riders, McGraw-Hill, Jones & Bartlett, Course Technology, and dozens more. For more information about Safari Books Online, please visit us online.

# How to Contact Us

Please address comments and questions concerning this book to the publisher:

O'Reilly Media, Inc.
1005 Gravenstein Highway North
Sebastopol, CA 95472
800-998-9938 (in the United States or Canada)
707-829-0515 (international or local)
707-829-0104 (fax)

We have a web page for this book, where we list errata, examples, and any additional information. You can access this page at *http://oreil.ly/Java_web_services*.

To comment or ask technical questions about this book, send email to *bookques tions@oreilly.com*.

For more information about our books, courses, conferences, and news, see our website at *http://www.oreilly.com*.

Find us on Facebook: *http://facebook.com/oreilly*

Follow us on Twitter: *http://twitter.com/oreillymedia*

Watch us on YouTube: *http://www.youtube.com/oreillymedia*

# Acknowledgments

Edward Yue Shung Wong and Ken Yu were generous enough to review this book and offer many insightful suggestions for its improvement. They made the book better than it otherwise would have been. I thank them heartily for the time and effort that they invested in this project. The remaining shortcomings are mine alone, of course. Meghan Blanchette, my editor, has provided invaluable support, and the book would not be without her help. My thanks go as well to the many behind-the-scenes people at O'Reilly Media who worked on this project.

This edition, like the first, is dedicated to Janet.

# Web Services Quickstart

Although the term *web service* has various, imprecise, and evolving meanings, a working definition should be enough for the upcoming code example, which consists of a service and a client, also known as a consumer or requester. As the name suggests, a web service is a kind of webified application—an application typically delivered over HTTP (HyperText Transport Protocol). HTTPS (HTTP Secure) adds a security layer to HTTP; hence, a service delivered over HTTPS likewise counts as a web service. Until the main topic of interest is web service security, HTTP should be understood to include HTTPS.

Amazon, a pioneer in web services, is well known for its various websites, among which is the E-Commerce site for shopping. Amazon has other popular websites as well. Of interest here is that the data and functionality available at Amazon websites are likewise available as Amazon web services. For example, someone can use a browser to shop interactively at the Amazon E-Commerce site, but this person also could write a program, as later examples show, to do the shopping through the corresponding Amazon E-Commerce web service. Amazon is particularly good at pairing off its websites with web services.

Web services can be programmed in a variety of languages, old and new. The obvious way to publish a web service is with a web server; a web service client needs to execute on a machine that has network access, usually over HTTP, to the web server. In more technical terms, a web service is a distributed software system whose components can be deployed and executed on physically distinct devices. Consider, for example, a web server *host1* that hosts a web service and a mobile device *host2* that hosts an application issuing requests against the service on *host1* (see Figure 1-1). Web services may be more architecturally complicated than this, of course; for one thing, a service may have many clients issuing requests against it, and the service itself may be composed of other services. For instance, a stock-picking web service might consist of several code components, each hosted on a separate commercial-grade web server, and any mix of PCs, handhelds, and other networked devices might host programs that consume the service. Although the building blocks of web services are relatively simple, the web services themselves can be arbitrarily complex.

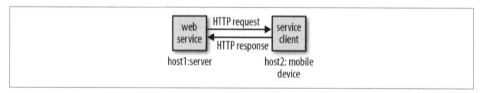

*Figure 1-1. A web service and one of its clients*

An HTTP request goes, by definition, from client to server, and an HTTP response goes, also by definition, from server to client. For web services over HTTP, the HTTP messages are the infrastructure, and these HTTP messages can be combined into basic conversational patterns that characterize a web service. For example, if the web service conversation starts with an HTTP request that expects an HTTP response, the pattern is the familiar *request/response* conversation. By contrast, if the conversation starts with an HTTP message from the server, a message that expects a message from the client in return, then the pattern is *solicit/response*. Richer conversational patterns can be composed out of such basic two-message patterns. Indeed, these two-message patterns are composed of even more primitive ones: a message from client to server without a response is a pattern known as *one-way,* and the reverse pattern, from server to client without a client response, is known as *notification*. Web services tend to be simple in structure. The four conversational patterns enumerated just now cover most modern web services, and request/response is the pattern that still dominates.

Web services come in two popular flavors: SOAP-based and REST-style. SOAP is an XML dialect with a grammar that specifies the structure that a document must have in order to count as SOAP. In a typical SOAP-based service, the client sends SOAP messages to the service and the service responds in kind, with SOAP messages. REST-style services are hard to characterize in a sentence or two, but with respect to pattern, these services tend to be request/response; the same holds for SOAP-based services. For now, a REST-style service is one that treats HTTP not only as transport infrastructure but also as a set of guidelines for designing service requests and service responses. In a REST-style service, HTTP itself can be seen as an API. SOAP has standards, toolkits, and bountiful software libraries. REST has no official standards, comparatively few toolkits, and uneven software libraries among programming languages. Yet there is growing support for REST-style services across programming languages; hence, it seems only a matter of time until toolkits and libraries for REST-style services mature.

From a historical perspective, the RESTful approach to web services can be viewed as an antidote to the creeping complexity of SOAP-based web services. SOAP-based services are designed to be transport-neutral; as a result, SOAP messaging may seem overly complicated if the transport is, in fact, HTTP. This book covers SOAP-based and

REST-style web services, starting with REST-style ones. This chapter ends with a sample REST-style service and sample client calls against the service. At present, the distinction between the two flavors of web service is not sharp, because a SOAP-based service delivered over HTTP can be seen as a special case of a REST-style service; HTTP remains the dominant transport for SOAP-based services.

SOAP originally stood for Simple Object Access Protocol and then, by serendipity but never officially, might have stood for Service-Oriented Architecture (SOA) Protocol. (SOA is discussed in the section "Web Services and Service-Oriented Architecture" on page 7.) The World Wide Web Consortium (hereafter, W3C) currently oversees SOAP, and SOAP is officially no longer an acronym.

# Web Service Miscellany

Except in test mode, the client of either a SOAP-based or REST-style service is rarely a web browser but, rather, usually an application without a graphical user interface. The client may be written in any language with the appropriate support libraries. Indeed, a major appeal of web services is language transparency: the service and its clients need not be written in the same language. Language transparency is a key contributor to web service interoperability—that is, the ability of web services and their consumers to interact seamlessly despite differences in programming languages, support libraries, operating systems, and hardware platforms. To underscore this appeal, my examples use a mix of languages besides Java, among them C#, JavaScript, and Perl. My sample clients in Java consume services written in languages other than Java; indeed, sometimes in languages unknown.

There is no magic in language transparency, of course. If a web service written in Java can have a Python or a Ruby consumer, there must be an intermediary layer that handles the differences in data types between the service and the client languages. XML technologies, which support structured document interchange and processing, act as one such intermediary level. Another intermediary level is JSON (JavaScript Object Notation). XML and JSON are both data-interchange formats, but JSON clearly has the upper hand with data receivers written in JavaScript because a JSON document is the text representation of a native JavaScript object. Web service clients are increasingly JavaScript programs embedded in HTML documents and executing in a browser; such clients process JSON with less fuss than they do XML. Even among non-JavaScript clients, JSON has gained in popularity; for one thing, JSON is more readable than XML because JSON has relatively less markup. Chapter 2 illustrates various ways in which REST-style services can generate XML and JSON payloads; Chapter 3 focuses on consuming XML and JSON payloads from RESTful web services. In SOAP-based services, XML remains the dominant format, although the DotNet framework is especially good at giving JSON equal status.

Several features distinguish web services from other distributed software systems. Here are three:

*Open infrastructure*

Web services are deployed using industry-standard, vendor-independent protocols and languages such as HTTP, XML, and JSON, all of which are ubiquitous and well understood. Web services can piggyback on networking, data formatting, security, and other infrastructures already in place, which lowers entry costs and promotes interoperability among services. Organizations that publish websites with production-grade web servers such as Apache2, IIS, and Nginx can publish web services with these very web servers. Firewalls and other security mechanisms that defend websites thereby defend web services as well.

*Platform and language transparency*

Web services and their clients can interoperate even if written in different programming languages. Languages such as C, C#, Go, Java, JavaScript, Perl, Python, Ruby, and others provide libraries, utilities, and even frameworks in support of web services. Web services can be published and consumed on various hardware platforms and under different operating systems. Web services are an excellent way to integrate diverse software systems while allowing the programmer to work in the programmer's language of choice. The web service approach to software development is not to rewrite but, rather, to integrate.

*Modular design*

Web services are meant to be modular in design so that new services can be composed out of existing ones. Imagine, for example, an inventory-tracking service integrated with an online ordering service to compose a service that automatically orders the appropriate products in response to inventory levels. Web services are the small software parts out of which arbitrarily large systems can be built. A guiding principle in web service design is to begin with very simple service operations, essentially uncomplicated functions, and then group these operations into services, which in turn can be orchestrated to work with other services, and so on indefinitely.

# What Good Are Web Services?

This obvious question has no simple answer, but the benefits and promises of web services can be clarified with examples. The first example underscores how the distinction between *websites* and *web services* continues to blur: the data and functionality available at one can be available at the other. (One web framework that emphasizes the blurring is Rails, which is discussed in more detail later.) The second example focuses on how web services can be used to integrate diverse software systems and to make legacy systems more widely accessible.

A visit to a website such as the Amazon E-Commerce (*http://www.amazon.com*) site is often interactive: a shopper uses a browser to search the Amazon site for desired items, places some of these in a shopping cart, checks out the cart, finalizes the order with a credit card or the equivalent, and receives a confirmation page and usually an email. Pioneers in web services, such as Amazon, expose the information and functionality of websites through web services as well. Searching and shopping against Amazon, as code examples in later chapters illustrate, are tasks that are automated readily because Amazon makes a point of coordinating its websites with its web services. In any case, here is a sketch of how a search-and-shop experience might be automated.

1. A shopper has a database table or even a simple text file, *wishList.txt*, that contains items of interest such as books, movies, or any other search-and-shop category that Amazon supports.

2. The database table or text file, which acts as a wish list with constraints, provides pertinent information such as the ISBN of a desired book, the maximum price the shopper is willing to pay, the number of items to order, and so on.

3. The shopper programs a client, in whatever language the shopper prefers, that reads the database table or text file, opens a connection to Amazon, searches Amazon for wishlist items, checks whether the items are available under the constraints in the wishlist, and orders the items that meet the constraints.

4. The client program checks an email account for the confirming email; if all goes well, the client places confirmation information in a data store such as a database table or another simple text file.

An interactive shopping experience thus gives way to an automated one. Of course, some shoppers derive as much pleasure from the activity as from the outcome. The point is not that shopping should be automated but, rather, that web services open up this possibility for many tasks, shopping included. At one time, *HTML screen scraping* was a popular way to have applications other than browsers hit a website, download HTML documents, and then parse the HTML for its informational content. As more sites follow the Amazon practice of exposing the same or, at least, nearly the same data and functionality as both websites and web services, this screen scraping becomes increasingly unnecessary. Later chapters illustrate, with code examples, the close relationship between websites and web services.

The second example of what makes web services attractive focuses on a major challenge in modern software development: systems integration. Modern software systems are written in a variety of languages—a variety that seems likely to increase. These software systems will continue to be hosted on a variety of platforms. Institutions large and small have significant investment in legacy software systems whose functionality is useful and perhaps mission critical; few of these institutions have the will and the resources, human or financial, to rewrite their legacy systems. How are such disparate software systems to interact? That these systems must interact is taken for granted nowadays; it is a rare software system that gets to run in splendid isolation.

A challenge, then, is to have a software system interoperate with others, which may reside on different hosts under different operating systems and may be written in different languages. Interoperability is not just a long-term challenge but also a current requirement of production software. Web services provide a relatively simple answer to question of how diverse software systems, written in many languages and executing on various platforms under different operating systems, can interoperate. In short, web services are an excellent way to integrate software systems.

Web services address the problem of interoperability directly because such services are, first and foremost, language- and platform-neutral. If a legacy COBOL system is exposed through a web service, the system is thereby interoperable with service clients written in other currently more widely used languages. Exposing a legacy COBOL system as a web service should be significantly less expensive than, say, rewriting the system from scratch. Legacy database systems are an obvious source of data and functionality, and these systems, too, can be made readily accessible, beyond the local machine that hosts the database, through web services.

In the past, data sources for applications were usually *data stores* such as relational database management systems (RDBMS) or even local filesystems. Nowadays web services also serve as data sources, at least as intermediate ones that are backed up ultimately with persistent data stores. Indeed, web services integrate readily with RDBMS and other data storage systems as frontends that are easier conversational partners than the data storage systems themselves—because web services, at least well-designed ones, have APIs that publish their functionality in high-level, language-neutral, and platform-independent terms. A web service thus can be viewed as a uniform access mechanism for divergent data stores. A web service can act as the frontend of a database system, a frontend that exposes, through a published API, the data and the functionality of the database system (see Figure 1-2).

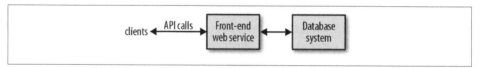

*Figure 1-2. A web service as the frontend of a data store*

Web services are inherently distributed systems that communicate mostly over HTTP but can communicate over other popular transports as well. The communication payloads of web services are typically structured text, usually XML or JSON documents, which can be inspected, transformed, persisted, and otherwise processed with widely and even freely available tools. When efficiency demands it, however, web services can also deliver compact binary payloads. Finally, web services are a work in progress with real-world distributed systems as their test bed. For all of these reasons, web services are an essential tool in any modern programmer's toolbox.

The examples that follow, in this and later chapters, are simple enough to isolate critical features of web services such as security but also realistic enough to illustrate the power and flexibility that such services bring to software development. The main service examples have an accompanying Ant script to compile and then publish the web service on a production-grade web server such as Tomcat or Jetty; many of the Java clients against web services are packaged as executable JAR files in order to reduce hassle.

As noted earlier, web services come in different flavors: SOAP-based and REST-style. SOAP and SOA, though related, remain distinct. The next section goes into detail about the relationship between SOA and REST-style and SOAP-based web services.

# Web Services and Service-Oriented Architecture

Web services and SOA are related but distinct. SOA, like REST, is more an architectural style—indeed, a mindset—than a body of precisely defined rules for the design and implementation of distributed systems; web services are a natural, important way to provide the services at the core of any SOA system. A fundamental idea in SOA is that an application results from integrating network-accessible services, which are interoperable because each has an interface that clearly defines the operations encapsulated in the service. Per operation, the interface specifies the number and type of each argument passed to the service operation together with the number and type of values returned from each service operation. The very point of a service interface is to publish the invocation syntax of each operation encapsulated in the service. One attraction of the SOA approach is that the ultimate building blocks of even large, complicated systems are structurally simple components; this simplicity at the base level makes it relatively easy to test, debug, deploy, extend, and otherwise maintain a software system.

In an SOA system, services as building block components may be characterized as *unassociated* and *loosely coupled*. Consider, for example, two primitive services, $S_1$ and $S_2$, in an SOA application. The two services are unassociated in that neither $S_1$ nor $S_2$ depends on the other: $S_1$ is not required to use $S_2$ or vice versa. The services are mutually independent but can be used together or orchestrated as parts of a larger software system. Following the same theme, components such as $S_1$ and $S_2$ are loosely coupled in that neither needs to know anything about the internal structure of the other in order for both of these services to work together as parts of a larger distributed system. A persistent theme in the many discussions of SOA is the modularity of SOA-based systems.

At the implementation level, a service operation is a function call: the function takes zero or more arguments and returns zero or more values. Although functions in many languages such as C and even Java technically return, at most, only a single value and therefore must resort to aggregate data structures such as a lists to return multiple values, newer languages such as Go have uncomplicated syntax for functions to return arbitrarily many values including, of course, none. This fact underscores the inherent richness and flexibility of the function as a system building block. Programmers fluent in virtually any language are thereby knowledgeable about the syntax and semantics of functions.

In an SOA system, a very simple service may consist of a single function. The implementation model is thus uncomplicated and familiar to programmers, and the simplicity of service operations promotes code reuse through the composition of new services out of existing ones. This ground-level simplicity also enables relatively straightforward troubleshooting because services reduce to primitive function calls. An SOA system can be quite complicated, of course, but the complication arises from the composition and not from the simple services into which the system ultimately decomposes.

Web services are well suited as components in an SOA system. Following best practices, a web service should consist of operations, each of which is implemented as a stateless function call: the call is *stateless* in that the return value(s) depend only on the arguments passed to the call. In an object-oriented language such as a Java, a well-designed web service is a class that has instance methods as service operations but no instance fields that impact the value returned from a particular method. In practice, *statelessness* is easier said than done, as the many examples in this book illustrate. In the context of SOA, it is common to distinguish between *providers* and *consumers* of web services: the provider furnishes the service's functionality, and the consumer is a client that issues requests against the service's operations. The provider/consumer pair is commonly used to describe web services and their clients, respectively.

Perhaps the best way to clarify SOA in the concrete is to contrast this approach to distributed systems with a quite different approach: DOA (Distributed Object Architecture). Web services came to fore as a reaction against the complexity of DOA systems. The next section provides a short history of web services, with emphasis on the kinds of software challenges that web services are meant to address.

# A Very Short History of Web Services

Web services evolved from the RPC (Remote Procedure Call) mechanism in DCE (Distributed Computing Environment), a framework for software development from the early 1990s. DCE includes a distributed filesystem (DCE/DFS) and a Kerberos-based authentication system. Although DCE has its origins in the Unix world, Microsoft quickly did its own implementation known as MSRPC, which in turn served as the infrastructure for interprocess communication in Windows. Microsoft's COM/OLE (Common Object Model/Object Linking and Embedding) technologies and services were built on a DCE/RPC foundation. There is irony here. DCE designed RPC as a way to do distributed computing (i.e., computing across distinct physical devices), and Microsoft cleverly adapted RPC to support interprocess communication, in the form of COM infrastructure, on a single device—a PC running Windows.

The first-generation frameworks for distributed object systems, CORBA (Common Object Request Broker Architecture) and Microsoft's DCOM (Distributed COM), are anchored in the DCE/RPC procedural framework. Java RMI (Remote Method Invocation) also derives from DCE/RPC, and the method calls in Java EE (Enterprise Edition), specifically in Session and Entity EJBs (Enterprise Java Bean), are Java RMI calls. Java EE (formerly J2EE) and Microsoft's DotNet are second-generation frameworks for distributed object systems, and these frameworks, like CORBA and DCOM before them, trace their ancestry back to DCE/RPC. By the way, DCE/RPC is not dead. Various popular system utilities (for instance, the Samba file and print service for Windows clients) use DCE/RPC.

## From DCE/RPC to XML-RPC

DCE/RPC has the familiar client/server architecture in which a client invokes a procedure that executes on the server. Arguments can be passed from the client to the server and return values can be passed from the server to the client. The framework is platform- and language- neutral in principle, although strongly tilted toward C in practice. DCE/RPC includes utilities for generating client and server artifacts (stubs and skeletons, respectively). DCE/RPC also provides software libraries that hide the transport details. Of interest now is the IDL (Interface Definition Language) document that acts as the service contract and is an input to utilities that generate artifacts in support of the DCE/RPC calls. An IDL document can be short and to the point (see Example 1-1).

*Example 1-1. A sample IDL document that declares the echo function*

```
/* echo.idl */
[uuid(2d6ead46-05e3-11ca-7dd1-426909beabcd), version(1.0)]
interface echo {
    const long int ECHO_SIZE = 512;
    void echo(
        [in]            handle_t h,
        [in,  string]   idl_char from_client[ ],
        [out, string]   idl_char from_server[ECHO_SIZE]
    );
}
```

The IDL interface named echo, identified with a machine-generated UUID (Universally Unique IDentifier), declares a single function with the same name, echo. The names are arbitrary and need not be the same. The echo function expects three arguments, two of which are in parameters (that is, inputs into the remote procedure) and one of which is an out parameter (that is, an output from the remote procedure). The first argument, of built-in type handle_t, is required and points to an RPC data structure. The function echo could but does not return a value, because the echoed string is returned instead as an out parameter. The IDL specifies the invocation syntax for the echo function, which is the one and only operation in the service. Except for annotations in square brackets to the left of the three echo parameters, the syntax of the IDL is essentially C syntax. The IDL document is a precursor of the WSDL (Web Service Description Language) document that provides a formal specification of a web service and its operations. The WSDL document is discussed at length in Chapter 4 on SOAP-based services.

There is a Microsoft twist to the IDL story as well. An ActiveX control under Windows is a DLL (Dynamic Link Library) with an embedded *typelib*, which in turn is a compiled IDL file. For example, suppose that a calendar ActiveX control is plugged into a browser. The browser can read the *typelib*, which contains the invocation syntax for each operation (e.g., displaying the next month) in the control. An ActiveX control is thus a chunk of software that embeds its own interface. This is yet another inspired local use of a technology designed for distributed computing.

In the late 1990s, Dave Winer of UserLand Software developed XML-RPC, a technology innovation that has as good a claim as any to mark the birth of web services. XML-RPC is a very lightweight RPC system with support for elementary data types (basically, the built-in C types together with a boolean and a datetime type) and a few simple commands. The original specification is about seven pages in length. The two key features are the use of XML marshaling/unmarshaling to achieve language neutrality and reliance on HTTP (and, later, SMTP) for transport. The term *marshaling* refers to the conversion of an in-memory object (for instance, an Employee object in Java) to some other format (for instance, an XML document); *unmarshaling* refers to the inverse process of generating an in-memory object from, in this example, an XML document. The marshal/unmarshal distinction is somewhere between close to and identical with the serialize/deserialize distinction. My habit is to use the distinctions interchangeably. In any case, the O'Reilly open-wire Meerkat service and the WordPress publishing platform are based on XML-RPC.

Two key differences separate XML-RPC, on the one side, from DCE/RPC and its offshoots, on the other side:

- XML-RPC payloads are text, whereas DCE/RPC payloads are binary. Text is relatively easy to inspect and process with standard, readily available tools such as editors and parsers.

- XML-RPC transport uses HTTP rather than a proprietary system. To support XML-RPC, a programming language requires only a standard HTTP library together with libraries to generate, parse, transform, and otherwise process XML.

As an RPC technology, XML-RPC supports the request/response pattern. Here is the XML request to invoke, on a remote machine, the Fibonacci function with an argument of 11. This argument is passed as a 4-byte integer, as the XML start tag <i4> indicates:

```
<?xml version="1.0">
<methodCall>
    <methodName>fib<methodName>
    <params>
      <param><value><i4>11</i4></value></param>
    </params>
</methodCall>
```

The integer 11 occurs in the XML-RPC message as text. An XML-RPC library on the receiving end needs to extract 11 as text and then convert the text into a 4-byte integer in the receiving language such as Go or Java. Even this short example illustrates the idea of having XML—in particular, data types expressed in XML—serve as the leveling mechanism between two different languages involved in an XML-RPC exchange.

XML-RPC is deliberately low fuss and lightweight. SOAP, an XML dialect derived straight from XML-RPC, is considerably heavier in weight. From inception, XML-RPC faced competition from second-generation DOA systems such as Java EE (J2EE) and AspNet. The next section considers the challenges inherent in DOA systems. These challenges sustained and eventually intensified interest in lighter-weight approaches to distributed computing—modern web services.

## Distributed Object Architecture: A Java Example

What advantages do web services have over DOA technologies such as Java RMI? This section addresses the question with an example. Java RMI (including the Session and Entity EJB constructs built on Java RMI) and DotNet Remoting are examples of second-generation distributed object systems. Consider what a Java RMI client requires in order to invoke a method declared in a service interface such as this:

```
import java.util.List;
public interface BenefitsService extends java.rmi.Remote {
    public List<Benefit> getBenefits(Emp emp) throws RemoteException;
}
```

The interface appears deceptively simple in that it declares only the method named `getBenefits`, yet the interface likewise hints at what makes a Distributed Object Architecture so tricky. A client against this `BenefitsService` requires a Java RMI stub, an instance of a class that implements the `BenefitsService` interface. The stub is downloaded automatically from the server to the client as part of the Java RMI setup (see Figure 1-3).

*Figure 1-3. Downloading a stub in Java RMI*

Once the stub setup is done, the `getBenefits` method is executed as a stub method; that is, the stub acts as the client-side object making a remote method call through one of stub's encapsulated methods. The call thus has the following syntax:

```
Emp fred = new Emp();
//...
List<Benefit> benefits = rmiStub.getBenefits(fred); // rmiStub = reference
```

Invoking the `getBenefits` method requires that the byte codes for various Java classes, standard and programmer-defined, be available on the client machine. To begin, the client needs the class `Emp`, the argument type for the `getBenefits` method, and the class `Benefit`, the member type for the `List` that the method `getBenefits` returns. Suppose that the class `Emp` begins like this:

```
public class Emp {
    private Department                       department;
    private List<BusinessCertification>  certifications;
    private List<ClientAccount>          accounts;
    private Map<String, Contact>         contacts;
    ...
}
```

The standard Java types such as `List` and `Map` are already available on the client side because the client is, by assumption, a Java application. The challenge involves the additional, programmer-defined types such as `Department`, `BusinessCertification`, `ClientAccount`, and `Contact` that are needed to support the client-side invocation of a remotely executed method. The setup on the client side to enable a remote call such as:

```
Emp fred = new Emp();
// set properties, etc.
List<EmpBenefits> fredBenefits = rmiStub.getBenefits(fred);
```

is significant, with lots and lots of bytes required to move from the server down to the client just for the setup. Anything this complicated is, of course, prone to problems such as versioning issues and outright errors in the remote method calls.

Java RMI uses proprietary marshaling/unmarshaling and proprietary transport, and DotNet does the same. There are third-party libraries for interoperability between the two frameworks. Yet a Java RMI service can be expected to have mostly Java clients, and a DotNet Remoting service can be expected to have mostly DotNet clients. Web services represent a move toward standardization, simplicity, and interoperability.

## Web Services to the Rescue

Web services simplify matters in distributed computing. For one thing, the client and service typically exchange XML or equivalent documents, that is, *text*. If needed, non-text bytes can be exchanged instead, but the preferred payloads are text. The exchanged text can be inspected, validated, transformed, persisted, and otherwise processed using readily available, nonproprietary, and often free tools. Each side, client and service, simply needs a local software library that binds language-specific types such as the Java String to XML Schema or comparable types, in this case xsd:string. (In the qualified name xsd:string, xsd is a namespace abbreviation and string is a local name. Of interest here is that xsd:string is an XML type rather than a Java type.) Given these Java/XML bindings, relatively uncomplicated library modules can convert from one to the other—from Java to XML or from XML to Java (see Figure 1-4).

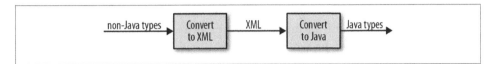

*Figure 1-4. Java/XML conversions*

Processing on the client side, as on the service side, requires only locally available libraries and utilities. The complexities, therefore, can be isolated at the endpoints—the service and the client applications together with their supporting libraries—and need not seep into the exchanged messages. Finally, web services are available over HTTP, a nonpropriety protocol that has become standard, ubiquitous infrastructure; HTTP in particular comes with a security extension, HTTPS, that provides multifaceted security services.

In a web service, the requesting client and the service need not be coded in the same language or even in the same style of language. Clients and services can be implemented in object-oriented, procedural, functional, and other language styles. The languages on either end may be statically typed (for instance, Java and Go) or dynamically typed (for example, JavaScript and Ruby). The complexities of stubs and skeletons, the serializing and deserializing of objects encoded in some proprietary format, give way to relatively simple text-based representations of messages exchanged over standard transports such as HTTP. The messages themselves are neutral; they have no bias toward a particular language or even family of languages.

The first code example in this chapter, and all of the code examples in Chapter 2 and Chapter 3, involve REST-style services. Accordingly, the next section looks at what REST means and why the REST-style service has become so popular. From a historical perspective, REST-style services can be viewed as a reaction to the growing complexity of SOAP-based ones.

# What Is REST?

Roy Fielding (*http://roy.gbiv.com*) coined the acronym REST in his PhD dissertation. Chapter 5 of Fielding's dissertation lays out the guiding principles for what have come to be known as REST-style or RESTful web services. Fielding has an impressive résumé.

He is, among other things, a principal author of the HTTP 1.1 specification and a cofounder of the Apache Software Foundation.

REST and SOAP are quite different. SOAP is a messaging protocol in which the messages are XML documents, whereas REST is a style of software architecture for distributed hypermedia systems, or systems in which text, graphics, audio, and other media are stored across a network and interconnected through hyperlinks. The World Wide Web is the obvious example of such a system. As the focus here is on *web* services, the World Wide Web is the distributed hypermedia system of interest. In the Web, HTTP is both a transport protocol and a messaging system because HTTP requests and responses are messages. The payloads of HTTP messages can be typed using the MIME (Multipurpose Internet Mail Extension) type system. MIME has types such as `text/html`, `applica tion/octet-stream`, and `audio/mpeg3`. HTTP also provides response status codes to inform the requester about whether a request succeeded and, if not, why. Table 1-1 lists some common status codes.

*Table 1-1. Sample HTTP status codes and their meanings*

| Status code | In English | Meaning |
| --- | --- | --- |
| 200 | OK | Request OK |
| 303 | See Other | Redirect |
| 400 | Bad Request | Request malformed |
| 401 | Unauthorized | Authentication error |
| 403 | Forbidden | Request refused |
| 404 | Not Found | Resource not found |
| 405 | Method Not Allowed | Method not supported |
| 415 | Unsupported Media Type | Content type not recognized |
| 500 | Internal Server Error | Request processing failed |

REST stands for REpresentational State Transfer, which requires clarification because the central abstraction in REST—the resource—does not occur in the acronym. A *re-source* in the RESTful sense is something that is accessible through HTTP because this thing has a name—URI (Uniform Resource Identifier). A URI has two subtypes: the familiar URL, which specifies a *location*, and the URN, which is a symbolic name but not a location. URIs are *uniform* because they must be structured in a certain way; there is a syntax (*http://tools.ietf.org/html/rfc3986*) for URIs. In summary, a URI is a stand-ardized name for a resource and, in this sense, a URI acts as noun.

In practical terms, a resource is a web-accessible, informational item that may have hyperlinks to it. Hyperlinks use URIs to do the linking. Examples of resources are plentiful but likewise misleading in suggesting that resources must have something in common other than identifiability through URIs. The gross national product of Lithuania is a resource, as is the Modern Jazz Quartet. Ernie Banks' baseball accomplishments count as a resource, as does the maximum flow algorithm. The concept of a resource is remarkably broad but, at the same time, impressively simple and precise.

As web-based informational items, resources are pointless unless they have at least one representation. In the Web, representations are MIME typed. The most common type of resource representation is probably still text/html, but nowadays resources tend to have multiple representations. For example, there are various interlinked HTML pages that represent the Modern Jazz Quartet but there are also audio and audiovisual representations of this resource.

Resources have state. Ernie Banks' baseball accomplishments changed during his career with the dismal Chicago Cubs from 1953 through 1971 and culminated in his 1977 induction into the Baseball Hall of Fame. A useful representation must capture a resource's state. For example, the current HTML pages on Ernie at the Baseball Reference website (*http://www.baseball-reference.com*) need to represent all of his major league accomplishments, from his rookie year in 1953 through his induction into the Hall of Fame.

A RESTful request targets a resource, but the resource itself typically is created on the service machine and remains there. A resource may be persisted in a data store such as a database system. Some mix of humans and applications may maintain the state of the resource. In the usual case of web service access to a resource, the requester receives a representation of the resource if the request succeeds. It is the representation that transfers from the service machine to the requester machine. In a REST-style web service, a client does two things in an HTTP request:

- Names the targeted resource by giving its URI, typically as part of a URL.
- Specifies a *verb* (HTTP method), which indicates what the client wishes to do; for example, *read* an existing resource, *create* a new resource from scratch, *edit* an existing resource, or *delete* an existing resource.

One of the basic cases is a *read* request. If a *read* request succeeds, a typed representation (for instance, text/html) of the resource is transferred from the server that hosts and maintains the resource to the client that issues the request. The client is an arbitrary application written in some language with support for REST-style requests. The representation returned from the service is a good one only if it captures the resource's state in some appropriate way. Figure 1-5 depicts a resource with its identifying URI together with a RESTful client and some typed representations sent back to the client in response to client requests.

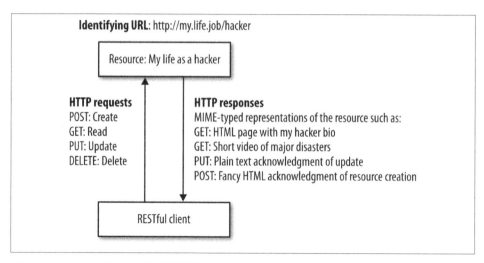

*Figure 1-5. A small slice of a RESTful system*

In summary, RESTful web services involve not just resources to represent but also client-invoked operations on such resources. At the core of the RESTful approach is the insight that HTTP, despite the occurrence of Transport in its name, acts as an API and not simply as a transport protocol. HTTP has its well-known verbs, officially known as *methods*. Table 1-2 lists the HTTP verbs that correspond to the CRUD (*Create, Read, Update, Delete*) operations so familiar throughout computing.

*Table 1-2. HTTP verbs and their CRUD operations*

| HTTP verb | CRUD operation |
|-----------|----------------|
| POST | Create |
| GET | Read |
| PUT | Update |
| DELETE | Delete |

Although HTTP is not case sensitive, the HTTP verbs are traditionally written in uppercase. There are additional verbs. For example, the verb HEAD is a variation on GET that requests only the HTTP headers that would be sent to fulfill a GET request.

HTTP also has standard response codes such as 404 to signal that the requested resource could not be found and 200 to signal that the request was handled successfully. In short, HTTP provides request verbs and MIME types for client requests and status codes (and MIME types) for service responses.:

Modern browsers generate only GET and POST requests. If a user enters a URL into the browser's input window, the browser generates a GET request. A browser ordinarily generates a POST request for an HTML form with a *submit* button. It goes against the spirit of REST to treat GET and POST interchangeably. In Java, for example, an `HttpServlet` instance has callback methods such as `doGet` and `doPost` that handle GET and POST requests, respectively. Each callback has the same parameter types: the `HttpServletRequest` type (the key/value pairs from the request) and the type `HttpServletResponse` (effectively a channel to communicate back to the requester). It is not unknown for a programmer to have the two callbacks execute the same code (for instance, by having one invoke the other), thereby conflating the original HTTP distinction between *read* and *create*. A key guiding principle of the RESTful style is to respect the original meanings of the HTTP verbs. In particular, any GET request should be side-effect free (*idempotent*) because a GET is a *read* rather than a *create*, *update*, or *delete* operation. A GET as a *read* with no side effects is called a *safe* GET.

The REST approach does not imply that either resources or the processing needed to generate adequate representations of them are simple. A REST-style web service might be every bit as subtle and complicated, in its functionality, as a SOAP-based service or a DOA application. The RESTful approach tries to simplify a service's implementation by taking what HTTP and the MIME type system already offer: built-in CRUD operations, uniformly identifiable resources, typed representations that can capture a resource's state, and status codes to summarize the outcome of a request. REST as a design philosophy tries to isolate application complexity at the endpoints—that is, at the client and at the service. A service may require lots of logic and computation to maintain resources and to generate adequate representation of resources, such as large and subtly formatted XML documents, and a client may require significant XML processing to extract the desired information from the XML representations transferred from the service to the client. Yet the RESTful approach keeps the complexity out of the transport level, as a resource representation is transferred to the client as the body of an HTTP response message. For the record, RESTful web services are Turing complete; that is, these services are equal in power to any computational system, including a system that consists of SOAP-based web services or DOA stubs and skeletons.

## Verbs and Opaque Nouns

In HTTP a URI is meant to be opaque, which means that the URI:

    http://bedrock/citizens/fred

has no inherent connection to the URI:

    http://bedrock/citizens

although Fred happens to be a citizen of Bedrock. These are simply two different, independent identifiers. Of course, a good URI designer will come up with URIs that are suggestive about what they are meant to identify. The point is that URIs have no intrinsic hierarchical structure. URIs can and should be interpreted, but these interpretations are imposed on URIs, not inherent in them. Although URI syntax looks like the syntax used to navigate a hierarchical filesystem, this resemblance is misleading. A URI is an opaque identifier, a logically proper name that should denote exactly one resource.

# Review of HTTP Requests and Responses

The next section has a REST-style sample service whose URL is:

```
http://localhost:8080/predictions/
```

If this URL is typed into a browser's window, the browser generates a request similar to:

```
GET /predictions/ HTTP/1.1
User-Agent: Mozilla/5.0 (X11; Linux x86_64) Chrome/24.0.1312.56
Host: localhost:8080
Accept: text/html
```

The browser parses the entered URL into these parts, with clarifications below:

- `GET /predictions/ HTTP/1.1`

  This is the HTTP request *start line*:

  — GET is the HTTP method (verb).

  — `/predictions/` is the URI (resource's name).

  — `HTTP/1.1` is the HTTP version that the requester is using.

- `User-Agent: Mozilla/5.0 (X11; Linux x86_64) Chrome/24.0`

  Immediately after the start line come the HTTP request header elements or *headers* for short. Each element is a key/value pair with a colon (:) separating the key on the left from the value on the right. In this element, `User-Agent` is the key, and everything to the right of the colon is the value. Chrome is the browser used in this request, and Mozilla/5.0 specifies a browser compatibility type. The `User-Agent` information also includes the operating system in use, 64-bit Linux. Of interest here is that key `User-Agent` captures the intended meaning: it is the application (agent) that a user employs to make a request.

- `Host: localhost:8080`

  In `localhost:8080`, the network address of the machine that hosts the resource is to the left of the colon; the port number, in this case 8080, is to the right. In this example, the network address is `localhost` and its dotted-decimal equivalent is 127.0.0.1. Because the network address is `localhost`, the web server and the requesting application are on the same machine, which is convenient during development. In a production environment, the web server might have a network address such as `dcequip.cti.depaul.edu`. Port numbers range from 0 to roughly 65000, with port numbers from 0 through 1023 typically reserved for standard applications such as web servers (port 80 for HTTP and port 443 for HTTPS), SMTP (email, port 25), SSH (secure shell, port 22), and so on. For convenience, the web servers Tomcat and Jetty use port 8080 by default, but the number can be changed (for example, to the standard HTTP port number 80). Under HTTP 1.1, the key/value pair, with `Host` as the key, is required. The other header elements are optional, although the ones shown here are typical.

- `Accept: text/html`

  This is the MIME type (`text`) and subtype (`html`), which the browser is ready to accept. The application running on the web server may not honor the requested type and respond instead with, for example, `text/plain` or `text/xml`.

In summary, the key/value pairs such as:

```
Accept: text/html
```

make up the HTTP request headers. These pairs may occur in any order and only the following pair:

```
Host: <network address>
```

is mandatory under HTTP 1.1.

Two newlines terminate the headers section. A GET request has no body; hence, a GET request consists only of the start line and the headers. A POST request always has a body, which may be empty. In a POST request, two newlines mark the end of the headers.

Because a GET request has no body, such a request often includes, in the URI, a query string that consists of key/value pairs. For example, this GET request:

```
http://.../products?id=27&category=boots
```

includes a query string with two key/value pairs: `id` is the first key and `27` is the value; `category` is the second key and `boots` is the value. The query string thus provides a way for a bodyless GET request to include information within the request. The query string data is encapsulated in the HTTP request headers. POST requests always have a body, which is usually nonempty. The body of a POST request holds key/value pairs as well.

If all goes well, sending an HTTP request to the URL:

```
http://localhost:8080/predictions/
```

leads to an HTTP response, which is similar to Example 1-2.

*Example 1-2. The HTTP response message from the predictions service*

```
HTTP/1.1 200 OK
Server: Apache-Coyote/1.1
Set-Cookie: JSESSIONID=35B1E3AA21EB7242FD2FC50044D2166A; Path=/predictions/;
Content-Type: text/html;charset=ISO-8859-1
Transfer-Encoding: chunked
```

```
<?xml version="1.0" encoding="UTF-8"?>
<java version="1.7.0" class="java.beans.XMLDecoder">
 <array class="predictions.Prediction" length="32">
  <void index="0">
   <object class="predictions.Prediction">
    <void property="what">
     <string>
        Managed holistic contingency will grow killer action-items.
     </string>
    </void>
    <void property="who">
     <string>
        Cornelius Tillman
     </string>
    </void>
   </object>
  </void>
  ...
</java>
```

The start line:

```
HTTP/1.1 200 OK
```

begins with the HTTP version in use on the server. Next comes the HTTP status code (SC for short) as a number (200) and in English (OK). Status codes in the 200 range signal success. Five header elements follow, including the name of the web server that sends the response and the content type of the response. Note that the response type is given as text/html rather than as what it actually is: text/xml. The reason is that my code, which generates the response, does not bother to set the content type; hence, the Apache-Coyote (that is, Tomcat) web server uses its default type of text/html. Two newline characters again separate the headers from the HTTP body, which can be empty. In this case, the body is an XML document that lists corporate predictions together with their predictors.

# HTTP as an API

HTTP can be viewed as an API. Among frameworks for developing websites and RESTful web services, Rails has pioneered this view of HTTP, which deliberately blurs the distinction between websites that deliver HTML and web services that deliver XML or JSON. In a well-designed Rails application, a GET request for the URI */products* is equivalent to the same request for */products.html*, and an HTML list of products is returned in response. A GET request against */products.json* or */products.xml* would return the same list but in JSON or XML, respectively. Rails has an often-copied idiom for combining URIs and HTTP verbs into a *RESTful route*—the route that a request takes to the code that handles the request. The Rails routing style is an elegant yet practical use of HTTP as an API. Table 1-3 is a summary of the Rails approach. In a

URI, a term such as *:id*, which begins with a colon character, indicates a placeholder or parameter, in this case a placeholder whose intended value is a numerical identifier such as 27.

*Table 1-3. Rails routing idioms*

| HTTP verb | URI (Name) | Meaning |
|-----------|------------|---------|
| GET | /products | Read all products |
| POST | /products | Create a new product from information in the POST body |
| GET | /products/new | Read the form to create a new product |
| GET | /products/:id/edit | Read the form to edit an existing product |
| GET | /products/:id | Read a single product |
| PUT | /products/:id | Update a product with information in the POST body |
| DELETE | /products:id | Delete the specified product |

These verb/name pairs are terse, precise, intuitive, and uniform in style. The pairs illustrate that RESTful conventions can yield simple, clear routing expressions about which operation should be performed on which resource. The POST and PUT verbs are used in requests that have an HTTP body; hence, the request data is in the HTTP message body. The GET and DELETE verbs are used in requests that have no body; hence, the request data, if any, is sent as query string key/value pairs.

The decision about whether to be RESTful in a particular application depends, as always, on practical matters that will come to the fore throughout this book. The current section looked at REST from on high; it is now time to descend into details with code examples. The next section summarizes the overview of HTTP with two Java clients. A first RESTful service follows.

## Two HTTP Clients in Java

The foregoing descriptions about HTTP can be fleshed out and summarized with two short Java clients, which can be run against any URL—for a website or a web service. The first client (see Example 1-3) takes a deliberately low-level approach by building up the HTTP request as a string, one chunk at a time. The second client (see Example 1-4) uses the Java utility class URLConnection, which shortens the code and makes the program more readable.

*Example 1-3. A simple Java client that makes an HTTP GET request*

```
import java.net.Socket;
import java.net.URL;
import java.net.MalformedURLException;
import java.net.UnknownHostException;
import java.io.IOException;
import java.io.PrintWriter;
import java.io.BufferedReader;
```

```
import java.io.InputStreamReader;

public class SimpleHttpClient {
    public static void main(String[ ] args) {
        // usage
        if (args.length < 1) {                                          ❶
            System.err.println("Usage: SimpleHttpClient <url>");
            return;
        }
        try {
            // Parse the URL.
            URL url = new URL(args[0]);                                  ❷
            String host = url.getHost();                                 ❸
            String path = url.getPath();                                 ❹
            int port = url.getPort();                                    ❺
            if (port < 0) port = 80;
            // Send the request.
            String request = "GET " + path + " HTTP/1.1\n";             ❻
            request += "host: " + host;                                 ❼
            request += "\n\n";
            Socket sock = new Socket(host, port);
            PrintWriter writer = new PrintWriter(sock.getOutputStream());
            writer.print(request);                                      ❽
            writer.flush();
            // Read and print the response.
            BufferedReader reader =                                     ❾
                new BufferedReader(new InputStreamReader(sock.getInputStream()));
            String next_record = null;
            while ((next_record = reader.readLine()) != null)           ❿
                System.out.println(next_record);
            sock.close();
        }
        catch(MalformedURLException e) {
            throw new RuntimeException("Please try again. Bad URL.\n" + e);
        }
        catch(UnknownHostException e) {
            throw new RuntimeException("Please try again. Unknown host.\n" + e);
        }
        catch(IOException e) {
            throw new RuntimeException("Please try again. Something's wrong.\n" + e);
        }
    }
}
```

The SimpleHttpClient expects, as a command-line argument (line 1), a URL such as
*http://www.amazon.com/index.html*. After constructing a URL instance from the string
URL (line 2), the client extracts the *host*, the *path* (URI), and the *port number* (lines 3,
4, and 5) so that an HTTP GET request can be built in chunks. Line 6, for example,
builds the following start line, given the sample Amazon URL:

```
GET /index.html HTTP/1.1
```

Only the required HTTP header is generated (line 7), with host as the key and the IP address of the server (in this case, www.amazon.com) as the value. After the request is sent (line 8), the response is read (lines 9 and 10) and the connection is closed.

*Example 1-4. A Java HTTP client that uses the utility URLConnection class*

```
import java.net.URL;
import java.net.URLConnection;
import java.net.MalformedURLException;
import java.io.IOException;
import java.io.InputStreamReader;
import java.io.BufferedReader;

public class UrlConnectionClient {
    public static void main(String[ ] args) {
        // usage
        if (args.length < 1) {
            System.err.println("Usage: UrlConnectionClient <url>");
            return;
        }

        try {
            // Parse the URL.
            URL url = new URL(args[0].trim());                              ❶

            // Connect.
            URLConnection sock = url.openConnection();                      ❷

            // Read and print.
            BufferedReader reader =
                new BufferedReader(new InputStreamReader(sock.getInputStream()));
            String next_record = null;
            while ((next_record = reader.readLine()) != null)              ❸
                System.out.println(next_record);

            // Close.
            reader.close();                                                ❹
        }
        catch(MalformedURLException e) { throw new RuntimeException(e); }
        catch(IOException e) { throw new RuntimeException(e); }
    }
}
```

The UrlConnectionClient (see Example 1-4) uses the class URLConnection, which simplifies the code. This client, like the first, expects a URL as a command-line argument. A URL instance (line 1) again is constructed but then used immediately (line 2) to open a connection. By default, the opened connection is a GET request against the site with the given URL. The response is read chunk by chunk (line 3) and printed. The connection then is closed (line 4).

Clients such as these occur throughout the forthcoming chapters, especially in examples that involve REST-style services. It is now time to introduce the first RESTful example.

# A First RESTful Example

As befits a first example, the implementation is simple but sufficient to highlight key aspects of a RESTful web service. The implementation consists of a JSP (Java Server Pages) script and two backend JavaBeans that the JSP script uses to get the data returned to the client (see Figure 1-6). The data is composed of sage corporate predictions. Here is a sample:

```
Decentralized 24/7 hub will target robust web-readiness.
Synergistic disintermediate policy will expedite backend experiences.
Universal fault-tolerant architecture will synthesize bleeding-edge channels.
```

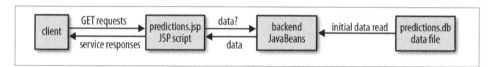

*Figure 1-6. The organization of the predictions web service*

There is an Ant script (see "An Ant script for service deployment" on page 31) that automates the deployment of this and other service examples. Here is a summary of the service parts and how the Ant script puts the parts together:

1.  The service consists of a JSP script together with two POJO (JavaBean) classes. The classes provide backend support for the JSP script. There is also a small configuration file, *web.xml*, that allows the URI to be shortened from:

    ```
    /predictions/predictions.jsp
    ```

    to:

    ```
    /predictions/
    ```

2.  The Ant script compiles the *.java* files and then packages the JSP script, the compiled *.class* files, and—only for convenience—the *.java* files into a JAR file with a *.war* extension (hereafter, a WAR file).

3.  The WAR file is copied to the Tomcat *webapps* subdirectory, which thereby deploys the service. The section "The Tomcat web server" on page 30 goes into the details of Tomcat installation and management.

In the *predictions* service, each prediction has an associated human predictor. The RESTful resource is thus a list of predictor names (e.g., Hollis McCullough) and their predictions (Hollis is responsible for the third prediction shown above). The resource name or URI is */predictions/*, and the only allowable HTTP verb is GET, which

---

corresponds to *read* among the CRUD operations. If the HTTP request is correct, the RESTful service returns an XML representation of the predictor/prediction list; otherwise, the service returns the appropriate HTTP status code (e.g., 404 for "Not Found" if the URI is incorrect or 405 for "Method Not Allowed" if the verb is not GET). Example 1-5 shows a slice of the XML payload returned upon a successful request.

*Example 1-5. The XML response from the predictions service*

```
<?xml version="1.0" encoding="UTF-8"?>
<java version="1.7.0" class="java.beans.XMLDecoder">
 <array class="predictions.Prediction" length="32">
  <void index="0">
   <object class="predictions.Prediction">
    <void property="what">
     <string>
      Managed holistic contingency will grow killer action-items.
     </string>
    </void>
    <void property="who">
     <string>Cornelius Tillman</string>
    </void>
   </object>
  </void>
  ...
  <void index="31">
   <object class="predictions.Prediction">
    <void property="what">
     <string>
      Versatile tangible application will maximize rich ebusiness.
     </string>
    </void>
    <void property="who">
     <string>Hiram Gulgowski</string>
    </void>
   </object>
  </void>
 </array>
</java>
```

## How the Predictions Web Service Works

When the *predictions* service is deployed to a web server such as Tomcat, the server translates the JSP script *predictions.jsp* (see Example 1-6) into a servlet instance. For now, this technical detail is overlooked because it is convenient to talk about the JSP script itself as the target of a request.

*Example 1-6. The JSP script predictions.jsp*

```
<jsp:useBean id    = "preds"                         ❶
             type  = "predictions.Predictions"
             class = "predictions.Predictions">
```

```
<% // Check the HTTP verb: if it's anything but GET,
   // return 405 (Method Not Allowed).
   String verb = request.getMethod();
   if (!verb.equalsIgnoreCase("GET")) {
     response.sendError(response.SC_METHOD_NOT_ALLOWED,
                        "Only GET requests are allowed.");
   }
   // If it's a GET request, return the predictions.
   else {
     preds.setServletContext(application);          ❷
     out.println(preds.getPredictions());
   }
%>
</jsp:useBean>
```

As requests come to the JSP script, the script first checks the request's HTTP method. If the method is GET, an XML representation of the predictions is returned to the requester. If the verb is not GET, the script returns an error message together with the HTTP status code. The relevant code follows:

```
String verb = request.getMethod();
if (!verb.equalsIgnoreCase("GET")) {
  response.sendError(response.SC_METHOD_NOT_ALLOWED,
                     "Only GET requests are allowed.");
}
```

JSP scripts have implicit object references such as request, response, and out; each of these is a field or a parameter in the servlet code into which the web server, such as Tomcat or Jetty, translates the JSP script. A JSP script can make the same calls as an HttpServlet.

On a successful request, the JSP script returns a list of predictions and their predictors, a list available from the backend JavaBean Predictions. The JSP code is pretty straightforward:

```
out.println(preds.getPredictions());
```

The object reference out, available in every JSP script, refers to an output stream through which the JSP script can communicate with the client. In this example, the object reference preds (line 1) refers to the backend JavaBean that maintains the collection of predictions; the getPredictions method in the backend bean converts the Java list of Predictions into an XML document.

The backend code consists of two POJO classes, Prediction (see Example 1-7) and Predictions (see Example 1-8). The Prediction class is quite simple, consisting of two properties: who (line 1) is the person making the prediction and what (line 2) is the prediction.

*Example 1-7. The backend* predictions.Prediction *class*

```
package predictions;
import java.io.Serializable;

public class Prediction implements Serializable {
    private String who;    // person
    private String what;   // his/her prediction
    public Prediction() { }
    public void setWho(String who) { this.who = who; }         ❶
    public String getWho() { return this.who; }
    public void setWhat(String what) { this.what = what; }     ❷
    public String getWhat() { return this.what; }
}
```

The Predictions class does the grunt work. For example, its populate method (line 3) reads the prediction data from a text file, *predictions.db*, encapsulated in the deployed WAR file, and the toXML method serializes a Java List<Prediction> into an XML document, which is sent back to the client. If there were problems reading or formatting the data, the *predictions* service would return null to the client.

*Example 1-8. The backend* predictions.Predictions *class*

```
package predictions;
import java.io.IOException;
import java.io.InputStream;
import java.io.InputStreamReader;
import java.io.BufferedReader;
import java.io.ByteArrayOutputStream;
import java.beans.XMLEncoder; // simple and effective
import javax.servlet.ServletContext;

public class Predictions {
    private int n = 32;
    private Prediction[ ] predictions;
    private ServletContext sctx;
    public Predictions() { }
    public void setServletContext(ServletContext sctx) { this.sctx = sctx; }  ❶
    public ServletContext getServletContext() { return this.sctx; }
    // getPredictions returns an XML representation of
    // the Predictions array
    public void setPredictions(String ps) { } // no-op
    public String getPredictions() {                                          ❷
        // Has the ServletContext been set?
        if (getServletContext() == null) return null;
        // Has the data been read already?
        if (predictions == null) populate();
        // Convert the Predictions array into an XML document
        return toXML();
    }
    private void populate() {                                                 ❸
        String filename = "/WEB-INF/data/predictions.db";
```

```
        InputStream in = sctx.getResourceAsStream(filename);
        // Read the data into the array of Predictions.
        if (in != null) {
            try {
                InputStreamReader isr = new InputStreamReader(in);
                BufferedReader reader = new BufferedReader(isr);
                predictions = new Prediction[n];
                int i = 0;
                String record = null;
                while ((record = reader.readLine()) != null) {
                    String[] parts = record.split("!");
                    Prediction p = new Prediction();
                    p.setWho(parts[0]);
                    p.setWhat(parts[1]);

                    predictions[i++] = p;
                }
            }
            catch (IOException e) { }
        }
    }
    private String toXML() {                                          ❹
        String xml = null;
        try {
            ByteArrayOutputStream out = new ByteArrayOutputStream();
            XMLEncoder encoder = new XMLEncoder(out);
            encoder.writeObject(predictions); // serialize to XML
            encoder.close();
            xml = out.toString(); // stringify
        }
        catch(Exception e) { }
        return xml;
    }
}
```

On a GET request, the JSP script invokes the method setServletContext (line 1 in the bean, line 2 in the JSP script) with an argument, the implicit object reference named application. The backend bean needs access to the servlet context in order to read data from a text file embedded in the deployed WAR file. The ServletContext is a data structure through which a servlet/JSP script can interact explicitly with the servlet container. The call to the setServletContext method sets up the subsequent call to the getPredictions method (line 2), which returns the XML representation shown in Example 1-5. Here is the getPredictions method without the comments:

```
public String getPredictions() {
    if (getServletContext() == null) return null;
    if (predictions == null) populate(); ❶
    return toXML();
}
```

The method populate (line 1 immediately above) reads the data. The predictions reference in the code segment above refers to the Map in which Prediction references are values. If the JSP script fails to set the servlet context, there is no way for the back-end Predictions bean to provide the requested data. The reason is that the populate method requires the servlet context (the reference is sctx, line 1, in the code below) in order to access the data:

```
private void populate() {
    String filename = "/WEB-INF/data/predictions.db";
    InputStream in = sctx.getResourceAsStream(filename); ❶
    ...
}
```

If the servlet context has been set but the predictions reference is null, then the data must be read from the *predictions.db* file into the Map that makes the data available to clients. Each entry in the Map is a Prediction, which again is a pair: who predicts what. Finally, the toXML method serializes the Java predictions into an XML document using the Java utility class XMLEncoder (line 1):

```
private String toXML() {
    String xml = null;
    try {
        ByteArrayOutputStream out = new ByteArrayOutputStream();
        XMLEncoder encoder = new XMLEncoder(out);              ❶
        encoder.writeObject(predictions); // serialize to XML
        encoder.close();
        xml = out.toString(); // stringify
    }
    catch(Exception e) { }
    return xml;                                                ❷
}
```

The XML document from the toXML method (line 2) becomes the body of the HTTP response to the client.

Although the XML from the *predictions* service is generated using the XMLEncoder class, Java does provide other ways to generate XML—but perhaps none quite as simple as XMLEncoder. The Prediction objects must be serializable in order to be encoded as XML using the XMLEncoder; hence, the Prediction class implements the empty (or *marker*) Serializable interface and defines the get/set methods for the properties who (the predictor) and what (the prediction). The Prediction properties are serialized into XML elements in the response document.

The predictions service can be deployed under the Tomcat web server using a provided Ant script (with % as the command-line prompt):

```
% ant -Dwar.name=predictions deploy
```

The deployed WAR file would be *predictions.war* in this case. The next section (see "The Tomcat web server" on page 30) elaborates on the Apache Tomcat server and explains how to install and use this server. The section "An Ant script for service deployment" on page 31 clarifies the Ant script, which is packaged with the book's code examples. The deployed WAR file *predictions.war* includes a standard web deployment document, *web.xml*, so that the URI can be shortened to */predictions/*.

## The Tomcat web server

Apache Tomcat (*http://tomcat.apache.org*) is a commercial-grade yet lightweight web server implemented in Java. Tomcat has various subsystems for administration, security, logging, and troubleshooting, but its central subsystem is Catalina, a container that executes servlets, including JSP and other scripts (e.g., JSF scripts) that Tomcat automatically translates into servlets. Tomcat is the popular name for the web server, and Catalina is the official name for the servlet container that comes with Tomcat.

Tomcat also includes a web console, tutorials, and sample code. This section focuses on installing Tomcat and on basic post-installation tasks such as starting and stopping the web server. The current version is 7.x, which requires Java SE 6 or higher. Earlier Tomcat versions are still available.

There are different ways to download Tomcat, including as a ZIP file. Tomcat can be installed in any directory. For convenience, let *TOMCAT_HOME* be the install directory. The directory *TOMCAT_HOME/bin* has startup and shutdown scripts for Unixy and Windows systems. For instance, the startup script is *startup.sh* for Unix and *startup.bat* for Windows. Tomcat is written in Java but does not ship with the Java runtime; instead, Tomcat uses the Java runtime on the host system. To that end, the environment variable *JAVA_HOME* should be set to the Java install directory (e.g., to */usr/local/java7*, *D:\java7*, and the like).

In summary, the key commands (with comments introduced with two semicolons) are:

```
% startup.sh   ;; or startup.bat on Windows to start Tomcat
% shutdown.sh  ;; or shutdown.bat on Windows to stop Tomcat
```

The commands can be given at a command-line prompt. On startup, a message similar to:

```
Using CATALINA_BASE:   /home/mkalin/tomcat7
Using CATALINA_HOME:   /home/mkalin/tomcat7
Using CATALINA_TMPDIR: /home/mkalin/tomcat7/temp
Using JRE_HOME:        /usr/local/java
Using CLASSPATH:       /home/mkalin/tomcat7/bin/bootstrap.jar
```

appears.

Under *TOMCAT_HOME* there is directory named *logs*, which contains various logfiles, and several other directories, some of which will be clarified later. A important directory for now is *TOMCAT_HOME/webapps*, which holds JAR files with a *.war* extension (hence the name WAR file). Subdirectories under *TOMCAT_HOME/webapps* can be added as needed. Deploying a web service under Tomcat is the same as deploying a website: a WAR file containing the site or the service is copied to the *webapps* directory, and a website or web service is undeployed by removing its WAR file.

Tomcat maintains various logfiles in *TOMCAT_HOME/logs*, one of which is especially convenient for ad hoc debugging. In standard configuration, Tomcat redirects output to System.err and System.out to *logs/catalina.out*. Accordingly, if a servlet executes:

```
System.err.println("Goodbye, cruel world!");
```

the farewell message will appear in the *catalina.out* logfile.

Apache Tomcat is not the only game in town. There is the related TomEE web server, basically Tomcat with support for Java EE beyond servlets. Another popular Java-centric web server is Jetty (*http://jetty.codehaus.org*). The sample services in this book can be deployed, as is, with either Tomcat or Jetty; the next chapter has a sidebar on how to install and run Jetty.

## An Ant script for service deployment

The first sample web service is published with a web server such as Tomcat or Jetty. The ZIP file with my code examples includes an Ant script to ease the task of deployment. The *Ant* utility, written in Java, is available on all platforms. My script requires Ant 1.6 or higher.

To begin, let the *current working directory* (*cwd*) be any directory on the local filesystem. The *cwd* holds the Ant script *build.xml*:

```
cwd: build.xml
```

The *cwd* has a subdirectory named *src* that holds the web service's artifacts. Suppose, for example, that a web service includes a JSP script, a backend JavaBean, the standard Tomcat or Jetty deployment file *web.xml*, and a JAR file that holds a JSON library. Here is a depiction:

```
cwd: build.xml
 |
src: products.jsp, json.jar, web.xml
```

Suppose, further, that the backend JavaBean has the fully qualified name:

```
acme.Products
```

The file structure is now:

```
cwd: build.xml
 |
src: products.jsp, json.jar, web.xml
 |
acme: Products.java
```

Finally, assume that the *src* directory also holds the datafile *new_products.db*. From the *cwd* command line, the command:

```
% ant -Dwar.name=products deploy
```

does the following:

- Creates the directory *cwd/build*, which holds copies of files in directory *src* and any subdirectories
- Compiles any *.java* files, in this case *acme.Products.java*
- Builds the WAR file, whose major contents are:

```
WEB-INF/web.xml
WEB-INF/classes/acme/Products.class
WEB-INF/data/new_products.db
WEB-INF/lib/json.jar
acme/Products.java
products.jsp
```

In the constructed WAR file:

- Any *.xml* file winds up in *WEB-INF*.
- Any *.jar* file winds up in *WEB-INF/lib*.
- Any *.db* file winds up in *WEB-INF/data*.
- Any *.java* or *.class* file winds up in its package/subdirectory.
- Other files, such as *.jsp* files, wind up in the WAR file's top level.

For convenience, the Ant script includes, in the WAR file, Java source (*.java*) and compiled (*.class*) files. In production, the source files would be omitted.

Finally, the Ant script copies the constructed WAR file to *TOMCAT_HOME/webapps* and thereby deploys the web service. The script also leaves a copy of the WAR file in *cwd*.

The command:

```
% ant
```

displays the three most useful commands. The command:

```
% ant clean
```

removes any *.war* files from the *cwd* and deletes the *build* directory. The command:

```
% ant compile
```

compiles any *.java* files but does not build or deploy a WAR file. The command:

```
% ant -Dwar.name=predictions deploy
```

first cleans and compiles; then the command builds and deploys the WAR file *predictions.war*.

The Ant file *build.xml* has extensive documentation and explains, in particular, what needs to be done to customize this file for your environment. Only one line in the file needs to be edited. Although the Ant script is targeted at Tomcat deployment, the WAR files that the script produces can be deployed as is to Jetty as well. As noted earlier, Chapter 2 goes into the details of installing and running Jetty.

## A Client Against the Predictions Web Service

Later examples introduce RESTful clients in Java and other languages; for now, either a browser or a utility such as *curl* (see "The curl Utility" on page 33) is good enough. On a successful *curl* request to the service:

```
% curl -v http://localhost:8080/predictions/
```

the response includes not only the XML shown earlier in Example 1-5 but also a trace (thanks to the *-v* flag) of the HTTP request and response messages. The HTTP request is:

```
GET /predictions/ HTTP/1.1
User-Agent: curl/7.19.7
Host: localhost:8080
Accept: */*
```

The HTTP response start line and headers are:

```
HTTP/1.1 200 OK
Server: Apache-Coyote/1.1
Set-Cookie: JSESSIONID=96C78773C190884EDE76C714728164EC; Path=/test1/;
Content-Type: text/html;charset=ISO-8859-1
Transfer-Encoding: chunked
```

Recall that an HTTP GET message has no body; hence, the entire message is the start line and the headers. The response shows the session identifier (a 128-bit statistically unique number, in hex, that Tomcat generates) in the header. In the JSP script, the session identifier could be disabled, as it is not needed; for now, the goal is brevity and simplicity in the code.

---

### The curl Utility

The *curl* utility (*curl.haxx.se*) is a command-line tool for requesting data using URL syntax. The tool supports a wide variety of protocols, including HTTP(S), SMTP, FTP(S), LDAP(S), and others. The tool is available on Unixy systems and there is port for Windows. This tool is useful for quick tests to determine whether a service is responding appropriately to requests.

---

If a POST request were sent to the RESTful *predictions* service:

```
% curl --request POST --data "foo=bar" http://localhost:8080/predictions/
```

the request message header becomes:

```
POST /predictions/ HTTP/1.1
User-Agent: curl/7.19.7
Host: localhost:8080
Accept: */*
Content-Length: 7
Content-Type: application/x-www-form-urlencoded
```

The response header is now:

```
HTTP/1.1 405 Method Not Allowed
Server: Apache-Coyote/1.1
Set-Cookie: JSESSIONID=34A013CDC5A9F9F8995A28E30CF31332; Path=/test1/;
Content-Type: text/html;charset=ISO-8859-1
Content-Length: 1037
```

The error message:

```
Only GET requests are allowed.
```

is in an HTML document that makes up the response message's body. Tomcat generates an HTML response because my code does not (but could) stipulate a format other than HTML, the default Tomcat format for a Tomcat response.

This first example illustrates how a JSP script is readily adapted to support web services in addition to websites. The next section goes into more detail on servlets and JSP scripts. In summary, the *predictions* web service is implemented as a JSP script with the two backend JavaBeans in support. This first example highlights key aspects of a REST-style service:

- The service provides access to resource under the URI */predictions/*.
- The service filters access on the HTTP request verb. In this example, only GET requests are successful; any other type of request generates a *bad method* error.
- The service responds with an XML payload, which the consumer now must process in some appropriate way.

# Why Use Servlets for RESTful Web Services?

Chapter 2 explores various ways to implement and publish RESTful services in Java, which has a rich set of built-in and third-party APIs. The current chapter introduces a tried-and-true way to do RESTful services in Java: the service is implemented as a JSP script, which a web server such as Tomcat or Jetty translates into a servlet, and the servlet then is published with the web server.

An `HttpServlet` is a natural, convenient way to implement RESTful web services for two main reasons. First, such servlets are close to the HTTP metal. For example, the `HttpServlet` class has methods such as `doGet`, `doPost`, `doPut`, and `doDelete` that match up with the HTTP verbs aligned with the CRUD operations. These servlet methods execute as callbacks that the servlet container, explained shortly, invokes as needed. The `HttpServlet` class also provides symbolic constants for HTTP status codes, for example, `SC_NOT_FOUND` for status code 404 and `SC_METHOD_NOT_ALLOWED` for status code 405. Each `HttpServlet` *do*-method has the same two arguments: an `HttpServletRequest` and an `HttpServletResponse`. The servlet request contains, as key/value pairs, all of the appropriate information encapsulated in the HTTP request, regardless of the request verb—for a GET request, the `HttpServletRequest` would include any key/value pairs in a query string; for a POST request, this data structure would include any key/value pairs in the POST request body. The `HttpServletRequest` map is easy to read and, if needed, easy to update and forward. The `HttpServletResponse` has methods to adjust the HTTP response message as needed, and this class encapsulates an output stream to communicate back to the client.

A second major advantage of servlets is that they execute in a servlet container, which is middleware that mediates between the application code of the servlet and the web server that provides the usual types of support: wire-level security in the form of HTTPS transport, user authentication and authorization, logging and troubleshooting support, server configuration, local or remote database access, naming services, application deployment and administration, and so on. In the Tomcat web server, the servlet container is named Catalina. Because the servlet container is such an integral part of a Java-based web server, it is common to conflate the container name (Catalina) and the server name (Tomcat), a practice followed here. (In Jetty, the server and the container have the same name: *Jetty*.) In any case, a Java-centric web server such as Tomcat is the natural way to publish real-world web services, including RESTful ones, written in Java. A servlet container typically houses several instances of executing servlets, each awaiting client requests (see Figure 1-7).

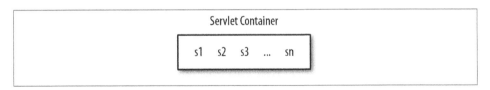

*Figure 1-7. A servlet container with servlet instances awaiting requests*

Here is a short, more technical review of servlets with emphasis on their use to deliver RESTful services. The class `HttpServlet` extends the class `GenericServlet`, which in turn implements the `Servlet` interface. All three types are in a package that is not included in core Java. (Tomcat and Jetty provide a JAR file *servlet-api.jar* that contains the required package.) The Servlet interface declares five methods, the most important of which is the service method that a web container invokes on every request to a servlet. The service method has a ServletRequest and a ServletResponse parameter. The request is a map that contains the request information from a client, and the response provides a stream to send responses back to the client. The GenericServlet class implements the Servlet methods in a transport-neutral fashion, whereas the HttpServlet subclass of GenericServlet implements these methods in an HTTP-specific way. Accordingly, the service parameters in the HttpServlet have the types HttpServletRequest and HttpServletResponse. The HttpServlet also provides request filtering that naturally supports a REST-style service: in an HttpServlet, the overridden service method dispatches a incoming GET request to the method doGet, an incoming POST request to the method doPost, and so on. Because HTTP is the dominant transport for websites and web services, the HttpServlet is an excellent choice for implementing either.

In the HttpServlet class, the *do*-methods such as doGet and doPost are defined as no-ops, (methods with empty bodies); these methods can be overridden as needed in a programmer-derived subclass. For example, if the class MyServlet extends HttpServlet and overrides doGet but not doPost, then doPost remains a no-op in MyServlet instances. A servlet programmer overrides the *do*-methods of interest and ignores the rest.

Servlets are written in Java and, therefore, have access to all of the Java libraries, standard and contributed. JSP scripts, by contrast, are an arbitrary mix of HTML and code. In the case of websites, JSP scripts typically serve as HTML templates and, under best practices, the major code segments involve references to backend JavaBeans. In the case of web services, by contrast, JSP scripts would consist predominantly or even exclusively of code because service clients do not expect HTML payloads as responses. The advantage of a JSP script over an HttpServlet is that the programmer does not need to compile a JSP script. The Java-aware web server assumes this responsibility. A JSP script is deployed as a text file but executes as a servlet because the web server automatically translates the script into an HttpServlet before loading one or more instances of the resulting servlet into the servlet container. For short examples and for the kind of experimentation typical of code development, JSP scripts are attractive. For deployment to production, the Java code of a servlet would be best practice. Some of the shorter servlet-based examples in this book use JSP scripts, but most of the examples use classes that explicitly extend HttpServlet.

# What's Next?

RESTful services are rich enough to warrant two dedicated chapters. Accordingly, the next chapter focuses on the service side by exploring options for implementing and publishing RESTful services. The web service APIs include:

- `HttpServlet` and its equivalents (e.g., JSP scripts)
- JAX-RS, which has various implementations
- Restlet, which is similar in style to JAX-RS
- JAX-WS `@WebServiceProvider`, which is a relatively low-level API

Web services using any of these APIs can be published with a production-grade web server such as Tomcat or Jetty; there are even command-line options for such publication, although these options vary significantly in ease of use. There are trade-offs among the APIs, and the next chapter highlights the pluses and minuses of each API.

The servlet approach represents a base-level API in that servlets have been a part of Java since the late 1990s, and they remain the foundation for websites written in Java. The servlet API is close to the HTTP metal in that, for example, an `HttpServletRequest` is a thin but likewise convenient wrapper around an HTTP request; in similar fashion, an `HttpServletResponse` is a thin and equally convenient wrapper around an HTTP response. At the same time, servlets provide high-level filtering of HTTP requests, and a data structure such as the `HttpServletRequest` collapses the distinction between the key/value pairs in a query string of a GET or DELETE request and the key/value pairs in the body of a POST or PUT request. All such pairs occur, without distinction, in the `HttpServletRequest` map. Servlets may seem old hat, but they are a hat worth trying on for REST-style services. The remaining APIs build upon what servlets offer and, in this sense, represent a layering on top of servlets.

JAX-RS and Restlet are roughly peers, although this comparison might stir heated denials from either camp. Both of these APIs emphasize the use of Java annotations to describe the RESTful access to a particular CRUD operation. For example, methods that handle GET requests are annotated with `@GET` or `@Get`, those that handle POST requests are annotated with `@POST` or `@Post`, and so on. In both frameworks there are symbolic constants to specify MIME types and status codes. Further, each framework supports the automated generation of XML and JSON payloads. These frameworks have a contemporary look and feel, but each represents, at the implementation level, a layer above the servlet layer. When published with a web server such as Tomcat or Jetty, JAX-RS and Restlet provide servlet interceptors that mediate between the client and the web service. The details are explored in Chapter 2.

JAW-WS is an API used mostly for SOAP-based services but can be used for REST-style services as well. In the latter case, the `@WebServiceProvider` annotation is central. The

@WebServiceProvider interface is sufficiently flexible that it can be used to annotate either a SOAP-based or a REST-style service; however, JAX-WS provides a related but higher level annotation, @WebService, for SOAP-based services. The @WebServicePro vider API is deliberately lower level than the servlet, JAX-RS, and Restlet APIs, and the @WebServiceProvider API is targeted at XML-based services. For programmers who need a low-level API, Java supports the @WebServiceProvider option. JAX-RS, Restlet, and @WebServiceProvider have both service-side and client-side APIs that can be used independently of one another. For example, a Restlet client could make calls against a JAX-RS service or vice versa.

In summary, Chapter 2 focuses on the server side of RESTful services. Chapter 3 shifts the focus to the client or consumer side of such services. The chapter includes client code against commercial RESTful services such as Amazon, Twitter, and the Chicago Transit Authority. The chapter also focuses on how the standard JAX-B (Java API for XML-Binding) packages and third-party libraries such as XStream can be put to good use by hiding the XML in the consumption of RESTful services. A dominant trend in contemporary web services is the occurrence of JavaScript clients against RESTful services. Such clients may be written in JavaScript or a dialect such as jQuery. In any case, these clients are usually embedded in HTML documents so that the clients execute in the context of a browser. JavaScript clients in general prefer JSON over XML payloads for the obvious reason that a JSON document is the text representation of a JavaScript object, even a JavaScript function. Chapter 3 also looks at various Java options for generating JSON as well as XML and plain-text responses, and the chapter explores different ways in which JavaScript clients can process the JSON payloads.

# RESTful Web Services: The Service Side

Java has options for implementing and publishing RESTful web services. On the publishing side, the choices range from very basic, command-line servers that are well suited for development, testing, and even low-volume production; through lightweight, Java-centric web servers such as Tomcat and Jetty; and up to full-blown Java Application Servers (JAS) such as GlassFish, JBoss, Oracle WebLogic, and WebSphere. This chapter introduces publication options in the first two categories, and Chapter 7 covers JAS publication.

There is also variety among the APIs and their implementations for RESTful services. Here is the list of APIs covered in this chapter:

- The `HttpServlet` and JSP APIs, introduced briefly in Chapter 1 and examined more thoroughly in this chapter
- The JAX-RS (Java API for XML-RESTful Services) API
- The third-party Restlet API, which is very similar to JAX-RS in look and feel
- The JAX-WS (Java API for XML-Web Services) API, the `@WebServiceProvider` interface in particular

For the most part, the API used to implement the web service does not constrain how this service can be published. The exception is the servlet API, as servlets need to be deployed in a servlet container such as Tomcat's Catalina or Jetty. (Jetty is the name of both the web server and its servlet container.) There are shortcuts for publishing JAX-RS and JAX-WS services but these, too, can be published with Tomcat or Jetty; the same goes for Restlet services.

The decision about how to publish a service depends on many factors. For example, if service deployment requires wire-level security in the form of HTTPS together with user authentication/authorization, then a web server such as Tomcat or Jetty is the obvious starting point. If the published web services are to interact with EJBs, which are deployed in an EJB container, then a souped-up web server such as TomEE (Tomcat with EE support) or a full JAS is a better choice. In development, simpler command-line options such as Endpoint, introduced later, are attractive.

# A RESTful Service as an HttpServlet

Chapter 1 has a sample RESTful service implemented as a JSP script and two backend classes: Prediction and Predictions. The JSP-based service supported only GET requests. This section revises the example to provide an HttpServlet implementation with support for the four CRUD operations:

- A new Prediction can be created with a POST request whose body should have two key/value pairs: a who key whose value is the name of the predictor and a what key whose value is the prediction.

- The Prediction objects can be read one at a time or all together with a GET request. If the GET request has a query string with an id key, then the corresponding Prediction, if any, is returned. If the GET request has no query string, then the full list of Predictions is returned. On any GET request, the client can indicate a preference for JSON rather than the default XML format.

- A specified Prediction can be updated with a PUT request that provides the identifier for the Prediction and either a new who or a new what.

- A specified Prediction can be deleted.

The earlier JSP service is *predictions* and the servlet revision is *predictions2*. The structure of *predictions2* differs from that of *predictions* in several ways. The most obvious change is that an explicit HttpServlet subclass replaces the JSP script. There are also changes in the details of the Prediction and Predictions classes, which still provide backend support. The details follow.

---

### The Jetty Web Server

The Jetty web server (*http://jetty.codehaus.org*) is available as a ZIP file. Let the install directory be *JETTY_HOME*. Its subdirectories are similar to those of *TOMCAT_HOME*. For example, there is a *webapps* subdirectory into which WAR files are deployed; a *logs* subdirectory; a *lib* subdirectory with various JAR files, including a versioned counterpart of Tomcat's *servlet-api.jar*; and others. Jetty ships with an executable JAR file *start.jar*; hence, Jetty can be started at the command line with the command:

```
% java -jar start.jar
```

---

In general, a WAR file deployable under Tomcat is deployable under Jetty and vice versa; my examples can be deployed under either. The Jetty web server, like Tomcat, listens by default on port 8080. Jetty is a first-rate web server that has a lighter feel than does Tomcat, and Jetty's simplicity makes embedding this web server in other systems relatively straightforward. It is hard to make a bad choice between Tomcat and Jetty.

## Implementation Details

There are small but important changes to the Prediction class (see Example 2-1), which now includes an id property (line 1), an auto-incremented integer that the service sets when a Prediction object is constructed.

*Example 2-1. The backend Prediction class*

```
package predictions2;
import java.io.Serializable;

public class Prediction implements Serializable, Comparable<Prediction> {
    private String who;   // person
    private String what;  // his/her prediction
    private int    id;    // identifier used as lookup key

    public Prediction() { }
    public void setWho(String who) { this.who = who; }
    public String getWho() { return this.who; }
    public void setWhat(String what) { this.what = what; }
    public String getWhat() { return this.what; }
    public void setId(int id) { this.id = id; }        ❶
    public int getId() { return this.id; }
    public int compareTo(Prediction other) { return this.id - other.id; }
}
```

The id property is used to sort the Prediction objects, which explains why the Prediction class implements the interface Comparable used in sorting:

```
public class Prediction implements Serializable, Comparable<Prediction> {
```

Implementing the Comparable interface requires that the compareTo method be defined:

```
public int compareTo(Prediction other) {
    return this.id - other.id;
}
```

The compareTo method uses the comparison semantics of the age-old C function qsort. For illustration, suppose that this.id in the code above is 7 and other.id is 12, where this is the current object and other is another Prediction object against which the current Prediction object is being compared. The difference of 7–12 is the negative integer –5, which signals that the current Prediction *precedes* the other Prediction because 7 precedes 12. In general:

- A returned negative integer signals that the current object *precedes* the other object.

- A returned positive integer signals that the current object *succeeds* the other object.

- A returned zero signals that the two objects are to be treated as equals with respect to sorting.

The implementation of the `compareTo` method means the sort is to be in ascending order. Were the `return` statement changed to:

```
return other.id - this.id;
```

the sort would be in descending order. The `Prediction` objects are sorted for ease of confirming that the CRUD operations work correctly. For example, if a `Prediction` object is created with the appropriate POST request, then the newly created `Predic tion` occurs at the *end* of the `Prediction` list. In similar fashion, it is easy to confirm that the other destructive CRUD operations—PUT (update) and DELETE—work as intended by inspecting the resulting sorted list of `Prediction` objects.

A `Prediction` is still `Serializable` so that a list of these can be serialized into XML using the `XmlEncoder` utility. An added feature is that this list can be formatted in JSON if the client so requests.

The utility class `Predictions` has changed as well (see Example 2-2). As explained in the sidebar about thread synchronization and servlets, the `Map` of the earlier JSP implementation gives way to a `ConcurrentMap` so that the code can avoid explicit locks in the form of `synchronized` blocks.

*Example 2-2. The backend `Predictions` class*

```
package predictions2;
import java.io.IOException;
import java.io.InputStream;
import java.io.InputStreamReader;
import java.io.BufferedReader;
import java.io.ByteArrayOutputStream;
import java.util.concurrent.ConcurrentMap;
import java.util.concurrent.ConcurrentHashMap;
import java.util.concurrent.atomic.AtomicInteger;
import java.util.Collections;
import java.beans.XMLEncoder; // simple and effective
import javax.servlet.ServletContext;

public class Predictions {
    private ConcurrentMap<Integer, Prediction> predictions;
    private ServletContext sctx;
    private AtomicInteger mapKey;

    public Predictions() {
        predictions = new ConcurrentHashMap<Integer, Prediction>();
```

```java
        mapKey = new AtomicInteger();
    }
    public void setServletContext(ServletContext sctx) {
        this.sctx = sctx;
    }
    public ServletContext getServletContext() { return this.sctx; }
    public void setMap(ConcurrentMap<String, Prediction> predictions) {
        // no-op for now
    }
    public ConcurrentMap<Integer, Prediction> getMap() {
        // Has the ServletContext been set?
        if (getServletContext() == null) return null;
        // Has the data been read already?
        if (predictions.size() < 1) populate();
        return this.predictions;
    }
    public String toXML(Object obj) {
        String xml = null;
        try {
            ByteArrayOutputStream out = new ByteArrayOutputStream();
            XMLEncoder encoder = new XMLEncoder(out);
            encoder.writeObject(obj); // serialize to XML
            encoder.close();
            xml = out.toString(); // stringify
        }
        catch(Exception e) { }
        return xml;
    }
    public int addPrediction(Prediction p) {
        int id = mapKey.incrementAndGet();
        p.setId(id);
        predictions.put(id, p);
        return id;
    }
    private void populate() {
        String filename = "/WEB-INF/data/predictions.db";
        InputStream in = sctx.getResourceAsStream(filename);
        // Read the data into the array of Predictions.
        if (in != null) {
            try {
                InputStreamReader isr = new InputStreamReader(in);
                BufferedReader reader = new BufferedReader(isr);
                int i = 0;
                String record = null;
                while ((record = reader.readLine()) != null) {
                    String[] parts = record.split("!");
                    Prediction p = new Prediction();
                    p.setWho(parts[0]);
                    p.setWhat(parts[1]);
                    addPrediction(p);
                }
            }
        }
```

```
            catch (IOException e) { }
        }
    }
}
```

The `Predictions` class now has an `addPrediction` method:

```
public int addPrediction(Prediction p) {
    int id = mapKey.incrementAndGet(); // AtomicInteger
    p.setId(id);
    predictions.put(id, p);
    return id;
}
```

to support POST requests. The servlet's `doPost` method creates a new `Prediction`, sets the who and what properties with data from the POST message's body, and then invokes `addPrediction` to add the newly constructed `Prediction` to the map whose object reference is `predictions`. The `mapKey`, a thread-safe `AtomicInteger`, gets incremented with each new `Prediction` and behaves like an auto-incremented integer in a database system; the `mapKey` value becomes the `id` of each newly constructed `Prediction`, thereby ensuring that each `Prediction` has a unique `id`.

The remaining `Predictions` code is slightly changed, if at all, from the earlier version. For example, the `populate` method is modified slightly to give each newly constructed `Prediction` an `id`, but the method's main job is still to read data from the text file encapsulated in the WAR—data that contain the who and what of each `Prediction`.

The `PredictionServlet` (see Example 2-3) replaces the JSP script and differs from this script in supporting all of the CRUD operations. The servlet offers new functionality by allowing the client to request the JSON format for the response of any GET request. Further, the earlier JSP script interpreted GET to mean *read all* but the servlet allows the client to request one specified `Prediction` or all of them. The code for the `Predic tionServlet` is long enough that it makes sense to isolate important code segments for clarification.

*Example 2-3. The `PredictionsServlet` with full support for the CRUD operations*

```
package predictions2;

import java.util.concurrent.ConcurrentMap;
import javax.servlet.ServletException;
import javax.servlet.http.HttpServlet;
import javax.servlet.http.HttpServletRequest;
import javax.servlet.http.HttpServletResponse;
import javax.xml.ws.http.HTTPException;
import java.util.Arrays;
import java.io.ByteArrayInputStream;
import java.io.ByteArrayOutputStream;
import java.io.OutputStream;
```

```java
import java.io.BufferedReader;
import java.io.InputStreamReader;
import java.beans.XMLEncoder;
import org.json.JSONObject;
import org.json.XML;

public class PredictionsServlet extends HttpServlet {
    private Predictions predictions; // backend bean

    // Executed when servlet is first loaded into container.
    // Create a Predictions object and set its servletContext
    // property so that the object can do I/O.
    @Override
    public void init() {
        predictions = new Predictions();
        predictions.setServletContext(this.getServletContext());
    }
    // GET /predictions2
    // GET /predictions2?id=1
    // If the HTTP Accept header is set to application/json (or an equivalent
    // such as text/x-json), the response is JSON and XML otherwise.
    @Override
    public void doGet(HttpServletRequest request, HttpServletResponse response) {
        String param = request.getParameter("id");
        Integer key = (param == null) ? null : new Integer(param.trim());
        // Check user preference for XML or JSON by inspecting
        // the HTTP headers for the Accept key.
        boolean json = false;
        String accept = request.getHeader("accept");
        if (accept != null && accept.contains("json")) json = true;
        // If no query string, assume client wants the full list.
        if (key == null) {
            ConcurrentMap<Integer, Prediction> map = predictions.getMap();
            // Sort the map's values for readability.
            Object[] list = map.values().toArray();
            Arrays.sort(list);
            String xml = predictions.toXML(list);
            sendResponse(response, xml, json);
        }
        // Otherwise, return the specified Prediction.
        else {
            Prediction pred = predictions.getMap().get(key);

            if (pred == null) { // no such Prediction
                String msg = key + " does not map to a prediction.\n";
                sendResponse(response, predictions.toXML(msg), false);
            }
            else { // requested Prediction found
                sendResponse(response, predictions.toXML(pred), json);
            }
        }
    }
}
```

```
// POST /predictions2
// HTTP body should contain two keys, one for the predictor ("who") and
// another for the prediction ("what").
@Override
public void doPost(HttpServletRequest request, HttpServletResponse response) {
    String who = request.getParameter("who");
    String what = request.getParameter("what");
    // Are the data to create a new prediction present?
    if (who == null || what == null)
        throw new HTTPException(HttpServletResponse.SC_BAD_REQUEST);
    // Create a Prediction.
    Prediction p = new Prediction();
    p.setWho(who);
    p.setWhat(what);
    // Save the ID of the newly created Prediction.
    int id = predictions.addPrediction(p);
    // Generate the confirmation message.
    String msg = "Prediction " + id + " created.\n";
    sendResponse(response, predictions.toXML(msg), false);
}
// PUT /predictions
// HTTP body should contain at least two keys: the prediction's id
// and either who or what.
@Override
public void doPut(HttpServletRequest request, HttpServletResponse response) {
    /* A workaround is necessary for a PUT request because neither Tomcat
       nor Jetty generates a workable parameter map for this HTTP verb. */
    String key = null;
    String rest = null;
    boolean who = false;
    /* Let the hack begin. */
    try {
        BufferedReader br =
            new BufferedReader(new InputStreamReader(request.getInputStream()));
        String data = br.readLine();
        /* To simplify the hack, assume that the PUT request has exactly
           two parameters: the id and either who or what. Assume, further,
           that the id comes first. From the client side, a hash character
           # separates the id and the who/what, e.g.,
               id=33#who=Homer Allision
        */
        String[] args = data.split("#");      // id in args[0], rest in args[1]
        String[] parts1 = args[0].split("="); // id = parts1[1]
        key = parts1[1];
        String[] parts2 = args[1].split("="); // parts2[0] is key
        if (parts2[0].contains("who")) who = true;
        rest = parts2[1];
    }
    catch(Exception e) {
        throw new HTTPException(HttpServletResponse.SC_INTERNAL_SERVER_ERROR);
    }
    // If no key, then the request is ill formed.
```

```
        if (key == null)
            throw new HTTPException(HttpServletResponse.SC_BAD_REQUEST);
        // Look up the specified prediction.
        Prediction p = predictions.getMap().get(new Integer(key.trim()));
        if (p == null) { // not found?
            String msg = key + " does not map to a Prediction.\n";
            sendResponse(response, predictions.toXML(msg), false);
        }
        else { // found
            if (rest == null) {
                throw new HTTPException(HttpServletResponse.SC_BAD_REQUEST);
            }
            // Do the editing.
            else {
                if (who) p.setWho(rest);
                else p.setWhat(rest);
                String msg = "Prediction " + key + " has been edited.\n";
                sendResponse(response, predictions.toXML(msg), false);
            }
        }
    }
}
// DELETE /predictions2?id=1
@Override
public void doDelete(HttpServletRequest request, HttpServletResponse response) {
    String param = request.getParameter("id");
    Integer key = (param == null) ? null : new Integer(param.trim());
    // Only one Prediction can be deleted at a time.
    if (key == null)
        throw new HTTPException(HttpServletResponse.SC_BAD_REQUEST);
    try {
        predictions.getMap().remove(key);
        String msg = "Prediction " + key + " removed.\n";
        sendResponse(response, predictions.toXML(msg), false);
    }
    catch(Exception e) {
        throw new HTTPException(HttpServletResponse.SC_INTERNAL_SERVER_ERROR);
    }
}
// Method Not Allowed
@Override
public void doTrace(HttpServletRequest request, HttpServletResponse response) {
    throw new HTTPException(HttpServletResponse.SC_METHOD_NOT_ALLOWED);
}
@Override
public void doHead(HttpServletRequest request, HttpServletResponse response) {
    throw new HTTPException(HttpServletResponse.SC_METHOD_NOT_ALLOWED);
}
@Override
public void doOptions(HttpServletRequest request, HttpServletResponse response) {
    throw new HTTPException(HttpServletResponse.SC_METHOD_NOT_ALLOWED);
}
// Send the response payload to the client.
```

```
        private void sendResponse(HttpServletResponse response,
                                  String payload,
                                  boolean json) {
    try {
        // Convert to JSON?
        if (json) {
            JSONObject jobt = XML.toJSONObject(payload);
            payload = jobt.toString(3); // 3 is indentation level for nice look
        }
        OutputStream out = response.getOutputStream();
        out.write(payload.getBytes());
        out.flush();
    }
    catch(Exception e) {
        throw new HTTPException(HttpServletResponse.SC_INTERNAL_SERVER_ERROR);
    }
  }
}
```

Recall that each of the *do*-methods in an `HttpServlet` take the same arguments: an `HttpServletRequest`; a map that contains the information encapsulated in the HTTP request; and an `HttpServletResponse`, which encapsulates an output stream for communicating back with the client. Here is the start of the doGet method:

```
public void doGet(HttpServletRequest request, HttpServletResponse response) {
```

The `HttpServletRequest` has a `getParameter` method that expects a string argument, a key into the request map, and returns either `null` if there is no such key or the key's value as a string otherwise. The `getParameter` method is agnostic about whether the key/value pairs are in the body of, for example, a POST request or in the query string of, for example, a GET request. The method works the same in either case. There is also a `getParameters` method that returns the parameter collection as a whole.

In the case of `PredictionsServlet`, the doGet method needs to answer two questions about the incoming request:

- Does the bodyless GET request include a key named `id` whose value identifies a particular `Prediction`?

  If the `id` is present, the doGet method uses the `id` to perform a lookup against the `ConcurrentMap`, which holds references to all of the `Prediction` objects. If the lookup fails, then the doGet method returns an XML message to that effect:

```
    Prediction pred = predictions.getMap().get(key);
    if (pred == null) { // no such Prediction
        String msg = key + " does not map to a prediction.\n";
        sendResponse(response, predictions.toXML(msg), false);
    }
```

The last argument to the sendResponse method indicates whether JSON rather than XML should be sent back to the client. In this example, XML is returned because the JSON flag is false. If the id parameter is not present, the doGet method assumes that the client wants to read a list of all Predictions and returns this list in either JSON or XML format:

```
ConcurrentMap<String, Prediction> map = predictions.getMap();
// Sort the map's values for readability.
Object[] list = map.values().toArray();
Arrays.sort(list); // other ways to sort shown later
...
```

- Does the client prefer JSON over XML?

In an HTTP request, the requester can express a preference for the MIME type of the returned representation. For example, the header element:

```
Accept: text/html
```

expresses a preference for the MIME type text/html. Among the MIME combinations is application/json that, together with several variants, expresses a preference for JSON. The doGet method therefore uses the getHeader method in the HttpServletRequest to inspect the HTTP header element with Accept as its key:

```
boolean json = false;
String accept = request.getHeader("accept");
if (accept != null && accept.contains("json")) json = true;
```

This check determines whether the client prefers JSON over XML. (Recall that HTTP is case insensitive; hence, the key could be Accept, accept, ACCEPT, and so on.) The json flag is the third argument to the sendResponse method:

```
private void sendResponse(HttpServletResponse res,
                          String payload,
                          boolean json) { // json format?
   try {
      if (json) {
        JSONObject jobt = XML.toJSONObject(payload);
        payload = jobt.toString(3); // 3 is indentation level
      }
      OutputStream out = res.getOutputStream();
      out.write(payload.getBytes());
      out.flush();
   }
   catch(Exception e) {
       throw new HTTPException(HttpServletResponse.SC_INTERNAL_SERVER_ERROR);
   }
}
```

Details about generating the JSON are considered next.

The deployed WAR file *predictions2.war* includes a lightweight, third-party JSON library in the JAR file *json.jar* (it is available at the JSON in Java website (*http://json.org/java*)). If the client prefers JSON over XML, then the response payload is converted to JSON. If anything goes awry in sending the response back to the client, the servlet throws an HTTPException, which in this case generates a response with HTTP status code 500 for *Internal Server Error*, a catchall for request-processing errors on the server.

The *doPost* and *doPut* operations are similar in that doPost creates an altogether new Prediction using data in the body of a POST request, whereas doPut updates an existing Prediction from data in the body of a PUT request. The main difference is that a PUT request needs to include the id of the Prediction to be updated, whereas a POST request creates a new Prediction and then sets its id to an auto-incremented integer. In implementation, however, doPost and doPut differ significantly because the servlet container's runtime does not generate a usable parameter map, the HttpServletRequest, on a PUT request; on a POST request, the map is usable. (This is the case in both Tomcat and Jetty.) As a result, the doPut implementation extracts the data directly from an input stream.

To begin, here is the doPost implementation, without the comments:

```
public void doPost(HttpServletRequest request, HttpServletResponse response) {
   String who = request.getParameter("who");                                ❶
   String what = request.getParameter("what");                              ❷
   if (who == null || what == null)
      throw new HTTPException(HttpServletResponse.SC_BAD_REQUEST);
   Prediction p = new Prediction();                                         ❸
   p.setWho(who);                                                           ❹
   p.setWhat(what);                                                         ❺
   int id = predictions.addPrediction(p);                                   ❻
   String msg = "Prediction " + id + " created.\n";
   sendResponse(response, predictions.toXML(msg), false);                   ❼
}
```

The two calls to the getParameter method extract the required data (lines 1 and 2). A new Prediction is then constructed, its who and what properties are set, and a confirmation is generated for the client (lines 3 through 7).

In the doPut method, the getParameter method does not work correctly because neither Tomcat nor Jetty builds a usable parameter map in HttpServletRequest. The workaround is to access directly the input stream encapsulated in the request structure:

```
BufferedReader br =
  new BufferedReader(new InputStreamReader(request.getInputStream()));
String data = br.readLine();
...
```

The next step is to extract the data from this stream. The code, though not pretty, gets the job done. The point of interest is that the HttpServletRequest does provide access to the underlying input stream from which the PUT data can be extracted. Using the getParameter method is, of course, much easier.

The body of doDelete method has simple logic:

```
String key = request.getParameter("id");
if (key == null)
    throw new HTTPException(HttpServletResponse.SC_BAD_REQUEST);
try {
    predictions.getMap().remove(key);                                    ❶
    String msg = "Prediction " + key + " removed.\n";
    sendResponse(response, predictions.toXML(msg), false);
}
catch(Exception e) {
    throw new HTTPException(HttpServletResponse.SC_INTERNAL_SERVER_ERROR);
}
```

If the id for the Prediction can be extracted from the parameter map, the prediction is effectively removed from the collection by removing the lookup key from the Con currentMap (line 1).

The PredictionsServlet also implements three other *do*-methods, and all in the same way. Here, for example, is the implementation of doHead:

```
public void doHead(HttpServletRequest request, HttpServletResponse response) {
    throw new HTTPException(HttpServletResponse.SC_METHOD_NOT_ALLOWED);
}
```

Throwing the HTTPException signals to the client that the underlying HTTP verb, in this case HEAD, is not supported. The numeric status code for Method Not Allowed is 405. The web service designer thus has an idiomatic way to reject particular HTTP verbs: throw a Method Not Allowed exception.

---

## Servlets and Thread Synchronization

A web server such as Tomcat can instantiate arbitrarily many instances of a servlet, although the number is typically small (e.g., 1 through 4). The web server itself makes the decision. For example, Tomcat by default loads one instance of a servlet to begin but may load more instances thereafter if simultaneous requests for the servlet are sufficient in number. Whatever the number of servlet instances, the number of client requests per instance is typically greater—and significantly so. For example, one servlet instance might handle tens of simultaneous requests. For reasons of efficiency, a web server such as Tomcat keeps the number of servlet instances as small as possible while supporting reasonable response time per request. A high-volume web server might have to handle hundreds of requests per second, distributed across many servlet instances; one servlet instance per request is out of the question in this real-world scenario. The upshot is that Java-based web servers rely on multithreading to handle simultaneous requests. The model is sometimes described as *one thread per request*.

---

For reasons of performance, a web server such as Tomcat creates a thread pool at startup; as requests come in, each is dispatched to a thread from the pool, which then handles the request and returns to the pool afterwards. The pooling amortizes the relatively expensive cost of thread creation across the web server's uptime. There are, of course, various ways to measure how well a web server is performing. One critical measure is response time. For example, a website might require that the upper bound on response time for 90% of all requests be, say, 10 *ms*.

The one-thread-per-request model poses challenges for the servlet/JSP programmer, in particular the challenge of thread coordination or *synchronization*. For example, if there are a dozen concurrent requests against the `PredictionsServlet` of the *predictions2* service, then each of these requests is implemented as a thread that executes the appropriate *do*-method in the servlet. On a multicore server (that is, a server with more than one CPU), one thread could be executing the `doGet` method at exactly the same time as another is executing the `doPut` method; the result is a simultaneous *read* and *write* operation on the same resource. There are various other concurrency scenarios, any one of which requires proper thread synchronization to avoid so-called *race conditions*, and the programmer rather than the servlet container must ensure that these scenarios remain thread safe.

A servlet container such as Catalina or Jetty, in contrast to an EJB container, does *not* ensure thread safety; instead, the programmer is responsible for proper thread coordination. A servlet must be programmed so that, for example, two requests—each executing as a separate thread—cannot simultaneously update the same resource such as a `Prediction`. In earlier Java versions, the mainstay of thread coordination was the `synchronized` block; later versions of Java have added higher level constructs, many in the `java.util.concurrent` package, for managing thread-based concurrency.

The *predictions2* service uses a thread-safe `ConcurrentMap` to coordinate simultaneous thread access to the `Predictions`. A `ConcurrentMap` segments its entries; as a result, the map usually needs to lock only a portion of its total entries to enforce synchronization. In any case, the `ConcurrentMap` synchronizes access to the `Predictions` collection and does so in an efficient manner. The `java.util.concurrent` package offers other thread-safe data structures; a later example in this chapter, the JAX-RS *predictions3* service, uses one of these data structures, the thread-safe `CopyOnWriteArrayList`. Finally, the *predictions2* service uses an integer counter to set the `id` for each newly created prediction. The counter is implemented with a thread-safe `AtomicInteger`.

## Sample Client Calls Against the predictions2 Service

Example 2-4 is a list of *curl* calls against the service. These calls serve as a very preliminary test of the service. Two semicolons introduce comments that explain the purpose of the *curl* call. Recall that the Ant script can be used to deploy the *predictions2* service under Tomcat:

```
% ant -Dwar.name=predictions2 deploy
```

*Example 2-4. A suite of curl calls against the predictions RESTful service*

```
;; GET all predictions (XML response)
% curl localhost:8080/predictions2/    ;; curl --request GET...
;; GET a specified saying (XML response)
% curl localhost:8080/predictions2?id=31
;; GET all predictions (JSON response)
% curl --header "Accept: application/json" localhost:8080/predictions2/
;; GET a specified saying (JSON response)
% curl --header "Accept: application/json" localhost:8080/predictions2?id=31
;; POST a new saying
% curl --request POST --data "who=TSEliot& \
        what=This is the way the world ends" localhost:8080/predictions2/
;; GET all predictions to confirm the POST (new saying is at the end)
% curl localhost:8080/predictions2/
;; PUT new data into an existing saying
% curl --request PUT \
        --data "id=33#what=This is an update" localhost:8080/predictions2/
;; GET all predictions to confirm the PUT (edited saying is at the end)
% curl localhost:8080/predictions2/
;; DELETE a specified saying
% curl --request DELETE localhost:8080/predictions2?id=33
;; GET all predictions to confirm the DELETE
% curl localhost:8080/predictions2/
```

The XML responses from the *predictions2* service are formatted exactly the same as in the original version, which did not support JSON responses. Here is a sample JSON response from a GET request on the Prediction with id 31:

```
{"java": {"class": "java.beans.XMLDecoder", "object": {"void": [
        {"int": 31, "property": "id"},
        {"string": "Balanced clear-thinking utilisation
                    will expedite collaborative initiatives.",
            "property": "what"}, {"string": "Deven Blanda", "property": "who"}],
    "class": "predictions2.Prediction"},
    "version": "1.7.0_17"}}
```

# A RESTful Web Service as a JAX-RS Resource

The servlet API, the grizzled workhorse for producing Java websites, is still nimble enough to support RESTful web services as well. There are more recent APIs, among them JAX-RS (Java API for XML-RESTful Services). JAX-RS relies upon Java annotations to advertise the RESTful role that a class and its encapsulated methods play. Jersey (*http://jersey-java.net*) is the *reference implementation* (RI) of JAX-RS. RESTEasy (*http://bit.ly/1d0ccZx*), a JBoss project; Apache Wink (*http://bit.ly/1527t4B*); and Apache CXF (*http://cxf.apache.org*) are other implementations. JAX-RS has APIs for programming RESTful services and clients against such services; the two APIs can be used independently. This section focuses on the service-side API. The first JAX-RS example supports only GET requests, but the second JAX-RS example supports all of the CRUD operations.

## A First JAX-RS Web Service Using Jersey

JAX-RS web services are resources that can be published with the Tomcat and Jetty web servers. The first example has one resource, the class Adages, and two supporting Java classes: the deployment class RestfulApplication and the POJO class Adage. Exactly how these three classes interact is covered next.

The RestfulAdage class (see Example 2-5) extends the JAX-RS Application class (line 2), which implements a getClasses method that enumerates the individual resources deployed in the WAR file (line 3). In this example, there is but one such resource, Adages, but there could be arbitrarily many (line 4).

*Example 2-5. The JAX-RS Application subclass that lists Adages.class as a resource*

```
package adages;

import java.util.Set;
import java.util.HashSet;
import javax.ws.rs.ApplicationPath;
import javax.ws.rs.core.Application;

@ApplicationPath("/resourcesA")                          ❶
public class RestfulAdage extends Application {           ❷
    @Override
    public Set<Class<?>> getClasses() {                  ❸
        Set<Class<?>> set = new HashSet<Class<?>>();
        set.add(Adages.class);                           ❹
        return set;
    }
}
```

Recall that any website or web service deployed under Tomcat has a URI that begins with the name of the deployed WAR file. In the RestfulAdage class, the annotation ApplicationPath (line 1) spells out how the URI continues. For example, assuming that the deployed WAR file is named *adages.war*, the ApplicationPath annotation indicates that the URI part of the URL continues with *resourcesA*:

```
http://localhost:8080/adages/resourcesA
```

The next part is tricky, so the low-level details are explained in a sidebar. At issue is how the programmer-defined RestfulAdage class interacts with the Jersey JAX-RS implementation under a Tomcat deployment. For context, recall that the getClasses method (line 3), a callback invoked when the RestfulAdage instance is loaded into the servlet container, specifies the JAX-RS resources available in the WAR file. Once again, there is but a single resource, Adages (see Example 2-7), in the example. The RestfulAdage class is a Jersey `Application` because the programmer-defined `RestfulAdage` class extends the JAX-RS `Application` class. If multiple JAX-RS resources were to be made available in the deployed WAR file, then the class name of each would occur in a `set.add` call in `RestfulAdage`. In the current example, there is only:

```
set.add(Adages.class);
```

because `Adages` is the only resource.

## Publishing JAX-RS Resources with a Java Application

"Publishing JAX-RS Resources with Tomcat" on page 56 explains how a JAX-RS resource can be published with a production-grade web server such as Tomcat; the section also explains how the JAX-RS libraries can be downloaded. For now, the point of interest is that the Jersey implementation of JAX-RS offers other ways to publish, which may be better suited for development. Here is a standalone Java application that publishes the *adages* service:

```
package adages;

import java.net.InetSocketAddress;
import javax.ws.rs.ext.RuntimeDelegate;
import com.sun.net.httpserver.HttpHandler;
import com.sun.net.httpserver.HttpServer;

public class AdagesPublisher{
    private static final int port = 9876;                              ❶
    private static final String uri = "/resourcesA/";                  ❷
    private static final String url = "http://localhost:" + port + uri;
    public static void main(String[ ] args) {
        new AdagesPublisher().publish();
    }
    private void publish() {
        HttpServer server = getServer();
        HttpHandler requestHandler =
            RuntimeDelegate.getInstance().createEndpoint(new RestfulAdage(),
                                                    HttpHandler.class);
        server.createContext(uri, requestHandler);
        server.start();
        msg(server);
    }
    private HttpServer getServer() {
        HttpServer server = null;
        int backlog = 8;
        try {
            server =
                HttpServer.create(new InetSocketAddress("localhost", port),
                              backlog);
        }
        catch(Exception e) { throw new RuntimeException(e); }
```

```
        return server;
    }

    private void msg(HttpServer server) {
        String out = "Publishing RestfulAdage on " + url +
                                     ". Hit any key to stop.";
        System.out.println(out);
        try {
            System.in.read();
        } catch(Exception e) { }
        server.stop(0); // normal termination
    }
}
```

For convenience, this `AdagesPublisher` class is in the `adages` package together with
`Adage`, `Adages`, and `RestfulAdage`. To compile, the JAR file *jersey-core.jar* must be on
the classpath; to run, that file and *jersey-server.jar* must be on the classpath. The ZIP
that contains the sample code has an executable JAR file *AdagesPublish.jar* that includes
all of the dependencies. The JAR can be executed from the command line:

```
% java -jar AdagesPublish.jar
```

The `AdagesPublisher` awaits connections on port 9876 (line 1), and the URI (line 2)
is `/resourcesA`. Accordingly, the base URL is:

```
http://localhost:9876/resourcesA/
```

The JAX-RS utility publisher uses classes such as `HttpServer` and `HttpHandler`, which
come with core Java. Later examples will put these and related classes to use. The point
for now is that there are options for publishing JAX-RS services, including a very lightweight option. The *adages* web service performs the same way regardless of how it is
published. The Jersey implementation does a nice job of cleanly separating JAX-RS
services from their publication.

## Publishing JAX-RS Resources with Tomcat

The JAX-RS and Jersey packages do not come with the core Java JDK; instead, the
relevant JAR files can be found at *jersey.java.net*. There is a Maven repository from
which a Maven script can install Jersey and its dependencies, but the standalone JAR
files are available as well. The Maven approach deliberately hides the deployment details
to make life easier for the developer. The goal here, however, is to understand how things
work under the hood. In any case, working directly with the JARs is straightforward.

JAX-RS resources can be published as usual with the Ant *build.xml* script. For example,
the command to deploy a JAX-RS resource in the WAR file named *adages* is:

```
% ant -Dwar.name=adages deploy
```

As usual, the relevant files would be in a *src* directory. In this example, the three *.java* files are in the *src/adages* subdirectory. The remaining files, including four Jersey JARs, are in *src*. The relevant JAR files, with approximate sizes, are:

```
asm.jar               ;;   43K bytes
jersey-core.jar       ;;  206K bytes
jersey-server.jar     ;;  595K bytes
jersey-servlet.jar    ;;  125K bytes
```

The last three JARs are available, for convenience, in a *jersey-bundle.jar*.

There are different ways to make these four JARs accessible to Tomcat. The JAR files could be copied to *TOMCAT_HOME/lib* and thereby be made available to any WAR file deployed under Tomcat. (Recall that Tomcat must be restarted after files are copied to its *lib* directory in contrast to its *webapps* directory.) The problem with this approach is version control. Should new versions of the JARs be installed as they come out? If so, will these new versions break already deployed web services? A more conservative approach is to *freeze* a deployed WAR file by packing the four JARs within the WAR file. This approach also makes it easier to port the WAR from one web server to another, for instance, from Tomcat on one machine to Tomcat on another machine, or from Tomcat to Jetty, and so on. The one downside to packing the JARs inside the WAR is, of course, that the WAR file becomes larger. My preference is to include the required JARs within the WAR file. With this approach, the contents of deployed WAR file *adages.war* are:

```
WEB-INF/web.xml
WEB-INF/classes/adages/Adage.class
WEB-INF/classes/adages/Adages.class
WEB-INF/classes/adages/RestfulAdage.class
WEB-INF/lib/asm.jar
WEB-INF/lib/jackson-annotations.jar
WEB-INF/lib/jackson-core.jar
WEB-INF/lib/jackson-databind.jar
WEB-INF/lib/jersey-core.jar
WEB-INF/lib/jersey-server.jar
WEB-INF/lib/jersey-servlet.jar
```

The three JAR files that begin with `jackson` handle the generation of JSON documents. Jackson (*http://jackson.codehaus.org*) is a collection of Java packages for producing and consuming JSON documents. The main text explains how Jackson works with the rest of the service.

The class `adages.RestfulAdage` (see Example 2-5) encapsulates a `getClasses` method, whose role can be clarified with reference to the deployment file *web.xml*. A JAX-RS service deployed under Tomcat needs a minimalist *web.xml* to set up communication between the servlet container and the service. Here is an example that can be used with any Jersey JAX-RS service published with Tomcat (or Jetty):

```
<?xml version="1.0" encoding="UTF-8"?>
<web-app>
```

```
<servlet>
  <servlet-name>jersey</servlet-name>
  <servlet-class>
    com.sun.jersey.spi.container.servlet.ServletContainer
  </servlet-class>
  <load-on-startup>1</load-on-startup>
</servlet>
</web-app>
```

The `load-on-startup` element prompts Tomcat to instantiate and load an instance of the Jersey `ServletContainer` during the WAR bootstrap process; the critical role of the `ServletContainer` is to scan the deployed WAR file for Jersey `Application` classes. Here is a slice of Tomcat's *catalina.out* logfile, edited for readability:

```
INFO: Deploying web application archive adages.war
INFO: Registering Jersey servlet application, named adages.RestfulAdage,   ❶
      at the servlet mapping, /resources/*, with the Application class
      of the same name
INFO: Scanning for root resource in the Web app resource paths:
INFO: Root resource classes found: class adages.Adages              ❷
INFO: Instantiated the Application class adages.RestfulAdage
```

The upshot of this log segment is that the Jersey `ServletContainer` finds the class `RestfulAdage` (line 1), which in turn identifies the JAX-RS resources in the WAR file (line 2). In this case, there is only one such resource: `Adages`. By the way, if multiple JAX-RS services are deployed to a servlet container, then each service should have a unique name for the class that extends `Application`. In this first example, the class is named `RestfulAdage`; in a later example, the name is `RestfulPrediction` to avoid conflict.

The JAX-RS service in the deployed WAR file, *adages.war*, is now ready to accept requests such as:

```
% curl http://localhost:8080/adages/resourcesA/
```

## The Adage Class

The `Adage` class (see Example 2-6) has an `import` for the JAX-B annotation `XmlRootElement`. The term *binding* refers, in this context, to linking a Java data type such as `String` to an XML type, in this case `xsd:string`.

*Example 2-6. The Adage POJO class annotated for XML generation through JAX-B*

```
package adages;

import javax.xml.bind.annotation.XmlRootElement;

@XmlRootElement(name = "adage")                                      ❶
public class Adage {
    private String words;
```

---

```
    private int wordCount;

    public Adage() { }
    @Override
    public String toString() {
        return words + " -- " + wordCount + " words";
    }
    public void setWords(String words) {
        this.words = words;
        this.wordCount = words.trim().split("\\s+").length;
    }
    public String getWords() { return this.words; }
    public void setWordCount(int wordCount) { }
    public int getWordCount() { return this.wordCount; }
}
```

The @XmlRootElement annotation (line 1) signals that an Adage object can be transformed into an XML document whose *document* or *root* (that is, outermost) element is named adage. For example, the XML document:

```
<?xml version="1.0" encoding="UTF-8" standalone="yes"?>
<adage>
  <wordCount>7</wordCount>
  <words>What can be shown cannot be said.</words>
</adage>
```

results from the JAX-B transformation of an in-memory Adage object.

The Adages class (see Example 2-7) is a JAX-RS resource that accepts RESTful requests, in this case only GET requests, and responds with payloads of these three MIME types: text/plain, application/json, and application/xml.

*Example 2-7. The Adages class as a JAX-RS resource*

```
package adages;

import javax.xml.bind.annotation.XmlElementDecl;
import javax.xml.bind.JAXBElement;
import javax.xml.namespace.QName;
import javax.ws.rs.GET;
import javax.ws.rs.Path;
import javax.ws.rs.Produces;
import javax.ws.rs.core.MediaType;
import java.util.Random;
import com.fasterxml.jackson.databind.ObjectMapper;

@Path("/")
public class Adages {
    // Add aphorisms to taste...
    private String[ ] aphorisms =
        {"What can be shown cannot be said.",
         "If a lion could talk, we could not understand him.",
```

```
                    "Philosophy is a battle against the bewitchment of " +
                    "our intelligence by means of language.",
                    "Ambition is the death of thought.",
                    "The limits of my language mean the limits of my world."};
        public Adages() { }
        @GET
        @Produces({MediaType.APPLICATION_XML}) // could use "application/xml"
        public JAXBElement<Adage> getXml() {
            return toXml(createAdage());
        }
        @GET
        @Produces({MediaType.APPLICATION_JSON})
        @Path("/json")
        public String getJson() {
            return toJson(createAdage());
        }
        @GET
        @Produces({MediaType.TEXT_PLAIN})
        @Path("/plain")
        public String getPlain() {
            return createAdage().toString() + "\n";
        }
        // Create an Adage and set the words property, which
        // likewise sets the wordCount property. The adage is
        // randomly selected from the array, aphorisms.
        private Adage createAdage() {
            Adage adage = new Adage();
            adage.setWords(aphorisms[new Random().nextInt(aphorisms.length)]);
            return adage;
        }
        // Java Adage --> XML document
        @XmlElementDecl(namespace = "http://aphorism.adage", name = "adage")
        private JAXBElement<Adage> toXml(Adage adage) {
            return new JAXBElement<Adage>(new QName("adage"), Adage.class, adage);
        }
        // Java Adage --> JSON document
        // Jersey provides automatic conversion to JSON using the Jackson
        // libraries. In this example, the conversion is done manually
        // with the Jackson libraries just to indicate how straightforward it is.
        private String toJson(Adage adage) {
            String json = "If you see this, there's a problem.";
            try {
                json = new ObjectMapper().writeValueAsString(adage);
            }
            catch(Exception e) { }
            return json;
        }
    }
}
```

Perhaps the best way to clarify how the three Java classes interact is through sample client calls. To begin, consider the request:

---

```
% curl localhost:8080/adages/resourcesA/plain
```

On a sample run, the output was:

```
What can be shown cannot be said. -- 7 words
```

The RESTful routing of the client's request works as follows:

- In the URI */adages/resources/plain*, the initial segment */adages* specifies the deployed WAR file *adages.war*.
- The next subsegment */resourcesA* represents the JAX-RS `ApplicationPath`, information that the WAR file's `RestfulAdage` provides to the web server.
- The next subsegment is */*. Recall that the RESTful resource in this web service is the `Adages` class, which begins:

  ```
  @Path("/")
  public class Adages {
  ...
  ```

  The `@Path("/")` annotation represents the last slash in the URI *adages/resources/*. Accordingly, this URI maps to the `Adages` class, which is the one and only JAX-RS resource in the deployed WAR file *adages.war*.
- The final subsegment in the URI is *plain*, so that the full URI is:

  ```
  /adages/resources/plain
  ```

The `Adages` method `getPlain` is:

```
@GET
@Produces({MediaType.TEXT_PLAIN})
@Path("/plain")
public String getPlain() {
    return createAdage().toString() + "\n";
}
```

The `@GET` annotation signals that the method/operation `getPlain`, an arbitrary name, is accessible through a GET request only. The `@Produces` annotation promises, in effect, to respond with the MIME type `text/plain`. This is a promise rather than a guarantee. The `@Path` annotation indicates that the URI subsegment */plain* completes the path to this service operation.

The RESTful routing idioms used in JAX-RS follow the spirit, if not the exact syntax, of those from the Rails framework. These idioms support clear, terse URIs such as:

```
/adages/resourcesA/plain
```

and:

```
adages/resourcesA/json
```

## JAX-RS Generation of XML and JSON Responses

The interaction between the JAX-RS resource class Adages and the POJO class Adage
needs clarification. Recall that class Adage begins:

```
@XmlRootElement(name = "adage")
public class Adage {
...
```

and that the annotation @XmlRootElement allows an Adage instance to be serialized into
an XML document with <adage> as its document-level start tag. In the language of JAX-
RS, the Adage class is a *provider* of XML. (See the "How JAX-B Can Transform a Java
Object into an XML Document" on page 62 for details about how JAX-B uses an XML
Schema to generate the XML.) Adage is likewise a POJO class with the familiar get/set
methods for two properties: words and wordCount. The only unusual detail is that the
setWords method also sets the wordCount for the adage:

```
public void setWords(String words) {
    this.words = words;
    this.wordCount = words.trim().split("\\s+").length; // word count
}
```

because this is a convenient way to do so.

---

### How JAX-B Can Transform a Java Object into an XML Document

The *adages* JAX-RS service uses the JAX-B library, under the hood, to transform a Java
object, an Adage instance, into an XML document such as:

```
<?xml version="1.0" encoding="UTF-8" standalone="yes"?>
<adage>
  <wordCount>14</wordCount>
  <words>
    Philosophy is a battle against the bewitchment of our intelligence
    by means of language.
  </words>
</adage>
```

The @XmlRootElement annotation on the Adage class guides the transformation by indicating that the outermost XML element is to be named adage; the return data type
JAXBElement<Adage> in the getXml method represents, in Java, an XML element—
*including* an entire XML document. This sidebar delves into the details.

---

The core Java JDK has a *schemagen* utility[1] that, when applied to a POJO source file such as *Adage.java*, generates an XML Schema. The utility can be invoked from the command line:

```
% schemagen Adage.java
```

The resulting XML Schema document is:

```
<?xml version="1.0" encoding="UTF-8" standalone="yes"?>
<xs:schema version="1.0" xmlns:xs="http://www.w3.org/2001/XMLSchema">
  <xs:complexType name="Adage">
    <xs:sequence>
      <xs:element name="words" type="xs:string"/>
      <xs:element name="wordCount" type="xs:int"/>
    </xs:sequence>
  </xs:complexType>
</xs:schema>
```

This XML Schema document has all of the information that JAX-B utilities would need to go from an XML `adage` document to a Java `Adage` instance:

- The XML Schema indicates that the data type, an XML `complexType`, is named `Adage`. In this context, a `complexType` is contrasted with a simple, built-in type such as `xsd:string`. The `Adage` class is programmer-defined rather than built-in as well. When an `Adage` instance is constructed, its two properties, `words` and `wordCount`, are available for setting.

- The XML Schema specifies an element named `words` and another element named `wordCount`, with the data type of each: a `word` in XML is an `xs:string`, which binds to a Java `String`; a `wordCount` in XML is an `xs:int`, which binds to a Java `int`. JAX-B thus works from the convention that the `Adage` elements in the XML Schema correspond to Java properties, with the corresponding *set*-methods—in this case `setWords` and `setWordCount`.

In summary, the JDK *schemagen* utility can generate an XML Schema instance from a Java class. A second JDK utility, *xjc*, works in the other direction. Given an XML Schema, *xjc* can generate Java classes to represent the XML types in the schema. Such processing details, which remain hidden in the Jersey implementation of JAX-RS, will be investigated carefully in Chapter 3. This first look at the Java-to-XML transformation sketches the kind of processing that Jersey must perform to transform an `Adage` into an XML document.

The `Adages` resource has three methods that define the web service operations: *getJson*, *getPlain*, and *getXml*. The operation names are arbitrary. The important routing infor-

---

1. In core Java 8, the functionality of the *schemagen* utility will give way to general annotation processing through *javac*.

mation for each operation comes from the annotations that describe the HTTP verb (in this case, only GET) and the @Path. The *getXml* operation has no @Path annotation, which means that the path for the resource, the Adages class, is the path for this operation; the path is */adages/resourcesA/*. In effect, *getXml* is the default operation.

The *getJson* and *getXml* operations could be combined into a single operation:

```
@GET
@Produces({MediaType.APPLICATION_XML, MediaType.APPLICATION_JSON})
...
```

because Jersey can coordinate directly with the Jackson libraries to process JSON. My implementation uses Jackson explicitly to show just how simple the API is. Further, if the two operations were combined into one, then a client would have to disambiguate the request by adding the HTTP header:

```
Accept: application/json
```

to the HTTP request. It seems cleaner to use two different URIs: */adages/resourcesA/* maps to the default *getXml* operation, whereas */adages/resourcesA/json* maps to the *getJson* operation. Here for review is the utility method that *getJson* calls to produce the JSON:

```
private String toJson(Adage adage) {
    String json = "If you see this, there's a problem.";
    try {
        json = new ObjectMapper().writeValueAsString(adage); ❶
    } catch(Exception e) { }
    return json;
}
```

The Jackson ObjectMapper encapsulates the method writeValueAsString (line 1), which serializes an Adage into a JSON document. The response for a sample request against the *toJson* operation, formatted for readability, would look like this:

```
{"words":    "The limits of my language mean the limits of my world.",
 "wordCount":11
}
```

Similar serialization occurs with respect to an Adage converted into an XML document. The default operation *getXml*:

```
@GET
@Produces({MediaType.APPLICATION_XML}) // could use "application/xml" instead
public JAXBElement<Adage> getXml() {
    return toXml(createAdage());
}
```

returns a JAXBElement<Adage>, an XML document that represents an Adage. Under the hood the JAX-B processor converts an Adage instance into an XML document. On a sample run the output was:

```
<?xml version="1.0" encoding="UTF-8" standalone="yes"?>
<adage>
  <wordCount>10</wordCount>
  <words>If a lion could talk, we could not understand him.</words>
</adage>
```

The POJO class Adage currently has but one annotation, @XmlRootElement. A variety
of others could be used to refine the XML output. Here is a sample refinement:

```
package adages;
...
@XmlRootElement(name = "adage")
@XmlAccessorType(XmlAccessType.FIELD)
@XmlType(propOrder = {"words", "wordCount"})  ❶
public class Adage {
    @XmlElement(required = true)
    protected String words;
    @XmlElement(required = true)
    protected int wordCount;
    ...
```

The @XmlType (line 1) is particularly useful if the order of elements in the generated
XML document matters. In the current implementation, the wordCount element precedes the words element, but this order could be reversed through the propOrder attribute in the @XmlType annotation (line 1).

This first JAX-RS example illustrates the style of implementing a RESTful web service
as a JAX-RS resource. The deployment under Tomcat is uncomplicated, and the
*adages.war* file also can be deployed, as is, under Jetty. The *adages* service supports only
GET requests. The forthcoming *adages2* service, implemented as a set of Restlet resources, supports all of the CRUD operations. The next section also shows, with a different example, how JAX-RS nicely supports all of the CRUD operations.

# Porting the Predictions Web Service to JAX-RS

The servlet-based *predictions2* service supports the four CRUD operations; hence,
the port from the servlet/JSP implementations to JAX-RS is an opportunity to show the
@POST, @PUT, and @DELETE annotations and to illustrate parametrized versions of the
@GET and @DELETE operations. This revision highlights again the JAX-RS idioms for
RESTful URIs. The revised service is called *predictions3*.

The JAX-RS *predictions3* service has four Java classes:

- The RestfulPrediction class extends the JAX-RS Application class. When the
  service WAR file is loaded into Tomcat or Jetty, the Jersey ServletContainer finds
  the RestfulPrediction instance and invokes its getClasses method to identify
  the RESTful resources in the WAR file. In the case of the RestfulPrediction
  service, there is only one resource: the PredictionsRS class.

- The `PredictionsRS` class is the RESTful resource, a POJO class whose methods carry annotations such as `@GET` and `@POST` in support of the standard CRUD operations. This resource supports MIME-typed requests for XML, JSON, and plain text. A GET request can ask for all predictions or for a specific one.

- The `Prediction` class is also a POJO class with two properties from before: `who` is the author of the prediction and `what` is the prediction itself. There is still an `id` property whose value uniquely identifies each `Prediction` instance; prediction instances are stored, in ascending order by `id`, in a `PredictionsList`, explained in the next bullet point. The `Prediction` class is annotated as an `@XmlRootElement` so that Jersey can automatically convert a single prediction into an XML document. The *get*-methods of the properties are annotated with `@XmlElement` for emphasis. A `Prediction` instance can be transformed into an XML or a JSON document; the `Prediction` override of the `toString` method supports a plain-text format as well. The `Prediction` class still implements the `Comparable` interface in case sorting is needed. The implementation logic of *predictions3* ensures, however, that the predictions are always sorted by `id` in ascending order; hence, additional sorting might put the predictions in descending order by `id`, ascending order by `who`, and so on.

- The `PredictionsList` is a class that represents a collection of `Prediction` instances, with the collection implemented as a thread-safe `CopyOnWriteArrayList`. The integer `id` of each prediction added to the list is generated with a thread-safe `AtomicInteger`. The class `PredictionsList` is annotated as an `@XmlRootElement` so that Jersey automatically serializes a list of predictions, as well as a single prediction, into XML. The `PredictionsList` class likewise overrides the `toString` method, yet again a convenient way to support a plain-text representation of a predictions list.

The `RestfulPrediction` class (see Example 2-8) is the JAX-RS `Application` class. To ensure that the *adages* JAX-RS service and this JAX-RS service can coexist in the same servlet container, the names of the two `Application` classes must differ: in the case of *adages*, the `Application` class is `RestfulAdage`; in this case, the `Application` class is `RestfulPrediction`.

*Example 2-8. Registering the `PredictionsRS` class as a JAX-RS resource*

```
package predictions3;

import java.util.Set;
import java.util.HashSet;
import javax.ws.rs.ApplicationPath;
import javax.ws.rs.core.Application;

@ApplicationPath("/resourcesP")
public class RestfulPrediction extends Application {
```

```
    public Set<Class<?>> getClasses() {
        Set<Class<?>> set = new HashSet<Class<?>>();
        set.add(PredictionsRS.class);
        return set;
    }
}
```

The backend support for the `PredictionsRS` source consists of two POJO classes: `Prediction` (see Example 2-9) and `PredictionsList` (see Example 2-10). The class `Prediction` is mostly unchanged from the *predictions2* version except for the added `@XmlRootElement` annotation, which means that the runtime can automatically convert a `Prediction` instance into an XML document. Details follow shortly.

*Example 2-9. The `Prediction` class with properties who, what, and id*

```
package predictions3;

import javax.xml.bind.annotation.XmlRootElement;
import javax.xml.bind.annotation.XmlElement;

@XmlRootElement(name = "prediction")
public class Prediction implements Comparable<Prediction> {
    private String who;    // person
    private String what;   // his/her prediction
    private int    id;     // identifier used as lookup key

    public Prediction() { }
    @Override
    public String toString() {
        return String.format("%2d: ", id) + who + " ==> " + what + "\n";
    }
    public void setWho(String who) { this.who = who; }
    @XmlElement
    public String getWho() { return this.who; }
    public void setWhat(String what) { this.what = what; }
    @XmlElement
    public String getWhat() { return this.what; }
    public void setId(int id) { this.id = id; }
    @XmlElement
    public int getId() { return this.id; }
    public int compareTo(Prediction other) { return this.id - other.id; }
}
```

The `PredictionsList` POJO class (see Example 2-10) in the *predictions3* service is simpler overall than the `Predictions` from class of *predictions2* because methods such as `populate` have moved into the core JAX-RS class. In any case, the `Predictions List` class has a `find` method to search for a particular `Prediction`, and the data structure used to store the predictions is now a thread-safe `CopyOnWriteArrayList`.

*Example 2-10. The PredictionsList class*

```java
package predictions3;

import java.util.List;
import java.util.concurrent.CopyOnWriteArrayList;
import java.util.concurrent.atomic.AtomicInteger;
import javax.xml.bind.annotation.XmlElement;
import javax.xml.bind.annotation.XmlElementWrapper;
import javax.xml.bind.annotation.XmlRootElement;

@XmlRootElement(name = "predictionsList")
public class PredictionsList {
    private List<Prediction> preds;
    private AtomicInteger predId;

    public PredictionsList() {
        preds = new CopyOnWriteArrayList<Prediction>();
        predId = new AtomicInteger();
    }
    @XmlElement
    @XmlElementWrapper(name = "predictions")
    public List<Prediction> getPredictions() {
        return this.preds;
    }
    public void setPredictions(List<Prediction> preds) {
        this.preds = preds;
    }
    @Override
    public String toString() {
        String s = "";
        for (Prediction p : preds) s += p.toString();
        return s;
    }
    public Prediction find(int id) {
        Prediction pred = null;
        // Search the list -- for now, the list is short enough that
        // a linear search is ok but binary search would be better if the
        // list got to be an order-of-magnitude larger in size.
        for (Prediction p : preds) {
            if (p.getId() == id) {
                pred = p;
                break;
            }
        }
        return pred;
    }
    public int add(String who, String what) {
        int id = predId.incrementAndGet();
        Prediction p = new Prediction();
        p.setWho(who);
        p.setWhat(what);
        p.setId(id);
```

```
        preds.add(p);
        return id;
    }
}
```

The `PredictionsRS` class (see Example 2-11) is the JAX-RS resource with annotations
that define the CRUD operations. The class is long enough that inspecting the code in
chunks may be helpful.

*Example 2-11. The JAX-RS resource `PredictionsRS`*

```
package predictions3;

import java.io.InputStream;
import java.io.BufferedReader;
import java.io.InputStreamReader;
import javax.ws.rs.GET;
import javax.ws.rs.POST;
import javax.ws.rs.PUT;
import javax.ws.rs.DELETE;
import javax.ws.rs.Path;
import javax.ws.rs.PathParam;
import javax.ws.rs.FormParam;
import javax.ws.rs.Produces;
import javax.ws.rs.core.MediaType;
import javax.ws.rs.core.Context;
import javax.ws.rs.core.Response;
import javax.ws.rs.core.Context;
import javax.servlet.ServletContext;
import com.fasterxml.jackson.databind.ObjectMapper;

@Path("/")
public class PredictionsRS {
    @Context
    private ServletContext sctx;          // dependency injection
    private static PredictionsList plist; // set in populate()

    public PredictionsRS() { }

    @GET
    @Path("/xml")
    @Produces({MediaType.APPLICATION_XML})
    public Response getXml() {
        checkContext();
        return Response.ok(plist, "application/xml").build();
    }
    @GET
    @Path("/xml/{id: \\d+}")
    @Produces({MediaType.APPLICATION_XML}) // could use "application/xml" instead
    public Response getXml(@PathParam("id") int id) {
        checkContext();
        return toRequestedType(id, "application/xml");
```

```java
}
@GET
@Produces({MediaType.APPLICATION_JSON})
@Path("/json")
public Response getJson() {
    checkContext();
    return Response.ok(toJson(plist), "application/json").build();
}
@GET
@Produces({MediaType.APPLICATION_JSON})
@Path("/json/{id: \\d+}")
public Response getJson(@PathParam("id") int id) {
    checkContext();
    return toRequestedType(id, "application/json");
}
@GET
@Path("/plain")
@Produces({MediaType.TEXT_PLAIN})
public String getPlain() {
    checkContext();
    return plist.toString();
}
@POST
@Produces({MediaType.TEXT_PLAIN})
@Path("/create")
public Response create(@FormParam("who") String who,
                       @FormParam("what") String what) {
    checkContext();
    String msg = null;
    // Require both properties to create.
    if (who == null || what == null) {
        msg = "Property 'who' or 'what' is missing.\n";
        return Response.status(Response.Status.BAD_REQUEST).
                                            entity(msg).
                                            type(MediaType.TEXT_PLAIN).
                                            build();
    }
    // Otherwise, create the Prediction and add it to the collection.
    int id = addPrediction(who, what);
    msg = "Prediction " + id +
        " created: (who = " + who + " what = " + what + ").\n";
    return Response.ok(msg, "text/plain").build();
}
@PUT
@Produces({MediaType.TEXT_PLAIN})
@Path("/update")
public Response update(@FormParam("id") int id,
                       @FormParam("who") String who,
                       @FormParam("what") String what) {
    checkContext();
    // Check that sufficient data is present to do an edit.
    String msg = null;
```

```
        if (who == null && what == null)
            msg = "Neither who nor what is given: nothing to edit.\n";
        Prediction p = plist.find(id);
        if (p == null)
            msg = "There is no prediction with ID " + id + "\n";

        if (msg != null)
            return Response.status(Response.Status.BAD_REQUEST).
                                             entity(msg).
                                             type(MediaType.TEXT_PLAIN).
                                             build();
        // Update.
        if (who != null) p.setWho(who);
        if (what != null) p.setWhat(what);
        msg = "Prediction " + id + " has been updated.\n";
        return Response.ok(msg, "text/plain").build();
    }
    @DELETE
    @Produces({MediaType.TEXT_PLAIN})
    @Path("/delete/{id: \\d+}")
    public Response delete(@PathParam("id") int id) {
        checkContext();
        String msg = null;
        Prediction p = plist.find(id);
        if (p == null) {
            msg = "There is no prediction with ID " + id + ". Cannot delete.\n";
            return Response.status(Response.Status.BAD_REQUEST).
                                             entity(msg).
                                             type(MediaType.TEXT_PLAIN).
                                             build();
        }
        plist.getPredictions().remove(p);
        msg = "Prediction " + id + " deleted.\n";
        return Response.ok(msg, "text/plain").build();
    }
    private void checkContext() {
        if (plist == null) populate();
    }
    private void populate() {
        plist = new PredictionsList();
        String filename = "/WEB-INF/data/predictions.db";
        InputStream in = sctx.getResourceAsStream(filename);
        // Read the data into the array of Predictions.
        if (in != null) {
            try {
                BufferedReader reader =
                    new BufferedReader(new InputStreamReader(in));
                int i = 0;
                String record = null;
                while ((record = reader.readLine()) != null) {
                    String[] parts = record.split("!");
                    addPrediction(parts[0], parts[1]);
```

```
                }
            }
            catch (Exception e) {
                throw new RuntimeException("I/O failed!");
            }
        }
    }
    private int addPrediction(String who, String what) {
        int id = plist.add(who, what);
        return id;
    }
    // Prediction --> JSON document
    private String toJson(Prediction prediction) {
        String json = "If you see this, there's a problem.";
        try {
            json = new ObjectMapper().writeValueAsString(prediction);
        }
        catch(Exception e) { }
        return json;
    }
    // PredictionsList --> JSON document
    private String toJson(PredictionsList plist) {
        String json = "If you see this, there's a problem.";
        try {
            json = new ObjectMapper().writeValueAsString(plist);
        }
        catch(Exception e) { }
        return json;
    }
    // Generate an HTTP error response or typed OK response.
    private Response toRequestedType(int id, String type) {
        Prediction pred = plist.find(id);
        if (pred == null) {
            String msg = id + " is a bad ID.\n";
            return Response.status(Response.Status.BAD_REQUEST).
                                              entity(msg).
                                              type(MediaType.TEXT_PLAIN).
                                              build();
        }
        else if (type.contains("json"))
            return Response.ok(toJson(pred), type).build();
        else
            return Response.ok(pred, type).build(); // toXml is automatic
    }
}
```

A summary of the major parts of this class follows:

- There are five operations annotated with @GET.

  Three of the @GET operations return the entire list of predictions: in XML, in JSON, and in plain-text format. In addition, there is a parametrized GET as follows:

```
@GET
@Path("/xml/{id: \\d+}")
@Produces({MediaType.APPLICATION_XML}) // could use "application/xml" instead
public Response getXml(@PathParam("id") int id) {
    ...
```

If successful, it returns a single prediction in XML. There is a similarly parametrized GET that, if successful, returns a single prediction in JSON. The @Path annotation:

```
@Path("/xml/{id: \\d+}")
```

contains a parameter, id, together with a regular expression that restricts the values of the parameter to one or more decimal digits. The regular expression also could be written as:

```
@Path("/xml/{id: [0-9]+}")
```

In either case, the regular expression requires at least one but perhaps more decimal digits. A request such as:

```
% curl http://localhost:8080/predictions3/resourcesP/xml/13
```

would succeed and return, as an XML document, the Prediction with id 13 because 13 matches the specified pattern. However, a request such as:

```
% curl http://localhost:8080/predictions3/resourcesP/xml/foo
```

would result in an HTTP 404 (Not Found) error because foo does not match the one-or-more-decimal-digits pattern. The JAX-RS support for precise data validation through regular expressions is, of course, convenient; the only complication comes in the regular expressions themselves.

The methods that implement parametrized GET operations use the @PathParam annotation to identify which argument in a method corresponds to the URI parameter. For example, the getJson method begins:

```
@GET
@Produces({MediaType.APPLICATION_JSON})
@Path("/json/{id: \\d+}")
public Response getJson(@PathParam("id") int id) { ❶
    ...
```

The @PathParam named id (line 1) corresponds, in this example, to the int parameter named id as well. The two names could differ. If a URI had multiple parameters:

```
http://...:8080/greetings/resourcesG/msg/fred/Hi
```

then the order of the Java method's parameters could differ from the order in the URI:

```
...
@Path("/msg/{who}/{what}
public Response echoMessage(@PathParam("what") String p1,
                            @PathParam("who") String p2) {
...
```

---

## Why Does the predictions3 RESTful Service Use Static Class Members?

In a production-grade service, the data typically would be persisted in a database of some kind. As the PredictionsRS resource in the *predictions3* service changes through POST, PUT, and DELETE operations, however, these changes are not persisted in a backend database; instead, a static collection is used to store—in memory—the changing data. My goal is to keep the focus on the APIs for RESTful services, minimizing distractions wherever possible, and database access would be one such distraction. In a production-grade service, of course, a persistent data store almost surely would be the way to go. Two later examples illustrate how the JPA (Java Persistence API) can be used to persist Predictions with two different relational database systems.

---

- The operations annotated with @POST, @PUT, and @DELETE implement the remaining CRUD operations: *create*, *update*, and *delete*, respectively.

In the *predictions3* service, most of the RESTfully annotated operations return the JAX-RS type Response. This gives the operations a common look and feel that accentuates critical features of an HTTP response—the HTTP status code together with the content type of the response. For simplicity, the getPlain method returns a String. Here is the return statement from the nonparametrized *getXml* operation, which returns all of the predictions in XML format:

```
return Response.ok(predictions, "application/xml").build();
```

Consider the contrast between this return statement and its counterpart in the *adages* JAX-RS service:

```
@GET
@Produces({MediaType.APPLICATION_XML}) // could use "application/xml" instead
public JAXBElement<Adage> getXml() {
    return toXml(createAdage());
}
```

In the *adages* case, the return type is JAXBElement, and there is an explicit call to the toXml method to convert an Adage instance into an XML document:

```
@XmlElementDecl(namespace = "http://aphorism.adage", name = "adage")
private JAXBElement<Adage> toXml(Adage adage) {
    return new JAXBElement<Adage>(new QName("adage"), Adage.class, adage);
}
```

By contrast, the *predictions3* service simply returns a `Predictions` instance as the `Response` without wrapping the `predictions` reference in a call to `toXml`:

```
//**** No need to invoke toXml on the predictions!
return Response.ok(toXml(predictions), "application/xml").build();
```

The reason for this simplification is that, with `Response` as the return type of the `getXml` method, the JAX-RS runtime automatically generates the XML, and JAX-RS runtime does so because the `@Produces` annotation gives `application/xml` as the MIME type of the HTTP response. Recall that the `Prediction` and `Predic tionsList` POJO classes are annotated with `@XmlRootElement`. The combination of this annotation and the `@Produces` annotation together automate the XML generation.

The *predictions3* service still has a `toJson` utility method to convert one `Prediction` or a collection of these into JSON. This is a design decision, not a necessity. The JAX-RS runtime also generates JSON automatically if the relevant Jackson libraries are included and if the HTTP request contains the header element `Accept: application/json`. The conversion to JSON is simple enough that *predictions3* does it manually, thereby sparing the client the responsibility of adding a specific header element to the HTTP request.

The request pattern in the *predictions3* service is uniform as there is no default URI—that is, a URI consisting solely of the slash (/). A request for an XML document ends with /xml for all predictions in XML or, for instance, /xml/7 to get prediction 7 in XML; a request for JSON ends with /json or, for example, /json/13; and a request for plain text ends with /plain. The JAX-RS patterns for URIs can adhere to the Rails URI patterns, now widely imitated, as closely as the programmer likes.

# A RESTful Web Service as Restlet Resources

The Restlet web framework supports RESTful web services, and the API is similar to JAX-RS; indeed, a Restlet application can use JAX-RS annotations such as `@Produces` instead of or in addition to Restlet annotations. This section adapts the earlier JAX-RS *adages* service to a Restlet implementation, which is published both with a web server and with a standalone Java application. The revised service, *adages2*, implements the four CRUD operations.

## Downloading and Using the Restlet Framework

The Restlet (*http://www.restlet.org*) JAR files are available for free to download. The current version is 2.x. There are editions for core and enterprise Java together with tutorials, documentation, and examples. Restlet, like JAX-RS, provides HTTP-method annotations for resources. Restlet has a client-side and a service-side API. A Restlet resource published under Tomcat or Jetty can be published, with little change, using a standard command-line application and a single Restlet JAR file. The framework does a first-rate job of decoupling the service-as-a-resource from its publication.

The Restlet framework includes JAR files to interoperate with other popular Java frameworks such as Spring and the Google Web Toolkit. Restlet even supports, through an extension, JAX-RS annotations such as @POST and @Produces. There are libraries for Apache's Velocity (*http://www.velocity.apache.org*) templating engine, email, SSL (Secure Sockets Layer), OAuth (*http://www.oauth.net*), and various other technologies. Anyone versatile in either JAX-RS or Restlet should have little trouble adapting to the other, and both approaches are worth a look.

A Restlet web service has three main parts, each of which consists of one or more Java classes:

- A programmer-defined class, in this example AdagesApplication, extends the Restlet Application class. The purpose of the extended class is to set up a *routing table*, which maps request URIs to resources. The resources are named or anonymous Java classes; the current example illustrates both approaches. The spirit of Restlet development is to have very simple resource classes.

- There are arbitrarily many resource classes, any mix of named or anonymous. In best practices, a resource implementation supports a very small number of operations on the resource—in the current example, only one operation per resource. For example, the *adages2* service has seven resources: six of these are named classes that extend the Restlet ServerResource class and the other is an anonymous class that implements the Restlet interface. The named classes are CreateResource, the target of a POST request; UpdateResource, the target of a PUT request; XmlAllRe source, the target of a GET request for all Adages in XML; JsonAllResource, the target of a GET request for all Adages in JSON; XmlOneResource, the target of a GET request for a specified Adage; and so on.

- The backend POJO classes are Adage and Adages, each slightly redefined from the earlier *adages* web service.

If the Restlet service is deployed with a web server such as Tomcat or Jetty, then the Restlet ServerServlet acts as an interceptor for requests against the Restlet service.

---

The interceptor servlet interacts with the Restlet `Application`, which contains the routing table, so that a properly formatted request winds up at the correct Restlet resource. The architecture is simple and clean. Deployment of *adages2* service requires a *web.xml* document (see Example 2-12) that sets up the Restlet interceptor (line 1) and links the interceptor to the Restlet `Application` (line 2).

*Example 2-12. The web.xml file for the adages2 Restlet service*

```
<?xml version="1.0" encoding="UTF-8"?>
<web-app>
   <!-- Restlet adapter -->
   <servlet>
     <servlet-name>RestletServlet</servlet-name>
     <servlet-class>org.restlet.ext.servlet.ServerServlet</servlet-class>    ❶
     <init-param>
       <!-- Application class name -->
       <param-name>org.restlet.application</param-name>
       <param-value>adages2.AdagesApplication</param-value>                   ❷
     </init-param>
   </servlet>
   <!-- Dispach all requests to the Restlet servlet. -->
   <servlet-mapping>
     <servlet-name>RestletServlet</servlet-name>
     <url-pattern>/*</url-pattern>
   </servlet-mapping>
</web-app>
```

---

## The Included JAR Files for the Restlet adages2 Web Service

The *adages2* service can be deployed to Tomcat in the usual way:

```
% ant -Dwar.name=adages2 deploy
```

The deployed WAR file includes these JAR files:

```
org.json.jar
org.restlet.ext.json.jar
org.restlet.ext.servlet.jar
org.restlet.ext.xml.jar
org.restlet.jar
```

The two main files are *org.restlet.jar* and *org.restlet.servlet.jar*. The remaining three files support formatting in XML and JSON. Restlet has various options for formatting responses; the current example illustrates two of these.

---

The `Adage` class (see Example 2-13) is mostly unchanged from the earlier version of the service. There is now an `id` property (line 1) to support searching for a specified `Adage` on a GET, PUT, or DELETE request.

*Example 2-13. The Adage POJO class in the adages2 Restlet service*

```
package adages2;

public class Adage {
    private String words;
    private int wordCount;
    private int id;

    public Adage() { }
    @Override
    public String toString() {
        return String.format("%2d: ", id) + words + " -- " + wordCount + " words";
    }
    public void setWords(String words) {
        this.words = words;
        this.wordCount = words.trim().split("\\s+").length;
    }
    public String getWords() { return this.words; }
    public void setWordCount(int wordCount) { }
    public int getWordCount() { return this.wordCount; }

    public void setId(int id) { this.id = id; }          ❶
    public int getId() { return this.id; }
}
```

The Adages class (see Example 2-14) has a `static` list (line 1) of the thread-safe type `CopyOnWriteArrayList`, which substitutes for a persistence store such as database. The class has a `toPlain` method (line 2) to support a `text/plain` response on a GET request to the *adages2* service. The `find` method (line 3) supports GET, PUT, and DELETE requests for a specified Adage in the list `adages`, and the `add` method (line 4) supports POST requests by adding a newly created Adage to the list.

*Example 2-14. The POJO class Adages in the adages2 Restlet service*

```
package aphorism2;

import java.util.concurrent.CopyOnWriteArrayList;
import java.util.concurrent.atomic.AtomicInteger;

public class Adages {
    private static CopyOnWriteArrayList<Adage> adages;          ❶
    private static AtomicInteger id;

    static {
        String[ ] aphorisms =
            {"What can be shown cannot be said.",
             "If a lion could talk, we could not understand him.",
             "Philosophy is a battle against the bewitchment of
              our intelligence by means of language.",
             "Ambition is the death of thought.",
```

```
               "The limits of my language mean the limits of my world."};
        adages = new CopyOnWriteArrayList<Adage>();
        id = new AtomicInteger();
        for (String str : aphorisms) add(str);
    }

    public static String toPlain() {                                ❷
        String retval = "";
        int i = 1;
        for (Adage adage : adages) retval += adage.toString() + "\n";
        return retval;
    }
    public static CopyOnWriteArrayList<Adage> getList() { return adages; }
    public static Adage find(int id) {                              ❸
        Adage adage = null;
        for (Adage a : adages) {
            if (a.getId() == id) {
                adage = a;
                break;
            }
        }
        return adage;
    }
    public static void add(String words) {                         ❹
        int localId = id.incrementAndGet();
        Adage adage = new Adage();
        adage.setWords(words);
        adage.setId(localId);
        adages.add(adage);
    }
}
```

The AdagesApplication class (see Example 2-15) extends the Restlet Application class
(line 1) and interacts with the service's publisher. In the case of a web server such as
Tomcat, this class works with the Restlet ServerServlet to dispatch incoming service
requests to the proper resource. The dispatching is done through a pattern-driven
routing table at the end of the class.

*Example 2-15. The Restlet Application class with the routing table*

```
package adages2;

import org.restlet.Application;
import org.restlet.Restlet;
import org.restlet.Request;
import org.restlet.Response;
import org.restlet.routing.Router;
import org.restlet.data.Status;
import org.restlet.data.MediaType;

public class AdagesApplication extends Application {               ❶
```

```
@Override
public synchronized Restlet createInboundRoot() {
    // To illustrate the different API possibilities, implement the
    // DELETE operation as an anonymous Restlet class. For the
    // remaining operations, follow Restlet best practices and
    // implement each as a Java class.
    // DELETE handler
    Restlet janitor = new Restlet(getContext()) {                        ❷
            public void handle(Request request, Response response) {
                String msg = null;
                String sid = (String) request.getAttributes().get("id");
                if (sid == null) msg = badRequest("No ID given.\n");
                Integer id = null;
                try {
                    id = Integer.parseInt(sid.trim());
                }
                catch(Exception e) { msg = badRequest("Ill-formed ID.\n"); }
                Adage adage = Adages.find(id);
                if (adage == null)
                    msg = badRequest("No adage with ID " + id + "\n");
                else {
                    Adages.getList().remove(adage);
                    msg = "Adage " + id + " removed.\n";
                }
                // Generate HTTP response.
                response.setEntity(msg, MediaType.TEXT_PLAIN);
            }
        };
    // Create the routing table.
    Router router = new Router(getContext());
    router.attach("/",           PlainResource.class);                   ❸
    router.attach("/xml",        XmlAllResource.class);                  ❹
    router.attach("/xml/{id}",   XmlOneResource.class);
    router.attach("/json",       JsonAllResource.class);                 ❺
    router.attach("/create",     CreateResource.class);                  ❻
    router.attach("/update",     UpdateResource.class);
    router.attach("/delete/{id}", janitor); // instance of anonymous class
    return router;
}
private String badRequest(String msg) {
    Status error = new Status(Status.CLIENT_ERROR_BAD_REQUEST, msg);
    return error.toString();
}
}
```

Each *adages2* resource could be written as an anonymous class encapsulated inside the Application class; however, under Restlet best practices, these resources should be implemented as relatively small, individual classes such as PlainResource (line 3), XmlAllResource (line 4), JsonAllResource (line 5), CreateResource (line 6), and so on. For illustration, however, the AdagesApplication class does include an anonymous class that implements the Restlet interface by defining the handle method, which has

Request and Response parameters; the Response and Request types are quite similar to the HttpServletRequest and HttpServletResponse types, respectively. The reference to an instance of this anonymous class is named janitor (line 2) because the class handles DELETE requests by removing a specified Adage from the list of adages.

The routing table at the end of AdagesApplication class follows a popular idiom for RESTful frameworks such as Restlet: a URI pattern maps to a specified resource. A routing table entry such as:

```
router.attach("/", PlainResource.class);
```

maps the URI /, the single slash, to the PlainResource, thereby making this resource the default one. By contrast, the entry:

```
router.attach("/xml/{id}", XmlOneResource.class); // {id} is a parameter
```

includes the parameter id in braces, where the numerical id identifies the desired Adage. The URI for the UpdateResource does not include the identifier for the Adage in question because this information is supplied in the body of the PUT request.

The resource classes are quite short because each has very specialized, hence limited, functionality. For example, the XmlAllResource is Example 2-16.

*Example 2-16. The XmlAllResource Restlet resource*

```
package adages2;

import org.restlet.resource.Get;
import org.restlet.resource.ServerResource;
import org.restlet.representation.Representation;
import org.restlet.ext.xml.DomRepresentation;
import org.w3c.dom.Document;
import org.w3c.dom.Element;
import org.restlet.data.Status;
import org.restlet.data.MediaType;
import java.util.List;

public class XmlAllResource extends ServerResource {
    public XmlAllResource() { }
    @Get                                                    ❶
    public Representation toXml() {
        List<Adage> list = Adages.getList();
        DomRepresentation dom = null;                       ❷
        try {
            dom = new DomRepresentation(MediaType.TEXT_XML);
            dom.setIndenting(true);
            Document doc = dom.getDocument();

            Element root = doc.createElement("adages");
            for (Adage adage : list) {
                Element next = doc.createElement("adage");
```

```
                next.appendChild(doc.createTextNode(adage.toString()));
                root.appendChild(next);
            }
            doc.appendChild(root);
        }
        catch(Exception e) { }
        return dom;
    }
}
```

There are various Java ways to generate XML, including the DOM (Document Object Model) or tree-based method shown in the XmlAllResource (line 2), which builds the XML tree out of the Adages. This resource is reachable, as the @Get annotation signals (line 1), only with a GET request.

The CreateResource class (see Example 2-17) highlights some nice features of the Restlet API. The argument to the create method, of Restlet type Representation (line 1), represents the HTTP request body. The Restlet class Form (line 2) makes it easy to search for specified keys, in this case words, with which the corresponding values can be accessed, in this case the text for the new Adage.

*Example 2-17. The CreateResource class in the adages2 service*

```
package adages2;

import org.restlet.resource.Post;
import org.restlet.resource.ServerResource;
import org.restlet.representation.Representation;
import org.restlet.representation.StringRepresentation;
import org.restlet.data.Status;
import org.restlet.data.MediaType;
import org.restlet.data.Form;

public class CreateResource extends ServerResource {
    public CreateResource() { }
    @Post
    public Representation create(Representation data) {        ❶
        Status status = null;
        String msg = null;
        // Extract the data from the POST body.
        Form form = new Form(data);                           ❷
        String words = form.getFirstValue("words");
        if (words == null) {
            msg = "No words were given for the adage.\n";
            status = Status.CLIENT_ERROR_BAD_REQUEST;
        }
        else {
            Adages.add(words);
            msg = "The adage '" + words + "' has been added.\n";
            status = Status.SUCCESS_OK;
        }
```

```
        setStatus(status);
        return new StringRepresentation(msg, MediaType.TEXT_PLAIN);
    }
}
```

A JAX-RS resource typically encapsulates several methods, each annotated with a distinct combination of HTTP verb (for instance, @GET or @POST) and URI (that is, @Path). In this sense, a JAX-RS resource class is multipurpose: its various methods handle various HTTP requests. The Restlet approach differs. Each resource class is, in best practices, single-purpose: one annotated method is the callback for an HTTP request targeted at a particular URI. The Restlet resource classes thus tend to be small, as the *adages2* service illustrates.

## Sample Calls Against the adages2 Service

The RESTful *adages2* service can be deployed to Tomcat in the usual way:

```
% ant -Dwar.name=adages2 deploy
```

Once the service is deployed, some *curl* calls can be used to confirm that the service is behaving correctly. Here is a series of test calls. Each begins with a comment, introduced with two semicolons, followed by the *curl* call itself, and ending with the output, which is formatted for readability.

```
;; GET all in plain text
% curl --request GET http://localhost:8080/adages2/
 1: What can be shown cannot be said. -- 7 words
 2: If a lion could talk, we could not understand him. -- 10 words
 ...
;; GET all in XML
% curl --request GET http://localhost:8080/adages2/xml
<?xml version="1.0" encoding="UTF-8" standalone="no"?>
<adages>
<adage> 1: What can be shown cannot be said. -- 7 words</adage>
<adage> 2: If a lion could talk, we could not understand him. -- 10 words</adage>
 ...
;; GET all in JSON
% curl --request GET http://localhost:8080/adages2/json
[ 1: What can be shown cannot be said. -- 7 words,
  2: If a lion could talk, we could not understand him. -- 10 words,
 ...
;; GET Adage with id of 2 in XML
% curl --request GET http://localhost:8080/adages2/xml/2
<?xml version="1.0" encoding="UTF-8" standalone="no"?>
<adage>
    2: If a lion could talk, we could not understand him. -- 10 words
</adage>
;; Create a new adage
% curl --request POST --data "words=This is a test" \
    http://localhost:8080/adages2/create
```

```
The adage 'This is a test' has been added.
;; Delete the newly added Adage
% curl --request DELETE http://localhost:8080/adages2/delete/6
Adage 6 removed.
```

## Publishing the adages2 Restlet Service Without a Web Server

Restlet is excellent at separating concerns: the web service is one concern and its publication is quite another. The *adages2* service can be deployed with Tomcat or Jetty but
also—and with ease—using a standard Java application (see Example 2-18).

*Example 2-18. A Java application to publish the Restlet adages2 web service*

```
package adages2;

import org.restlet.Component;                                           ❶
import org.restlet.data.Protocol;                                       ❷

public class Main {
    public static void main(String[ ] args) throws Exception {
        // Create a new Component.
        Component component = new Component();
        // Add a new HTTP server listening on port 8182.
        component.getServers().add(Protocol.HTTP, 8182);               ❸
        // Attach the application.
        component.getDefaultHost().attach("/adages", new AdagesApplication()); ❹
        // Start the web server.
        component.start();
    }
}
```

The two import statements (lines 1 and 2) in Main require only the *org.restlet.jar* file to
compile and run, but the various Restlet resource classes such as XmlAllResource and
JsonAllResource require other JARs. The command-line server listens to HTTP connections on port 8182 (line 3) for requests against the URI that begins with */adages*
(line 4).

The ZIP file with the sample applications includes *Main.jar*, an executable JAR file that
can be used instead of Tomcat or Jetty to publish the service:

```
% java -jar Main
```

The built-in server listens for requests indefinitely, and the functionality of the *ad-
ages2* service is unchanged in this command-line option for publication. For example,
here is a request for the adages in plain text together with the response:

```
% curl localhost:8182/adages/

1: What can be shown cannot be said. -- 7 words
2: If a lion could talk, we could not understand him. -- 10 words
3: Philosophy is a battle against the bewitchment of our intelligence
```

```
        by means of language. -- 14 words
    4: Ambition is the death of thought. -- 6 words
    5: The limits of my language mean the limits of my world. -- 11 words
```

The URI begins with */adages*, in effect the counterpart of the WAR filename under Tomcat or Jetty. The URI ends with the slash, giving */adages/*, which maps to the `Plain Resource` in the *adages2* service.

The command-line option for publishing is nicely suited for development. In a production environment, web servers such as Tomcat and Jetty or application servers such as GlassFish and WebSphere provide levels of support that a standalone Java application simply cannot match.

# A RESTful Service as a @WebServiceProvider

JAX-WS includes APIs for RESTful and SOAP-based web services, although JAX-WS seems to be used mostly for the latter. The reference implementation is Metro (*http://metro.java.net*), which is part of the GlassFish project. Although JAX-WS technically belongs to enterprise rather than core Java, the core Java JDK (1.6 or greater) includes enough of the Metro distribution to compile and publish RESTful and SOAP-based services. JAX-RS and Restlet are state-of-the-art, high-level APIs for developing RESTful services; by contrast, the JAX-WS API for RESTful services is low-level. Nonetheless, JAX-WS support for RESTful services deserves a look, and the JAX-WS API for SOAP-based services will be the centerpiece in Chapter 4 and Chapter 5.

The JAX-WS stack reflects the view that SOAP-based services over HTTP are refinements of RESTful services. The JAX-WS API has two main annotations. A POJO class annotated as a `@WebService` delivers a SOAP-based service, whereas a POJO class annotated as a `@WebServiceProvider` usually delivers a RESTful one; however, a class annotated as a `@WebServiceProvider` can deliver a SOAP-based service as well. Yet another revision of the *adages* RESTful service, *adages3*, introduces the JAX-WS API for RESTful services.

In the revised *adages3* service, the `Adage` and `Adages` classes are mostly unchanged from the *adages2* version. One small change is that the package name goes from `adages2` to `adages3`; another change is that the `Adage` list is returned as array, which then is serialized into XML. The `toPlain` method in the `Adages` class could be dropped because the revised service deals only in `application/xml` and not in `text/plain` HTTP payloads. The `AdagesProvider` class (see Example 2-19) supports the four CRUD operations against the RESTful service.

*Example 2-19. The AdagesProvider class that supports the CRUD operations*

```
package adages3;

import java.beans.XMLEncoder;
```

```
import java.io.ByteArrayOutputStream;
import java.io.ByteArrayInputStream;
import java.io.StringReader;
import java.util.ArrayList;
import java.util.Arrays;
import javax.annotation.Resource;
import javax.xml.transform.Source;
import javax.xml.transform.stream.StreamSource;
import javax.xml.transform.Transformer;
import javax.xml.transform.TransformerFactory;
import javax.xml.transform.stream.StreamResult;
import javax.xml.ws.handler.MessageContext;
import javax.xml.ws.WebServiceContext;
import javax.xml.ws.WebServiceProvider;
import javax.xml.ws.Provider;
import javax.xml.ws.BindingType;
import javax.xml.ws.http.HTTPBinding;
import javax.xml.ws.ServiceMode;
import javax.xml.ws.http.HTTPException;
import javax.xml.xpath.XPathFactory;
import javax.xml.xpath.XPath;
import javax.xml.xpath.XPathConstants;
import org.xml.sax.InputSource;

@WebServiceProvider                               // generic service provider       ❶
@ServiceMode(javax.xml.ws.Service.Mode.MESSAGE) // entire message available        ❷
@BindingType(HTTPBinding.HTTP_BINDING)           // versus SOAP binding            ❸
public class AdagesProvider implements Provider<Source> {
    @Resource
    protected WebServiceContext wctx;  // dependency injection

    public AdagesProvider() { }
    // Implement the Provider interface by defining invoke, which expects an XML
    // source (perhaps null) and returns an XML source (perhaps null).
    public Source invoke(Source request) {                                         ❹
        if (wctx == null) throw new RuntimeException("Injection failed on wctx.");
        // Grab the message context and extract the request verb.
        MessageContext mctx = wctx.getMessageContext();                            ❺
        String httpVerb = (String) mctx.get(MessageContext.HTTP_REQUEST_METHOD);
        httpVerb = httpVerb.trim().toUpperCase();
        // Dispatch on verb to the handler method. POST and PUT have non-null
        // requests so only these two get the Source request.
        if      (httpVerb.equals("GET"))    return doGet(mctx);                     ❻
        else if (httpVerb.equals("POST"))   return doPost(request);
        else if (httpVerb.equals("PUT"))    return doPut(request);
        else if (httpVerb.equals("DELETE")) return doDelete(mctx);
        else throw new HTTPException(405);  // bad verb
    }
    private Source doGet(MessageContext mctx) {
        // Parse the query string.
        String qs = (String) mctx.get(MessageContext.QUERY_STRING);
        // Get all Adages.
```

```
        if (qs == null) return adages2Xml();
        // Get a specified Adage.
        else {
            int id = getId(qs);
            if (id < 0) throw new HTTPException(400); // bad request
            Adage adage = Adages.find(id);
            if (adage == null) throw new HTTPException(404); // not found
            return adage2Xml(adage);
        }
    }
}
private Source doPost(Source request) {
    if (request == null) throw new HTTPException(400); // bad request
    InputSource in = toInputSource(request);
    String pattern = "//words/text()"; // find the Adage's "words"
    String words = findElement(pattern, in);
    if (words == null) throw new HTTPException(400); // bad request
    Adages.add(words);
    String msg = "The adage '" + words + "' has been created.";
    return toSource(toXml(msg));
}
private Source doPut(Source request) {
    if (request == null) throw new HTTPException(400); // bad request
    InputSource in = toInputSource(request);
    String pattern = "//words/text()";   // find the Adage's "words"
    String words = findElement(pattern, in);
    if (words == null) throw new HTTPException(400); // bad request
    // Format in XML is: <words>!<id>
    String[ ] parts = words.split("!");
    if (parts[0].length() < 1 || parts[1].length() < 1)
        throw new HTTPException(400); // bad request
    int id = -1;
    try {
        id = Integer.parseInt(parts[1].trim());
    }
    catch(Exception e) { throw new HTTPException(400); } // bad request
    // Find and edit.
    Adage adage = Adages.find(id);
    if (adage == null) throw new HTTPException(404); // not found
    adage.setWords(parts[0]);
    String msg = "Adage " + adage.getId() + " has been updated.";
    return toSource(toXml(msg));
}
private Source doDelete(MessageContext mctx) {
    String qs = (String) mctx.get(MessageContext.QUERY_STRING);
    // Disallow the deletion of all teams at once.
    if (qs == null) throw new HTTPException(403); // illegal operation
    else {
        int id = getId(qs);
        if (id < 0) throw new HTTPException(400); // bad request
        Adage adage = Adages.find(id);
        if (adage == null) throw new HTTPException(404); // not found
        Adages.remove(adage);
```

```
                String msg = "Adage " + id + " removed.";
                return toSource(toXml(msg));
        }
    }
    private int getId(String qs) {
        int badId = -1; // bad ID
        String[ ] parts = qs.split("=");
        if (!parts[0].toLowerCase().trim().equals("id")) return badId;
        int goodId = badId; // for now
        try {
            goodId = Integer.parseInt(parts[1].trim());
        }
        catch(Exception e) { return badId; }
        return goodId;
    }
    private StreamSource adages2Xml() {
        String str = toXml(Adages.getListAsArray());
        return toSource(str);
    }
    private StreamSource adage2Xml(Adage adage) {
        String str = toXml(adage);
        return toSource(str);
    }
    private String toXml(Object obj) {
        ByteArrayOutputStream out = new ByteArrayOutputStream();
        XMLEncoder enc = new XMLEncoder(out);
        enc.writeObject(obj);
        enc.close();
        return out.toString();
    }
    private StreamSource toSource(String str) {
        return new StreamSource(new StringReader(str));
    }
    private InputSource toInputSource(Source source) {
        InputSource input = null;
        try {
            Transformer trans = TransformerFactory.newInstance().newTransformer();
            ByteArrayOutputStream bos = new ByteArrayOutputStream();
            StreamResult result = new StreamResult(bos);
            trans.transform(source, result);
            input = new InputSource(new ByteArrayInputStream(bos.toByteArray()));
        }
        catch(Exception e) { throw new HTTPException(500); } // internal server error
        return input;
    }
    private String findElement(String expression, InputSource source) {
        XPath xpath = XPathFactory.newInstance().newXPath();
        String retval = null;
        try {
            retval =
                (String) xpath.evaluate(expression, source, XPathConstants.STRING);
        }
```

```
        catch(Exception e) { throw new HTTPException(400); } // bad request
        return retval;
    }
}
```

Even a glance at the AdagesProvider code looks low-level. Much of this code transforms one type to another, for example, a Source to an InputSource or an Adage to a Stream Source. The Source types are *sources of XML*. The JAX-P (Java API for XML-Processing) packages, used in the *adages3* service, support *transforms* that convert a *source* into a *result* (see Figure 2-1).

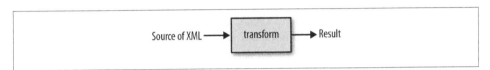

*Figure 2-1. A JAX-P transform*

For example, a generic Source might be transformed into a specific type such as Stream Result. The need for such transformations in the *adages3* service is explained shortly. First, however, it will be helpful to consider the overall structure of the AdagesProvider.

Three annotations adorn the AdagesProvider class:

- @WebServiceProvider (line 1) indicates that the AdagesProvider class implements a templated Provider interface, in this case a Provider<Source> interface, where Source is a source precisely of XML. The templated Provider interface requires that the implementing class define the method:

    ```
    public Source invoke(Source input) { /*...*/ }
    ```

    This method expects a Source of XML as an argument and returns a Source of XML. The AdagesProvider class defines the invoke method (line 2), which is the target of every HTTP request against the *adages3* service. The invoke method implements a simple routing table. After extracting the HTTP verb from the incoming request, using the MessageContext map (line 5) that the runtime provides, the invoke method calls one of four AdagesProvider methods (line 6), each of which returns a Source of XML for the HTTP response body:

    ```
    // mctc --> MessageContext, request --> Source
    if      (httpVerb.equals("GET"))    return doGet(mctx);
    else if (httpVerb.equals("POST"))   return doPost(request);
    else if (httpVerb.equals("PUT"))    return doPut(request);
    else if (httpVerb.equals("DELETE")) return doDelete(mctx);
    else throw new HTTPException(405);  // bad verb
    ```

This table mimics, in the method names, an `HttpServlet` with its encapsulated `doGet`, `doPost`, `doPut`, and `doDelete` methods. The difference here is that each *do*-method takes only one argument. The GET and DELETE have no bodies, which means that the incoming `Source` is empty. In any case, the `doGet` and `doDelete` methods need only information in the query string, which is stored in the HTTP headers; hence, `doGet` and `doDelete` are passed the `MessageContext` as the argument. By contrast, the `doPost` and `doPut` methods require information in the HTTP request body, a nonempty `Source`; these methods therefore are passed the request `Source` as their single argument.

- The `@ServiceMode` annotation (line 2) has two possible values: `MESSAGE` (the entire request message) or `PAYLOAD` (the body, if any, of the request message). The *adages3* service needs access to both the HTTP headers and, for POST and PUT requests, the HTTP body; hence, the service mode is `MESSAGE`.

- The `@BindingType` (line 3) refers to the type of payload in an HTTP message. The default type is SOAP, which means that the body of an HTTP message (for instance, a POST request or any response) is a SOAP document. The `AdagesProvider` specifies an HTTP binding, which means that the HTTP payload is to be arbitrary XML, not exclusively the SOAP variant of XML. Even with this binding type, however, a SOAP document could be a payload because SOAP still counts as XML.

This overview should help in the more detailed analysis that follows. In the *adages3* service, the `doGet` method needs to handle two cases:

- If there is no query string, this method assumes that the client means *read all* with the GET request. In this case, the entire list of adages, encoded as XML using the `XMLEncoder`, is returned.

- If there is a query string, it should have a key/value pair such as:

    id=4

    where 4 is then interpreted as the `id` of the single message to be returned. Here, for quick review, is the `doGet` method:

```
private Source doGet(MessageContext mctx) {
    // Parse the query string.
    String qs = (String) mctx.get(MessageContext.QUERY_STRING);
    if (qs == null) return adages2Xml(); // all adages        ❶
    else {                               // one adage
        int id = getId(qs);
        if (id < 0) throw new HTTPException(400); // bad request
        Adage adage = Adages.find(id);
        if (adage == null) throw new HTTPException(404); // not found
        return adage2Xml(adage);
    }
}
```

Utility methods such as `adages2Xml` (line 1) handle the transformation of `Adage` objects into XML documents (text), which in turn are transformed into `Stream Source` instances sent back to the client.

The `doPost` method is:

```
private Source doPost(Source request) {
    if (request == null) throw new HTTPException(400); // bad request
    InputSource in = toInputSource(request);                          ❶
    String pattern = "//words/text()"; // find the Adage's "words"    ❷
    String words = findElement(pattern, in);
    if (words == null) throw new HTTPException(400); // bad request
    Adages.add(words);
    String msg = "The adage '" + words + "' has been created.";
    return toSource(toXml(msg));
}
```

This method relies on utility methods, in particular on the tricky `toInputSource` method (line 1) that transforms a `Source` request, which is likely but not necessarily a `Stream Source`, into an `InputSource`. The reason is that, for convenience, the `doPost` method uses an `XPath` instance to search the incoming XML document for the `words` in the `Adage` to be created. For example, the XML document might look like this in a POST request:

```
<ns1:foo xmlns:ns1='http://sample.org'>
    <words>This is the way the world ends.</words>
</ns1:foo>
```

An `XPath` search requires a pattern, in this example (line 2):

```
//words/text()
```

The two opening slashes mean *anywhere in the document* and the specific search term is the literal `words`. The `text()` at the end signals `XPath` to return the text node in the XML document that contains the new adage; in this case, the phrase:

```
This is the way the world ends.
```

The search is flexible in that the XML tag *words* could be anywhere in the document, in this example nested inside the root element named *ns1:foo*. Now let me get back to the point about needing to transform a `Source` into an `InputSource`. The `XPath` method `evaluate` searches an XML document for a pattern such as *//words* but requires, as a second argument, an `InputSource`; hence, the transformation of the incoming but generic `Source` to an `InputSource` sets up the `XPath` search. There are other ways in which the `XPath` search might be supported but any of these would require a transformation of some kind.

The `doPut` method in the `AdagesProvider` class is similar in structure to the `doPost` method because, of course, creating a new `Adage` (POST) and updating an existing one

(PUT) are similar operations. However, the doPut implementation allows only the words of the Adage to be changed; the id property, which the Adages class manages, cannot be changed through a PUT operation.

---

## Publishing the adages3 Service with Tomcat and Endpoint

With core Java 1.6 or greater, publishing a @WebServiceProvider service (and, for that matter, a SOAP-based @WebService) from the command line requires very little code. Here is a sample publisher, included in the ZIP with the sample code:

```
package adages3;

import javax.xml.ws.Endpoint;
public class Publisher {
    public static void main(String[ ] args) {
        int port = 8888;
        String url = "http://localhost:" + port + "/";
        System.out.println("Restfully publishing on port " + port);
        Endpoint.publish(url, new AdagesProvider());
    }
}
```

Once published, the AdagesProvider service awaits requests indefinitely on port 8888. For example, the request:

```
% curl localhost:8888/?id=3
```

elicits the response:

```
<java version="1.7.0" class="java.beans.XMLDecoder">
 <object class="adages3.Adage">
  <void property="id">
   <int>3</int>
  </void>
  <void property="wordCount">
   <int>14</int>
  </void>
  <void property="words">
   <string>
     Philosophy is a battle against the bewitchment of our intelligence
     by means of language.
   </string>
  </void>
 </object>
</java>
```

Publishing with Tomcat or Jetty is likewise straightforward, although two configuration files are needed: the usual *web.xml* and the additional *sun-jaxws.xml*. Here is the *web.xml* for the *adages3* service:

---

```
<?xml version="1.0" encoding="UTF-8"?>
<web-app>
  <listener>
    <listener-class>
      com.sun.xml.ws.transport.http.servlet.WSServletContextListener   ❶
    </listener-class>
  </listener>
  <servlet>
    <servlet-name>jaxws</servlet-name>
    <servlet-class>
      com.sun.xml.ws.transport.http.servlet.WSServlet
    </servlet-class>                                                    ❷
    <load-on-startup>1</load-on-startup>
  </servlet>
  <servlet-mapping>
    <servlet-name>jaxws</servlet-name>
    <url-pattern>/*</url-pattern>
  </servlet-mapping>
</web-app>
```

The Metro classes `WSServletContextListener` (line 1) and `WSServlet` (line 2) are in the JAR file currently named *webservices-rt.jar*, which can be downloaded with the rest of Metro JARs (*http://metro.java.net*). This JAR should be in the *src* directory so that the Ant script can package it in the deployed WAR file. In any case, the `WSServletContextListener` parses the *sun-jaxws.xml* file, with more details shortly. The `WSServlet` acts as the interceptor: the servlet receives incoming requests and dispatches these to the *AdagesProvider* service. This architecture is quite similar to the Restlet version.

The second configuration file, *sun-jaxws.xml*, is:

```
<?xml version="1.0" encoding="UTF-8"?>
<endpoints version="2.0"
           xmlns="http://java.sun.com/xml/ns/jax-ws/ri/runtime">  ❶
  <endpoint implementation="adages3.AdagesProvider"                ❷
            name="AdagesProvider"
            url-pattern="/*"/>
</endpoints>
```

This file completes the routing by notifying the `WSServletContextListener` that the `WSServlet` should dispatch requests to an `AdagesProvider` instance (line 2). By the way, the `xmlns` attribute in the `endpoints` element (line 1) is important and should not be changed or omitted.

With the two configuration files and the Metro library JAR in the *src* directory, the *adages3* service can be deployed to Tomcat in the usual way:

```
% ant -Dwar.name=adages3 deploy
```

Sample requests then can be sent to the service:

```
% curl localhost:8080/adages3?id=3
```

The JAX-WS @WebServiceProvider is a low-level, XML-centric API. Java is well known for providing options, and this API is among the Java options for delivering REST-style services. Chapter 7 introduces the client-side API, based on the Dispatch interface, for RESTful services implemented with @WebServiceProvider.

# What's Next?

This chapter focused on programming and publishing RESTful services; the next chapter focuses on consuming such services, or the client side. Some of the sample clients make requests against major RESTful sites such as Amazon and Twitter, whereas others make requests against the services developed in this chapter. Once again, the goal is to illustrate, with working code, the various client-side APIs at the Java programmer's disposal.

Four different APIs were considered in this chapter, but these APIs fall into three general groups:

- The HttpServlet API, which has been around since the late 1990s, remains an excellent way to implement RESTful services. Servlets are HTTP-aware and provide convenient filtering of requests by HTTP verb. Programmers accustomed to implementing websites with servlets, JSP, and related scripting languages such as JSF or Struts, should find servlets a natural and appealing way to deliver web services as well. The servlet API is at once uncomplicated and powerful.

- The JAX-RS and Restlet APIs take full advantage of Java annotations to advertise the RESTful aspects of implemented services. These frameworks integrate well with JAX-B technologies to automate the conversion of Java types into XML and JSON documents. JAX-RS and Restlet services, like servlet-based servlets, can be published with production-grade web servers such as Tomcat and Jetty. These APIs also mimic the routing idioms that have become so popular because of frameworks such as Rails and Sinatra.

- The JAX-WS API, with the @WebServiceProvider at its center, is lower level than the other options but well suited for programmers who need to be close to the HTTP and XML metal. This API is sufficiently rich to deliver real-world RESTful services, but the rival APIs are more appealing in that they hide many of the details that a JAX-WS service must handle explicitly. For SOAP-based services, the JAX-WS API is as good as any and will be the focus in Chapters 4 and 5.

# CHAPTER 3

# RESTful Web Services: The Client Side

Consider a familiar scenario in which a client accesses a RESTful web service:

1. The client issues a GET request against a RESTful service. In general, a request to a RESTful service targets a named resource, with a URI as the name.

2. If successful, this GET request results in a response document, a representation of the resource targeted in the request. The document is usually in XML or JSON, although other formats might be available. In any case, the response should be MIME-typed.

3. The client extracts from the document whatever information is required for the client's application logic.

For example, the client might be a jQuery script embedded in an HTML document. This client requests data, such as a product list, from a web service. If the request succeeds, the client extracts relevant information; for instance, the client might extract the name, category, price, and in-stock quantity of each product in the list. The client then processes the information in some appropriate way; for example, the JavaScript client might build and display an HTML table that represents the product list, with one row per product.

Each step in this sample scenario poses a challenge. The GET request must be formatted properly, and the status code of the response should be inspected to determine whether the request succeeded and, if not, why not. The toughest challenge for the client, however, may be extracting required information from the document: the client may have to parse the returned document to get the information in a usable format. To build an HTML table from an XML document, for example, a JavaScript client would need to extract information items as text *without* the XML markup; an XML parse would be the standard way to extract such information. It would be easier if the JavaScript client received a JSON payload so that the XML parse could be avoided altogether. The

@WebServiceProvider service in Chapter 2 illustrates the problem of parsing XML because successful POST and PUT operations against this service must send, as an XML document, the data required to construct or edit an Adage, and the service code parses the document to extract the words that make up the Adage. A dominant theme in this chapter is how to avoid the explicit parsing of documents, XML or JSON, returned from RESTful services.

All of the CRUD verbs used in RESTful services pose challenges, although these differ in degree, for both the service and the client. This chapter focuses on the client side and pays particular attention to the challenge of extracting usable information from an HTTP response whose payload is an XML or JSON document. Some examples parse documents to extract such information, and other examples show how explicit parsing can be avoided. Java has various libraries, standard and contributed, for dealing with XML and JSON documents; the examples illustrate such libraries.

Web services in general purport to be language-neutral. Accordingly, the proof of the pudding is whether a client written in one language can consume, without undue fuss, a service written in a different language. My first example illustrates how this can be done with a Perl client against a Java RESTful service. Most of the other examples focus on Java clients against various services, including two Java clients against Amazon's RESTful E-Commerce service. The E-Commerce examples highlight the complexities encountered in targeting real-world services.

# A Perl Client Against a Java RESTful Web Service

The Perl client (see Example 3-1) against the Java *predictions2* RESTful service, implemented as an HttpServlet, makes various calls that cover the CRUD operations. (The *predictions2* service is from Chapter 2.) Perl comes with most Unixy systems and is available on Windows (see, for example, ActiveState (*http://www.activestate.com*)). Although Perl has a quirky syntax—it has been called *line-noise interpreted* and even worse —its excellent libraries, standard and contributed, more than compensate. In any case, the point of the example is to provide a first look at how a client interacts with a RESTful service. The *curl* clients from the two previous chapters illustrated all of the CRUD operations against several services; all of the CRUD requests received at least a minimal document in return. Yet the *curl* utility is meant for making HTTP requests, not processing HTTP responses. The Perl client takes the second step; that is, this client performs all of the CRUD operations and then highlights the challenge of processing response documents. In the case of response documents in XML, the Perl client parses the XML to extract usable information, in this case the id, who, and what of a specified Prediction or of the entire PredictionsList returned from the service.

*Example 3-1. A Perl client making CRUD calls against the RESTful predictions2 service*

```perl
#!/usr/bin/perl -w

# packages
use strict;
use LWP;
use XML::XPath;
use List::MoreUtils qw(each_array);

my $baseUrl = 'http://localhost:8080/predictions2/';
my $ua = LWP::UserAgent->new;
runTests();

## Run CRUD tests against the service.
sub runTests {
    getTest($baseUrl);                  ## GET all (xml)
    getTest($baseUrl . '?id=4');        ## GET one (xml)
    getTestJson($baseUrl);              ## GET all (json)
    getTestJson($baseUrl . '?id=4');    ## GET one (json)
    postTest($baseUrl);                 ## POST
    getTest($baseUrl);                  ## GET all (xml)
    putTest($baseUrl);                  ## PUT
    getTest($baseUrl . '?id=4');        ## GET one (xml)
    deleteTest($baseUrl . '?id=31');    ## DELETE
    getTest($baseUrl);                  ## GET one (xml)
}
sub getTest {
    my ($url) = @_;
    my $request = HTTP::Request->new(GET => $url);
    my $response = $ua->request($request);
    handleResponse($response, \&parseXml); # pointer to a function
}
sub getTestJson {
    my ($url) = @_;
    my $request = HTTP::Request->new(GET => $url,
                        HTTP::Headers->new('Accept' => 'application/json'));
    my $response = $ua->request($request);
    handleResponse($response, \&parseJson);
}
sub postTest {
    my ($url) = @_;
    my $request = HTTP::Request->new(POST => $url);
    $request->content_type('application/x-www-form-urlencoded');
    $request->content('who=TS Eliot&what=This is the way the world ends.');
    my $response = $ua->request($request);
    handleResponse($response, undef);
}
sub putTest {
    my ($url) = @_;
    my $request = HTTP::Request->new(PUT => $url);
    $request->content_type('application/x-www-form-urlencoded');
    $request->content('id=4#who=FOOBAR');
```

```perl
    my $response = $ua->request($request);
    handleResponse($response, undef);
}
sub deleteTest {
    my ($url) = @_;
    my $request = HTTP::Request->new(DELETE => $url);
    my $response = $ua->request($request);
    handleResponse($response, undef);
}
sub parseXml {
    my ($rawXml) = @_;
    # print "Raw XML response:\n" . $rawXml . "\n";
    # Set up the XPath search.
    my $xp = XML::XPath->new(xml => trim($rawXml));
    # Extract a list apiece of ids, whos, and whats.
    my @ids = $xp->find('//object/void[@property="id"]/int')->get_nodelist;
    my @whos = $xp->find('//object/void[@property="who"]/string')->get_nodelist;
    my @whats = $xp->find('//object/void[@property="what"]/string')->get_nodelist;
    # Iterate over the lists to print the data.
    my $it = each_array(@ids, @whos, @whats);
    while (my ($id, $who, $what) = $it->()) {
        print sprintf("%2d: ", $id->string_value) .
            $who->string_value . " -> '" .
            $what->string_value . "'\n";
    }
}
sub parseJson {
    my ($json) = @_;
    print "JSON document:\n$json\n";
    # ...
}
sub trim {
    my $string = shift;
    $string =~ s/^\s+//;
    $string =~ s/\s+$//;
    return $string;
}
sub handleResponse {
    my ($response, $callback) = @_;
    if ($response->is_success) {
        if (defined $callback) {
            $callback->($response->content);
        }
        else {
            print $response->content . "\n";
        }
    }
    else {
        print STDERR $response->status_line . "\n";
    }
}
```

The Perl client can make a GET request for all predictions or just a specified one, and the client can express a preference for XML or JSON in either case. Here is the function getTest, which requests all predictions in XML:

```perl
sub getTest {
    my ($url) = @_;                                      ❶
    print "\nGET request against $url\n\n";
    my $request = HTTP::Request->new(GET => $url);       ❷
    my $response = $ua->request($request);               ❸
    handleResponse($response, \&parseXml);               ❹
}
```

In line 1 the $url variable (in Perl, a scalar variable starts with a $) has, as its value, a string URL that targets the *predictions2* service, whose GET operation is the doGet method in the HttpServlet. The Perl client generates, in line 2, a request object (the reference is $request) and then issues this request through a LWP::UserAgent instance, with $ua as the reference (line 3). The client then invokes, in line 4, the function named handleResponse with two arguments: the $response reference, which gives access to the entire HTTP response, including the status code, the headers, and the body; and a reference to a response-processing function, in this case parseXml, which parses the returned XML if the request succeeds.

The function parseXml illustrates the challenge of extracting usable information from the XML payload. Perl, like most general-purpose languages, has various ways to parse XML. In this example, the Perl XPath library is used. Here is the parsing function without the comments:

```perl
sub parseXml {
    my ($rawXml) = @_;
    print "Raw XML response:\n" . $rawXml . "\n"; # raw xml        ❶
    my $xp = XML::XPath->new(xml => trim($rawXml));                ❷
    my @ids = $xp->find('//object/void[@property="id"]/int')
        ->get_nodelist;                                            ❸
    my @whos = $xp->find('//object/void[@property="who"]/string')
        ->get_nodelist;                                           ❹
    my @whats = $xp->find('//object/void[@property="what"]/string')
        ->get_nodelist;                                           ❺
    my $it = each_array(@ids, @whos, @whats);
    while (my ($id, $who, $what) = $it->()) {
      print sprintf("%2d: ", $id->string_value) . $who->string_value . " -> '" .
            $what->string_value . "'\n";
    }
}
```

The function prints the raw XML from the *predictions2* service (line 1) and then uses XPath (line 2) to get three lists: @ids, @whos, and @whats (lines 3, 4, and 5). (Perl lists begin with @.) The while loop then prints the text representation of each Prediction, giving the values of its id, who, and what properties. Here is a slice of the output:

```
 1: Cornelius Tillman ->
    'Managed holistic contingency will grow killer action-items.'
 2: Conner Kulas ->
    'Vision-oriented zero administration timeframe will generate
     backend interfaces.'
...
23: Lottie Marks ->
    'Open-source multitasking timeframe will monetize rich partnerships.'
```

In a production example, the application logic might be considerably more complicated than simply printing the extracted information. The extracted `Prediction` instances might be inserted into a database, mined for relevant patterns, integrated with other information, sent out as email greetings, and so on. Nonetheless, the XML parsing would be the first step in support of any such additional processing.

The other requests from the Perl client are very similar to the *curl* commands used in Chapters 1 and 2. For example, the *predictions2* service returns JSON rather than XML on a GET request if the appropriate header element is in the HTTP message. The Perl client inserts the `Accept` key/value pair, issues the request, and then parses the returned JSON (line 1):

```
my $request = HTTP::Request->new(GET => $url,
                         HTTP::Headers->new('Accept' => 'application/json')); ❶
my $response = $ua->request($request);
handleResponse($response, \&parseJson);
```

A POST or a PUT request requires that relevant data about a `Prediction` be inserted into the body of the HTTP request. Here is the POST test:

```
sub postTest {
    my ($url) = @_;
    my $request = HTTP::Request->new(POST => $url);
    $request->content_type('application/x-www-form-urlencoded');       ❶
    $request->content('who=TS Eliot&what=This is the way the world ends.'); ❷
    my $response = $ua->request($request);                             ❸
    handleResponse($response, undef); # undef means no callback function  ❹
}
```

Line 1 sets the content type of the HTTP request for x-www-form-urlencoded, the standard type for the body of a POST request; this type is commonly abbreviated as the *HTTP form*. The form holds two key/value pairs, one for the who and the other for the what property of a `Prediction` (line 2). Line 3 sends the request and awaits the response. In line 4, the call to `handleResponse`, the Perl value `undef` (short for *undefined*) serves roughly the same purpose as `null` in Java. In the call to `handleResponse`, a second argument with `undef` as its value signals that the HTTP response should be printed rather than processed further; for example, on a successful POST, the printed response would be similar to:

```
<?xml version="1.0" encoding="UTF-8"?>
<java version="1.7.0" class="java.beans.XMLDecoder">
```

```
<string>Prediction 36 created.</string>
</java>
```

The Perl example illustrates language neutrality in RESTful web services because the *predictions2* service is written in Java. At the same time, this example focuses on a central question in this chapter: How can a RESTful client minimize or even avoid XML/JSON parsing? Even the relatively short Perl client makes clear that the tricky code involves XML parsing, although the Perl XPath library has an API that eases the task. The next section addresses the issue of response-document parsing with two examples, each a Java client against the Amazon E-Commerce service. The first client contends with the XML that the Amazon service returns, whereas the second client uses JAX-B to transform the XML into native Java objects, which are then manipulated with the familiar *get/set* methods.

# A Client Against the Amazon E-Commerce Service

Amazon Web Services (*http://aws.amazon.com*) is an umbrella for Amazon's pioneering contributions, in infrastructure and applications, to web services. From early on, Amazon pushed hard to make its web sites for shopping, storage (S3, Simple Storage Service), utility-priced cloud computing (EC2), and so on available as web services, too. Among the prominent hosts of web services, Amazon is unusual in offering both SOAP-based and REST-style versions of such services. This chapter and later ones have code examples that involve Amazon's E-Commerce or shopping service (see "Registering with Amazon" on page 101), which requires an *accessId* and a *secretKey* for access. The *accessId* is inserted, as is, into any request against the E-Commerce service; the *secret-Key* is used to create what Amazon calls a *signature*, which is likewise inserted into every request and then verified on the Amazon side. The *secretKey* itself is not inserted into a request.

---

## Registering with Amazon

Amazon's E-Commerce web service (*http://affiliate-program.amazon.com*) is free of charge but requires registration. In particular, a web service client requires both an *access key id* (*accessId* for short) and a *secret access key* (*secretKey* for short), each of which comes from Amazon after registration. The sample clients against the E-Commerce service, in this and later chapters, require the *accessId* and the *secretKey* as command-line arguments.

---

The RestfulAmazon client (see Example 3-2) is relatively clean code but only because the messy details are isolated in the utility class RequestHelper. Amazon requires, in a RESTful request for item lookups against the E-Commerce service, that the verb be GET and that the required data be in a strictly formatted query string. Here are some details:

- The keys in the query string must be in lexicographical order with respect to the first byte in the key's name.

- The query string must include an ISO-8601 timestamp.

- The query string must be URL-encoded under RFC 3986.

- The query string must include a *hash-based message authentication code* using the SHA-256 hash algorithm. This hash value is what Amazon calls the signature.

- The authentication code must be base64-encoded.

Amazon's RESTful service is fussy about the format of requests against it. The utility class RequestHelper ensures that a GET request against the E-Commerce service has the required query string format.

*Example 3-2. The RestfulAmazon client against the Amazon E-Commerce web service*

```
package restful;

import java.net.URL;
import java.net.URLConnection;
import java.io.BufferedReader;
import java.io.InputStreamReader;
import java.io.ByteArrayInputStream;
import java.util.HashMap;
import java.util.Map;
import javax.xml.parsers.DocumentBuilderFactory;
import javax.xml.parsers.DocumentBuilder;
import org.w3c.dom.Document;
import org.w3c.dom.Element;
import org.w3c.dom.Node;
import org.w3c.dom.NodeList;

public class RestfulAmazon {
    private static final String endpoint = "ecs.amazonaws.com";
    private static final String itemId = "0545010225"; // Harry Potter        ❶

    public static void main(String[ ] args) {
        if (args.length < 2) {
            System.err.println("RestfulAmazon <accessKeyId> <secretKey>");
            return;
        }
        new RestfulAmazon().lookupStuff(args[0].trim(), args[1].trim());
    }
    private void lookupStuff(String accessKeyId, String secretKey) {
        RequestHelper helper = new RequestHelper(endpoint, accessKeyId, secretKey);
        String requestUrl = null;
        String title = null;
        // Store query string params in a hash.
        Map<String, String> params = new HashMap<String, String>();
        params.put("Service", "AWSECommerceService");
```

```
        params.put("Version", "2009-03-31");
        params.put("Operation", "ItemLookup");                    ❷
        params.put("ItemId", itemId);
        params.put("ResponseGroup", "Small");
        params.put("AssociateTag", "kalin");   // any string should do
        requestUrl = helper.sign(params);
        String response = requestAmazon(requestUrl);
        // The string "null" is returned before the XML document.
        String noNullResponse = response.replaceFirst("null", "");
        System.out.println("Raw xml:\n" + noNullResponse);
        System.out.println("Author: " + getAuthor(noNullResponse));
    }
    private String requestAmazon(String stringUrl) {
        String response = null;
        try {
            URL url = new URL(stringUrl);
            URLConnection conn = url.openConnection();
            conn.setDoInput(true);
            BufferedReader in =
                new BufferedReader(new InputStreamReader(conn.getInputStream()));
            String chunk = null;
            while ((chunk = in.readLine()) != null) response += chunk;
            in.close();
        }
        catch(Exception e) { throw new RuntimeException("Arrrg! " + e); }
        return response;
    }
    private String getAuthor(String xml) {
        String author = null;
        try {
            ByteArrayInputStream bais = new ByteArrayInputStream(xml.getBytes());
            DocumentBuilderFactory fact = DocumentBuilderFactory.newInstance();
            fact.setNamespaceAware(true);
            DocumentBuilder builder = fact.newDocumentBuilder();
            Document doc = builder.parse(bais);
            NodeList results = doc.getElementsByTagName("Author");
            for (int i = 0; i < results.getLength(); i++) {
                Element e = (Element) results.item(i);
                NodeList nodes = e.getChildNodes();
                for (int j = 0; j < nodes.getLength(); j++) {
                    Node child = nodes.item(j);
                    if (child.getNodeType() == Node.TEXT_NODE)
                        author = child.getNodeValue();
                }
            }
        }
        catch(Exception e) { throw new RuntimeException("Xml bad!", e); }
        return author;
    }
}
```

The RestfulAmazon application expects two command-line arguments: an Amazon *accessId* and *secretKey,* in that order. The client application then sets various properties such as the requested Amazon operation (in this example, ItemLookup in line 2), the item's identifier (in this example, 0545010225 in line 1, which is a Harry Potter novel), the Amazon associate's name, and so on. After the RequestHelper utility formats the request according to Amazon's requirements, the RestfulAmazon client then opens a URLConnection to the Amazon service, sends the GET request, and reads the response, chunk by chunk. The relevant code segment is:

```
URL url = new URL(stringUrl);
URLConnection conn = url.openConnection();                              ❶
conn.setDoInput(true);
BufferedReader in =                                                      ❷
  new BufferedReader(new InputStreamReader(conn.getInputStream()));
String chunk = null;
while ((chunk = in.readLine()) != null) response += chunk;               ❸
```

The code first creates a URLConnection (line 1) and then wraps a BufferedReader around the connection's InputStream (line 2). A while loop is used to read the Amazon response chunk by chunk (line 3). On a successful GET request, the payload in the HTTP response body is an XML document. Here is a slice from a sample run:

```
<?xml version="1.0" ?>
<ItemLookupResponse
   xmlns="http://webservices.amazon.com/AWSECommerceService/2011-08-01">
  <OperationRequest>
    <HTTPHeaders>
      <Header Name="UserAgent" Value="Java/1.7"></Header>
    </HTTPHeaders>
    <RequestId>591ac8db-0435-4c53-9b01-e3756ea9c55d</RequestId>
    <Arguments>
      <Argument Name="Operation" Value="ItemLookup"></Argument>
      <Argument Name="Service" Value="AWSECommerceService"></Argument>
      ...
      <Argument Name="ResponseGroup" Value="Small"></Argument>
    </Arguments>
    <RequestProcessingTime>0.0083090000000000</RequestProcessingTime>
  </OperationRequest>
  <Item>
    <Request>
      <IsValid>True</IsValid>
      <ItemLookupRequest>
        <IdType>ASIN</IdType>
        <ItemId>0545010225</ItemId>
        ...
      </ItemLookupRequest>
    </Request>
    <Item>
      <ASIN>0545010225</ASIN>
      <DetailPageURL>
```

```
        http://www.amazon.com/Harry-Potter-Deathly-Hallows-Book...
      </DetailPageURL>
      <ItemLinks>
        <ItemLink>
          <Description>Technical Details</Description>
          <URL>http://www.amazon.com/Harry-Potter-Deathly-Hallows-Book...</URL>
        </ItemLink>
        ...
        <ItemLink>
          <Description>Add To Wedding Registry</Description>              ❶
          <URL>http://www.amazon.com/gp/registry/wedding/add-item.html...</URL>
        </ItemLink>
        ...
      </ItemLinks>
      <ItemAttributes>
        <Author>J. K. Rowling</Author>
        <Creator Role="Illustrator">Mary GrandPré</Creator>
        <Manufacturer>Arthur A. Levine Books</Manufacturer>
        <ProductGroup>Book</ProductGroup>
        <Title>Harry Potter and the Deathly Hallows (Book 7)</Title>
      </ItemAttributes>
    </Item>
  </Items>
</ItemLookupResponse>
```

Even a cursory look at the XML makes clear, to anyone who has searched on the Amazon website, that the web service response contains essentially the same information as the corresponding HTML page viewed in a browser visit. For example, there is an XML element labeled:

```
Add To Wedding Registry (line 1)
```

Amazon's goal is to make the website and the web service deliver the same information and the same functionality but in different formats: the website delivers HTML documents, whereas the web service delivers XML documents.

With the response XML in hand, the `RestfulAmazon` client then parses the document to extract, as proof of concept, the author's name, J. K. Rowling. The code uses the relatively old-fashioned DOM parser, implemented as the standard Java `Document Builder` class. Here is the relevant code segment:

```
Document doc = builder.parse(bais);                              ❶
NodeList results = doc.getElementsByTagName("Author");           ❷
for (int i = 0; i < results.getLength(); i++) {
    Element e = (Element) results.item(i);
    NodeList nodes = e.getChildNodes();
        for (int j = 0; j < nodes.getLength(); j++) {
            Node child = nodes.item(j);
            if (child.getNodeType() == Node.TEXT_NODE)           ❸
                author = child.getNodeValue();
        }
}
```

The code first builds the DOM tree structure from the Amazon response bytes (line 1) and then gets a list, in this case a list of one element, from DOM elements tagged as Author. The author's name, J. K. Rowling, occurs as the contents of a TEXT_NODE (line 3). The parse deals with the usual complexities of the tree structure that a DOM represents. Similar DOM searches could extract from Amazon's XML response document any other information of interest, for example, the book's ISBN number.

The RequestHelper class (see Example 3-3) has one job: format the HTTP GET request in accordance with Amazon's strict requirements. This class acts as a utility that hides many low-level details, but a quick overview should provide some insight about what the E-Commerce service requires in a well-formed request. Recall that a request against the E-Commerce service requires both an *accessId* and a *secretKey* but the two play quite different roles in the request. The *accessId* occurs as a value in a key/value pair, with AWSAccessKeyId as the key (line 2). There is also a key/value pair for the timestamp that the E-Commerce service requires (line 3); hence, the *accessId* and the timestamp are peers. Amazon uses the timestamp to ensure that the requests are timely—that is, recently constructed.

*Example 3-3. The utility class RequestHelper, which supports the RestfulAmazon class*

```
package restful;

import java.io.UnsupportedEncodingException;
import java.net.URLDecoder;
import java.net.URLEncoder;
import java.text.DateFormat;
import java.text.SimpleDateFormat;
import java.util.Calendar;
import java.util.HashMap;
import java.util.Iterator;
import java.util.Map;
import java.util.SortedMap;
import java.util.TimeZone;
import java.util.TreeMap;
import javax.crypto.Mac;
import javax.crypto.spec.SecretKeySpec;
import org.apache.commons.codec.binary.Base64;

public class RequestHelper {
    private static final String utf8 = "UTF-8";
    private static final String hmacAlg = "HmacSHA256";
    private static final String requestUri = "/onca/xml";
    private static final String requestMethod = "GET";
    private String endpoint = null;
    private String accessKeyId = null;
    private String secretKey = null;
    private SecretKeySpec secretKeySpec = null;
    private Mac mac = null;
```

```
public RequestHelper(String endpoint,
                     String accessKeyId,
                     String secretKey) {
    if (endpoint == null || endpoint.length() == 0)
        throw new RuntimeException("The endpoint is null or empty.");
    if (null == accessKeyId || accessKeyId.length() == 0)
        throw new RuntimeException("The accessKeyId is null or empty.");
    if (null == secretKey || secretKey.length() == 0)
        throw new RuntimeException("The secretKey is null or empty.");
    this.endpoint = endpoint.toLowerCase();
    this.accessKeyId = accessKeyId;
    this.secretKey = secretKey;
    try {                                                              ❶
        byte[ ] secretKeyBytes = this.secretKey.getBytes(utf8);
        this.secretKeySpec = new SecretKeySpec(secretKeyBytes, hmacAlg);
        this.mac = Mac.getInstance(hmacAlg);
        this.mac.init(this.secretKeySpec);
    }
    catch(Exception e) { throw new RuntimeException(e); }
}
public String sign(Map<String, String> params) {
    params.put("AWSAccessKeyId", this.accessKeyId);                    ❷
    params.put("Timestamp", this.timestamp());                        ❸
    // The parameters need to be processed in lexicographical order, with
    // sorting on the first byte: a TreeMap is perfect for this.
    SortedMap<String, String> sortedParamMap =                        ❹
        new TreeMap<String, String>(params);
    // Ensure canonical form of the query string, as Amazon REST is fussy.
    String canonicalQS = this.canonicalize(sortedParamMap);           ❺
    // Prepare the signature with grist for the mill.
    String toSign =
        requestMethod + "\n"
        + this.endpoint + "\n"
        + requestUri + "\n"
        + canonicalQS;
    String hmac = this.hmac(toSign);
    String sig = null;
    try {
        sig = URLEncoder.encode(hmac, utf8);
    }
    catch(UnsupportedEncodingException e) { System.err.println(e); }
    String url =                                                      ❻
        "http://" + this.endpoint + requestUri + "?" + canonicalQS +
        "&Signature=" + sig;
    return url;
}
public String sign(String queryString) {
    Map<String, String> params = this.createParameterMap(queryString);
    return this.sign(params);
}
private String hmac(String stringToSign) {
    String signature = null;
```

```
        byte[ ] data;
        byte[ ] rawHmac;
        try {
            data = stringToSign.getBytes(utf8);
            rawHmac = mac.doFinal(data);
            Base64 encoder = new Base64();                              ❼
            signature = new String(encoder.encode(rawHmac));
        }
        catch (UnsupportedEncodingException e) {
            throw new RuntimeException(utf8 + " is unsupported!", e);
        }
        return signature;
    }
    // Amazon requires an ISO-8601 timestamp.
    private String timestamp() {
        String timestamp = null;
        Calendar cal = Calendar.getInstance();
        DateFormat dfm = new SimpleDateFormat("yyyy-MM-dd'T'HH:mm:ss'Z'");
        dfm.setTimeZone(TimeZone.getTimeZone("GMT"));
        timestamp = dfm.format(cal.getTime());
        return timestamp;
    }
    private String canonicalize(SortedMap<String, String> sortedParamMap) {
        if (sortedParamMap.isEmpty()) return "";
        StringBuffer buffer = new StringBuffer();
        Iterator<Map.Entry<String, String>> iter =
                sortedParamMap.entrySet().iterator();
        while (iter.hasNext()) {
            Map.Entry<String, String> kvpair = iter.next();
            buffer.append(encodeRfc3986(kvpair.getKey()));
            buffer.append("=");
            buffer.append(encodeRfc3986(kvpair.getValue()));
            if (iter.hasNext()) buffer.append("&");
        }
        return buffer.toString();
    }
    // Amazon requires RFC 3986 encoding, which the URLEncoder may not get right.
    private String encodeRfc3986(String s) {
        String out;
        try {
            out = URLEncoder.encode(s, utf8)
                .replace("+", "%20")
                .replace("*", "%2A")
                .replace("%7E", "~");
        }
        catch (UnsupportedEncodingException e) { out = s; }
        return out;
    }
    private Map<String, String> createParameterMap(String queryString) {
        Map<String, String> map = new HashMap<String, String>();
        String[ ] pairs = queryString.split("&");
        for (String pair : pairs) {
```

```
                if (pair.length() < 1) continue;
                String[ ] tokens = pair.split("=", 2);
                for(int j = 0; j < tokens.length; j++) {
                    try {
                        tokens[j] = URLDecoder.decode(tokens[j], utf8);
                    }
                    catch (UnsupportedEncodingException e) { }
                }
                switch (tokens.length) {
                    case 1: {
                        if (pair.charAt(0) == '=') map.put("", tokens[0]);
                        else map.put(tokens[0], "");
                        break;
                    }
                    case 2: {
                        map.put(tokens[0], tokens[1]);
                        break;
                    }
                }
            }
        }
        return map;
    }
}
```

The *secretKey* plays a different role than does the *accessId*. The *secretKey* is used to initialize a *message authentication code* (MAC), which the Java `javax.crypto.Mac` class represents. (The initialization occurs in the `try` block that begins on line 1.) Amazon requires a particular type of MAC, an HMAC (Hash Message Authentication Code) that uses the SHA-256 algorithm (Secure Hash Algorithm that generates a 256-bit hash). The important security point is that the *secretKey* itself does not go over the wire from the client to Amazon. Instead the *secretKey* is used to initialize the process that generates a message digest (hash value). Finally, this hash value is encoded in base64 (line 7). Amazon calls the result a signature, which occurs as the value in a key/value pair whose key is `Signature` (line 6).

There is a final preparatory step. The E-Commerce service expects, in a GET request, that the query string key/value pairs be in sorted order. The `RequestHelper` uses a `TreeMap`, as this data structure is ideally suited for the task (line 4). The properly formatted query string results from a call to `canonicalize`; this query string is then appended to the base URL for the Amazon E-Commerce service.

Not every commercial site is as fussy as Amazon when it comes to request formatting. This first Amazon example shows that generating a correctly formatted RESTful request may be nontrivial. This client also explicitly parses the returned XML. The next client addresses the issue of how to avoid such parsing. Before looking at the code for the second client, however, it will be useful to focus on the JAX-B utilities used in the second client.

# A Standalone JAX-B Example

Recall that the *B* in *JAX-B* stands for data binding, the associating of a Java data type such as String to an XML Schema (or equivalent) type, in this case xsd:string. There are built-in bindings for the Java primitive types such as int and double together with String and Calendar; arrays (including Collections) of any such types; and programmer-defined types that reduce, via properties, to any of the preceding. The surprising omission is the Map, a collection of key/value pairs, but a Map is readily handled as two coordinated collections: a collection of *keys* and a corresponding collection of *values*. An example of JAX-B in action may help to drive these points home.

The Skier class (see Example 3-4) is annotated with @XmlRootElement to inform the JAX-B utilities that a Skier instance should be transformed into an XML document that has skier as its root or document (that is, outermost) element. In the default Java naming convention, the root element is the lowercase version of the class name; hence, Skier becomes skier. The annotation could be amended:

```
@XmlRootElement(name = "NordicSkier")
```

so that the root element has a specified name, in this example NordicSkier.

*Example 3-4. The annotated Skier POJO class*

```
import javax.xml.bind.annotation.XmlRootElement;
import java.util.Collection;

@XmlRootElement
public class Skier  {
    private Person person;
    private String nationalTeam;
    private Collection majorAchievements;
    public Skier() { } // required for unmarshaling
    public Skier (Person person,
                  String nationalTeam,
                  Collection<String> majorAchievements) {
        setPerson(person);
        setNationalTeam(nationalTeam);
        setMajorAchievements(majorAchievements);
    }
    // properties
    public Person getPerson() { return this.person; }
    public void setPerson (Person person) { this.person = person; }

    public String getNationalTeam() { return this.nationalTeam; }
    public void setNationalTeam(String nationalTeam) {
        this.nationalTeam = nationalTeam;
    }
    public Collection getMajorAchievements() { return this.majorAchievements; }
```

```
    public void setMajorAchievements(Collection majorAchievements) {
        this.majorAchievements = majorAchievements;
    }
}
```

The Skier class has a property of programmer-defined type Person (see Example 3-5), which in turn is a POJO class with three properties: name, age, and gender. Two of the Person properties are of Java type String, which binds to XML type xsd:string. The third Person property is of Java type int, which binds to the XML type xsd:int.

*Example 3-5. The annotated Person POJO class with three properties*

```
import javax.xml.bind.annotation.XmlType;

@XmlType
public class Person  {
    private String name;
    private int     age;
    private String gender;

    public Person() { }
    public Person(String name, int age, String gender){
        setName(name);
        setAge(age);
        setGender(gender);
    }
    public String getName() { return name; }
    public void setName(String name) { this.name = name; }
    public int getAge() { return age;  }
    public void setAge(int age) { this.age = age; }
    public String getGender() { return gender; }
    public void setGender(String gender) { this.gender = gender; }
}
```

The annotation XmlType declares that a Person instance can be transformed into an XML type, a type that an XML Schema specifies in detail. The upshot of the annotated Skier and Person classes is this: an in-memory Skier object, which encapsulates a Person, can be transformed into a single XML document, whose root element is tagged skier, and the skier document encapsulates a person element.

The application class Marshal (see Example 3-6) does the following:

- Creates a Skier instance
- Marshals this instance into an XML document, which is saved to a file and also printed to the standard output
- Unmarshals the XML document in the file into a separate Skier instance, an instance that effectively clones the original Skier instance

Recall that, in this context, *marshaling* is the process of serializing an in-memory object into an XML document; *unmarshaling* is the inverse process of creating an in-memory object from an XML document.

*Example 3-6. The Marshal application that marshals and unmarshals a Skier*

```java
import java.io.File;
import java.io.OutputStream;
import java.io.FileOutputStream;
import java.io.InputStream;
import java.io.FileInputStream;
import java.io.IOException;
import javax.xml.bind.JAXBContext;
import javax.xml.bind.Marshaller;
import javax.xml.bind.Unmarshaller;
import javax.xml.bind.JAXBException;
import java.util.List;
import java.util.ArrayList;

class Marshal {
    private static final String fileName = "bd.mar";

    public static void main(String[ ] args) {
        new Marshal().runExample();
    }
    private void runExample() {
        try {
            JAXBContext ctx = JAXBContext.newInstance(Skier.class);    ❶
            Marshaller m = ctx.createMarshaller();                     ❷
            m.setProperty(Marshaller.JAXB_FORMATTED_OUTPUT, true);
            // Marshal a Skier object: 1st to stdout, 2nd to file
            Skier skier = createSkier();
            m.marshal(skier, System.out);
            FileOutputStream out = new FileOutputStream(fileName);
            m.marshal(skier, out);                                     ❸
            out.close();
            // Unmarshal as proof of concept
            Unmarshaller u = ctx.createUnmarshaller();                 ❹
            Skier bdClone = (Skier) u.unmarshal(new File(fileName));
            System.out.println();
            m.marshal(bdClone, System.out);
        }
        catch(JAXBException e) { System.err.println(e); }
        catch(IOException e) { System.err.println(e); }
    }
    private Skier createSkier() {
        Person bd = new Person("Bjoern Daehlie", 49, "Male");
        List<String> list = new ArrayList<String>();
        list.add("12 Olympic Medals");
        list.add("9 World Championships");
        list.add("Winningest Winter Olympian");
        list.add("Greatest Nordic Skier");
```

```
        return new Skier(bd, "Norway", list);
    }
}
```

In the Marshal class, the critical step is the creation of a JAXBContext (line 1), in this case a structure built from Java reflection on the type Skier. (The one-argument method newInstance can take, as its argument, a single class or a package identifier.) The utility class JAXBContext then guides the marshaling and unmarshaling: the Marshaller and the Unmarshaller are created with JAXBContext methods (lines 2 and 4). By the way, there is no agreement about whether marshaling and unmarshaling should be spelled with one *l* or two.

The marshaling (line 3) produces an XML document (see Example 3-7) that serves as the source of the unmarshaling (line 4). The only complexity is in the elements tagged majorAchievement, which include three attributes apiece. The reason is that a majorAchievement is, in Java, a Collection type—in particular, an Array List<String>. The corresponding XML type is an array of xs:string objects; the majorAchievement elements cite the XML Schema grammar (lines 1 and 2), which includes rules about arrays. By default, the Java marshaling produces an XML document in which the properties of the source Java object are in alphabetical order.

*Example 3-7. The XML document generated from marshaling a sample Skier*

```
<?xml version="1.0" encoding="UTF-8" standalone="yes"?>
<skier>
    <majorAchievements xmlns:xsi="http://www.w3.org/2001/XMLSchema-instance"   ❶
                       xmlns:xs="http://www.w3.org/2001/XMLSchema"              ❷
                       xsi:type="xs:string">12 Olympic Medals
    </majorAchievements>
    <majorAchievements xmlns:xsi="http://www.w3.org/2001/XMLSchema-instance"
                       xmlns:xs="http://www.w3.org/2001/XMLSchema"
                       xsi:type="xs:string">9 World Championships
    </majorAchievements>
    <majorAchievements xmlns:xsi="http://www.w3.org/2001/XMLSchema-instance"
                       xmlns:xs="http://www.w3.org/2001/XMLSchema"
                       xsi:type="xs:string">Winningest Winter Olympian
    </majorAchievements>
    <majorAchievements xmlns:xsi="http://www.w3.org/2001/XMLSchema-instance"
                       xmlns:xs="http://www.w3.org/2001/XMLSchema"
                       xsi:type="xs:string">Greatest Nordic Skier
    </majorAchievements>
    <nationalTeam>Norway</nationalTeam>
    <person>
        <age>49</age>
        <gender>Male</gender>
        <name>Bjoern Daehlie</name>
    </person>
</skier>
```

This JAX-B example implies, of course, that the conversion between Java and XML could be automated. Accordingly, a Java client against a RESTful service could:

- Issue a request whose response is an XML document
- Use JAX-B to unmarshal the XML document into a Java object
- Manipulate the Java object in the usual ways (for instance, with *get/set* methods) to serve the application logic

In this scenario, the XML is transparent. The second Amazon example goes into the details of how this can be done. First, however, an alternative to the standard Java XML utilities deserves a look.

## The XStream Option

Java comes with standard packages for Java-to-XML conversions and XML-to-JSON conversions. There are also various contributed libraries, among them XStream (*http://xstream.codehaus.org*). This section examines the XStream option for serializing Java objects to XML/JSON documents and deserializing Java objects from such documents. XStream includes a persistence API and has extensions in support of the Hibernate ORM (Object Relation Mapper). Among the more interesting features of XStream is that its API does not center on the *get/set* methods that define Java properties. XStream can serialize into XML an instance of a Java class that has nothing but `private` fields. XStream emphasizes its ease of use, which the following examples try to capture.

The `PersonNoProps` class (see Example 3-8) illustrates the ease of `XStream` use. The class has three `private` fields and only a three-argument constructor; of interest is that the class has no properties—no `public get/set` methods. Nonetheless, an instance of the `PersonNoProps` class can be serialized or deserialized straightforwardly. Line 1 in the code listing constructs an `XStream` instance with a DOM driver. Line 2 provides an alias for the document element's tag, in this case `skier`. If an alias were not provided, then the document element would have a tag named after the class; hence, line 2 is optional. The serialization in line 3 and the deserialization in line 4 are quick and easy.

*Example 3-8. An XStream example with a class that has no properties*

```
import com.thoughtworks.xstream.XStream;
import com.thoughtworks.xstream.io.xml.DomDriver;

public class PersonNoProps  {
    private String name;
    private int     age;
    private String gender;

    public PersonNoProps(String name, int age, String gender){
        this.name = name;
        this.age = age;
```

```
                this.gender = gender;
        }
}
class Main {
        public static void main(String[ ] args) {
                PersonNoProps bd = new PersonNoProps("Bjoern Daehlie", 49, "Male");
                // setup
                XStream xstream = new XStream(new DomDriver());              ❶
                xstream.alias("skier", PersonNoProps.class); // for readability ❷
                // serialize
                String xml = xstream.toXML(bd);                             ❸
                System.out.println(xml);
                // deserialize and confirm
                PersonNoProps bdClone = (PersonNoProps) xstream.fromXML(xml);  ❹
                System.out.println(xstream.toXML(bdClone));
        }
}
```

The output for both `println` calls is:

```
<skier>
  <name>Bjoern Daehlie</name>
  <age>49</age>
  <gender>Male</gender>
</skier>
```

The generated XML is minimalist. Compiling and running this code requires the core XStream packages, which come in a single JAR file: *xstream.jar*.

The first XStream example begins with the serialization of an entire PersonNoProps instance and ends with the deserialization of a clone. XStream also supports selective or fine-grained serialization and deserialization. The next example (see Example 3-9) illustrates this.

*Example 3-9. The PersonPropsConverter class for customized marshaling*

```
import com.thoughtworks.xstream.converters.Converter;
import com.thoughtworks.xstream.converters.MarshallingContext;
import com.thoughtworks.xstream.converters.UnmarshallingContext;
import com.thoughtworks.xstream.io.HierarchicalStreamReader;
import com.thoughtworks.xstream.io.HierarchicalStreamWriter;

public class PersonPropsConverter implements Converter {
        public boolean canConvert(Class c) {
                return c.equals(PersonProps.class);                         ❶
        }
        // As proof of concept, marshal/unmarshal only the name.
        public void marshal(Object object,
                            HierarchicalStreamWriter writer,
                            MarshallingContext context) {
                PersonProps person = (PersonProps) object;
                writer.startNode("Person");
```

```
        writer.setValue(person.getName());                            ❷
        writer.endNode();
    }
    public Object unmarshal(HierarchicalStreamReader reader,
                            UnmarshallingContext context) {
        PersonProps person = new PersonProps();
        reader.moveDown();
        person.setName(reader.getValue());                             ❸
        reader.moveUp();
        return person;
    }
}
```

The PersonPropsConverter class (see Example 3-9) serializes and deserializes, as proof of concept, only one property in a PersonProps instance: the name property. An implementation of the Converter interface must define three methods:

canConvert

This method (line 1) returns a boolean to indicate which types are eligible for the customized serialization and deserialization defined in the methods marshal and unmarshal (lines 2 and 3, respectively). In this example, an object must be of type PersonProps (see Example 3-10), which includes any descendants of this class, in order to be convertible.

marshal

This method (line 2) supports customized serialization (marshaling) of a Person Props object. In the current example, only the person's name property is serialized, but any subset of the properties, including all of them, could be serialized.

unmarshal

This method (line 3), the inverse of marshal, supports customized deserialization (unmarshaling).

*Example 3-10. The code to illustrate customized XStream marshaling/unmarshaling*

```
import com.thoughtworks.xstream.XStream;
import com.thoughtworks.xstream.io.xml.DomDriver;

public class PersonProps {
    private String name;
    private int    age;
    private String gender;

    // constructor
    public PersonProps() { }
    // properties
    public void setName(String name) { this.name = name; }          ❶
    public String getName() { return this.name; }
    public void setAge(int age) { this.age = age; }                 ❷
    public int getAge() { return this.age; }
```

```
    public void setGender(String gender) { this.gender = gender; } ❸
    public String getGender() { return this.gender; }
}

class Main {
    public static void main(String[ ] args) {
        // Create a person and set only the name.
        PersonProps person = new PersonProps();
        person.setName("Bruno");
        XStream xstream = new XStream(new DomDriver());
        xstream.registerConverter(new PersonPropsConverter());    ❹
        xstream.alias("name", PersonProps.class);
        String xml = xstream.toXML(person);                        ❺
        System.out.println(xml);
        PersonProps clone = (PersonProps) xstream.fromXML(xml);    ❻
        System.out.println(clone.getName()); // Bruno
    }
}
```

The PersonProps class (see Example 3-10) revises the PersonNoProps class by adding properties. The revised class has three conventional Java properties, each defined as a pair of get/set methods. The properties are name (type String) in line 1, age (type int) in line 2, and gender (type String) in line 3. The revised class has a no-argument constructor.

The tester class Main creates an XStream instance as before but now registers a customized Converter (line 4), a PersonPropsConverter (see Example 3-9). In the call to toXML (line 5), the customized converter takes over and serializes only the name property. The output is:

```
<person>
  <name>Bruno</name>
</person>
```

The deserialization (line 6) creates a new PersonProps instance and sets the name property to Bruno. The other properties, age and gender, have the default values for fields, in this case 0 and null, respectively.

The core XStream library also supports the conversion of Java objects to and from JSON. There are various JSON drivers available in this library, the simplest of which is the JsonHierarchicalStreamDriver. This driver supports the serialization of Java objects to JSON but not the inverse operation. If deserialization from JSON to Java is needed, then a driver such as Jettison (*http://jettison.codehaus.org*) is a good choice because it interoperates cleanly with XStream.

The JsonTest code (see Example 3-11) illustrates basic JSON serialization in XStream. An XStream instance is now constructed with a JSON driver (line 1), in this case an instance of a JsonHierarchicalStreamDriver, which comes with the core XStream JAR file. The serializing method is still named toXML (line 2), but the output is JSON rather than XML because of the JSON driver.

*Example 3-11. An example of XStream serialization to JSON*

```java
import com.thoughtworks.xstream.XStream;
import com.thoughtworks.xstream.io.xml.DomDriver;
import com.thoughtworks.xstream.io.json.JsonHierarchicalStreamDriver;

public class JsonTest {
    public static void main(String[ ] args) {
        PersonNoProps bd = new PersonNoProps("Bjoern Daehlie", 49, "Male");
        XStream xstream = new XStream(new JsonHierarchicalStreamDriver()); ❶
        String json = xstream.toXML(bd); // it's really toJson now        ❷
        System.out.println(json);
    }
}
```

Here is the output:

```json
{"PersonNoProps": {
  "name": "Bjoern Daehlie",
  "age": 49,
  "gender": "Male"
}}
```

XStream supports customized JSON serialization. For example, a programmer might not want the root element PersonNoProps included in the JSON, and the JSON serializer can be programmed to exclude this element.

The XStream API is remarkably low fuss but likewise powerful. This API has gained steadily in popularity among Java developers who are looking for quick and easy ways to convert between Java objects on the one side and either XML or JSON documents on the other side.

The JAX-B and XStream examples illustrate serialization from Java to XML or JSON and deserialization from XML or JSON to Java. In the context of clients against RESTful web services, the deserialization side of the coin is of primary interest because these clients need to process the response payloads, in XML or JSON, that come from the RESTful service. Accordingly, the next section returns to Amazon's E-Commerce service but this time with the goal of hiding the XML that this service returns in response to a successful HTTP request.

# Another Client Against the Amazon E-Commerce Service

The second client against the Amazon E-Commerce service does not deal explicitly with any XML but otherwise has the same functionality as the first client. The steps for setting up the second client are listed below, but the ZIP file with the sample code includes JAR *Amazon2.jar* that can be executed directly:

```
% java -jar Amazon2.jar <accessId> <secretKey>
```

Here are the steps for setting up the second Amazon client. These steps that would be copied for a Java client against any RESTful service that provides an XML Schema—and most services do provide a schema. For a depiction of the process and the role of Java's *xjc* utility, see Figure 3-1.

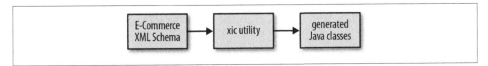

*Figure 3-1. Using the xjc utility to transform an XML Schema into Java classes*

1. Download the XML Schema for the E-Commerce service. The URL is:

   ```
   http://webservices.amazon.com/AWSECommerceServices/AWSECommerceService.xsd
   ```

   The downloaded schema is about 55K in size. (This is the same schema used in the SOAP-based versions of the Amazon services.) Put the downloaded document in a local file such as *amazon2/amazon.xsd*. The local filename is arbitrary.

2. The *amazon.xsd* needs some tweaking so that the Java JAX-B utilities can use this file without complaining. The downloaded XML Schema begins as follows:

   ```
   <?xml version="1.0" encoding="UTF-8"?>
   <xs:schema
     xmlns:xs="http://www.w3.org/2001/XMLSchema"                             ❶
     xmlns:tns="http://webservices.amazon.com/AWSECommerceService/2011-08-01"
     targetNamespace=
       "http://webservices.amazon.com/AWSECommerceService/2011-08-01"
     elementFormDefault="qualified">
     <xs:element name="Bin">                                                  ❷
       <xs:complexType>                                                       ❸
         <xs:sequence>                                                        ❹
           ...
   ```

   The problem lies with the namespace identifier xs, which occurs once to the right of the colon (line 1) in:

   ```
   xmlns:xs="http://www.w3.org/2001/XMLSchema"
   ```

   It also occurs on the second line and everywhere else to the left of the colon (lines 2, 3, and 4). The identifier xs should be changed globally to xsd; any reasonable text editor can make this change. The result should be:

   ```
   <?xml version="1.0" encoding="UTF-8"?>
   <xsd:schema
     xmlns:xsd="http://www.w3.org/2001/XMLSchema"
     xmlns:tns="http://webservices.amazon.com/AWSECommerceService/2011-08-01"
     targetNamespace=
       "http://webservices.amazon.com/AWSECommerceService/2011-08-01"
   ```

```
      elementFormDefault="qualified">
      <xsd:element name="Bin">
        <xsd:complexType>
          <xsd:sequence>
          ...
```

The *xjc* utility should not be this brittle, of course; Java itself generates schemas that use the namespace abbreviation xs.

3. Execute the *xjc* utility, which ships with the core Java JDK, against the schema. In this example, the command is:

```
% xjc -p restful2 amazon.xsd
```

The *-p* flag stands for *package*. The *xjc* utility creates the package/subdirectory named *restful2* and fills the subdirectory with, at present, 84 Java source files. The files have names such as *CartAddRequest.java*, *ItemLookup.java*, *ItemSearch.java*, *LoyaltyPoints.java*, and so on. These files, in compiled form, are the Java types that correspond to the XML Schema types in *amazon.xsd*.

4. This step is optional but recommended for convenience. Copy the source files *RestfulAmazon.java* and *RequestHelper.java* from the first Amazon example into the *restful2* subdirectory. The package name in both files needs to change from restful to restful2. The *xjc*-generated files could be kept in a separate package, of course.

5. Compile the *.java* files in *restful2*.

The nearly 85 Amazon files in *restful2* have JAX-B annotations such as @XmlType. These *xjc*-generated files automate the translation between an XML data type such as tns:Item Search and the corresponding Java type, in this case restful2.ItemSearch. The XML types are defined in the Amazon schema, and the corresponding Java types are the classes generated with the *xjc* utility. The process (see Figure 3-1) of generating Java artifacts is relatively uncomplicated.

Programming involves trade-offs, and the revised Amazon client illustrates one such trade-off. On the plus side, the revised RestfulAmazon client no longer needs *explicit-ly* to parse XML; hence, the various import directives that support DOM parsing can be removed because the getAuthor method no longer uses the imported types such as DocumentBuilder and NodeList. On the minus side, the *xjc*-generated classes bring a new API into play, and this API involves some Russian-doll nesting, as a look at the new code will show.

The revised client requires no changes to the RequestHelper except for the change in the package name. The revised RestfulAmazon client (see Example 3-12) is largely the same as the original; hence, unchanged code is marked with an ellipsis.

---

*Example 3-12. The revised `RestfulAmazon` that uses JAX-B to avoid XML parsing*

```
package restful2;

...
import javax.xml.transform.stream.StreamSource;
import javax.xml.validation.SchemaFactory;
import javax.xml.validation.Schema;
import javax.xml.XMLConstants;
import javax.xml.validation.Validator;
import javax.xml.bind.JAXBContext;
import javax.xml.bind.Marshaller;
import javax.xml.bind.Unmarshaller;
import javax.xml.bind.JAXBException;

public class RestfulAmazon {
    ...
    public static void main(String[ ] args) {
        ...
    }
    private void lookupStuff(String accessKeyId, String secretKey) {
        ...
    }
    private String requestAmazon(String string_url) {
        ...
    }
    private String getAuthor(String xml) {
      String author = null;
      try {
        // Create an XML Schema object
        final String fileName = "amazon.xsd"; // downloaded XML Schema
        final String schemaUri = XMLConstants.W3C_XML_SCHEMA_NS_URI;
        SchemaFactory factory = SchemaFactory.newInstance(schemaUri);
        Schema schema = factory.newSchema(new StreamSource(fileName));     ❶
        // Create a JAX-B context for unmarshaling
        JAXBContext ctx = JAXBContext.newInstance(ItemLookupResponse.class);  ❷
        Unmarshaller um = ctx.createUnmarshaller();                        ❸
        um.setSchema(schema);                                             ❹
        // Generate a Java ItemSearchResponse instance.
        ItemLookupResponse ilr = (ItemLookupResponse)
            um.unmarshal(new ByteArrayInputStream(xml.getBytes()));        ❺
        // Use the standard POJO idiom to extract the author.
        List<Items> itemsList = ilr.getItems(); // list of lists          ❻
        for (Items items : itemsList) {          // outer list            ❼
          List<Item> list = items.getItem();   // inner list              ❽
          for (Item item : list) {              // items in inner list
            ItemAttributes attributes = item.getItemAttributes();
            List<String> authors = attributes.getAuthor(); // could be several
            author = authors.get(0); // in this case, only one            ❾
          }
        }
      }
      catch(JAXBException e ) { throw new RuntimeException(e); }
```

```
        catch(Exception e) { throw new RuntimeException(e); }
        return author;
    }
}
```

In the revised RestfulAmazon client, the getAuthor method is invoked with an XML
document as the argument but the XML is not parsed. Instead, the method does the
following:

- A JAXBContext is used to get information about the class of interest, in this case
  the *xjc*-generated class, ItemLookupResponse (line 2). This class represents the
  E-Commerce response from a lookup operation against the service.

- The JAXBContext instance is used to create an unmarshaler (line 3), which is initialized with the E-Commerce schema (lines 1 and 4).

- The unmarshaler transforms the bytes from the E-Commerce response document,
  which is XML, into an instance of the ItemLookupResponse class. At this point,
  there is no need to parse any XML because the ItemLookupResponse object can be
  used instead to find desired information, in this case the author's name.

- In the current example, the RestfulAmazon client looks up only one item, a book.
  In general, however, a look-up request against the E-Commerce service might yield
  many hits instead of just one. At the data structure level, the result is lists nested
  inside lists; hence, code lines 6 through 8 work from the outermost to the innermost
  list. Here, for a closer look, is the looping in isolation:

```
List<Items> itemsList = ilr.getItems(); // list of lists        ❶
for (Items items : itemsList) {          // outer list
    List<Item> list = items.getItem();   // inner list
        for (Item item : list) {         // items in inner list ❷
            ItemAttributes attributes = item.getItemAttributes(); ❸
                List<String> authors = attributes.getAuthor();
                author = authors.get(0); // in this case, only one ❹
        }
    }
```

The getItems method encapsulated in the ItemLookupResponse object returns a
List<Items> (line 1) but each element in this list is itself a list. In the second for
loop (line 2), individual items are finally available; indeed, in this response there is
exactly one such Item, whose ItemAttributes (line 3) include the name of the
author, J. K. Rowling. Her name occurs as the first and only name in a list of authors
(line 4) because, of course, even a single book might have multiple authors.

The two clients against the Amazon RESTful service highlight a typical choice con-
fronted in programming RESTful clients. The choice can be summarized as follows:

- Should the client deal directly with the returned XML (or JSON), using parsing and similar tools to extract the required information?

- Should the client invest in utilities such as JAX-B that can hide the XML but thereby require the client to work in yet another API?

Is there a compelling answer to either question? For one-off client applications, working directly with the XML may be the way to go. Tools such as XPath make it relatively easy to extract information from XML documents, at least XML documents that are of a reasonable size. It is very hard to define *reasonable size* in this context, of course. The problem is that tools such as XPath require a DOM—a tree structure—in order to work. Building a tree from, say, an XML stream of gigabyte size may be prohibitively slow; searching the built tree may be the same. For client applications that regularly target a particular service such as Amazon E-Commerce, working with JAX-B artifacts means working in familiar Java idioms such as *get/set* methods. The benefit of using JAX-B is that the XML effectively disappears into the JAX-B infrastructure.

# The CTA Bus-Tracker Services

The Amazon websites for shopping, storage, and cloud computing are rich in content and functionality—and the corresponding web services inherit these very attributes. Amazon, moreover, is a pioneer and a major player in web services, SOAP-based and REST-style. Social networking sites such as Facebook, Twitter, and Tumblr support RESTful services against their sites. Indeed, the trend among serious websites, large or small, is to provide RESTful access and an API in support of such access. For contrast, this section considers a relatively recent and, in comparison with Amazon, small-scale effort at RESTful web services: bus tracking at the CTA (Chicago Transit Authority).

The Amazon E-Commerce service has a standard design in that a single service encapsulates many operations, for instance, operations to search, look up, order, clear a shopping cart, and so on. The CTA takes a different approach in that each service consists of a single operation; there is a separate XML Schema per service. The services are thus quite simple, and the schemas range in size from about 12 to 36 lines. The simplest service returns the current local time; more complicated services report on buses en route and on their routes, expected bus arrival times at particular locations, vehicles in operation, and the like.

Use of the bus-tracking service, through the website or a web service, requires a *key* (see Registering with the CTA) from the CTA. The key occurs as a query string attribute in a GET request, the only type of HTTP request supported. The sample BusTracker client (see Example 3-13) first targets the *gettime* service whose XML Schema is Example 3-14.

*Example 3-13. A sample client against the CTA's RESTful bus-tracking services*

```java
package ctaBT;

import java.net.URL;
import java.net.URLConnection;
import java.io.BufferedReader;
import java.io.InputStreamReader;

public class BusTracker {
    private static final String baseUrl =
        "http://www.ctabustracker.com/bustime/api/v1/";

    public static void main(String[ ] args) {
        if (args.length < 1) {
            System.err.println("BusTracker <CTA key>");
            return;
        }
        new BusTracker().demo("?key=" + args[0]);
    }
    private void demo(String key) {
        // Current official CTA time.
        String url = baseUrl + "gettime" + key;
        makeRequest(url);
        url = baseUrl + "getvehicles" + key;
        makeRequest(url);
        String sampleRoute = "&rt=20&pid=954";
        url = baseUrl + "getpatterns" + key + sampleRoute;
        makeRequest(url);
    }
    private void makeRequest(String stringUrl) {
        String response = null;
        try {
            URL url = new URL(stringUrl);
            URLConnection conn = url.openConnection();
            conn.setDoInput(true);
            BufferedReader in =
                new BufferedReader(new InputStreamReader(conn.getInputStream()));
            String chunk = null;
            while ((chunk = in.readLine()) != null) response += chunk;
            in.close();
        }
        catch(Exception e) { throw new RuntimeException("Arrrg! " + e); }
        report(stringUrl, response);
    }
    private void report(String url, String xml) {
        String msg = url + "\n" + xml;
        System.out.println(msg);
    }
}
```

**Registering with the CTA**

The CTA bus-tracker web services (*http://www.ctabustracker.com*) are free of charge but do require registration. A client call against any service requires a *key*, which the CTA provides upon registration.

*Example 3-14. The XML Schema for the CTA time service*

```xml
<?xml version="1.0" encoding="utf-8" ?>
<xs:schema xmlns:xs="www.w3.org/2001/XMLSchema">
  <xs:element name="bustime-response" type=" bustime-response" />
  <xs:complexType name="bustime-response">
    <xs:sequence>
      <xs:element name="error" type="error"
                  minOccurs="0" maxOccurs="unbounded"/>
      <xs:element name="tm" type="xs:string"
                  minOccurs="0" maxOccurs="1"/>
    </xs:sequence>
  </xs:complexType>
  <xs:complexType name="error">
    <xs:sequence>
      <xs:element name="msg" type="xs:string"
                  minOccurs="1" maxOccurs="1"/>
    </xs:sequence>
  </xs:complexType>
</xs:schema>
```

On a successful GET request, the response is similar to:

```xml
<?xml version="1.0"?>
<bustime-response>
  <tm>20130302 16:38:49</tm>
</bustime-response>
```

The invocation syntax for other services is only slightly more complicated. For example, the GET request with this URL:

```
http://www.ctabustracker.com/bustime/api/v1/getpatterns?key=...&rt=20&pid=954:
```

is asking for the traffic patterns of buses en route. A sample response would look like this:

```xml
<bustime-response>
  <ptr>
    <pid>954</pid>
    <ln>40902.0</ln>
    <rtdir>West Bound</rtdir>
    <pt>
      <seq>1</seq>
      <lat>41.882134908777</lat>
      <lon>-87.624528408051</lon>
    </pt>
```

```
        ...
    </ptr>
  </bustime-response>
```

The bus-tracker services are deliberately small and simple, which encourages developers to experiment with composing other services out of these. The CTA services illustrate a refreshing trend to make data available on websites equally accessible through web services. The CTA itself currently has a beta release of train-tracking services modeled after the bus-tracking ones.

# RESTful Clients and WADL Documents

At the core of a SOAP-based service is the *service contract*, a WSDL document. WSDL is an XML dialect. In modern web services, the WSDL plays the role that the IDL document plays in the DCE/RPC services introduced in Chapter 1. In any case, the WSDL document has various sections, all of which are required except for the *types* section that contains an XML Schema or equivalent; modern WSDLs almost always include a schema. The information in the WSDL specifies the invocation syntax for every operation encapsulated in the service. SOAP frameworks such as Java Metro and DotNet provide tools that, given a WSDL, can generate client-side library code, which facilitates the programming of a client against the service. The WSDL itself is language-neutral, and the publisher of the service typically generates at least the first draft of this service contract, which can then be refined as needed. In principle, a WSDL document could describe either a SOAP-based or a REST-style service; in practice, however, the WSDL is used predominantly for SOAP-based services. Chapter 4, which introduces SOAP-based examples, looks closely at the WSDL document. For now, the similarity between a WSDL document and a WADL (Web Application Description Language) document is of interest.

As noted, WSDL documents can describe either category of web service, SOAP-based or REST-style, but there seems to be little interest in WSDLs and WSDL-based tools for RESTful services. JAX-RS implementations such as Metro do provide a WSDL counterpart, the WADL document that describes a JAX-RS service and can be used to generate client-side code. The *wadl2java* (*http://wadl.java.net*) tool download includes Unixy and Windows versions. As the name indicates, this tool generates Java code from a WADL document. The publisher of JAX-RS service generates the WADL dynamically, although a WADL, like a WSDL, can be edited as needed—or even written from scratch. The syntax for getting the WADL differs slightly among JAX-RS implementations. In the Jersey implementation, the document is available as *application.wadl*. As an example, recall the *predictions3* JAX-RS service from Chapter 2 whose base URL is:

```
http://localhost:8080/predictions3/resourcesP/
```

The WADL document for this service is available under Jersey with the URL:

```
http://localhost:8080/predictions3/resourcesP/application.wadl
```

---

If the implementation were Apache CXF instead of Jersey, the URL would be:

```
http://localhost:8080/predictions3/resourcesP?wadl
```

The WADL document for the *predictions3* service (see Example 3-15) is a page or so in size. The document links the HTTP verb for a CRUD operation with the URI for the code that implements the operation; the document section also includes information about the parameters passed into the operation. For example, here is a segment for creating a new `Prediction` in the *predictions3* service:

```
<resource path="/create">                                          ❶
   <method name="POST" id="create">                                ❷
      <request>
         <representation mediaType="application/x-www-form-urlencoded">  ❸
            <param xmlns:xs="http://www.w3.org/2001/XMLSchema"
                   type="xsd:string" style="query" name="who"/>
            <param xmlns:xs="http://www.w3.org/2001/XMLSchema"
                   type="xsd:string" style="query" name="what"/>
         </representation>
      </request>
      <response>
         <representation mediaType="text/plain"/>                   ❹
      </response>
   </method>
</resource>
```

The `resource` element (line 1) specifies the `path` or URI, in this case `/create`, that identifies the RESTful resource. Next comes the HTTP method (line 2), in this case POST, together with the implementing Java method, in this case `create`. The *wadl2java* utility gets the names of the resource path and the implementing Java method from the source code. The WADL segment also gives the MIME types of the request (line 3) and the response (line 4): the request type `application/x-www-form-urlencoded` specifies a URL-encoded form (that is, collection of key/value pairs) in the body of the POST request; the response type `text/plain` is, if the request succeeds, a confirmation message.

*Example 3-15. The WADL document for the predictions3 JAX-RS web service*

```
<?xml version="1.0" encoding="UTF-8" standalone="yes"?>
<application xmlns="http://wadl.dev.java.net/2009/02">
   <doc xmlns:jersey="http://jersey.java.net/"
        jersey:generatedBy="Jersey: 1.10 11/02/2011 03:53 PM"/>
   <grammars/>
   <resources base="http://localhost:8080/predictions3/resourcesP/">
      <resource path="/">
         <resource path="/delete/{id: \d+}">
            <param xmlns:xsd="http://www.w3.org/2001/XMLSchema"
                   type="xsd:int" style="template" name="id"/>
            <method name="DELETE" id="delete">
               <response>
                  <representation mediaType="application/json"/>
```

```
        </response>
      </method>
    </resource>
    <resource path="/create">
      <method name="POST" id="create">
        <request>
          <representation mediaType="application/x-www-form-urlencoded">
            ...
          </representation>
        </request>
        <response>
          <representation mediaType="text/plain"/>
        </response>
      </method>
    </resource>
    ...
    <resource path="/xml/{id: \d+}">
      <param xmlns:xsd="http://www.w3.org/2001/XMLSchema"
             type="xsd:int" style="template" name="id"/>
          <method name="GET" id="getXml">
            <response>
              <representation mediaType="application/xml"/>
            </response>
          </method>
    </resource>
    <resource path="/json">
      <method name="GET" id="getJson">
        <response>
          <representation mediaType="application/json"/>
        </response>
      </method>
    </resource>
    <resource path="/json/{id: \d+}">
      <param xmlns:xsd="http://www.w3.org/2001/XMLSchema"
             type="xsd:int" style="template" name="id"/>
      <method name="GET" id="getJson">
        <response>
          <representation mediaType="application/json"/>
        </response>
      </method>
    </resource>
    ...
  </resources>
</application>
```

The WADL document is language-neutral but its use is confined basically to the Java world. Other languages and frameworks have their counterparts; for example, Rails has the ActiveResource construct that lets a client program interact with a service but without dealing explicitly with documents in XML or JSON. The *wadl2java* utility serves the same general purpose for the Java programmer.

WADL-derived code (see Example 3-16) is not everyday Java code, as the class named `Localhost_Predictions3ResourcesP` indicates. This code, like most that comes from utilities, is not pretty but does support a Java client against the JAX-RS *predictions3* service. Perhaps the best way to appreciate the usefulness of the *wadl2java* tool is to program a *predictions3* client that uses the *wadl2java*-generated artifacts.

*Example 3-16. A segment of the Java source file generated with the wadl2java utility*

```
package predictions3;

import java.net.URI;
import java.util.HashMap;
import java.util.Map;
import javax.annotation.Generated;
import javax.ws.rs.core.UriBuilder;
import com.sun.jersey.api.client.Client;
import com.sun.jersey.api.client.ClientResponse;
import com.sun.jersey.api.client.GenericType;
import com.sun.jersey.api.client.WebResource;
...
public class Localhost_Predictions3ResourcesP {
    public final static URI BASE_URI;
    static {
        URI originalURI =
            URI.create("http://localhost:8080/predictions3/resourcesP/");
        java.io.InputStream is =
          Localhost_Predictions3ResourcesP.class.getResourceAsStream(
            "/META-INF/jax-rs-catalog.xml");
        if (is != null) {
            ...
        }
        BASE_URI = originalURI;
    }
    ...
    public static class Root {
        public Localhost_Predictions3ResourcesP.Root.DeleteIdD
                    deleteIdD(String idD) {
            return new Localhost_Predictions3ResourcesP.Root.DeleteIdD(_client,
                _uriBuilder.buildFromMap(_templateAndMatrixParameterValues), idD);
        }
        public Localhost_Predictions3ResourcesP.Root.Create create() {
            return new Localhost_Predictions3ResourcesP.Root.Create(_client,
                _uriBuilder.buildFromMap(_templateAndMatrixParameterValues));
        }
        public Localhost_Predictions3ResourcesP.Root.Update update() {
            return new Localhost_Predictions3ResourcesP.Root.Update(_client,
                _uriBuilder.buildFromMap(_templateAndMatrixParameterValues));
        }
        ...
        public static class Create {
            private Client _client;
            private UriBuilder _uriBuilder;
```

```
            private Map<String, Object> _templateAndMatrixParameterValues;
            private URI _uri;

            public Create(Client client, URI uri) {
                _client = client;
                _uri = uri;
                _uriBuilder = UriBuilder.fromUri(uri);
                _uriBuilder = _uriBuilder.path("/create");
                _templateAndMatrixParameterValues = new HashMap<String, Object>();
            }
            ...
            public<T >T postXWwwFormUrlencodedAsTextPlain(Object input,
                                              GenericType<T> returnType) {
                UriBuilder localUriBuilder = _uriBuilder.clone();
                WebResource resource =
                   _client.resource(localUriBuilder.buildFromMap(
                                     _templateAndMatrixParameterValues));
                com.sun.jersey.api.client.WebResource.Builder resourceBuilder =
                   resource.getRequestBuilder();
                resourceBuilder = resourceBuilder.accept("text/plain");
                ...
                return response.getEntity(returnType);
            }
            ...
        }
        ...
    }
```

---

## From the predictions3.wadl File to the wadl2java-Generated Classes

The *wadl2java* (*http://wadl.java.net*) utility for Jersey downloads as a ZIP file, which includes sample Ant and Maven scripts that can be adapted as needed. (The sample Ant script builds client-support code for the Yahoo News Service, a RESTful service that Yahoo no longer publishes.) Let *WADL_HOME* be the base directory for the contents of the unzipped file. *WADL_HOME* has a *bin* subdirectory, with *wadl2java* utilities for Unixy and Windows systems, and a *lib* directory that contains almost all of the JAR files required. The missing JAR file, as of version WADL 1.1.3, is *jersey-bundle.jar*, which should be copied into the *WADL_HOME/lib* directory.

The Jersey-generated WADL document for the *predictions3* service uses xs instead of xsd as a namespace identifier. Here are the first two occurrences in *predictions.wadl*, with one xs to the left of the colon and the other to the right:

```
<param xmlns:xs="http://www.w3.org/2001/XMLSchema"
       type="xs:int"
...
```

The xs should be changed globally to xsd.

Compiling a *wadl2java*-generated file such as *Localhost_Predictions3ResourcesP.java* requires two JAR files: *jersey-bundle.jar* and *jersey-core.jar*. The ZIP file that contains the sample code includes the Ant script *runWADL.xml*, which compiles and executes the WADL-based client against the *predictions3* service.

The `Predictions3Client` (see Example 3-17) is the source code for a sample client against the *predictions3* JAX-RS service. For convenience, the client is in the same package, `predictions`, as the *wadl2java*-generated code. The `Predictions3Client` underscores again the trade-off in using a tool such as *wadl2java* to avoid dealing explicitly with XML or similar payloads:

- The upside is avoiding an XML or comparable parse.

- The downside is learning yet another API.

*Example 3-17. The `Predictions3Client`, which uses the wadl2java-generated classes*

```
package predictions3;

import java.net.URI;

public class Predictions3Client {
    public static void main(String[]  args) {
        new Predictions3Client().demo();
    }
    private void demo() {
        // Get a reference to the Localhost_Predictions3ResourcesP.Root defined
        // inside Localhost_Predictions3ResourcesP, as the "root" provides access
        // to other classes, which in turn support the CRUD functionalities.
        Localhost_Predictions3ResourcesP.Root root =               ❶
            Localhost_Predictions3ResourcesP.root();
        // The xmlGetter can make GET requests against the service.
        Localhost_Predictions3ResourcesP.Root.Xml xmlGetter = root.xml();   ❷
        String xml = xmlGetter.getAsXml(String.class); // String returned    ❸
        System.out.println("The raw XML:\n" + xml);      // predictions in XML
    }
}
```

The setup in the `Predictions3Client` seems clumsy because the *wadl2java*-generated artifacts are nested `static` classes, an idiom that is uncommon in quotidian Java. The good news is that, once the clumsiness recedes, the method calls are refreshingly simple. For instance, the calls to the `root` (line 1) and `xml` (line 2) methods take no arguments, and the call to `getAsXml` (line 3) takes but one argument, the Java type for the returned XML document. The *wadl2java*-generated code would be even easier to use if XML Schema documents were produced with, for example, the *schemagen* utility and then referenced in the `grammars` section of *predictions3.wadl*, which is currently empty. With this refinement, the call to:

```
xmlGetter.getAsXml(String.class)
```

could be changed to the friendlier:

```
xmlGetter.getAsXml(PredictionsList.class)
```

Chapter 4 covers the WSDL document and WSDL-based utilities for generating helpful client-side code. At that point it will be easier to assess the usefulness of WADL documents and the related utilities. For now, it is enough to name WADL-related technologies as yet another part of the Java support for RESTful web services.

# The JAX-RS Client API

JAX-RS, Restlet, and the JAX-WS @WebServiceProvider frameworks for RESTful services include client-side APIs. These APIs are meant to simplify the task of writing RESTful clients in general, not just clients against a RESTful service implemented in a particular framework. To underscore the point, this section takes a look at the JAX-RS client-side API (see Example 3-18); the client, however, goes against the servlet-based *predictions2* RESTful service from Chapter 2.

*Example 3-18. A sample client using the JAX-RS client-side API*

```
package jerseyClient;

import com.sun.jersey.api.client.Client;
import com.sun.jersey.api.client.WebResource;
import javax.ws.rs.core.MediaType;
import com.sun.jersey.api.representation.Form;

public class JerseyClient {
    private static final String baseUrl = "http://localhost:8080/predictions2";

    public static void main(String[ ] args) {
        new JerseyClient().demo();
    }
    private void demo() {
        Client client = Client.create();
        client.setFollowRedirects(true); // in case the service redirects
        WebResource resource = client.resource(baseUrl);
        getAllDemo(resource);
        postDemo(resource); // same resource but different verb
        String url = baseUrl + "?id=32";
        resource = client.resource(url);
        getOneDemo(resource);
        deleteDemo(resource); // delete id = 32
    }
    private void getAllDemo(WebResource resource) {
        // GET all XML
        String response =
            resource.accept(MediaType.APPLICATION_XML_TYPE).get(String.class);
        report("GET all in XML:\n", response);
```

```
    // GET all JSON
    response =
        resource.accept(MediaType.APPLICATION_JSON_TYPE).get(String.class);
    report("GET all in JSON:\n", response);
}
private void getOneDemo(WebResource resource) {
    String response =
        resource.accept(MediaType.APPLICATION_XML_TYPE).get(String.class);
    report("GET one in XML:\n", response);
    response =
        resource.accept(MediaType.APPLICATION_JSON_TYPE).get(String.class);
    report("GET one in JSON:\n", response);
}
private void postDemo(WebResource resource) {
    Form form = new Form(); // HTTP body, a simple hash
    form.add("who", "William Butler Yeats");
    form.add("what", "I know that I shall meet my fate");

    String response =
        resource.type(MediaType.APPLICATION_FORM_URLENCODED_TYPE)
        .accept(MediaType.TEXT_PLAIN_TYPE)
        .post(String.class, form);
    report("POST:\n", response);
}
private void deleteDemo(WebResource resource) {
    String response =
        resource.accept(MediaType.TEXT_PLAIN_TYPE).delete(String.class);
    report("DELETE:\n", response);
}
private void report(String msg, String response) {
    System.out.println("\n" + msg + response);
}
}
```

The `JerseyClient` (see Example 3-18) against the servlet-based *predictions2* RESTful
service supports all of the CRUD operations. (An executable JAR with the client is
included in the ZIP with the sample code.) This client underscores that the JAX-RS
client API is not restricted to JAX-RS services. In any case, the `JerseyClient` uses some
nice features of the JAX-RS client-side API. For example, the *predictions2* service uses
the same URI in a GET request that returns XML as in one that returns JSON. What
differentiates the two requests is that the one for JSON has the key/value pair:

```
accept: application/json
```

or the equivalent in the HTTP headers of a GET request. In the `getAllDemo` method of
the `JerseyClient`, the two forms of the GET request are expressed at a high level:

```
resource.accept(MediaType.APPLICATION_XML_TYPE).get(String.class);  // XML
resource.accept(MediaType.APPLICATION_JSON_TYPE).get(String.class); // JSON
```

There is no need for the programmer to inject, using a low-level API, inject this key/value pair into the HTTP headers using a low-level API:

```
accept: application/json
```

By the way, the get(String.class) at the end of each statement signals that the response to the GET request should be text, a Java String. The API accepts JAX-B types as well so that, for example, a GET request could indicate that it expects a Prediction object rather than a String one.

The setup for making CRUD calls is uncomplicated. A Client instance is created, which can be used to create arbitrarily many WebResource instances, each of which wraps a URL. Here, for review, is a slice of the JerseyClient:

```
Client client = Client.create();
client.setFollowRedirects(true); // in case the service redirects
WebResource resource = client.resource(baseUrl); // service URL
```

In version 2, the JAX-RS client API introduces some advanced features such as filters and asynchronous requests. These features will be examined in the next chapter but in the context of SOAP-based web services. Restlet has a client API comparable to the one in JAX-RS. The JAX-WS client API for calls against the @WebServiceProvider is at a lower level than both JAX-RS and Restlet. This is appropriate in that the @WebService Provider service-side API is deliberately low-level. All of these client-side APIs add a RESTful layer to the familiar Java classes such as URLConnection.

# JSON for JavaScript Clients

JavaScript clients, often written in a dialect such as jQuery, are now a major force in RESTful web services. Gone are the bad old days when a browser downloaded a page generated on the server and did no further client-side processing. A modern website typically integrates client-side and server-side processing to serve the overall goal of high performance combined with professional look and feel, and JavaScript—in a sense broad enough to encompass languages/frameworks such as Dojo, Enyo, Meteor, midori, jQuery, and SmartClient—is the dominant language for client-side processing.

At one time, the data displayed on a HTML page typically came from a database through a server-side application down to a browser. Web services are now a prevalent source of data, a source accessible directly from a client-side script embedded in an HTML page. Data flows into an HTML page need not originate, at least not immediately, in a server-side application connected to a database. These changes further blur the distinction between websites and web services because the HTML pages that remain a key part of any website embed scripts that can act as web service clients. Pioneering Java-Script frameworks such as Meteor (*http://www.meteor.com*) aim at virtually collapsing the difference between client-side and server-side functionality by allowing client-side scripts direct access to a server-side database. These changes and trends together open new possibilities for web services and their clients; these changes likewise point to an even greater role for JavaScript processing and JSON representations in web services.

## JSONP and Web Services

Contemporary web services regularly support not only JSON payloads but also JSONP, where the **P** stands for *with padding*. JSONP originally signified a way to work around the traditional *same domain policy* that prevents a page downloaded from a domain such as *server.foo.org* from communicating with a domain other than *foo.org*; JSONP still serves this purpose. The JSONP workaround involves `script` elements in a page, as these elements allow code to be downloaded from anywhere; the downloaded code can then perform arbitrary processing, which includes communicating with servers in arbitrary domains. JSONP works nicely with web services.

JSONP brings an event-driven API to client-side processing (Example 3-19). Using JSONP, the programmer can do the following:

- Provide a URL to a data source.
- Specify a callback function to be executed, in browser context, once the data from the specified source arrives.

*Example 3-19. A JSONP call against the RESTful Twitter search*

```
<!DOCTYPE html>
<html>
<head>
    <title>Twittering</title>
    <script type = "text/javascript"
            src = "http://code.jquery.com/jquery-latest.min.js">
    </script>
    <script type = 'text/javascript'>
        function cBack(data) { alert(JSON.stringify(data)); } ❶
        (function($) {
            var url = "http://search.twitter.com/search.json?q=skiing&rpp=4";
            $.ajax({
                type: 'GET',
                url: url,
                async: false,
                jsonpCallback: 'cBack',                        ❷
                contentType: "application/json",
                dataType: 'jsonp',                             ❸
                success: function(json) { console.dir(json.sites); },
                error: function(e) { console.log(e.message); }
            });
        })(jQuery);
    </script>
</head>
<body></body>
</html>
```

The HTML document in Example 3-19 embeds jQuery code, which illustrates a JSONP call against Twitter's RESTful search service. The three code lines of interest are numbered. The GET request to Twitter has `jsonp` as its `dataType` (line 3), and the `jsonpCallback` is a function named `cBack` (lines 1 and 2) that takes one argument: the data returned from the Twitter search. The Twitter response can be depicted in text as follows:

```
cBack({...})
```

This is the invocation syntax for a JavaScript function that takes one argument: a JavaScript object. (It should be noted that a JavaScript function is likewise a JavaScript *object*, as JavaScript treats functions as first-class objects.) The curly braces, { and }, mark the start and the end of the JavaScript argument to the function. This argument is a mix of metadata about the search and a list (that is, a JavaScript array) of information about skiing images. Here is a small slice of the argument, with personal data obscured with ellipses:

```
{"completed_in":0.009, "max_id":308446633115385860,
 ...
 "query":"skiing","refresh_url":"?
 ...
 [{"created_at": "Mon, 04 Mar 2013 05:19:42 +0000",
   "from_user": "...", "from_user_id": ...,
   "from_user_id_str": "...", "from_user_name" : "... ",
   "geo":null,
   ...
}
```

The JavaScript callback function `cBack`, upon receipt of the Twitter data, pops up an alert window that shows the text representation of the downloaded JSON object.

The JSONP exchange between the client-side script and the Twitter search service can be summarized as follows. The script, written in the jQuery dialect of JavaScript, makes a JSONP call that specifies a callback function; the Twitter service accommodates by returning, as the HTTP response, the name of the callback function together with the requested data as the argument to the function. The browser executes the function call, which displays the returned JSON in a pop-up window. This small example thus illustrates the event-driven character of a JSONP request.

With respect to RESTful web services, JSON is an ideal format for JavaScript clients because JSON is the text representation of a native JavaScript object. With two additional examples, this section covers the basics and sketches some possibilities. The first example involves a *composed* web service—a service that includes another service as a component. This example also illustrates a common task in web services—reformatting data, in this case reformatting XML as JSON. The second example focuses on Ajax calls: jQuery embedded in an HTML page regularly polls a server so that the partially updated page reflects the current state of the resource.

# A Composed RESTful Service with jQuery

The first jQuery example, named *cds*, is a composed RESTful service. Here is an overview:

- The HTML page, downloaded from the *cds* service to a browser, contains embedded jQuery that makes a GET request against *getCDs.jsp*, a JSP script with support from a backend JavaBean. This JSP script and the backend bean together implement the web service that delivers JSON back to a jQuery or comparable script.

- The backend JavaBean, an instance of the `FetchXML` class, makes its own GET request, in this case against a RESTful service that the W3C maintains. This service delivers a list of CD titles from the 1980s, in XML format, back to the `FetchXML` instance, which then converts the XML to JSON.

- The JSP script *getCDs.jsp*, with the JSON from the backend bean, completes the service by sending the JSON list of CDs back to the jQuery script embedded in the HTML page. Here is slice of the returned JSON:

```
[{"title":"empire burlesque",
  "price":10.9,
  "company":"columbia",
  "year":1985,
  "artist":"bob dylan",
  "country":"usa"},
  ...
```

- The jQuery script displays, as confirmation, the downloaded JSON in a pop-up window and then iterates over the JSON array of CDs, displaying the `title` and the `artist` for each CD as an HTML element in an unordered list. The entire scenario (see Figure 3-2) consists of two GET requests and two response payloads, one in XML and the ultimate one in JSON.

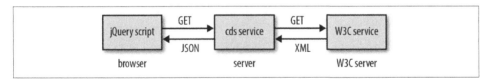

*Figure 3-2. The composed cds service*

Perhaps the best way to clarify the architecture is to start with the jQuery client, which expects the data to come in JSON format. The catch is that the W3C service provides the data in XML format. The intermediary *cds* service takes on the job of format converter (Example 3-20).

*Example 3-20. The jQuery RESTful client embedded in an HTML page*

```html
<!DOCTYPE html>
<html>
  <head>
    <title>JSON</title>
    <script type = "text/javascript"
            src = "http://code.jquery.com/jquery-latest.min.js">
    </script>
    <script type = "text/javascript">
      $.getJSON('http://localhost:8080/cds/getCDs.jsp', function(response) {
        var cds = response.catalog.cd;
        alert(JSON.stringify(cds));
        $.each(cds, function(ind, val) {                                    ❶
          $('#container').append('<li>' + cds[ind].title + ': ' +          ❷
                                  cds[ind].artist + '</li>'); } );          ❸
      });
    </script>
  </head>
  <body>
    <ul id = 'container'></ul>
  </body>
</html>
```

The HTML page with the embedded jQuery in Example 3-20 is short, and the embedded jQuery is likewise terse compared to the earlier Twitter sample (see Example 3-19). The current example shows a jQuery shortcut method, in this example getJSON, that can be used in place of the generic jQuery ajax method. Of particular interest here, however, is that the jQuery code does not parse the JSON document returned from the RESTful service but, rather, treats the JSON document as a native JavaScript array. In the body of the each iteration (line 1), for example, the jQuery extracts the title and the artist using regular JavaScript syntax:

```
cds[ind].title  /* line 2: ind is the index into the array */
cds[ind].artist /* line 3 */
```

No parsing is required.

In the composed *cds* service, the W3C service is the ultimate data source. The other service, which consists of the very short JSP script *getCDs.jsp* (see Example 3-21) and the backend POJO class FetchXML (see Example 3-22), is the fetch-and-convert module: a jQuery client hits the JSP script, which returns JSON from the FetchXML instance method getJson, and the JSON is the result of transforming XML from the W3C service into JSON.

*Example 3-21. The getCDs.jsp script in the cds service*

```jsp
<jsp:useBean id    = "fetcher"
             type  = "cds.FetchXML"
             class = "cds.FetchXML">
```

```
</jsp:useBean>
<jsp:getProperty name = "fetcher" property = "json" /> ❶
```

When a client request hits the *getCDs.jsp* script (technically, the servlet instance into which this JSP script is ultimately transformed), the client gets in response the value returned from the FetchXML method getJson, named in the JSP script as the property json (line 1).

*Example 3-22. The backend POJO class `FetchXML` and its getJson method*

```
package cds;

import org.json.JSONObject;
import org.json.XML;
import java.io.BufferedReader;
import java.io.InputStreamReader;
import java.io.InputStream;
import java.net.URL;
import java.net.URLConnection;

public class FetchXML {
    public void setJson(String json) { }
    public String getJson() {
        JSONObject json = null;
        try {
            // Fetch the XML document from the W3C site.
            String xml = "";
            URL url = new URL("http://www.w3schools.com/xml/cd_catalog.xml");     ❶
            URLConnection conn  = url.openConnection();                           ❷
            BufferedReader in =
                new BufferedReader(new InputStreamReader(conn.getInputStream()));
            // Read the document records.
            String line = null;
            while ((line = in.readLine()) != null) xml += line;                   ❸
            in.close();
            xml = xml.replace("'", ""); // Clean up the XML.                      ❹
            // Transform the XML document into a JSON object.
            json = XML.toJSONObject(xml.toLowerCase());                           ❺
        }
        catch(Exception e) { throw new RuntimeException(e); }
        return json.toString(); // JSON document                                 ❻
    }
}
```

The FetchXML method getJson uses a URLConnection (line 2) to communicate with the W3C service at the designated URL (line 1). The W3C service returns the CD list as an XML document, which the FetchXML instance reads line by line (line 3). For readability, the XML document is converted to lowercase and otherwise cleaned up (lines 4 and 5) before being converted into a JSON document (line 6), which is returned to the jQuery script. A JSON library deployed in the WAR file converts the XML to JSON, and the jQuery script, which invokes the composed RESTful service to begin, benefits from receiving JSON rather than XML. If the jQuery script dealt directly with the W3C service, then this script would take on the task of either parsing the returned XML document or transforming the XML into JSON.

## An Ajax Polling Example

The JAX-RS *predictions3* web service in Chapter 2 supports all of the CRUD operations, which means that the resource can change state over time. How should clients against this RESTful service keep abreast of the changes? Two general ways are available:

- The service itself might maintain a list of connected clients and automatically *push* to these clients any changes in the resource.
- The clients might periodically poll the service with GET requests and thereby *pull* the current representation of the resource.

The example in this section illustrates the second approach with a jQuery client that continually polls the *predictions3* service with GET requests for a JSON response. The *predictions3* service is unchanged from Chapter 2.

The HTML page *poll.html* (see Example 3-23) embeds a jQuery script that continually polls the *predictions3* service. The workhorse function is `fetch` (line 1), which makes an Ajax call against the RESTful *predictions3* service. The URL ends with /`json`, which signals that the response should be JSON rather than XML or plain text. As the key named `method` and its value indicate (line 2), the Ajax call is essentially a GET request. This example thus goes back to the generic `ajax` call rather than a shortcut call such as `getJSON`.

*Example 3-23. The poll.html page with jQuery to poll the predictions3 service*

```
<!DOCTYPE html>
<html>
  <head>
    <title>Ajax polling example</title>
    <script type = "text/javascript"
            src  = "http://code.jquery.com/jquery-latest.min.js">
    </script>
    <script type = "text/javascript">
      var url = 'http://localhost:8080/predictions3/resourcesP/json';
      function displayPreds(preds) {
         $('#container').empty(); // clear the old list, if any
         $.each(preds, function(ind, val) {
            $('#container').append('<li>' + preds[ind].who + ': ' +
                                      preds[ind].what + '</li>'); } );
      }
      function fetch() {
         $.ajax({                                                    ❶
```

```
                url:         url,
                method:      'GET',                                        ❷
                dataType:    'json',
                contentType: "application/json; charset=utf-8",
                cache:       false,
                success:     function(res) { displayPreds(res.predictions); },
                error:       function(res) { console.log(res); },
                complete:    function () {                                  ❸
                                 setTimeout(function() { fetch() }, 5000)}}); ❹
      }
      $(document).ready(fetch); // invoked after DOM is built and loaded    ❺
    </script>
  </head>
  <body>
    <ul id = 'container'></ul>
  </body>
</html>
```

The Ajax request from `fetch` has two possible outcomes:

- If the request succeeds, then the predictions are displayed on the HTML page as elements in an unordered list.

- If the request fails, the response message is logged.

In either case, the `complete` key (line 3) has as its value a function (lines 4 and 5) that invokes the jQuery `setTimeout` function, and the `setTimeout` function pauses for five seconds before invoking `fetch` yet again. The `complete` function executes *after* either the `success` or the `error` function has executed. The jQuery script thus polls the *predictions3* service repeatedly, with brief pauses in between each polling operation; the *poll.html* page displays, to within five seconds or so, the current state of the *predictions3* resource.

The deployed *poll.html* page (see the sidebar) can be tested as follows:

- The page can be displayed and thereby checked in a browser. If none of the predictions has been deleted and no new one has been added, there should be 32 predictions in all, the last of which should be:

  ```
  Hiram Gulgowski: Versatile tangible application will maximize...
  ```

- A *curl* call can then be used, for example, to delete this prediction, whose `id` is 32:

  ```
  % curl --request DELETE localhost:8080/predictions3/resourcesP/delete/32
  ```

In about five seconds or so, the *poll.html* page can be inspected again in the browser to confirm that the Hiram Gulgowski prediction is gone. Similar *curl* tests involving POST and PUT requests should have the expected impact on the browser-displayed *poll.html*.

## Why Deploy the poll.html Page as a One-Page Website?

The ZIP file with the sample code includes a simple website (*ch3/poll*) consisting of two files, *poll.html* and *web.xml*. The site can be deployed in the usual way:

```
% ant -Dwar.name=ajax deploy
```

After deployment, a browser hits the site with the URL:

```
http://localhost:8080/ajax/
```

It is tempting to avoid the deployment altogether and, instead, load the local file *poll.html* into the browser with a URL such as:

```
file:///home/kalin/jwsur2/ch3/poll/poll.html
```

In some browsers this may be all right, but in others (for example, Chrome), the *same origin policy*, discussed earlier with respect to JSONP, comes into play. In the case of Chrome, even two local files in the same directory are treated as having different origins. The upshot is that Ajax calls in an HTML page such as *poll.html* should be tested by deploying the page as part of a website. Accordingly, the *poll.html* page is deployed in the *ajax.war* file and a browser is then directed to this WAR file.

The Ajax polling example, like the earlier *cds* service, shows the benefit that a jQuery or other JavaScipt client enjoys from a JSON response. In the polling example, the who and the what attributes of a JSON prediction are extracted straightforwardly. Here, for review, is the code snippet that displays a prediction as an HTML element in an unordered list:

```
$('#container').append('<li>' + preds[ind].who + ': ' +
                        preds[ind].what + '</li>'); } );
```

In an expression such as:

```
preds[ind].who
```

preds refers to the JSON array, ind is an integer index into this array, and who is a field in the JSON representation of a JavaScript prediction object. The jQuery script can access the information of interest in a natural way precisely because the script deals with JSON rather than, say, XML.

JavaScript clients of RESTful web services, such as the jQuery clients illustrated in the three examples of this section, are becoming increasingly popular. RESTful services are sufficiently flexible to generate response payloads in whatever format a client prefers. In the case of JavaScript clients, the preferred format is clear: JSON.

# What's Next?

The focus in the first three chapters has been on RESTful web services and their clients. The next chapter turns to SOAP-based services delivered over HTTP(S), which can be viewed as a special case of RESTful services. The normal request and response payloads in a SOAP-based service are *SOAP envelopes*, XML documents whose root element has a tag with `Envelope` as the local name. An example is:

```
<soap:Envelope xmlns:soap = '...'>
  ...
</soap:Envelope>
```

In a typical SOAP-based exchange, a client sends an `Envelope` to a service and gets an `Envelope` in return. SOAP, like XML in general, is programming-language neutral, and any language with the appropriate libraries can support SOAP-based services and clients. At present, however, only Java and DotNet have strong support for SOAP; the other language systems have spotty support at best.

There is much to be said for SOAP over HTTP. The HTTP handles the transport and, in the case of HTTPS, addresses major wire-level security concerns. The SOAP libraries on the service and the client side typically hide the SOAP, although the SOAP is available to inspect or even manipulate if a service or a client requires this. Chapter 4 looks at the service and the client sides of SOAP-based services; this look includes two SOAP-based clients against the Amazon E-Commerce service. Chapter 5 then examines the *handler level* in SOAP-based services. At the *application level* in SOAP-based services, the SOAP itself is transparent; at the handler level, the SOAP is exposed for examination and manipulation.

# SOAP-Based Web Services

JAX-WS is an API for producing and consuming REST-style and SOAP-style services. Chapter 2 introduced, with a RESTful example, the JAX-WS @WebServiceProvider annotation, which can be used for either a REST-style or a SOAP-based service. This chapter introduces the @WebService annotation, in effect a refinement of @WebService Provider; a @WebService is emphatically SOAP-based. JAX-WS is thus sufficiently rich and varied that it might better be described as a collection of APIs. JAX-WS is the successor to JAX-RPC, which derives from the XML-RPC discussed in Chapter 1. The reference implementation for JAX-WS is part of the open source GlassFish project and is named GlassFish Metro or just Metro (*http://metro.java.net*) for short. The current version of JAX-WS is 2.2.x. JAX-WS is officially part of enterprise Java but, with JDK 1.6 or greater, JAX-WS services can be compiled and published using only core Java. SOAP-based services in JAX-WS can be published with a standard Java web server such as Tomcat or Jetty; there is also a convenient Endpoint publisher, used earlier to publish a RESTful service.

Apache Axis2 (*http://axis.apache.org*) is an alternative implementation of JAX-WS. Axis2, the successor to Axis, is based on JAX-WS but has additional features. Yet another JAX-WS implementation is Apache CXF (*http://cxf.apache.org*). This chapter focuses on the Metro implementation of JAX-WS, but the next chapter includes an Axis2 service and client. The Metro, Axis2, and Apache CXF implementations of JAX-WS are sufficiently close that a programmer fluent in one implementation should be able to move easily into any other implementation.

SOAP is an XML dialect that has two W3C-sanctioned versions: 1.1 and 1.2; SOAP is officially no longer an acronym. The differences between the versions of SOAP are more about infrastructure than API. For example, the media type for a SOAP 1.1 message is text/xml, whereas this type changes in SOAP 1.2 to application/soap+xml. The SOAP 1.2 processing model is more thoroughly and precisely specified than is the SOAP 1.1 model; SOAP 1.2 has an official *binding framework* that opens the way to using transport protocols other than HTTP for delivering SOAP messages. In practice, however, HTTP remains the dominant transport for both SOAP 1.1 and SOAP 1.2. In the major SOAP frameworks of Java and DotNet, SOAP 1.1 is the default, but both systems support SOAP 1.2 as well.

SOAP has a *basic profile*, which comes from the WS-I (Web Services Interoperability) consortium to encourage and support interoperability among web service languages and technologies. Beyond the basic profile are various initiatives, some of which are covered in later chapters; these initiatives (for instance, WS-Reliability and WS-Security) often are grouped under the acronym WS-*. WSIT (Web Services Interoperability Technology) is a related set of guidelines that promotes interoperability specifically between Java and DotNet, in particular DotNet's WCF (Windows Communication Foundation). WCF is a framework for developing service-oriented applications that would include but also go beyond SOAP-based web services *(metro.java.net/ guide)*. From time to time, this chapter refers to one or another SOAP specification in order to clarify a particular service or client, but the emphasis in this chapter remains on coding services and their clients. Unless otherwise specified, the examples are in SOAP 1.1.

# A SOAP-Based Web Service

JAX-WS, like JAX-RS, uses annotations, and machine-generated JAX-WS code is awash with these. The first example is stingy in its use of annotations in order to underscore exactly what is required for a SOAP-based service. Later examples introduce additional annotations.:

The RandService class (see Example 4-1) defines a SOAP-based service with two operations, each an annotated Java method:

- Operation *next1* takes no arguments and returns one randomly generated integer.
- Operation *nextN* takes one argument, the number of randomly generated integers desired, and returns a list (in this implementation, an array) of integers.

*Example 4-1. A SOAP-based service with two operations*

```
package rand;

import javax.jws.WebService;
import javax.jws.WebMethod;
import java.util.Random;

@WebService                                                    ❶
public class RandService {
    private static final int maxRands = 16;

    @WebMethod // optional but helpful annotation              ❷
```

```
    public int next1() { return new Random().nextInt(); }
    @WebMethod // optional but helpful annotation              ❸
    public int[ ] nextN(final int n) {
        final int k = (n > maxRands) ? maxRands : Math.abs(n);
        int[ ] rands = new int[k];
        Random r = new Random();
        for (int i = 0; i < k; i++) rands[i] = r.nextInt();
        return rands;
    }
}
```

The @WebService annotation (line 1) marks the RandService POJO class as a web ser-vice, and the @WebMethod annotation (lines 2 and 3) specifies which of the encapsulated methods is a service operation. In this example, the RandService class has only two methods and each of these is annotated as @WebMethod. The @WebMethod annotation is optional but recommended. In a class annotated as a @WebService, a public instance method is thereby a service *operation* even if the method is not annotated. This SOAP service code is compiled in the usual way, assuming JDK 1.6 or greater.

Recall that core Java 6 or greater includes the Endpoint class for publishing web services, SOAP-based (@WebService) and REST-style (@WebServiceProvider) alike. The class RandPublisher (see Example 4-2) is the Endpoint publisher for the RandService.

*Example 4-2. An Endpoint published for the RandService SOAP-based web service*

```
package rand;

import javax.xml.ws.Endpoint;
public class RandPublisher {
    public static void main(String[ ] args) {
        final String url = "http://localhost:8888/rs";              ❶
        System.out.println("Publishing RandService at endpoint " + url);
        Endpoint.publish(url, new RandService());                   ❷
    }
}
```

The publish method used here (line 2) takes two arguments: a URL that specifies the service endpoint (line 1) and an instance of the service implementation class, in this case the RandService class (line 2). In the URL, the port number 8888 and the URI /rs are arbitrary, although a port number greater than 1023 is recommended be-cause modern operating systems typically reserve port numbers below 1024 for partic-ular applications (e.g., port 80 is typically reserved for HTTP requests to a web server). The RandPublisher as coded here runs indefinitely, but there are various way to control an Endpoint publisher's life span.

The web service publisher can be executed in the usual way:

```
% java rand.RandPublisher
```

The output should be similar to this:

```
Publishing RandService at endpoint http://localhost:8888/rs

com.sun.xml.internal.ws.model.RuntimeModeler getRequestWrapperClass
INFO: Dynamically creating request wrapper Class rand.jaxws.Next1
com.sun.xml.internal.ws.model.RuntimeModeler getResponseWrapperClass
Dynamically creating response wrapper bean Class rand.jaxws.Next1Response
com.sun.xml.internal.ws.model.RuntimeModeler getRequestWrapperClass
INFO: Dynamically creating request wrapper Class rand.jaxws.NextN
com.sun.xml.internal.ws.model.RuntimeModeler getResponseWrapperClass
INFO: Dynamically creating response wrapper bean Class rand.jaxws.NextNResponse
```

The first line of output is from the RandPublisher but the others are from the Java run-time. The dynamically created wrapper classes such as Next1 and Next1Response are JAX-B artifacts that represent the incoming SOAP request (Next1) and the outgoing SOAP response (Next1Response).

Once the service is published, a utility such as *curl* can be used to confirm that the service is indeed up and running:

```
% curl http://localhost:8888/rs?xsd=1
```

This *curl* request contains the query string entry xsd=1 that asks for the XML Schema associated with this service; the schema, like the JAX-B artifacts, is generated dynamically (see Example 4-3).

*Example 4-3. The XML Schema generated dynamically for the RandService*

```
<?xml version="1.0" encoding="UTF-8"?>
<xs:schema xmlns:tns="http://rand/" xmlns:xs="http://www.w3.org/2001/XMLSchema"
          version="1.0" targetNamespace="http://rand/">
  <xs:element name="next1" type="tns:next1"></xs:element>
  <xs:element name="next1Response" type="tns:next1Response"></xs:element>
  <xs:element name="nextN" type="tns:nextN"></xs:element>
  <xs:element name="nextNResponse" type="tns:nextNResponse"></xs:element>
  <xs:complexType name="next1"><xs:sequence></xs:sequence></xs:complexType>
  <xs:complexType name="next1Response">
    <xs:sequence>
      <xs:element name="return" type="xs:int"></xs:element>
    </xs:sequence>
  </xs:complexType>
  <xs:complexType name="nextN">
    <xs:sequence>
      <xs:element name="arg0" type="xs:int"></xs:element>
    </xs:sequence>
  </xs:complexType>
  <xs:complexType name="nextNResponse">
    <xs:sequence>
      <xs:element name="return" type="xs:int" minOccurs="0" maxOccurs="unbounded">
      </xs:element>
    </xs:sequence>
```

```
    </xs:complexType>
</xs:schema>
```

The schema will be studied carefully later. For now, the point of interest is that the schema provides a data type for each SOAP message that travels, in either direction, between the service and the client. Each message is of an XML Schema `complexType` as opposed to an simple type such as `xsd:date`, `xsd:string`, or `xsd:integer`.

In the `RandService` there are two SOAP messages (for instance, the messages `Next1` and `Next1Response`) per web service operation (in this case, the *next1* operation) because each operation implements the familiar *request/response* pattern: a client issues a request, delivered to the service as a `Next1` SOAP message, and gets a response, in this case a `Next1Response` message, in return. Accordingly, the schema contains four typed SOAP messages because the `RandService` has two operations in the request/response pattern, which means two messages per operation. The number of `complexType` occurrences in the XML Schema may exceed the total number of messages needed to implement the service's operations because special error messages, SOAP *faults*, also may be defined in the XML Schema. SOAP faults are covered in the next chapter.

The XML Schema types such as `Next1` and `Next1Response` are the XML counterparts to the JAX-B artifacts, noted earlier, with the same names. The schema types and the JAX-B types together allow the SOAP libraries to transform Java objects into XML documents (in particular, SOAP `Envelope` instances) and SOAP `Envelope` instances into Java objects. The `Endpoint` publisher's underlying SOAP libraries handle the generation of the JAX-B artifacts and the generation of the XML Schema.

---

## Publishing a SOAP-Based Service with a Standalone Web Server

Publishing a `@WebService` with Tomcat or Jetty is almost the same as publishing a `@WebServiceProvider` (see "A RESTful Service as a @WebServiceProvider" on page 85) with these web servers. Here, for quick review, are the details.

Two configuration files are needed: the usual file *web.xml* and the additional file *sun-jaxws.xml*. Here is the *web.xml*, which would work for any implementation annotated as `@WebService` or `@WebServiceProvider`:

```
<?xml version="1.0" encoding="UTF-8"?>
<web-app>
  <listener>
    <listener-class>
      com.sun.xml.ws.transport.http.servlet.WSServletContextListener
    </listener-class>
  </listener>
  <servlet>
    <servlet-name>jaxws</servlet-name>
    <servlet-class>
```

---

```
      com.sun.xml.ws.transport.http.servlet.WSServlet
    </servlet-class>
    <load-on-startup>1</load-on-startup>
  </servlet>
  <servlet-mapping>
    <servlet-name>jaxws</servlet-name>
    <url-pattern>/*</url-pattern>
  </servlet-mapping>
</web-app>
```

The Metro classes `WSServletContextListener` and `WSServlet` are in the JAR file currently named *webservices-rt.jar*, which can be downloaded (*http://metro.java.net*) with the rest of Metro JARs. A second Metro library file *webservices-api.jar* is also required. The JAR files in question should be in the *src* directory so that the Ant script can package them in the deployed WAR file. In any case, the `WSServletContextListener` parses the *sun-jaxws.xml* file. The `WSServlet` acts as the interceptor: the servlet receives incoming requests and dispatches these to the `RandService`.

The second configuration file, *sun-jaxws.xml*, is:

```
<?xml version="1.0" encoding="UTF-8"?>
<endpoints version="2.0"
           xmlns="http://java.sun.com/xml/ns/jax-ws/ri/runtime">
  <endpoint implementation="rand.RandService" ❶
            name="RandService"
            url-pattern="/*" />
</endpoints>
```

This file completes the routing by notifying the `WSServletContextListener` that the `WSServlet` should dispatch requests to a `RandService` instance (line 1).

With the two configuration files and the Metro library JARs in the *src* directory, the `RandService` can be deployed to Tomcat in the usual way:

```
% ant -Dwar.name=rand deploy
```

Once the `@WebService` has been deployed, a *curl* call or a browser can be used to verify that the service is up and running:

```
% curl http://localhost:8080/myWarFileName?xsd=1
```

If successful, this command returns the XML Schema associated with the service.

Even this first and rather simple example underscores a major appeal of SOAP-based services: underlying SOAP libraries handle the conversions between native language types (in this case, Java types) and XML Schema types. Figure 4-1 depicts the architecture.

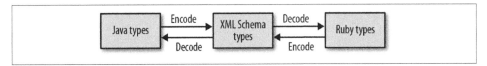

*Figure 4-1. The architecture of a typical SOAP-based service*

# The RandService in Two Files

The RandService in the first example (see Example 4-1) combines, in a single source file, what JAX-WS calls the SEI (Service Endpoint Interface) and the SIB (Service Implementation Bean). The SEI specifies, at a high level that befits an interface, the service operations, and the SIB provides an implementation of the operations. A SIB can be one of the following:

- A POJO class such as RandService annotated as @WebService and encapsulating service operations, each annotated as a @WebMethod.

- A @Stateless Session EJB that is likewise annotated as a @WebService. EJBs in general predate JAX-WS; hence, this second type of SIB is an inviting way to expose legacy EJBs as web services.

Chapter 7 covers the EJB implementation of a @WebService. For now, the SIBs will be POJO classes. For convenience, most of my examples take the single-file approach, which combines the SEI and the SIB into one class annotated as a @WebService. The two-file approach is illustrated with the SEI RandService (see Example 4-4) in one file and the SIB RandImpl (see Example 4-5) in another file. The RandService is now an interface, whereas the RandImpl is a class that implements this interface.

*Example 4-4. The Service Endpoint Interface for the revised RandService*

```
package rand2;

import javax.jws.WebService;
import javax.jws.WebMethod;
import java.util.Random;

@WebService
public interface RandService {
    @WebMethod
    public int next1();
    @WebMethod
    public int[ ] nextN(final int n);
}
```

*Example 4-5. The Service Implementation Bean for the revised RandService*

```
package rand2;

import javax.jws.WebService;
import javax.jws.WebMethod;
import java.util.Random;

@WebService(endpointInterface = "rand2.RandService")
public class RandImpl implements RandService {
    private static final int maxRands = 16;

    @WebMethod
    public int next1() { return new Random().nextInt(); }
    @WebMethod
    public int[ ] nextN(final int n) {
        final int k = (n > maxRands) ? maxRands : Math.abs(n);
        int[ ] rands = new int[k];
        Random r = new Random();
        for (int i = 0; i < k; i++) rands[i] = r.nextInt();
        return rands;
    }
}
```

In the SIB class RandImpl, the @WebService interface has an attribute, the key/value pair:

```
endpointInterface = "rand2.RandService"
```

that names the SEI. It is still important for the class RandImpl to employ the standard implements clause because only the implements clause prompts the compiler to make sure that the public methods declared in the SEI, in this case the two methods annotated with @WebMethod, are defined appropriately in the SIB.

The revised RandService has the same functionality as the original. The Endpoint publisher changes slightly:

```
Endpoint.publish(url, new RandImpl()); // SIB, not SEI
```

The second argument to the publish changes to RandImpl precisely because, in the revision, RandService is an interface. In general, the second argument to the static version of publish is always the SIB. In a single-file case such as the original version of RandService, a single class is the combined SEI and SIB.

# Clients Against the RandService

The claim that SOAP-based services are language-neutral needs to be taken on faith a bit longer. The first client against the RandService is in Java but the two thereafter are in C# and Perl. Starting with a Java client will help to clarify how the critical service contract, the WSDL document, can be put to good use in writing a client. The WSDL will be studied in detail, but putting the WSDL to work first should help to motivate the detailed study.

## A Java Client Against the RandService

Recall the XML Schema (see Example 4-3) that the Endpoint publisher generates dynamically when the RandService is published. The publisher likewise generates a WSDL, which can be requested as follows:

```
% curl http://localhost:8888/rs?wsdl
```

JDK 1.6 and greater ship with a utility, *wsimport*, that uses a WSDL to generate Java classes in support of programming a client against the service described in the WSDL. Here is how the utility can be used in the current example:

```
% wsimport -p client -keep http://localhost:8888/rs?wsdl
```

The -p flag stands for "package": the utility creates a directory named *client* and puts the generated Java code in this directory/package. The -keep flag generates source (*.java*) as well as compiled (*.class*) files; without this flag, only compiled files would be in the *client* directory. Sixteen files are generated in total, half source and half compiled. Among these are files with names such as Next1 and Next1Response, the very names of the classes generated at the publication of the RandService. In any case, these client-side artifacts correspond to SOAP types described in the XML Schema document for the RandService.

How are the *wsimport*-generated files to be used? Two of these are of special interest:

- The class RandServiceService begins with the name of the published SOAP service, RandService, and has another Service stuck on the end. The @WebService annotation could be used to specify a less awkward name but, for now, the key point is that this class represents, to the client, the deployed web service.

- The interface RandService has the same name as the published service but there is a critical difference: this RandService is an *interface*, whereas the published Rand Service is a *class*. This interface, like any Java interface, declares methods—hence, the interface declares the operations encapsulated in published service and thereby specifies the invocation syntax for each operation. In this example, there are two such operations: *next1* and *nextN*.

The RandServiceService and RandService types are used in an idiomatic way to write the Java client against the service. The RandClient (see Example 4-6) is a sample client that illustrates the idiom.

*Example 4-6. A Java client built with wsimport-generated artifacts*

```
import client.RandServiceService;
import client.RandService;
import java.util.List;

public class RandClient {
    public static void main(String[ ] args) {
        // set-up
        RandServiceService service = new RandServiceService(); ❶
        RandService port = service.getRandServicePort();        ❷
        // sample calls
        System.out.println(port.next1());                       ❸
        System.out.println();
        List<Integer> nums = port.nextN(4);                     ❹
        for (Integer num : nums) System.out.println(num);       ❺
    }
}
```

The `RandClient` imports two types from the *wsimport*-generated artifacts: the class `RandServiceService` and the interface `RandService`. In the setup phase of the client code, the class's no-argument constructor is invoked to create an object that represents, on the client side, the service itself (line 1). Once this object is constructed, there is a *get* call with a distinct pattern:

```
service.get<name of interface type>Port() // line 2 pattern
```

In this case, the interface is named `RandService` and so the call is:

```
service.getRandServicePort() // line 2
```

This *get* method returns a reference to an object that encapsulates the two operations in the `RandService`, *next1* and *nextN*. The reference is named `port`, although any name would do, for reasons that will become clear once the WSDL is studied in detail. The `port` reference is then used to make two sample calls against the service. On a sample run, the output was:

```
53378846        // from line 3
-818435924      // from lines 4 and 5
104886422
1714126390
-2140389441
```

The first integer is returned from the call to `next1` and the next four integers from the call to `nextN`.

The `RandClient` does reveal an oddity about the *wsimport*-generated artifacts. In the `RandService`, the method `nextN` begins:

```
public int[ ] nextN(...
```

The return type is int[ ], an array of int values. In the *wsimport*-generated interface RandService, the method nextN begins:

```
public List<Integer> nextN(...
```

The *wsimport* utility is within its rights to replace int[ ] with List<Integer>, as a List has a toArray method that returns an array; with automatic boxing/unboxing, the Java types Integer and int are interchangeable in the current context. The point is that the programmer typically needs to inspect at least the *wsimport*-generated interface, in this example RandService, in order to determine the argument and return types of every operation.

---

## Companion Utilities: wsimport and wsgen

The *wsimport* utility eases the task of writing a Java client against a service that has a WSDL as the service contract. This utility has a client-side focus, although the utility can be helpful on the server side as well; a later example illustrates. The *wsgen* utility, which also ships with core Java 1.6 or greater, has a server-side focus. For example, *wsgen* can be used to generate a WSDL. The command:

```
% wsgen -cp . -wsdl rand.RandService
```

generates a WSDL file named *RandServiceService.wsdl*. However, this WSDL has a placeholder for the service endpoint rather than a usable URL:

```
...
<soap:address location="REPLACE_WITH_ACTUAL_URL"/>
...
```

When a service publisher such as Endpoint, Tomcat, Jetty, and the like generate the WSDL, the WSDL includes a usable URL.

The *wsgen* utility has another use. When the RandService is published with Endpoint, the publisher outputs information about dynamically generated classes, in this case Next1, Next1Response, NetxN, and NextNResponse. As noted earlier, these are JAX-B artifacts that the Java runtime uses to convert Java types into XML types and vice versa. The *wsgen* utility can be used to generate the JAX-B artifacts as files on the local system. For example, the command:

```
% wsgen -cp . rand.RandService
```

automatically creates a package/directory *rand/jaxws* and then populates this directory with *Next1.class*, *Next1Response.class*, *NextN.class*, and *NextNResponse.class*. Now if the Endpoint publisher is started after these files have been created, the publisher does not generate the JAX-B artifacts dynamically but instead uses the ones that *wsgen* already created.

---

A final, obvious point about the interaction between the Java client and the Java service deserves mention: the SOAP is completely transparent. The underlying SOAP libraries generate the SOAP on the sending side and parse the SOAP on the receiving side so that the Java code on both sides can remain agnostic about what type of payload is being sent and received. SOAP transparency is a major selling point for SOAP-based services.

## A C# Client Against the RandService

The next client is in C#, a DotNet language similar to Java; DotNet has a *wsdl* utility similar to Java's *wsimport* utility. The *wsdl* utility can be targeted at the dynamically generated WSDL for the RandService:

```
% wsdl http://localhost:8888/rs?wsdl
```

This command generates a single file with an awkward name: *RandServiceService.cs* (see Example 4-7).

*Example 4-7. A C# client, built with wsdl-generated code, against the RandService*

```
using System;
using System.ComponentModel;
using System.Diagnostics;
using System.Web.Services;
using System.Web.Services.Protocols;
using System.Xml.Serialization;

// This source code was auto-generated by wsdl, Version=4.0.30319.1.
...
public partial class RandServiceService :
        System.Web.Services.Protocols.SoapHttpClientProtocol {
    private System.Threading.SendOrPostCallback next1OperationCompleted;
    private System.Threading.SendOrPostCallback nextNOperationCompleted;

    public RandServiceService() { this.Url = "http://localhost:8888/rs"; }
    ...
    public int next1() {
        object[] results = this.Invoke("next1", new object[0]);
        return ((int)(results[0]));
    }
    ...
    public System.Nullable<int>[]
            nextN([System.Xml.Serialization.XmlElementAttribute(
                Form=System.Xml.Schema.XmlSchemaForm.Unqualified)] int arg0) {
        object[] results = this.Invoke("nextN", new object[] {arg0});
        return ((System.Nullable<int>[])(results[0]));
    }
    ...
}
...
```

The code excised from the C# RandServiceService class supports asynchronous calls against the Java RandService. Java, too, supports both synchronous (blocking) and asynchronous (nonblocking) calls against a web service's operations, as a sample client against the RandService later illustrates. For now, only synchronous calls are of interest. Here is a sample C# client that uses the *wsdl*-generated code to make calls against the RandService:

```
class RandClient {
  static void Main() {
    RandServiceService service = new RandServiceService();    ❶
    Console.WriteLine("Call to next1():\n" + service.next1());  ❷
    Console.WriteLine("\nCall to nextN(4):");
    int?[] nums = service.nextN(4);                            ❸
    foreach (int num in nums) Console.WriteLine(num);
  }
}
```

The C# client code is simpler than its Java counterpart because the new operation with the no-argument constructor RandServiceService() (line 1) creates an object that encapsulates the client-side operations *next1* and *nextN*. The C# code does not require the getRandServicePort() call from the Java client. The call to *next1* (line 2) is basically the same in the C# and Java clients, but the C# call to *nextN* has unusual syntax. The return type int?[] (line 3) signifies an integer array that may have null as its value; the type int[] signifies an integer array that cannot be null. On a sample run, the C# client output is:

```
Call to next1():
680641940
Call to nextN(4):
1783826925
260390049
-48376976
-914903224
```

The C# example does illustrate language interoperability for SOAP-based services, although C# and Java are at least cousins among programming languages. The next sample client is written in a language quite different from Java.

## A Perl Client Against the RandService

The final client (see Example 4-8) against the Java RandService is in Perl. This client makes it easy to display the SOAP messages that go back and forth between client and service; the Perl library SOAP::Lite has an excellent, easy-to-use tracer.

*Example 4-8. A Perl client against the RandService*

```
#!/usr/bin/perl -w

use SOAP::Lite +trace => 'debug';
```

```
use strict;

my $soap =                                                                      ❶
    SOAP::Lite->uri('http://rand/')->proxy('http://localhost:8888/rs/');
my $num = $soap->next1()->result();                                             ❷
print "Response is: $num\n";                                                    ❸
```

In line 1, the Perl client constructs a SOAP::Lite object (the reference is $soap) that communicates with the RandService. The uri value of http://rand/ is the namespace that identifies a particular service available at the proxy (that is, the URL) value of http://localhost:8888/rs. A given service endpoint, a URL, could host any number of services, with a URI identifying each. In line 2, the call to next1 returns a SOAP message:

```
<?xml version="1.0" ?>
<S:Envelope
    xmlns:S="http://schemas.xmlsoap.org/soap/envelope/">
  <S:Body>
    <ns2:next1Response xmlns:ns2="http://rand/">
      <return>1774649411</return>
    </ns2:next1Response>
  </S:Body>
</S:Envelope>
```

The cascaded call to result (also line 2) extracts the value 1774649411 from the SOAP envelope, and the value is assigned to the variable $num. The client program prints the value and exits. This Perl-to-Java request again confirms the language transparency of a SOAP-based service.

The Perl client is especially useful because of its trace capabilities. Example 4-9 is the HTTP request that the Perl client generates on a sample run; Example 4-10 is the HTTP response from the Java service. In the request, the body of the POST request contains a SOAP envelope, so named because of the local name Envelope in the XML tag's qualified name soap:Envelope.

*Example 4-9. The HTTP request from the Perl client to the RandService*

```
POST http://localhost:8888/rs HTTP/1.1
Accept: text/xml
Accept: multipart/*
Accept: application/soap
Content-Length: 420
Content-Type: text/xml; charset=utf-8
SOAPAction: ""

<?xml version="1.0" encoding="UTF-8"?>
<soap:Envelope xmlns:xsi="http://www.w3.org/2001/XMLSchema-instance"
               xmlns:soapenc="http://schemas.xmlsoap.org/soap/encoding/"
               xmlns:tns="http://rand/"
               xmlns:xsd="http://www.w3.org/2001/XMLSchema"
```

```
                 soap:encodingStyle="http://schemas.xmlsoap.org/soap/encoding/"
                 xmlns:soap="http://schemas.xmlsoap.org/soap/envelope/">
    <soap:Body>
      <tns:next1 xsi:nil="true" /> ❶
    </soap:Body>
</soap:Envelope>
```

*Example 4-10. The HTTP response from the* `RandService` *to the Perl client*

```
HTTP/1.1 200 OK
Content-Type: text/xml;charset="utf-8"
Client-Peer: 127.0.0.1:8888
Client-Response-Num: 1
Client-Transfer-Encoding: chunked

<?xml version="1.0" ?>
<S:Envelope xmlns:S="http://schemas.xmlsoap.org/soap/envelope/">
   <S:Body>
      <ns2:next1Response xmlns:ns2="http://rand/">
         <return>1774649411</return>                    ❶
      </ns2:next1Response>
   </S:Body>
</S:Envelope>
```

Also in the request, this code in line 1 means that the *next1* operation takes no arguments:

```
<tns:next1 xsi:nil="true"/>
```

The HTTP response is more complicated than the request because there is a return value (line 1):

```
<return>1774649411</return>
```

The WSDL document specifies that the response from the `RandService` occurs in an element tagged `return`.

---

## Why Does the Perl Client Not Invoke nextN as Well as next1?

The Perl client invokes the *next1* operation but not the parametrized *nextN* operation in the `RandService`. Were the Perl client to invoke *nextN*, the response from the Rand Service would be an empty list. When the published `RandService` receives a request, the Java runtime uses a SAX (Simple API for XML) parser to parse the incoming request; this parser belches on the SOAP request that the Perl library generates. In particular, the SAX parser fails to extract the *nextN* argument, which specifies how many randomly generated integers are to be returned. A glitch such as this is not uncommon in web services, including SOAP-based ones. Web services, REST-style and SOAP-based alike, are remarkably but not perfectly interoperable among programming languages.

---

The examples so far illustrate that the WSDL document can be used even if its detailed structure remains unknown. Now is the time to take a close look at how the WSDL is structured.

# The WSDL Service Contract in Detail

The WSDL document, which is XML, is structured as follows:

- The document or root element is named `definitions`. This is appropriate because the WSDL defines the web service thoroughly enough that utilities such as *wsimport* can use the WSDL to generate code, typically but not exclusively client-side support code.

- The first child element of `definitions`, named `types`, is technically optional but almost always present in a modern WSDL. This element contains (or links to) an XML Schema or the equivalent—a grammar that specifies the data types for the messages involved in the service. In a modern SOAP-based web service, the arguments passed to web service operations are typed—but the SOAP messages themselves are also typed. For this reason, the receiver of a SOAP message can check, typically at the library level, whether the received message satisfies the constraints that the message's type impose.

- Next come one or more `message` elements, which list the messages whose data types are given in the `types` section immediately above. Every `message` has a corresponding `complexType` entry in the schema from the `types` section, assuming that the `types` section is nonempty.

- The `portType` section comes next. There is always exactly one `portType` element. The `portType` is essentially the service *interface*: a specification of the service's operations and the message patterns that the operations exemplify. For example, in the request/response pattern, the client begins the conversation with a request message and the service counters with a response message. In the solicit/response pattern, by contrast, the service starts the conversation with a solicitation message and the client counters with a response. There is also the one-way pattern (client to server only) and the notification pattern (server to client only). Richer conversational patterns can be built out of these simpler ones. The `message` items in the preceding section are the components of an operation, and the `portType` section defines an `operation` by placing `message` items in a specific order.

- Next come one or more `binding` sections, which provide implementation detail such as the transport used in the service (for instance, HTTP rather than SMTP), the service *style*, and the SOAP version (that is, 1.1 or 1.2). By default, Java generates a single `binding` section but DotNet generates two: one for SOAP 1.1 and another for SOAP 1.2.

- The last section, named `service`, brings all of the previous details together to define key attributes such as the *service endpoint*—that is, the URL at which the service can be accessed. Nested in the `service` element are one or more `port` subelements, where a `port` is a `portType` plus a `binding`:

  ```
  port = portType + binding
  ```

  Since there is only one `portType` in a WSDL, the number of `port` subelements equals the number of `binding` elements.

The biggest section in a WSDL is typically the `types` section because an XML Schema tends to be wordy. An example from Amazon, introduced shortly, illustrates. For now, the WSDL (see Example 4-11) for the `RandService` is only about a page or so in size.

*Example 4-11. The dynamically generated WSDL for the RandService*

```
<?xml version="1.0" encoding="UTF-8"?>
<definitions xmlns:soap="http://schemas.xmlsoap.org/wsdl/soap/"
             xmlns:tns="http://rand/"
             xmlns:xsd="http://www.w3.org/2001/XMLSchema"
             xmlns="http://schemas.xmlsoap.org/wsdl/"
             targetNamespace="http://rand/" name="RandServiceService">
  <types>
    <xsd:schema>
      <xsd:import namespace="http://rand/"
                  schemaLocation="http://localhost:8888/rs?xsd=1"></xsd:import>
    </xsd:schema>
  </types>
  <message name="next1">
    <part name="parameters" element="tns:next1"></part>
  </message>
  <message name="next1Response">
    <part name="parameters" element="tns:next1Response"></part>
  </message>
  <message name="nextN">
    <part name="parameters" element="tns:nextN"></part>
  </message>
  <message name="nextNResponse">
    <part name="parameters" element="tns:nextNResponse"></part>
  </message>
  <portType name="RandService">
    <operation name="next1">
      <input message="tns:next1"></input>
      <output message="tns:next1Response"></output>
    </operation>
    <operation name="nextN">
      <input message="tns:nextN"></input>
      <output message="tns:nextNResponse"></output>
    </operation>
  </portType>
  <binding name="RandServicePortBinding" type="tns:RandService">
```

```
                <soap:binding transport="http://schemas.xmlsoap.org/soap/http"
                              style="document"></soap:binding>
        <operation name="next1">
          <soap:operation soapAction=""></soap:operation>
          <input>
            <soap:body use="literal"></soap:body>
          </input>
          <output>
            <soap:body use="literal"></soap:body>
          </output>
        </operation>
        <operation name="nextN">
          <soap:operation soapAction=""></soap:operation>
          <input>
            <soap:body use="literal"></soap:body>
          </input>
          <output>
            <soap:body use="literal"></soap:body>
          </output>
        </operation>
      </binding>
      <service name="RandServiceService">
        <port name="RandServicePort" binding="tns:RandServicePortBinding">
          <soap:address location="http://localhost:8888/rs"></soap:address>
        </port>
      </service>
    </definitions>
```

The first three WSDL sections (`types`, `message`, and `portType`) present the service ab‐
stractly in that no implementation details are present. The `binding` and `service` sections
provide the concrete detail by specifying, for example, the type of transport used in the
service as well as the service endpoint.

The `portType` is of particular interest because it characterizes the service in terms of
operations, not simply messages; operations consist of one or more messages exchanged
in a specified pattern. The two areas of immediate interest in the WSDL for a program‐
mer writing a client against a service would be the `portType` and the `service`; the
`portType` section informs the programmer about what calls can be made against the
service, and the `service` section gives the service endpoint, the URL through which the
service can be reached.

XML is not fun to read, but the basic profile WSDL for the `RandService` is not unduly
forbidding. Perhaps the best way to read the document is from top to bottom.

## The types Section

This section contains or links to an XML Schema or equivalent. (In the case of Java, the
schema is a separate document shown in Example 4-3; in the case of DotNet, the schema

is included in the WSDL.) To understand how the schema relates to its WSDL, consider this segment of the XML Schema from Example 4-3:

```
<xs:element name="nextNResponse" type="tns:nextNResponse">    ❶
</xs:element>
...
<xs:complexType name="nextNResponse">                         ❷
  <xs:sequence>
    <xs:element name="return"                                 ❸
               type="xs:int" minOccurs="0" maxOccurs="unbounded">
    </xs:element>
  </xs:sequence>
</xs:complexType>
```

The xs:element in line 1 has a specified type, in this case tns:nextNResponse. The type is the complexType in line 2. XML Schema has built-in simple types such as xsd:int and xsd:string, but XML Schema is also *extensible* in that new complex types can be added as needed. The complexType in this case is for the nextNResponse message that the service returns to the client. Here is that message from the WSDL in Example 4-11:

```
<message name="nextNResponse">
  <part name="parameters" element="tns:nextNResponse"></part>   ❶
</message>
```

The message has an element attribute (line 1) with tns:nextNResponse as the value; tns:nextNResponse is the name of the element in line 1 of the XML Schema. The WSDL, in defining a message, points back to the XML Schema section that provides the data type for the message.

The complexType section of the WSDL indicates that a nextNResponse message returns zero or more integers (XML type xs:int). The zero leaves open the possibility that the service, in this case written in Java, might return null instead of an actual array or equivalent (e.g., List<Integer>). At this point a human editor might intervene by changing the minOccurs in line 3 from 0 to 1. (If the minOccurs attribute were dropped altogether, the value would default to 1.) The dynamically generated WSDL may not capture the intended design of a service; hence, the WSDL may need to be edited by hand.

## The message Section

Each message element in the WSDL points to an element and, more important, to a complexType in the WSDL's XML Schema. The result is that all of the messages are typed. The RandService exposes two operations and each follows the request/response pattern; hence, the WSDL has four message elements: two for the next1 and nextN requests and two for the corresponding responses named next1Response and nextNResponse, respectively.

## The portType Section

This section contains one or more `operation` elements, each of which defines an operation in terms of messages defined in the immediately preceding section. For example, here is the definition for the *nextN* operation:

```
<operation name="nextN">
  <input message="tns:nextN"></input>
  <output message="tns:nextNResponse"></output>
</operation>
```

The `input` message precedes the `output` message, which signals that the pattern is request/response. Were the order reversed, the pattern would be solicit/response. The term *input* is to be understood from the service's perspective: an `input` message goes into the service and an `output` message comes out from the service. Each `input` and `output` element names the message defined in a `message` section, which in turn refers to an XML Schema `complexType`. Accordingly, each `operation` can be linked to the typed messages that make up the `operation`.

## The binding Section

This section and the next, `service`, provide implementation details about the service. In theory, but rarely in practice, there are several options or *degrees of freedom* with respect to the service that the WSDL defines, and a `binding` section selects among these options. One option for a SOAP-based service such as the `RandService` is the SOAP version: 1.1 or 1.2. SOAP 1.1 is the default in Java; hence, the one and only `binding` section is for SOAP 1.1. In DotNet, a dynamically generated WSDL usually has two `binding` sections: one for SOAP 1.1 and the other for SOAP 1.2. However, the very same DotNet WSDL typically has only one service endpoint or URL; this means the same deployed service is for SOAP 1.1 and SOAP 1.2, thereby signaling that no difference between the two SOAP versions comes into play for the service.

There are three other options to be considered: transport (line 1) and style (line 2) are two of the three. Here is the first subelement in the `binding` section, a subelement that makes choices on these two options:

```
<soap:binding transport="http://schemas.xmlsoap.org/soap/http"   ❶
              style="document"></soap:binding>                   ❷
```

The `transport` value is a URI that ends with `soap/http`, which can be summed up as *SOAP over HTTP*. Another option would be SMTP (Simple Mail Transport Protocol) or even TCP (Transmission Control Protocol, which underlies HTTP), but in practice, HTTP is the dominant transport. HTTP in this context includes HTTPS. The other option (line 2) concerns the service `style`, in this case set to `document`. A web service in `document` style always has an XML Schema or equivalent that types the service's constituent messages. The other choice for `style` is misleadingly named `rpc`, which is short for *remote procedure call*. The name is misleading because a document-style service such as the RandService can and typically does follow the request/response pattern, which is the RPC pattern. In the context of a WSDL, rpc style really means that messages themselves are not typed, only their arguments and return values are typed. The WSDL for an rpc style service may have no types section at all or only an abbreviated one. In modern SOAP-based services, document style dominates and represents best practice. Indeed, both Java and DotNet toyed for a time with the idea of dropping support altogether for rpc style. The issue of rpc style will come up again later but only briefly.

The document style deserves to be the default. This style can support services with rich, explicitly defined Java data types such as Employee or ChessTournament because the service's WSDL can define, for the XML side, the required types in an XML Schema. Any service pattern, including request/response, is possible under the document style.

The last option concerns use, more accurately called *encoding*, because the choice determines how the service's data types are to be encoded and decoded. The WSDL has to specify how the data types used in an implementation language such as Java are to be serialized into and deserialized out of WSDL-compliant types—the types laid out in the WSDL's XML Schema or equivalent (see Example 4-12). For example, Java and Ruby have similar but subtly different data types. In a conversation based on SOAP messages, a conversation in which the SOAP remains transparent, the two languages would need the ability to serialize from instances of native types to XML and to deserialize from XML to instances of native types.

*Example 4-12. Encoding and decoding XML*

```
            encode                      decode
Java types-------->XML Schema types-------->Ruby types

Java types<--------XML Schema types<--------Ruby types
            decode                      encode
```

The attribute

```
    use = 'literal'
```

means the service's type definitions in the WSDL *literally* follow the WSDL's schema. The alternative to literal is named encoded, which means that the service's type definitions come from implicit encoding rules, typically the rules in the SOAP 1.1 specification. However, the use of encoded does not comply with WS-I (Web Services Interoperability) standards (*http://www.ws-i.org*).

# The service Section

This section brings the pieces together. Recall that a WSDL has but one portType section but may have multiple binding sections. The service element has port subelements, where a `port` is a `portType` linked to a `binding`; hence, the number of `port` subelements equals the number of `binding` sections in the WSDL. In this example, there is one `binding` and, therefore, one `port` subelement:

```
<port name="RandServicePort" binding="tns:RandServicePortBinding">
    <soap:address location="http://localhost:8888/rs"></soap:address> ❶
</port>
```

The `address` subelement specifies a `location` (line 1), whose value is commonly called the service endpoint. A web service with two significantly different bindings (for instance, one for HTTP and another for SMTP) would have different `location` values to reflect the different bindings.

## Java and XML Schema Data Type Bindings

The foregoing examination of the WSDL, and in particular its XML Schema, prompts an obvious question: Which Java data types bind to which XML Schema data types? Table 4-1 summarizes the bindings.

*Table 4-1. Java and XML Schema data type bindings*

| Java data type | XML schema data type |
| --- | --- |
| boolean | xsd:boolean |
| byte | xsd:byte |
| short | xsd:short |
| short | xsd:unsignedByte |
| int | xsd:int |
| int | xsd:unsignedShort |
| long | xsd:long |
| long | xsd:unsignedInt |
| float | xsd:float |
| double | xsd:double |
| byte[ ] | xsd:hexBinary |
| byte[ ] | xsd:base64Binary |
| java.math.BigInteger | xsd:integer |
| java.math.BigDecimal | xsd:decimal |
| java.lang.String | xsd:string |
| java.lang.String | xsd:anySimpleType |
| javax.xml.datatype.XMLGregorianCalendar | xsd:dateTime |
| javax.xml.datatype.XMLGregorianCalendar | xsd:time |
| javax.xml.datatype.XMLGregorianCalendar | xsd:date |
| javax.xml.datatype.XMLGregorianCalendar | xsd:g |

| Java data type | XML schema data type |
|---|---|
| javax.xml.datatype.Duration | xsd:duration |
| javax.xml.namespace.QName | xsd:QName |
| javax.xml.namespace.QName | xsd:NOTATION |
| java.lang.Object | xsd:anySimpleType |

The bindings in Table 4-1 are automatic in the sense that, in a JAX-WS service, the SOAP infrastructure does the conversions without application intervention. Conversions also are automatic for arrays of any type in Table 4-1. For example, an array of BigInteger instances converts automatically to an array of xsd:integer instances, and vice versa. Programmer-defined classes whose properties reduce to any type in Table 4-1 or to arrays of these likewise convert automatically. For example, an Employee class that has properties such as firstName (String), lastName (String), id (int), salary (float), age (short), hobbies (String[ ]), and the like would convert automatically to XML Schema types. The upshot is that the vast majority of the data types used in everyday Java programming convert automatically to and from XML Schema types. The glaring exception is the Map—a collection of key/value pairs. However, a Map is readily implemented as a pair of coordinated arrays: one for the keys, the other for the values.

# Code First or Contract First?

Should the web service code be used to generate the WSDL or should the WSDL, designed beforehand, be used to guide the coding of the web service? This question sums up the *code first versus contract first* controversy. The examples so far take the code-first approach: the service publisher (for example, Endpoint or Tomcat) automatically generates the WSDL for the service. The code-first approach has the obvious appeal of being easy. Yet the code-first approach has drawbacks, including:

- If the service changes under a code-first approach, the WSDL thereby changes— and client code generated from the WSDL (using, for instance, *wsimport*) needs to be regenerated. In this sense, the code-first approach is not client friendly. The code-first approach compromises a basic principle of software development: a service contract, once published, should be treated as immutable so that client-side code written against a published service never has to be rewritten.

- The code-first approach goes against the *language neutrality* at the core of web services. If a service contract is done first, the implementation language remains open.

- The code-first approach does not address tricky but common problems such as null arguments or return values. Consider, for example, a very simple service that includes an operation to return the current time as a string:

```
@WebMethod
public String getTime() { return new java.util.Date().toString(); }
```

Here is the relevant entry in the XML Schema from the automatically generated WSDL:

```
<xs:element name="return" type="xs:string" minOccurs="0"></xs:element>
```

The `minOccurs` value of 0 allows the *getTime* operation to return `null`. Suppose, however, the service needs to ensure that returned string has no fewer than, say, 28 characters, which rules out `null` as a return value. (In Java, a stringified `Date` has 28 characters.) The relevant schema section might look like this:

```
<xs:element minOccurs = "1"
            maxOccurs = "1"
            nillable  = "false"
            name      = "currentTime">
   <simpleType>
     <restriction base  = "string">
       <minLength value = "28"/>
     </restriction>
   </simpleType>
</xs:element>
```

By the way, the `minOccurs` and `maxOccurs` elements, each with a value of 1, could be dropped altogether because 1 is the default value for these attributes. The point here is that a schema entry such as this must be handcrafted. Even a clever use of Java annotations is not sufficient to produce this entry automatically.

Given the ease of the code-first approach—not to mention the economic pressures and hectic pace of software development—there seems to be little chance that a contract-first approach to web services will eclipse the dominant code-first approach. Nonetheless, a code-first-generated WSDL and its accompanying schema can be refined as needed to ensure that this contract document reflects service requirements.

## Wrapped and Unwrapped Document Style

The source for the `RandService` class begins as follows:

```
@WebService
public class RandService {
...
```

The default style, `document`, could be overridden with an additional annotation:

```
@WebService
@SOAPBinding(style = Style.RPC) // versus Style.DOCUMENT, the default
public class RandService {
...
```

The RandService is simple enough that the difference would be transparent to clients against the service. Of interest here is how the different styles impact the underlying SOAP messages.

Consider a very simple SOAP-based service with operations named add, subtract, multiply, and divide. Each operation expects two arguments, the numbers on which to operate. Under the original SOAP 1.1 specification, a request message for document style—what is now called *unwrapped* or *bare* document style—would look like Example 4-13:

*Example 4-13. Unwrapped document style*

```
<?xml version="1.0" ?>
<!-- Unwrapped document style -->
<soapenv:Envelope
    xmlns:soapenv="http://schemas.xmlsoap.org/soap/envelope/"
    xmlns:xsd="http://www.w3.org/2001/XMLSchema">
  <soapenv:Body>
    <num1 xmlns:ans="http://arith/">27</num1>
    <num2 xmlns:ans="http://arith/">94</num2>
  </soapenv:Body>
</soapenv:Envelope>
```

The Body of the SOAP message contains two elements at the same level, the elements tagged num1 and num2; each element is a child of the soapenv:Body element. The glaring omission is the name of the operation, for instance, add. This name might occur instead, for example, in the request URL:

```
http://some.server.org/add
```

It is peculiar that the SOAP envelope should contain the named arguments but not the named operation. Under rpc style, however, the operation would be the one and only child of the Body element; the operation then would have, as its own child elements, the arguments. Here is the contrasting SOAP message in *rpc* style or, what now comes to the same thing, *wrapped document style* (Example 4-14).

*Example 4-14. Wrapped document style, the same as rpc style*

```
<?xml version="1.0" ?>
<!-- Wrapped document or rpc style -->
<soapenv:Envelope
    xmlns:soapenv="http://schemas.xmlsoap.org/soap/envelope/"
    xmlns:xsd="http://www.w3.org/2001/XMLSchema">
  <soapenv:Body>
    <add xmlns:ans="http://arith/">  ❶
      <num1>27</num1>
      <num2>94</num2>
    </addNums>
  </soapenv:Body>
</soapenv:Envelope>
```

The add element (line 1) now acts as a *wrapper* for the argument elements, in this case num1 and num2. The wrapped convention, unofficial but dominant in SOAP frameworks, gives a document-style service the look and feel of an rpc-style service—at the message level. The document style still has the advantage of a full XML Schema that types the messages. In Java as in DotNet, the default style for any SOAP-based service is *wrapped document*; hence, a service such as RandService, with only the @WebService annotation, is wrapped document in style. This style is often shortened to *wrapped doc/lit*: wrapped document style with literal encoding.

## Another Practical Use for the WSDL and Its XML Schema

A utility such as *wsimport* consumes a WSDL and produces Java classes that ease the task of writing a client against the service defined in the WSDL. However, the *wsimport* utility can also be used to generate service-side code (see the section, "wsimport Artifacts for the Service Side" on page 171). There are other practical uses for the WSDL. Consider a scenario (see Figure 4-2) in which incoming SOAP requests target operations encapsulated in a document-style SOAP-based service.

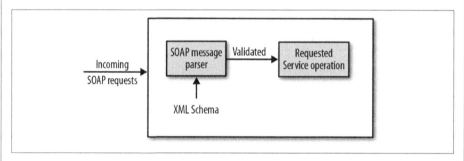

*Figure 4-2. Using the WSDL's XML Schema for message validation*

If the service is *doc/lit*, there is a WSDL with an attendant XML Schema; this schema can be used in a validating parse of the incoming SOAP messages. In XML, a *validating parse* checks whether a document, in this case a SOAP document, is syntactically correct but also whether the document conforms to a grammar, the XML Schema. If the parser does not validate the incoming message, there is no point in wasting CPU cycles on the execution of the service operation. Every document-style service has an XML Schema or equivalent as part of service's WSDL. Accordingly, this schema can be used to check whether SOAP messages satisfy the grammar that the schema represents.

# wsimport Artifacts for the Service Side

The *wsimport* utility produces, from a WSDL document, code that directly supports client calls against a web service. This same code can be used, with a few adjustments, to program a service. This section illustrates with a simple example.

Here are two operations for a temperature conversion service written in C#:

```
[WebMethod]
public double c2f(double t) { return 32.0 + (t * 9.0 / 5.0); }
[WebMethod]
public double f2c(double t) { return (5.0 / 9.0) * (t - 32.0); }
```

The c2f operation converts from centigrade to fahrenheit and the f2c method converts from fahrenheit to centigrade.

DotNet, by default, generates a WSDL with SOAP 1.1 and SOAP 1.2 bindings. This temperature conversion service is simple enough that the two bindings have the same implementation. In general, however, the *wsimport* utility can handle multiple bindings with the *-extension* flag. Assuming that the WSDL for the service is in the file *tc.wsdl*, the command:

```
% wsimport -p tempConvert -keep -extension tc.wsdl
```

generates the usual artifacts: Java *.class* files that represent the c2f and f2c request messages and their corresponding responses, together with various support files. Of interest here is the interface—the Java file that represents the portType section of the WSDL. Here is the file, cleaned up for readability:

```
package tempConvert;

import javax.jws.WebMethod;
import javax.jws.WebParam;
import javax.jws.WebResult;
import javax.jws.WebService;
import javax.xml.bind.annotation.XmlSeeAlso;
import javax.xml.ws.RequestWrapper;
import javax.xml.ws.ResponseWrapper;

@WebService(name = "ServiceSoap",
            targetNamespace = "http://tempConvertURI.org/")
@XmlSeeAlso({
    ObjectFactory.class
})
public interface ServiceSoap {
    @WebMethod(operationName = "c2f",
               action = "http://tempConvertURI.org/c2f")
    @WebResult(name = "c2fResult",
               targetNamespace = "http://tempConvertURI.org/")
    @RequestWrapper(localName = "c2f",
                    targetNamespace = "http://tempConvertURI.org/",
```

```
                        className = "tempConvert.C2F")
        @ResponseWrapper(localName = "c2fResponse",
                        targetNamespace = "http://tempConvertURI.org/",
                        className = "tempConvert.C2FResponse")
        public double c2F(
            @WebParam(name = "t",
                        targetNamespace = "http://tempConvertURI.org/")
            double t);
        @WebMethod(operationName = "f2c",
                    action = "http://tempConvertURI.org/f2c")
        @WebResult(name = "f2cResult",
                    targetNamespace = "http://tempConvertURI.org/")
        @RequestWrapper(localName = "f2c",
                        targetNamespace = "http://tempConvertURI.org/",
                        className = "tempConvert.F2C")
        @ResponseWrapper(localName = "f2cResponse",
                        targetNamespace = "http://tempConvertURI.org/",
                        className = "tempConvert.F2CResponse")
        public double f2C(
            @WebParam(name = "t",
                        targetNamespace = "http://tempConvertURI.org/")
            double t);
    }
```

The ServiceSoap interface, like any interface, *declares* but does not *define* methods, which in this case represent service operations. If the semantics of these two operations c2f and f2c are understood, then converting this *wsimport* artifact to a web service is straightforward:

- Change the interface to a POJO class.

  ```
  ...
  public class ServiceSoap {
  ...
  ```

- Implement the *c2f* and *f2c* operations by defining the methods. Java and C# are sufficiently close that the two implementations would be indistinguishable. For example, here is the body of *c2f* in either language.

  ```
  public double c2f(double t) { return 32.0 + (t * 9.0 / 5.0); }
  ```

  Not every language is as close to Java as C#, of course. Whatever the original implementation of a service, the challenge is the same: to understand what a service operation is supposed to do so that the operation can be re-implemented in Java.

- Publish the service with, for example, Endpoint or a web server such as Tomcat or Jetty.

  Although the *wsimport* utility could be used to help write a SOAP-based service in Java, the main use of this utility is still in support of clients against a SOAP-based service. The point to underscore is that the WSDL is sufficiently rich in detail to support useful code on either the service or the client side. The next section returns to the Amazon E-Commerce service to illustrate this very point.

# SOAP-Based Clients Against Amazon's E-Commerce Service

Chapter 3 has two Java clients against the RESTful Amazon E-Commerce service. The first client parses the XML document from Amazon in order to extract the desired information, in this case the author of a specified Harry Potter book, J. K. Rowling. The second client uses JAX-B to deserialize the returned XML document into a Java object, whose *get*-methods are then used to extract the same information. This section introduces two more clients against the E-Commerce service; in this case the service is SOAP-based and, therefore, the clients are as well. The SOAP-based clients use a *handler*, Java code that has access to every outgoing and incoming SOAP message. In the case of Amazon, the handler's job is to inject into the SOAP request the authentication information that Amazon requires, in particular a digest based on the *secretKey* used in both of the RESTful clients of Chapter 2. A message digest generated with the *secretKey*, rather than the *secretKey* itself, is sent from the client to the Amazon service; hence, the *secretKey* itself does not travel over the wire. SOAP handlers are the focus of the next chapter; for now, a handler is used but not analyzed.

The SOAP-based clients against Amazon's E-Commerce service, like the other SOAP-based Java clients in this chapter, rely upon *wsimport*-generated classes as building blocks. There are some key points about the SOAP-based service and its clients:

- The WSDL and *wsimport*.

  The WSDL for the SOAP-based version of Amazon's E-Commerce service is available at:

      http://webservices.amazon.com/AWSECommerceService/AWSECommerceService.wsdl

  This WSDL is more than 1,500 lines in size, with most of these lines in the XML Schema. The *wsimport* utility can be applied to this WSDL in the usual way:

      % wsimport -p amazon -keep \
        http://webservices.amazon.com/AWSECommerceService/AWSECommerceService.wsdl\
        -b custom.xml

  The result is a directory/package named *amazon* filled with client-support classes generated from the WSDL. The part at the end, with *custom.xml*, is explained shortly.

- Client-side API styles.

  The Amazon SOAP-based service follows best design practices and is, therefore, *wrapped doc/lit*. However, *wsimport* can generate different *client* APIs from one and the same Amazon WSDL. This point deserves elaboration. Consider a very simple operation in a SOAP-based service, which takes two arguments, text and a pattern, and returns the number of times that the pattern occurs in the text. For example, the text might be the novel *War and Peace* and the pattern might be the name of one of the heroines, *Natasha*. The operation is named *getCount*. There are different ways in which this operation might be implemented in Java. Perhaps the obvious implementation would have the declaration:

```
public int getCount(String text, String pattern);
```

This version takes two arguments, the text and the pattern, and returns the count as an `int`. Yet the client of a SOAP-based web service, following in the footsteps of DCE/RPC, can distinguish between *in* and *out* parameters—arguments passed *into* the service and ones passed *out of* this same service and back to the client. This possibility opens the way to a quite different version of *getCount*:

```
public void getCount(String text, String pattern, Holder result);
```

The return type for `getCount` is now `void`, which means that the *count* must be returned in some other way. The third parameter, of the special type `Holder`, embeds the desired count of `pattern` occurrences in the `text`. This programming style is uncommon in Java and, accordingly, might be judged inferior to the two-argument version of `getCount` that returns the *count* directly as an `int`. The point of interest is that *wsimport* can generate client-side artifacts in either style, and, perhaps surprisingly, the second style is the default for *wsimport*. In Java, the first style is:

```
SOAPBinding.ParameterStyle.BARE
```

and the second style is:

```
SOAPBinding.ParameterStyle.WRAPPED
```

The critical point is that these *parameter styles* refer to the *wsimport* artifacts generated from a service WSDL—the parameter styles do not refer to the structure of the service itself, which remains *wrapped doc/lit*. Java's *wsimport* utility can present this service style, on the client side, in different ways, known as parameter styles in Java.

• Authentication credentials in a SOAP-based client.

A SOAP-based client against E-Commerce must send the same authentication credentials as a RESTful client: a registered user's *accessId* and a hash value generated with the *secretKey*. In a REST-style client, these credentials are sent in the query string of a GET request. A SOAP-based client is different in that its requests are all POSTs, even if the intended web service operation is a *read*. In a SOAP-based exchange over HTTP, the request is a SOAP envelope that is the body of a POST request. Accordingly, a SOAP-based client must process the required credentials in a different way. In this section, the credential processing is partly the job of a SOAP handler, which is examined carefully in the next chapter.

In Chapter 3, the clients against the RESTful E-Commerce service did *lookup* operations. For contrast, the SOAP-based client does a *search* against the Amazon E-Commerce service. The `AmazonClientBareStyle` (see Example 4-15) is the first and friendliest SOAP-based client.

*Example 4-15. A SOAP-based Amazon client in bare parameter style*

```
package amazon;

import amazon.AWSECommerceService;
import amazon.AWSECommerceServicePortType;
import amazon.ItemSearchRequest;
import amazon.ItemSearchResponse;
import amazon.ItemSearch;
import amazon.Items;
import amazon.Item;
import amazon.AwsHandlerResolver;
import java.util.List;

class AmazonClientBareStyle {
    public static void main(String[ ] args) {
        if (args.length < 2) {
            System.err.println("AmazonClientBareStyle <accessId> <secretKey>");
            return;
        }
        final String accessId = args[0];
        final String secretKey = args[1];

        AWSECommerceService service = new AWSECommerceService();            ❶
        service.setHandlerResolver(new AwsHandlerResolver(secretKey));      ❷
        AWSECommerceServicePortType port = service.getAWSECommerceServicePort();  ❸
        ItemSearchRequest request = new ItemSearchRequest();               ❹
        request.setSearchIndex("Books");
        request.setKeywords("Austen");
        ItemSearch itemSearch= new ItemSearch();                           ❺
        itemSearch.setAWSAccessKeyId(accessId);
        itemSearch.setAssociateTag("kalin");
        itemSearch.getRequest().add(request);
        ItemSearchResponse response = port.itemSearch(itemSearch);         ❻
        List<Items> itemsList = response.getItems();                       ❼
        int i = 1;
        for (Items next : itemsList)
           for (Item item : next.getItem())
               System.out.println(String.format("%2d: ", i++) +
                               item.getItemAttributes().getTitle());
    }
}
```

The ZIP file with the sample code includes an executable JAR with the code from Example 4-15 and its dependencies. The JAR can be executed as follows:

```
% java -jar AmazonClientBare.jar <accessId> <secretKey>
```

The `AmazonClientBareStyle` highlights what SOAP-based services have to offer to their clients. The *wsimport*-generated classes include the `AWSECommerceService` with a no-argument constructor. This class represents, to the client, the E-Commerce service. The usual two-step occurs: in line 1 an `AWSECommerceService` instance is constructed and in line 3 the `getAWSECommerceServicePort` method is invoked. The object reference `port` can now be used, in line 6, to launch a search against the E-Commerce service, which results in an `ItemSearchResponse`. Line 2 in the setup hands over the user's *secretKey* to the client-side handler, which uses the *secretKey* to generate a hash value as a message authentication code, which Amazon can then verify on the service side.

The remaining code, from line 7 on, resembles the code in the second RESTful client against the E-Commerce service. Here is a quick review of the SOAP-based code:

```
List<Items> itemsList = response.getItems();                    ❶
int i = 1;
for (Items next : itemsList)
    for (Item item : next.getItem())                           ❷
        System.out.println(String.format("%2d: ", i++) +
                        item.getItemAttributes().getTitle());  ❸
```

The `ItemSearchResponse` from Amazon encapsulates a list of `Items` (line 1), each of whose members is itself a list. The nested `for` loop iterates (line 2) over the individual `Item` instances, printing the title of each book found (line 3). By the way, the search returns the default number of items found, 10; it is possible to ask for all of the items found. On a sample run, the output was:

```
 1: Persuasion (Dover Thrift Editions)
 2: Pride and Prejudice (The Cambridge Edition of the Works of Jane Austen)
 3: Emma (Dover Thrift Editions)
 4: Northanger Abbey (Dover Thrift Editions)
 5: Mansfield Park
 6: Love and Friendship
 7: Jane Austen: The Complete Collection (With Active Table of Contents)
 8: Lady Susan
 9: Jane Austen Collection: 18 Works, Pride and Prejudice, Love and Friendship,
        Emma, Persuasion, Northanger Abbey, Mansfield Park, Lady Susan & more!
10: The Jane Austen Collection: 28 Classic Works
```

Now is the time to clarify the *custom.xml* file used in the *wsimport* command against the Amazon WSDL. The filename *custom.xml* is arbitrary and, for review, here is the *wsimport* command:

```
% wsimport -p amazon -keep \
   http://webservices.amazon.com/AWSECommerceService/AWSECommerceService.wsdl \
   -b custom.xml
```

The file *custom.xml* is:

```
<jaxws:bindings
   wsdlLocation =
```

```
        "http://ecs.amazonaws.com/AWSECommerceService/AWSECommerceService.wsdl"
          xmlns:jaxws="http://java.sun.com/xml/ns/jaxws">
        <jaxws:enableWrapperStyle>false</jaxws:enableWrapperStyle>  ❶
    </jaxws:bindings>
```

The key element in the file sets the enableWrapperStyle for the parameters to false (line 1). The result is the bare parameter style evident in the AmazonClientBareStyle code. The alternative to this style is the default one, the client-side wrapped style. The AmazonClientWrappedStyle (see Example 4-16) is a SOAP-based Amazon client in the default style.

*Example 4-16. A SOAP-based Amazon client in wrapped parameter style*

```
package amazon2;

import amazon2.AWSECommerceService;
import amazon2.AWSECommerceServicePortType;
import amazon2.ItemSearchRequest;
import amazon2.ItemSearch;
import amazon2.Items;
import amazon2.Item;
import amazon2.OperationRequest;
import amazon2.SearchResultsMap;
import amazon2.AwsHandlerResolver;

import javax.xml.ws.Holder;
import java.util.List;
import java.util.ArrayList;

class AmazonClientWrappedStyle {
    public static void main(String[ ] args) {
        if (args.length < 2) {
            System.err.println("java AmazonClientWrappedStyle <accessId> <secretKey>");
            return;
        }
        final String accessId = args[0];
        final String secretKey = args[1];

        AWSECommerceService service = new AWSECommerceService();
        service.setHandlerResolver(new AwsHandlerResolver(secretKey));
        AWSECommerceServicePortType port = service.getAWSECommerceServicePort();
        ItemSearchRequest request = new ItemSearchRequest();
        request.setSearchIndex("Books");
        request.setKeywords("Austen");
        ItemSearch search = new ItemSearch();
        search.getRequest().add(request);
        search.setAWSAccessKeyId(accessId);
        search.setAssociateTag("kalin");
        Holder<OperationRequest> operationRequest = null;          ❶
        Holder<List<Items>> items = new Holder<List<Items>>();     ❷
        port.itemSearch(search.getMarketplaceDomain(),             ❸
                        search.getAWSAccessKeyId(),
```

```
                    search.getAssociateTag(),
                    search.getXMLEscaping(),
                    search.getValidate(),
                    search.getShared(),
                    search.getRequest(),
                    operationRequest,                    ❹
                    items);                              ❺
        Items retval = items.value.get(0);              ❻
        int i = 1;
        List<Item> item_list = retval.getItem();        ❼
        for (Item item : item_list)
            System.out.println(String.format("%2d: ", i++) +
                        item.getItemAttributes().getTitle());
    }
}
```

The AmazonClientWrappedStyle code uses *wsimport*-generated classes created with the following command:

```
% wsimport -p amazon2 -keep \
  http://webservices.amazon.com/AWSECommerceService/AWSECommerceService.wsdl
```

The WSDL is the same as in previous examples, but the style of the *wsimport*-classes changes from bare to wrapped, a change reflected in the AmazonClientWrappedStyle code. The change is evident at lines 1 and 2, which declare two object references of type Holder. As the name suggests, a Holder parameter is meant to hold some value returned from the E-Commerce service: the operationRequest holds metadata about the request, whereas items holds the book list that results from a successful search. This idiom is common in C or C++ but rare—and, therefore, clumsy—in Java. The Holder parameters are the last two (lines 4 and 5) of the nine parameters in the revised itemSearch (line 3). On a successful search, items refers to a value (line 6) from which a list of Items is extracted. This code, too, is awkward in Java. This list of Items has a getItem method (line 7), which yields a List<Item> from which the individual Item instances, each representing a Jane Austen book, can be extracted.

The AmazonClientWrappedStyle client is clearly the clumsier of the two clients against SOAP-based E-Commerce service, a service that has a single WSDL and whose response payloads to the two clients are identical in structure. The two clients differ markedly in their APIs, however. The bare style API would be familiar to most Java programmers, but the wrapped style, with its two Holder types, would seem a bit alien even to an experienced Java programmer. Nonetheless, the wrapped style remains the default in Java and in DotNet.

# Asynchronous Clients Against SOAP-Based Services

All of the SOAP-based clients examined so far make *synchronous* or *blocking* calls against a web service. For example, consider these two lines from the bare style client against the E-Commerce service:

```
ItemSearchResponse response = port.itemSearch(itemSearch); ❶
List<Items> itemsList = response.getItems();               ❷
```

The call in line 1 to `itemSearch` *blocks* in the sense that line 2 does not execute until `itemSearch` returns a value, perhaps `null`. There are situations in which a client might need the invocation of `itemSearch` to return immediately so that other application logic could be performed in the meantime. In this case, a *nonblocking* or *asynchronous* call to `itemSearch` would be appropriate.

The `RandClientAsync` (see Example 4-17) is an asynchronous client against the `Rand Service` (see Example 4-1).

*Example 4-17. A client that makes asynchronous requests against the `RandService`*

```
import javax.xml.ws.AsyncHandler;
import javax.xml.ws.Response;
import java.util.List;
import clientAsync.RandServiceService;
import clientAsync.RandService;
import clientAsync.NextNResponse;

public class RandClientAsync {
    public static void main(String[ ] args) {
        RandServiceService service = new RandServiceService();
        RandService port = service.getRandServicePort();
        port.nextNAsync(4, new MyHandler());                      ❶
        try {
            Thread.sleep(5000); // in production, do something useful!
        }
        catch(Exception e) { }
        System.out.println("\nmain is exiting...");
    }
    static class MyHandler implements AsyncHandler<NextNResponse> {   ❷
        public void handleResponse(Response<NextNResponse> future) {  ❸
            try {
                NextNResponse response = future.get();               ❹
                List<Integer> nums = response.getReturn();           ❺
                for (Integer num : nums) System.out.println(num);    ❻
            }
            catch(Exception e) { System.err.println(e); }
        }
    }
}
```

Although an asynchronous client also could be coded against the E-Commerce service, the far simpler RandService makes the client itself relatively straightforward; it is then easier to focus on the asynchronous part of the API. No changes are required in the RandService or its publication, under either Endpoint or a web server such as Tomcat. The *wsimport* command again takes a customization file, in this example *customAsync.xml*; the filename is arbitrary. The *wsimport* command is:

```
wsimport -p clientAsync -keep http://localhost:8888/rs?wsdl -b customAsync.xml
```

The customized binding file is:

```
<jaxws:bindings
    wsdlLocation="http://localhost:8888/rs?wsdl"
    xmlns:jaxws="http://java.sun.com/xml/ns/jaxws">
  <jaxws:enableAsyncMapping>true</jaxws:enableAsyncMapping>  ❶
</jaxws:bindings>
```

The customized binding sets the enableAsyncMapping to true (line 1). The *wsimport* utility generates the same classes as in the earlier examples: Next1, Next1Response, and so on. The request/response classes such as Next1 and Next1Response have additional methods, however, to handle the asynchronous calls, and these classes still have the methods that make synchronous calls.

The setup in the asynchronous client is the familiar two-step: first create a service instance and then invoke the getRandService method on this instance. The dramatic change is line 1, the asynchronous call, which now takes two arguments:

```
port.nextNAsync(4, new MyHandler());
```

Although the nextNAsync method does return a value, my code does not bother to assign this value to a variable. The reason is that the Java runtime passes the NextNResponse message from the RandService to the client's event handler, an instance of MyHandler, which then extracts and prints the randomly generated integers from the service.

The call to nextNAsync, a method declared together with nextN in the *wsimport*-generated RandService interface, takes two arguments: the number of requested random numbers and an event handler, in this case a MyHandler instance. The handler class MyHandler must implement the AsyncHandler interface (line 2) by defining the handleResponse method (line 3). The handleResponse method follows the standard Java pattern for event handlers: the method has void as its return type and it expects one argument, an event triggered by a Response<NextNResponse> that arrives at the client.

When the client runs, the main thread executes the asynchronous call to nextNAsync, which returns immediately. To prevent the main thread from exiting main and thereby ending the application, the client invokes Thread.sleep. This is contrived, of course; in a production environment, the main thread presumably would go on to do meaningful work. In this example, the point is to illustrate the execution pattern. When the

`RandService` returns the requested integers, the Java runtime starts a (daemon) thread to execute the `handleResponse` callback, which prints the requested integers. In the meantime, the `main` thread eventually wakes up and exits `main`, thereby terminating the client's execution. On a sample run, the output was:

```
1616290443
-984786015
1002134912
311238217
main is exiting...
```

The daemon thread executing `handleResponse` prints the four integers, and the `main` thread prints the good-bye message.

Java and DotNet take different approaches toward generating, from a WSDL, support for asynchronous calls against a service. DotNet automatically generates methods for synchronous and asynchronous calls against the service; Java takes the more conservative approach of generating the asynchronous artifacts only if asked to do so with a customized binding such as the one used in this example. The key point is that Java API, like its DotNet counterpart, fully supports synchronous and asynchronous calls against SOAP-based services such as the `RandService`.

---

## How Are WSDL and UDDI Related?

WSDL documents, as service contracts, should be publishable and discoverable, as are the services that they describe. A UDDI (Universal Description Discovery and Integration) registry is one way to publish a WSDL so that potential clients can discover the document and ultimately consume the web service that the WSDL describes. UDDI has a type system that accommodates WSDL documents as well as other kinds of formal service contracts. From a UDDI perspective, a WSDL appears as a two-part document. One part, which comprises the `types` through the `binding` sections, is the UDDI *service interface*. The other part, which comprises any `import` directives and the `service` section, is the UDDI *service implementation*. In WSDL, the service interface (`portType` section) and service implementation (`binding` sections) are two parts of the same document. In UDDI, they are two separate documents, and these UDDI terms do not match up exactly with their WSDL counterparts.

A WSDL does not explain service semantics or, in plainer terms, what the service is about. The WSDL does explain, in a clear and precise way, the service's invocation syntax: the names of the service operations (e.g., an operation such as *getTime*); the operation pattern (e.g., request/response rather than solicit/response); the number, order, and type of arguments that each operation expects; faults, if any, associated with a service operation; and the number, order, and types of response values from an operation. The W3C is pursuing initiatives in web semantics under the rubric of WSDL-S (Semantics) (*http://bit.ly/16X5hKD*).

---

> As of now, however, a WSDL is useful only if a programmer already understands what the service is about. The WSDL can guide you through technical aspects of a web service, but this document presupposes rather than provides an insight into service semantics.

# What's Next?

JAX-WS has two distinct but related APIs for SOAP-based web services. One API, with annotations such as @WebService and @WebMethod, focuses on what might be called the application level. On the service side, annotations are used to create web services and to specify their operations. Additional annotations such as @WebParam are available for fine-tuning and documenting different aspects of a service and its operations. On the client side, the application API enables clients to draw upon *wsimport*-generated classes to access a SOAP-based service and to invoke its operations. A central feature of the application level is the WSDL contract, which captures in XML the service and its operations, including essential details such as the invocation syntax for the service operations, the encoding/decoding scheme for data types, the transport used for messages, and the service endpoint. Frameworks such as JAX-WS and DotNet come with utilities that put the WSDL to practical use.

A major appeal of the application level in JAX-WS is that the SOAP itself—the XML—remains hidden on the service and the client sides. The underlying SOAP libraries serialize from Java into XML and deserialize from XML into Java, thereby allowing both service and service client to work in Java data structures and in familiar Java programming idioms. JAX-B and related utilities allow REST-style services in Java to work around the XML or JSON payloads typical of REST-style services, but JAX-WS, which uses JAX-B under the hood, takes the further step of automating the serialization/deserialization. JAX-WS is programmer-friendly on both the service and client side.

The examples in this chapter have remained, for the most part, at the JAX-WS application level but have touched on another level, the handler level. A second JAX-WS API, with the Handler interface and its two subinterfaces LogicalHandler and SOAPHandler, provides access to the underlying SOAP. A SOAPHandler gives the programmer access to the entire SOAP message, whereas the convenient LogicalHandler gives the programmer access to the payload of the SOAP body. A SOAPHandler often is called a *message handler* and a LogicalHandler is called simply a *logical handler*.

The handler API allows the programmer to inspect and, if needed, to manipulate the SOAP that the underlying libraries generate. The distinction between the JAX-WS application and handler APIs in web services corresponds roughly to the distinction between the *servlet* and *filter* API in Java-based websites. (One important difference is that JAX-WS handlers are available on both the client and the service side.) This chapter introduced but did not explore the handler API in the clients against Amazon's E-Commerce service. In the REST-style clients of Chapter 3 against the E-Commerce service, the clients made GET requests, and critical pieces of information (e.g., the user's *accessId* and an HMAC hash generated from the user's *secretKey*) had to be sent in the query string. The very same pieces of information are required in a SOAP-based client, but such a client, even when invoking a *read* operation on the E-Commerce service, sends a POST request whose body is a SOAP envelope. The JAX-WS libraries generate the SOAP envelope, but a client-side handler, an instance of the mentioned but not listed `AwsServiceHandler` class, inserts the user's *accessId*, the HMAC hash, and a strictly formatted timestamp into the SOAP envelope, in particular into the SOAP body. The next chapter takes a close look at the `AwsServiceHandler` class.

The next chapter goes down to the JAX-WS handler level by explaining, first, how the class `AwsServiceHandler` works in the E-Commerce service clients. This chapter then does a full example with a client-side and a service-side handler, an example that deliberately mimics the way that Amazon's more complicated E-Commerce service works. JAX-WS also exposes to the programmer the *transport level*, which is almost always HTTP(S). On either the client side or the service side, JAW-WS code can inspect and, if appropriate, modify the HTTP messages that carry SOAP messages as their payloads. JAX-WS thus covers three distinct levels of SOAP-based web services: the application level, the handler level, and the transport level. Chapter 5 also looks at some miscellaneous but related topics: SOAP faults in the application and handler levels, binary payloads in SOAP services, and the Axis2 implementation of JAX-WS, which is an alternative to the Metro implementation.

# CHAPTER 5

# SOAP Handlers and Faults

SOAP messages have some similarity to the HTTP messages that commonly transport them. Each type of message, SOAP and HTTP, can have a header and a body, although the header in a SOAP message is optional. In HTTP 1.1, there must be a header with at least the one key/value pair, with `Host` as the key, but HTTP headers usually contain at least a half dozen or so header elements. A SOAP message must have a body, which can be, but typically is not, empty. Not every HTTP message has a body, of course, with GET and DELETE messages as two bodyless examples. In each kind of message, the header, if present, is meant to contain metadata; the body, if present, is meant to contain data.

SOAP has a messaging architecture that centers on the different uses envisioned for the SOAP header and the SOAP body. At the base level of this architecture is the SOAP message, a one-way transmission from a sender to a receiver. The fundamental *message exchange pattern* (MEP) is thus one-way. SOAP-based applications such as web services are free to establish conversational patterns that combine one-way messaging in richer ways, for example, in the familiar request/response pattern that involves two one-way messages in the opposite direction. Even request/response and solicit/response are brief conversational patterns but these, too, can be combined to construct even richer patterns. There is no limit to how complex a SOAP conversational pattern may become.

A SOAP message has a *sender* and targets a *receiver*, but the SOAP messaging architecture allows for *intermediaries*, which are nonterminal recipients along the route from the sender to the ultimate receiver. The sender, the receiver, and the intermediaries are alike in being *nodes* along the path from the sender to the receiver. Figure 5-1 depicts this architecture with a sender, a receiver, and two intermediaries.

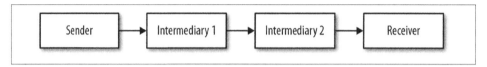

*Figure 5-1. SOAP message architecture: sender, intermediary, and receiver nodes*

Along the route from sender to receiver, an intermediary node is supposed to inspect and otherwise process elements in the SOAP message's header, known as *header blocks*; the SOAP message's body, which contains the data, is supposed to be reserved for the receiver alone. By contrast, the sender and the receiver are meant to enjoy access to the entire SOAP message, including the body. The SOAP specification does not prescribe how an intermediary node is to process a header block, as this is an application-specific rather than a SOAP requirement. Consider, for example, an application in which a sender inserts a security credential into the SOAP message's header. An intermediary node might access this credential in order to verify it: if the verification succeeds, the intermediary node might add a verification block to the SOAP message's header and then send the message on its way; if the verification fails, the intermediary node might throw a SOAP fault, thereby terminating the message. The intermediaries thus can function as filters that screen out messages that should not make their way to the terminal receiver.

In summary, the header/body distinction plays a key role in SOAP's message architecture, and JAX-WS has an API that supports this architecture. This chapter focuses on the JAX-WS *handler* API, which gives the nodes in the SOAP messaging architecture low-level access to the entire SOAP message: header, body, and attachments. The chapter also covers SOAP faults and SOAP attachments.

Chapter 4 introduced but did not clarify handlers. In the SOAP-based API for Amazon's E-Commerce service, a handler is used in order to insert critical information into a SOAP request: an HMAC hash value generated from the user's *secretKey* and a properly formatted timestamp. Although such information counts as metadata, Amazon requires that it be inserted into a SOAP request's *body*, in particular as two children of the wrapper element, which names the operation (for instance, lookup or search) that the request targets. If the information is not inserted into the request body, then Amazon generates a SOAP fault—an error message sent back to the client in place of a normal response. Figure 5-2 depicts this situation.

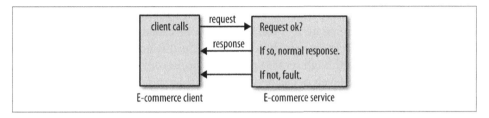

*Figure 5-2. A SOAP fault versus a normal SOAP response*

SOAP faults can be generated in two different contexts: from within the service code itself or from within a handler. Examples of both are presented in this chapter.

# The Handler Level in SOAP-Based Services and Clients

Figure 5-3 shows the structure of a SOAP message. In SOAP over HTTP, such a message is itself the body of either an HTTP request, typically a POST request, or an HTTP response. The message consists of:

- The *SOAP part*, which comprises the SOAP envelope, which in turn consists of an optional header and a required body. The body can be, but typically is not, empty. The header and the body are text, in particular XML.
- Arbitrarily many *attachments*, including none. Attachments are an efficient way to transport media types such as audio or video as binary payloads belonging to a SOAP message.

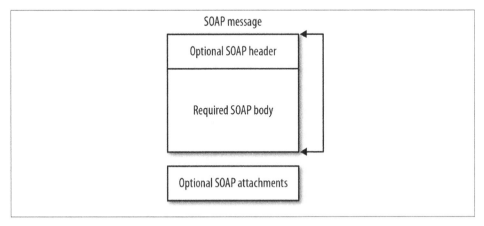

*Figure 5-3. The structure of a SOAP message*

SOAP attachments are covered later in this chapter. For now, the distinction between the SOAP header and the SOAP body is of interest because this difference is a way to focus on two related but separate SOAP APIs: an API for what might be called the application level and a separate API for what might be called the handler level. (This distinction roughly mirrors, in Java-based websites, the distinction between the servlet API and the filter API, although servlets and filters occur only on the server side.) The application and handler levels occur on the service side and on the client side. In the examples so far, the focus has been on the application level with the use of annotations such as @WebService and @WebMethod. The Amazon E-Commerce clients in Chapter 4 touched on the handler level because a hash generated from the user's *secretKey* together with a timestamp had to be inserted in a specified location within a SOAP message; a handler did the required work. This section introduces the handler level in two steps: first, by examining the AwsHandlerResolver class used in the two SOAP-based E-Commerce clients of Chapter 4, and second, with an example that has code at the handler level on both the client and the service side.

A quick look at how the application and handler levels interact may be useful before a full code example. Recall the RandClient from Chapter 4, in particular these three lines of code:

```
RandServiceService service = new RandServiceService();
RandService port = service.getRandServicePort();
System.out.println(port.next1());  // invoke next1
```

The first two lines set up the call to next1, which returns a randomly generated integer. When this call executes, the underlying SOAP libraries generate the appropriate SOAP envelope and send it, over HTTP, to the RandService. The three lines of code are at the application level. The RandClient does not use any handlers; hence, nothing happens at the handler level. Suppose that there was a handler; for now, the code details can be ignored, but a depiction (see Figure 5-4) may be helpful.

A handler is inherently bidirectional: on either side, client or service, a handler handles incoming and outgoing messages. A handler can detect whether a given SOAP message is coming in or going out and react accordingly. Figure 5-4 depicts a single handler, but multiple ones, a *handler chain*, are possible on either side. The service side in the figure has no handlers.

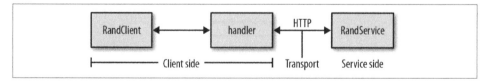

*Figure 5-4. The RandClient with an assumed handler*

Handlers come in two types:

- A SOAPHandler, abbreviated as a message handler, has access to the entire SOAP message: headers, body, and attachments.

- A LogicalHandler has access only to the payload in the body of a SOAP message.

A SOAPHandler can do anything that a LogicalHandler can do because the former has access to the entire SOAP message, but a LogicalHandler is convenient if the handler code requires access only to the payload in the body of a SOAP message. Examples of both LogicalHandler code and SOAPHandler code are forthcoming. How handlers of different types can be chained together also is covered in the examples.

Handlers are close to the metal in that they have access to either the entire SOAP message or just the payload in the body. In Figure 5-4, the SOAP libraries that underlie the RandClient generate a SOAP request message in calls to next1 or nextN. By default, these libraries create a message without a SOAP header. The message then goes to the handler *before* being handed over to HTTP for transport to the service. The handler can perform arbitrary logic on the SOAP message. For example, the handler could add a SOAP header if the SOAP message did not have one already. The handler could add, edit, remove, and otherwise process elements in the SOAP message—header, body, and attachments. JAX-WS confines such low-level processing to the handler level so that the application level remains a high level at which service operations are invoked and response values are processed. In short, the handler/application distinction represents a separation of concerns.

The AwsHandlerResolver and AwsSoapHandler classes (see Example 5-1) make up the handler-level code mentioned but not explained in Chapter 4.

*Example 5-1. The AwsHandlerResolver and AwsSoapHandler classes*

```
package amazon;

import java.text.SimpleDateFormat;
import java.util.ArrayList;
import java.util.Calendar;
import java.util.List;
import java.util.Set;
import java.util.TimeZone;
import javax.crypto.Mac;
import javax.crypto.spec.SecretKeySpec;
import javax.xml.namespace.QName;
import javax.xml.soap.SOAPBody;
import javax.xml.soap.SOAPMessage;
import javax.xml.ws.handler.Handler;
import javax.xml.ws.handler.HandlerResolver;
import javax.xml.ws.handler.MessageContext;
import javax.xml.ws.handler.PortInfo;
import javax.xml.ws.handler.soap.SOAPHandler;
import javax.xml.ws.handler.soap.SOAPMessageContext;
```

```
import org.apache.commons.codec.binary.Base64;
import org.w3c.dom.Element;
import org.w3c.dom.Node;

public class AwsHandlerResolver implements HandlerResolver {
    private String awsSecretKey;

    public AwsHandlerResolver(String awsSecretKey) {
        this.awsSecretKey = awsSecretKey;
    }
    public List<Handler> getHandlerChain(PortInfo portInfo) {
        List<Handler> handlerChain = new ArrayList<Handler>();
        QName serviceQName = portInfo.getServiceName();
        if(serviceQName.getLocalPart().equals("AWSECommerceService")) {
            handlerChain.add(new AwsSoapHandler(awsSecretKey));
        }
        return handlerChain;
    }
}

class AwsSoapHandler implements SOAPHandler<SOAPMessageContext> {
    private byte[ ] secretBytes;

    public AwsSoapHandler(String awsSecretKey) {
        secretBytes = getBytes(awsSecretKey);
    }
    public void close(MessageContext mCtx) { }
    public Set<QName> getHeaders() { return null; }
    public boolean handleFault(SOAPMessageContext mCtx) {
        return true;
    }
    public boolean handleMessage(SOAPMessageContext mCtx) {
        Boolean outbound =
            (Boolean) mCtx.get(MessageContext.MESSAGE_OUTBOUND_PROPERTY);
        if (outbound) {
            try {
                SOAPMessage soapMessage = mCtx.getMessage();
                SOAPBody soapBody = soapMessage.getSOAPBody();
                Node firstChild = soapBody.getFirstChild(); // operation name
                String timeStamp = getTimestamp();
                String signature = getSignature(firstChild.getLocalName(),
                                                timeStamp,
                                                secretBytes);
                append(firstChild, "Signature", signature);
                append(firstChild, "Timestamp", timeStamp);
            }
            catch(Exception e) {
                throw new RuntimeException("SOAPException thrown.", e);
            }
        }
        return true; // continue down the handler chain
    }
```

```
    private String getSignature(String operation, String timeStamp,
                                byte[ ] secretBytes) {
        try {
            String toSign = operation + timeStamp;
            byte[] toSignBytes = getBytes(toSign);
            Mac signer = Mac.getInstance("HmacSHA256");
            SecretKeySpec keySpec = new SecretKeySpec(secretBytes, "HmacSHA256");
            signer.init(keySpec);
            signer.update(toSignBytes);
            byte[ ] signBytes = signer.doFinal();
            String signature = new String(Base64.encodeBase64(signBytes));
            return signature;
        }
        catch(Exception e) { throw new RuntimeException(e); }
    }
    private String getTimestamp() {
        Calendar calendar = Calendar.getInstance();
        SimpleDateFormat dateFormat =
            new SimpleDateFormat("yyyy-MM-dd'T'HH:mm:ss'Z'");
        dateFormat.setTimeZone(TimeZone.getTimeZone("UTC"));
        return dateFormat.format(calendar.getTime());
    }
    private void append(Node node, String elementName, String elementText) {
        Element element = node.getOwnerDocument().createElement(elementName);
        element.setTextContent(elementText);
        node.appendChild(element);
    }
    private byte[ ] getBytes(String str) {
        try {
            return str.getBytes("UTF-8");
        }
        catch(Exception e) { throw new RuntimeException(e); }
    }
}
```

The code in the `AwsHandlerResolver` class registers handlers with the runtime, and the `AwsSoapHandler` is the *message* rather than a logical handler that gets registered. The handler API is event-driven: the application registers a handler chain, which may be a chain with just one handler, with the Java runtime; the runtime then invokes the appropriate handler methods on incoming and outgoing messages. The handler itself can detect a message's direction and react accordingly.

In the E-Commerce clients of Chapter 4, the `AwsHandlerResolver` class is used in this context (line 1):

```
AWSECommerceService service = new AWSECommerceService();
service.setHandlerResolver(new AwsHandlerResolver(secretKey));   ❶
AWSECommerceServicePortType port = service.getAWSECommerceServicePort();
```

Line 1 links the `service` with an `AwsHandlerResolver` instance that encapsulates the user's *secretKey*. As the name suggests, the `AwsHandlerResolver` resolves which handlers, if any, are to be in play.

To implement the `HandlerResolver` interface, a class must define one method:

```
public List<Handler> getHandlerChain(PortInfo portInfo);
```

In this case, the implementation is short because there is only one handler to put into the chain:

```
public List<Handler> getHandlerChain(PortInfo portInfo) {
    List<Handler> handlerChain = new ArrayList<Handler>();          ❶
    QName serviceQName = portInfo.getServiceName();
    if (serviceQName.getLocalPart().equals("AWSECommerceService"))  ❷
        handlerChain.add(new AwsSoapHandler(awsSecretKey));         ❸
    return handlerChain;
}
```

The `getHandlerChain` method creates an empty `List<Handler>` (line 1) and then checks whether the service in question is Amazon's `AWSECommerceService`, the official name for the E-Commerce service (line 2). If so, an instance of the `AwsSoapHandler` class, initialized with the user's *secretKey*, is constructed (line 3). The Java runtime now ensures that the handlers in the list, in this case just one, are invoked *after* the SOAP message has been built but *before* this message is handed off to HTTP for transport to the service.

The handler class `AwsSoapHandler`, which the resolver registers with the runtime, is a `SOAPHandler` rather than a `LogicalHandler`:

```
class AwsSoapHandler implements SOAPHandler<SOAPMessageContext> {
    ...
```

The reason is that the `AwsSoapHandler` needs to add elements to the message body, and a `LogicalHandler` provides access only to the current *payload* in the body. The methods in the `AwsSoapHandler` class add to this initial payload. To implement the `SOAPHandler` interface and its superinterface `Handler`, the `AwsSoapHandler` class must define four methods:

getHeaders
: This is a convenience method that gives the handler access to the SOAP header elements or headers for short. The runtime invokes this method first. In the current example, the method is minimally defined but not used. Later examples use the `getHeaders` method.

close
: As the name suggests, this method is the last one that the runtime invokes. Once again, the current example minimally defines but does not use this method.

handleMessage *and* handleFault

> The runtime invokes exactly one of these. For example, the two E-Commerce clients in Chapter 4 send a search request to the Amazon service with one of two results: the Amazon service accepts the request, conducts the search, and returns the results; or the Amazon service generates a SOAP fault. Either a standard SOAP response message or a fault message returns to the client: if a standard response, then the runtime invokes handleMessage in the handler; if a SOAP fault, then the runtime invokes handleFault in the handler.

The return type for the methods handleMessage and handleFault is boolean. A return value of true means *continue executing other handlers, if any, in the chain*; a return value of false means *do not execute other handlers, if any, in the chain*. The logic is similar to the logic of filters in servlet-based websites. In this example, handleFault is minimally defined (that is, the method simply returns true), but handleMessage has logic to make the SOAP request comply with the requirements of the E-Commerce service.

The handleMessage method deserves a closer look. Here is the main part of the code, slightly reformatted:

```
Boolean outbound = (Boolean) mCtx.get(MessageContext.MESSAGE_OUTBOUND_PROPERTY);
if (outbound) {                                                      ❶
   try {
      SOAPMessage soapMessage = mCtx.getMessage();
      SOAPBody soapBody = soapMessage.getSOAPBody();                 ❷
      Node firstChild = soapBody.getFirstChild(); // operation name  ❸
      String timeStamp = getTimestamp();
      String signature = getSignature(firstChild.getLocalName(),
                                      timeStamp,
                                      secretBytes);
      append(firstChild, "Signature", signature);                   ❹
      append(firstChild, "Timestamp", timeStamp);                   ❺
   }
   ...
```

The handleMessage method first checks, in line 1, whether it is being invoked on an outgoing (that is, request) or incoming (that is, response) SOAP message. Incoming messages are of no interest to this handler. For an outgoing or request SOAP message, the method uses the mCtx argument (of type SOAPMessageContext) to get the full SOAP message from which the SOAPBody is extracted (line 2). The *first child* in the SOAP body is the wrapper element, the name of the E-Commerce service operation (in this example, the search operation), because the E-Commerce service uses wrapped document style (line 3). Two utility methods provide the current time in the required format and an HmacSHA256 digest generated from the user's *secretKey* and other information (lines 4 and 5). These low-level operations are not of particular interest right now, but they are required in any SOAP-based request to E-Commerce service. (Chapter 6, on security, goes into the details of a hash such as HmacSHA256, and the next example in this chapter clarifies HmacSHA256 further.)

Once the required timestamp and hash value are in hand, the handleMessage method appends two XML elements to the wrapper element in the SOAP body: one with the so-called signature, which is the message digest or hash value, and another with the time-stamp. After handleMessage returns true, the runtime invokes the close method—and then hands the amended SOAP message off to the HTTP transport. Example 5-2 depicts the before and after situation with respect to the work of the AwsSoapHandler: this handler adds lines 1 and 2 to the already created SOAP request message.

*Example 5-2. A before/after depiction of how the AwsSoapHandler works*

```
<Soap:Envelope>                        <Soap:Envelope>
  <Soap:Body>          handler           <Soap:Body>
    <ItemSearch>      ==========>           <ItemSearch>
                                              <Signature>...</Signature> ❶
       ...                                    <Timestamp>...</Timestamp> ❷
    </ItemSearch>                             ...
  </Soap:Body>                              </ItemSearch>
<Soap:Envelope>                           </Soap:Body>
                                        </Soap:Envelope>


  # Before handler runs                 # After handler runs
```

The SOAP-based version of Amazon's E-Commerce service enforces strict conditions on the structure of a SOAP request message. In particular, this service requires that a message digest (the signature) and a timestamp be in the request body as children of the wrapper element.

JAX-WS handlers are a way to separate low-level concerns, which require inspection and even manipulation of SOAP messages, from the high-level concerns of invoking, as transparently as possible, web service operations. At the application level, the SOAP is completely hidden; at the handler level, the SOAP is exposed for whatever processing is required. The next example uses handlers on the client and on the service side; this example also introduces SOAP faults, which can be thrown at either the application or the handler level.

# Handlers and Faults in the predictionsSOAP Service

This section ports the various REST-style versions of the *predictions* web service to a SOAP-based version. The new version is *predictionsSOAP*, whose structure can be summarized as follows:

- There is a service client and a client-side message handler. The handler inserts an HMAC hash into every client request against the *predictionsSOAP* service.

However, the handler departs from the Amazon practice by inserting the hash into the SOAP header rather than the SOAP body.

- The client, built atop *wsimport*-generated classes, invokes various CRUD operations in the *predictionsSOAP* service.

- There is a service-side message handler whose job is to verify the HMAC hash from the client.

- The service implements the standard CRUD operations.

- The service throws SOAP faults from both the handler and the application level in order to contrast the two different APIs. As the name suggests, a SOAP fault signals an error condition; the fault is a special message sent back to the client in place of an error-free SOAP response. The service WSDL indicates, in the `portType` section, that a client request may result in a fault message rather than a standard response. The architecture of the *predictionsSOAP* service is sketched in Figure 5-5.

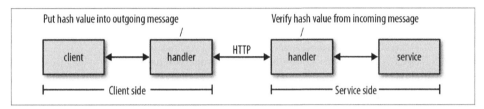

*Figure 5-5. The architecture of the predictionsSOAP service*

The *predictionsSOAP* service mirrors, in its structure, the SOAP-based version of Amazon's E-Commerce service. In each case, a client-side handler modifies an outgoing SOAP message by inserting a security credential; a service-side handler then verifies the credential before dealing with the request itself.

The `PredictionsSOAP` class (see Example 5-3), the main class for the *predictionsSOAP* service, has five service operations: *getAll*, *getOne*, *create*, *edit*, and *delete*.

*Example 5-3. The `PredictionsSOAP` class with two methods that throw SOAP faults*

```
package predictions;

import javax.annotation.Resource;
import javax.jws.WebService;
import javax.jws.WebMethod;
import javax.jws.HandlerChain;
import javax.xml.ws.WebServiceContext;
import javax.xml.ws.handler.MessageContext;
import java.util.List;
import javax.servlet.ServletContext;
```

```java
@WebService
@HandlerChain(file = "../../../WEB-INF/serviceHandler.xml")
public class PredictionsSOAP {
    @Resource
    private WebServiceContext wsCtx;
    private ServletContext sCtx;
    private static final Predictions predictions= new Predictions();
    private static final int maxLength = 16;
    @WebMethod
    public List<Prediction> getAll() {
        init();
        return predictions.getPredictions();
    }
    @WebMethod
    public Prediction getOne(int id) {
        init();
        return predictions.getPrediction(id);
    }
    @WebMethod
    public String create(String who, String what) throws VerbosityException {       ❶
        int count = wordCount(what);
        if (count > maxLength)
            throw new VerbosityException(count + " is too verbose!",
                                         "Max words: " + maxLength);
        init();
        Prediction p = new Prediction();
        p.setWho(who);
        p.setWhat(what);
        int id = predictions.addPrediction(p);
        String msg = "Prediction " + id + " created.";
        return msg;
    }
    @WebMethod
    public String edit(int id, String who, String what) throws VerbosityException {❷
        int count = wordCount(what);
        if (count > maxLength)
            throw new VerbosityException(count + " is too verbose!",
                                         "Max words: " + maxLength);
        init();
        String msg = "Prediction " + id + " not found.";
        Prediction p = predictions.getPrediction(id);
        if (p != null) {
            if (who != null) p.setWho(who);
            if (what != null) p.setWhat(what);
            msg = "Prediction " + id + " updated.";
        }
        return msg;
    }
    @WebMethod
    public String delete(int id) {
        init();
        String msg = "Prediction " + id + " not found.";
```

```
        Prediction p = predictions.getPrediction(id);
        if (p != null) {
            predictions.getMap().remove(id);
            msg = "Prediction " + id + " removed.";
        }
        return msg;
    }
    private void init() {
        if (wsCtx == null) throw new RuntimeException("DI failed on wsCtx!");
        if (sCtx == null) { // ServletContext not yet set?
            MessageContext mCtx = wsCtx.getMessageContext();
            sCtx = (ServletContext) mCtx.get(MessageContext.SERVLET_CONTEXT);
            predictions.setServletContext(sCtx);
        }
    }
    private int wordCount(String words) {
        if (words == null) return -1;
        return words.trim().split("\\s+").length;
    }
}
```

Two of the implementing methods, *create* and *edit* (lines 1 and 2), throw an exception named VerbosityException if the creation of a new Prediction or the editing of an existing one results in a candidate prediction that exceeds the maximum length, currently set to 16 words. Each of the methods *create* and *edit* is annotated as a @WebMethod and each throws a VerbosityException, which becomes a fault at the SOAP level. As a result, the service's WSDL now contains an extra message in the portType section for the *create* and *edit* operations. Here is a WSDL segment that includes the portion for *create* and, for contrast, *delete*:

```
<portType name="PredictionsSOAP">
  <operation name="delete">
    <input wsam:Action="http://predictions/PredictionsSOAP/deleteRequest"  ❶
        message="tns:delete" />
    <output wsam:Action="http://predictions/PredictionsSOAP/deleteResponse"
        message="tns:deleteResponse" />
  </operation>
  <operation name="create">
    <input wsam:Action="http://predictions/PredictionsSOAP/createRequest"
        message="tns:create" />
    <output wsam:Action="http://predictions/PredictionsSOAP/createResponse"
        message="tns:createResponse" />
    <fault message="tns:VerbosityException"                                 ❷
        name="VerbosityException"
        wsam:Action=
        "http://predictions/PredictionsSOAP/create/Fault/VerbosityException"/>
  </operation>
  ...
```

The *delete* operation has the usual input and output messages (line 1), whereas the *create* operation now has, in addition to the usual two, a fault message as well (line 2); the fault message, like all of the other messages, is defined in the XML Schema.

A VerbosityException is thrown at the application rather than at the handler level. Accordingly, the underlying SOAP libraries handle the details of converting a Java Exception into a SOAP fault message. The VerbosityException class is standard Java:

```
package predictions;
public class VerbosityException extends Exception {
    private String details;
    public VerbosityException(String reason, String details) {
        super(reason);                                          ❶
        this.details = details;
    }
    public String getFaultInfo() { return this.details; }       ❷
}
```

A VerbosityException has a reason (line 1) to explain why the fault occurred together with details (line 2) that provide additional information. Both the reason and the details become part of the SOAP fault message.

Generating a VerbosityException is standard Java—a throw clause is used to generate an exception. The bodies of the create and edit methods begin in the same way—with a check of whether the submitted Prediction (the parameter name is what) is too long:

```
int count = wordCount(what);
if (count > maxLength)
    throw new VerbosityException(count + " is too verbose!",  ❶
                                 "Max words: " + maxLength);
```

If a candidate Prediction exceeds the maximum length, a VerbosityException is thrown (line 1) with the regular Java syntax. Generating a SOAP fault at the application level requires just two conditions:

- A service operation (that is, a @WebMethod) throws a customized Exception, in this case a VerbosityException.

- The customized Exception should invoke the superclass constructor with the reason for the fault (line 1 in the full listing) and also should implement the method getFaultInfo (line 2 in the full listing), which can provide additional detail about the fault.

For the fault message returned from the *PredictionsSOAP* service when a submitted prediction is 18 words in length, see Example 5-4.

*Example 5-4. A fault generated from a verbose prediction*

```
<S:Envelope xmlns:S="http://schemas.xmlsoap.org/soap/envelope/">
  <S:Header/>
  <S:Body>
    <S:Fault xmlns:ns4="http://www.w3.org/2003/05/soap-envelope">
      <faultcode>S:Server</faultcode>
      <faultstring>18 is too verbose!</faultstring>
      <detail>
        <ns2:VerbosityException xmlns:ns2="http://predictions/">
          <faultInfo>Max words: 16</faultInfo>
          <message>18 is too verbose!</message>
        </ns2:VerbosityException>
      </detail>
    </S:Fault>
  </S:Body>
</S:Envelope>
```

## The Backend Support Classes

The PredictionsSOAP class has backend classes in support, in particular Prediction
(see Example 5-5) and Predictions (see Example 5-6). Neither the PredictionsSOAP
class nor any of the backend classes does any explicit XML processing, of course, because
the underlying SOAP libraries handle the serialization and deserialization automatically.

*Example 5-5. The Prediction supporting class*

```
package predictions;

import java.io.Serializable;

public class Prediction implements Serializable, Comparable<Prediction> {
    private String who;    // person
    private String what;   // his/her prediction
    private int    id;     // identifier used as lookup key
    public Prediction() { }
    public void setWho(String who) { this.who = who; }
    public String getWho() { return this.who; }
    public void setWhat(String what) { this.what = what; }
    public String getWhat() { return this.what; }
    public void setId(int id) { this.id = id; }
    public int getId() { return this.id; }
    public int compareTo(Prediction other) {
        return this.id - other.id;
    }
}
```

The Prediction class implements Comparable and, therefore, defines the compareTo
method so that a client against the *predictionsSOAP* service can get a sorted list of
Predictions on a getAll request. Otherwise, the Prediction class is a POJO class with

three properties: id, which identifies a Prediction; who, which names the author of the Prediction; and what, which consists of the actual words in the Prediction.

*Example 5-6. The Predictions supporting class*

```
package predictions;

import java.io.IOException;
import java.io.InputStream;
import java.io.InputStreamReader;
import java.io.BufferedReader;
import java.io.ByteArrayOutputStream;
import java.util.Arrays;
import java.util.List;
import java.util.ArrayList;
import java.util.concurrent.ConcurrentMap;
import java.util.concurrent.ConcurrentHashMap;
import java.util.concurrent.atomic.AtomicInteger;
import javax.servlet.ServletContext;

public class Predictions {
    private ConcurrentMap<Integer, Prediction> predictions;        ❶
    private ServletContext sctx;
    private AtomicInteger mapKey;

    public Predictions() {
        predictions = new ConcurrentHashMap<Integer, Prediction>();
        mapKey = new AtomicInteger();
    }
    public void setServletContext(ServletContext sctx) {
        this.sctx = sctx;
    }
    public ServletContext getServletContext() { return this.sctx; }
    public void setMap(ConcurrentMap<String, Prediction> predictions) { }
    public ConcurrentMap<Integer, Prediction> getMap() {
        if (good2Go()) return this.predictions;
        else return null;
    }
    public int addPrediction(Prediction p) {                       ❷
        int id = mapKey.incrementAndGet();
        p.setId(id);
        predictions.put(id, p);
        return id;
    }
    public Prediction getPrediction(int id) {
        return predictions.get(id);
    }
    public List<Prediction> getPredictions() {                     ❸
        List<Prediction> list;
        if (good2Go()) {
            Object[] preds = predictions.values().toArray();
            Arrays.sort(preds);
```

```
            list = new ArrayList<Prediction>();
            for (Object obj : preds) list.add((Prediction) obj);
            return list;
        }
        else
            return null;
    }
    private boolean good2Go() {
        if (getServletContext() == null) return false;
        if (predictions.size() < 1) populate();
        return true;
    }
    private void populate() {
        String filename = "/WEB-INF/data/predictions.db";
        InputStream in = sctx.getResourceAsStream(filename);
        // Read the data into the array of Predictions.
        if (in != null) {
            try {
                InputStreamReader isr = new InputStreamReader(in);
                BufferedReader reader = new BufferedReader(isr);
                int i = 0;
                String record = null;
                while ((record = reader.readLine()) != null) {
                    String[] parts = record.split("!");
                    Prediction p = new Prediction();
                    p.setWho(parts[0]);
                    p.setWhat(parts[1]);
                    addPrediction(p);
                }
            }
            catch (IOException e) { }
        }
    }
}
```

The Predictions class provides the supporting data structures, in particular a thread-safe ConcurrentMap (line 1), together with convenience methods such as the method getPredictions (line 3), which returns a sorted List<Prediction>, and the method addPrediction (line 2), which adds a newly created Prediction to the existing collection. The *predictionsSOAP* service invokes these methods as needed. As in the earlier versions, the service initializes the Prediction collection from the *predictions.db* file in the deployed WAR file.

## From the Client to the Service

There remains one more service-side class to discuss, the ServiceHashHandler. Perhaps the best way to clarify this handler, however, is to switch first to the client side. The reason is that the service-side handler extracts and verifies a credential that a client-side handler needs to inject into every SOAP request message. One motivation behind the *predictionsSOAP* example is to mimic the authentication scheme used in Amazon's E-Commerce service.

The `PredictionsClient` class (see Example 5-7) is a client against the *predictions-SOAP* service.

*Example 5-7. The `PredictionsClient` against the predictionsSOAP service*

```
import clientSOAP.PredictionsSOAP;
import clientSOAP.PredictionsSOAPService;
import clientSOAP.Prediction;
import clientSOAP.ClientHandlerResolver;
import java.util.List;

public class PredictionsClient {
    public static void main(String[ ] args) {
        if (args.length < 2) {
            System.err.println("Usage: PredictionsClient <name> <key>");   ❶
            return;
        }
        new PredictionsClient().runTests(args[0], args[1]);
    }
    private void runTests(String name, String key) {
        PredictionsSOAPService service = new PredictionsSOAPService();
        service.setHandlerResolver(new ClientHandlerResolver(name, key));
        PredictionsSOAP port = service.getPredictionsSOAPPort();

        getTests(port);
        postTest(port);
        getAllTest(port);      // confirm the POST
        deleteTest(port, 33); // delete the just POSTed prediction
        getAllTest(port);      // confirm the POST
        putTest(port);
    }
    private void getTests(PredictionsSOAP port) {
        getAllTest(port);
        getOneTest(port);
    }
    private void getAllTest(PredictionsSOAP port) {
        msg("getAll");
        List<Prediction> preds = port.getAll();
        for (Prediction pred : preds)
            System.out.println(String.format("%2d: ", pred.getId()) +
                               pred.getWho() + " predicts: " + pred.getWhat());
    }
    private void getOneTest(PredictionsSOAP port) {
        msg("getOne (31)");
        System.out.println(port.getOne(31).getWhat());
    }
    private void postTest(PredictionsSOAP port) {
        msg("postTest");
        String who = "Freddy";
```

```
        String what = "Something bad may happen.";
        String res = port.create(who, what);
        System.out.println(res);
    }
    private void putTest(PredictionsSOAP port) {
        msg("putTest -- here's the record to be edited");
        getOneTest(port);
        msg("putTest results");
        String who = "FooBar";
        String what = null;   // shouldn't change
        int id = 31;
        String res = port.edit(id, who, what);
        System.out.println(res);
        System.out.println("Confirming:");
        Prediction p = port.getOne(31);
        System.out.println(p.getWho());
        System.out.println(p.getWhat());
    }
    private void deleteTest(PredictionsSOAP port, int id) {
        msg("deleteTest");
        String res = port.delete(id);
        System.out.println(res);
    }
    private void msg(String s) {
        System.out.println("\n" + s + "\n");
    }
}
```

As usual, the PredictionsClient uses *wsimport*-generated artifacts, which are in the clientSOAP package. This client, together with dependencies, is packaged in the executable JAR file *PredictionsClient.jar*:

```
% java -jar PredictionsClient.jar
Usage: PredictionsClient <name> <key>
```

The client expects two command-line arguments (line 1): a *name* (in Amazon E-Commerce, the *accessId*) and a key (in Amazon E-Commerce, the *secretKey*). The *predictionsSOAP* service includes a DataStore class that mimics a database with a map with *names* as the lookup keys and secret *keys* as their values. Accordingly, the command:

```
% java -jar PredictionsClient.jar moe MoeMoeMoe
```

provides the required pair of command-line arguments, with *moe* as the name and *MoeMoeMoe* as the key.

The PredictionsClient dynamically sets the client-side handler whose job is to turn the command-line arguments into a credential that the service-side handler can verify. Here is the relevant code segment:

```
PredictionsSOAPService service = new PredictionsSOAPService();
service.setHandlerResolver(new ClientHandlerResolver(name, key)); ❶
PredictionsSOAP port = service.getPredictionsSOAPPort();
```

In line 1, name and key are the two command-line arguments. After setting the handler, the PredictionsClient runs the expected tests against the CRUD operations that the *predictionsSOAP* service implements: *getAll*, *getOne*, *create*, *edit*, and *delete*. It should be noted that the PredictionsClient, like the *predictionsSOAP* service, does absolutely no XML processing but instead works exclusively with Java data structures such as List<Prediction>.

The ClientHandlerResolver class (see Example 5-8) registers an instance of the class ClientHashHandler with the runtime system. Before digging into the details, it may be helpful to do a before/after comparison with respect to the handler.

*Example 5-8. The ClientHandlerResolver and ClientHashHandler classes*

```
package clientSOAP;

import java.text.SimpleDateFormat;
import java.util.ArrayList;
import java.util.Calendar;
import java.util.List;
import java.util.Set;
import java.util.TimeZone;
import javax.crypto.Mac;
import javax.crypto.spec.SecretKeySpec;
import javax.xml.namespace.QName;
import javax.xml.soap.SOAPMessage;
import javax.xml.soap.SOAPEnvelope;
import javax.xml.soap.SOAPHeader;
import javax.xml.ws.handler.Handler;
import javax.xml.ws.handler.HandlerResolver;
import javax.xml.ws.handler.MessageContext;
import javax.xml.ws.handler.PortInfo;
import javax.xml.ws.handler.soap.SOAPHandler;
import javax.xml.ws.handler.soap.SOAPMessageContext;
import org.apache.commons.codec.binary.Base64;
import org.w3c.dom.Element;
import org.w3c.dom.Node;

public class ClientHandlerResolver implements HandlerResolver {
    private String name;
    private String key;

    public ClientHandlerResolver(String name, String key) {
        this.name = name;
        this.key = key;
    }
    public List<Handler> getHandlerChain(PortInfo portInfo) {
        List<Handler> handlerChain = new ArrayList<Handler>();
```

```
        handlerChain.add(new ClientHashHandler(this.name, this.key));
        return handlerChain;
    }
}

class ClientHashHandler implements SOAPHandler<SOAPMessageContext> {
    private byte[ ] secretBytes;
    private String name;

    public ClientHashHandler(String name, String key) {
        this.name = name;
        this.secretBytes = getBytes(key);
    }
    public void close(MessageContext mCtx) { }                              ❶
    public Set<QName> getHeaders() { return null; }                        ❷
    public boolean handleFault(SOAPMessageContext mCtx) {                  ❸
        try {
            SOAPMessage msg = mCtx.getMessage();
            msg.writeTo(System.err);
        }
        catch(Exception e) { throw new RuntimeException(e); }
        return true;
    }
    public boolean handleMessage(SOAPMessageContext mCtx) {                ❹
        Boolean outbound =
            (Boolean) mCtx.get(MessageContext.MESSAGE_OUTBOUND_PROPERTY);
        if (outbound) {                                                    ❺
            try {
                SOAPMessage soapMessage = mCtx.getMessage();
                SOAPEnvelope envelope = soapMessage.getSOAPPart().getEnvelope();
                // Ensure there is a header and add a 'wrapper' element.
                if (envelope.getHeader() == null) envelope.addHeader();   ❻
                SOAPHeader header = envelope.getHeader();
                QName qn = new QName("http://predictionsSOAP", "credentials");
                header.addHeaderElement(qn);                              ❼
                // Now insert credentials into the header.
                String timeStamp = getTimestamp();
                String signature = getSignature(this.name,
                                                timeStamp,
                                                this.secretBytes);
                Node firstChild = header.getFirstChild();
                append(firstChild, "Name",      this.name);              ❽
                append(firstChild, "Signature", signature);             ❾
                append(firstChild, "Timestamp", timeStamp);             ❿
                soapMessage.saveChanges();
            }
            catch(Exception e) {
                throw new RuntimeException("SOAPException thrown.", e);
            }
        }
        return true; // continue down the handler chain
    }
```

```java
    private String getSignature(String name, String timestamp, byte[ ] secretBytes) {
        try {
            System.out.println("Name ==      " + name);
            System.out.println("Timestamp == " + timestamp);
            String toSign = name + timestamp;
            byte[] toSignBytes = getBytes(toSign);
            Mac signer = Mac.getInstance("HmacSHA256");
            SecretKeySpec keySpec = new SecretKeySpec(secretBytes, "HmacSHA256");
            signer.init(keySpec);
            signer.update(toSignBytes);
            byte[] signBytes = signer.doFinal();
            String signature = new String(Base64.encodeBase64(signBytes));
            return signature;
        }
        catch(Exception e) {
            throw new RuntimeException("NoSuchAlgorithmException thrown.", e);
        }
    }
    private String getTimestamp() {
        Calendar calendar = Calendar.getInstance();
        SimpleDateFormat dateFormat =
            new SimpleDateFormat("yyyy-MM-dd'T'HH:mm:ss'Z'");
        dateFormat.setTimeZone(TimeZone.getTimeZone("UTC"));
        return dateFormat.format(calendar.getTime());
    }
    private void append(Node node, String elementName, String elementText) {
        Element element = node.getOwnerDocument().createElement(elementName);
        element.setTextContent(elementText);
        node.appendChild(element);
    }
    private byte[ ] getBytes(String str) {
        try {
            return str.getBytes("UTF-8");
        }
        catch(Exception e) { throw new RuntimeException(e); }
    }
}
```

As an example, consider the first test that the `PredictionsClient` runs: the client invokes `getAll` on the service to get a list of all of the predictions. Here is what happens:

- The underlying SOAP libraries generate the appropriate SOAP message:

```xml
<S:Envelope xmlns:S="http://schemas.xmlsoap.org/soap/envelope/">
  <S:Body><ns2:getAll xmlns:ns2="http://predictions/"/></S:Body>
</S:Envelope>
```

  This automatically generated SOAP message has no header.

- Before this message is handed over to HTTP for transport to the service, the runtime invokes the `ClientHashHandler`, which amends the outgoing message to:

```
<S:Envelope xmlns:S="http://schemas.xmlsoap.org/soap/envelope/">
  <S:Header>
    <credentials xmlns="http://predictionsSOAP">
      <Name xmlns="">moe</Name>
      <Signature xmlns="">
          vkIQm8isdpomHeQ1aFqckzQawlZakj+hWOQaxsQcPgU=
      </Signature>
      <Timestamp xmlns="">2014-03-26T01:12:47Z</Timestamp>
    </credentials>
  </S:Header>
  <S:Body>
    <ns2:getAll xmlns:ns2="http://predictions/"/>
  </S:Body>
</S:Envelope>
```

A SOAP header together with a `credentials` element is added; the `credentials` element has three subelements tagged `Name`, `Signature`, and `Timestamp` in that lexicographical order. The `Name` is the command-line argument `moe` and the `Signature` is an `HmacSHA256` hash encoded in base64, the same kind of hash used in Amazon's E-Commerce service. The `Signature` hash is generated from the provided key value `MoeMoeMoe`, but this *secretKey* cannot be recovered from the hash. (Chapter 6, on security, explains why.) Accordingly, Moe's secret key is not in jeopardy of being hijacked when the SOAP request is sent over the wire.

The `ClientHashHandler` class implements the `SOAPHandler` interface and, therefore, defines the four methods `getHeaders`, `close`, `handleFault`, and `handleMessage` (lines 1 through 4 in the code listing). Only `handleFault` and `handleMessage` are of interest here. Recall that handlers are inherently bidirectional; that is, they handle incoming and outgoing messages alike, and only one of these methods is invoked in either case: if there is a fault, the runtime invokes `handleFault`; otherwise, the runtime invokes handleMessage.

The `handleMessage` method has work to do only on outgoing messages or requests; hence, this method checks the direction of the message (line 5). If the message is indeed outgoing, the handler does the following:

- Checks whether there is a SOAP header and, if not, adds one (line 6).

- Adds, as the first child of the SOAP header, an element tagged `credentials` (line 7).

- Adds, as children of the `credentials` element, three elements tagged `Name` (with a value such as `moe`), `Signature` (whose value is an `HmacSHA256` hash generated with, in this case, Moe's secret key), and `Timestamp` (whose value is a properly formatted timestamp).

The outgoing SOAP message, a request, is now properly structured. The SOAP body names the operation of interest (for instance, getOne) and includes any required arguments (in this example, the integer identifier of the Prediction to get). The SOAP header contains the requester's name, a hash value that serves as a signature, and a timestamp.

The handler method handleFault does not check the message direction because a fault would arrive, in any case, as a response from the *predictionsSOAP* service. This service generates a SOAP fault as a VerbosityException if a candidate Prediction is excessively wordy. At present, handleFault simply prints the SOAP fault to the standard error; in a production environment, more elaborate logic might be brought into play—for instance, the fault might be saved in a data store for later analysis.

Handlers, especially SOAP handlers, are powerful in that they can amend the SOAP message created at the application level. In this example, a SOAP rather than a Logical handler is needed because the handler needs access to the SOAP header. On the service side, the handler also needs to be a SOAP handler.

The ServiceHashHandler (see Example 5-9) is a service-side SOAP handler. On any incoming message, this handler checks for the following:

- Does the message include a SOAP header? If not, generate a SOAP fault (line 1).

- Are there at least three children of the element tagged credentials? If not, generate a SOAP fault (line 2).

- Are the Name, Signature, and Timestamp values all non-null? If not, generate a SOAP fault (line 3).

- Does the Name, used as a lookup key in the service-side data store, have a value? (The value should be the user's secret key.) If not, generate a SOAP fault (line 4).

- Does the Signature generated on the service side match the Signature sent in the client request? If not, generate a SOAP fault (line 5).

*Example 5-9. The service-side ServiceHashHandler, which verifies the credentials in a request*

```
package predictions;

import java.text.SimpleDateFormat;
import java.util.ArrayList;
import java.util.Calendar;
import java.util.List;
import java.util.Set;
import java.util.Map;
import java.util.HashMap;
import java.util.TimeZone;
import java.util.Iterator;
```

```
import java.util.Arrays;
import javax.crypto.Mac;
import javax.crypto.spec.SecretKeySpec;
import javax.xml.namespace.QName;
import javax.xml.soap.SOAPHeader;
import javax.xml.soap.SOAPBody;
import javax.xml.soap.SOAPFault;
import javax.xml.soap.SOAPMessage;
import javax.xml.ws.soap.SOAPFaultException;
import javax.xml.soap.SOAPException;
import javax.xml.ws.handler.Handler;
import javax.xml.ws.handler.MessageContext;
import javax.xml.ws.handler.soap.SOAPHandler;
import javax.xml.ws.handler.soap.SOAPMessageContext;
import org.apache.commons.codec.binary.Base64;
import org.w3c.dom.Node;
import org.w3c.dom.NodeList;

public class ServiceHashHandler implements SOAPHandler<SOAPMessageContext> {
    private byte[ ] secretBytes;

    public ServiceHashHandler() { }
    public void close(MessageContext mCtx) { }
    public Set<QName> getHeaders() { return null; }
    public boolean handleFault(SOAPMessageContext mCtx) {
        return true;
    }
    public boolean handleMessage(SOAPMessageContext mCtx) {
        Boolean outbound =
            (Boolean) mCtx.get(MessageContext.MESSAGE_OUTBOUND_PROPERTY);
        if (!outbound) {
            try {
                SOAPMessage msg = mCtx.getMessage();
                SOAPHeader soapHeader = msg.getSOAPHeader();
                if (soapHeader == null)                                      ❶
                    generateFault(msg, "No header!");
                Node node = soapHeader.getFirstChild();    // credentials
                NodeList nodeList = node.getChildNodes(); // Name, Timestamp, Sig.
                if (nodeList.getLength() < 3)                                ❷
                    generateFault(msg, "Too few header nodes!");
                // Extract the required attributes.
                String name = nodeList.item(0).getFirstChild().getNodeValue();
                String signature = nodeList.item(1).getFirstChild().getNodeValue();
                String timestamp = nodeList.item(2).getFirstChild().getNodeValue();
                if (name == null || timestamp == null || signature == null)  ❸
                    generateFault(msg, "Missing header key/value pairs!");
                // Generate comparison signature and compare against what's sent.
                String secret = DataStore.get(name);
                if (secret == null)
                    generateFault(msg, name + " not registered!");           ❹
                byte[ ] secretBytes = getBytes(secret);
                String localSignature = getSignature(name, timestamp, secretBytes);
```

```
                if (!verify(signature, localSignature))
                    generateFault(msg, "HMAC signatures do not match.");         ❺
            }
            catch(Exception e) {
                throw new RuntimeException("SOAPException thrown.", e);
            }
        }
        return true; // continue down the handler chain
    }
    private boolean verify(String sig1, String sig2) {
        return Arrays.equals(sig1.getBytes(), sig2.getBytes());
    }
    private String getSignature(String name, String timestamp, byte[ ] secretBytes) {
        try {
            System.err.println("Name ==     " + name);
            System.err.println("Timestamp == " + timestamp);
            String toSign = name + timestamp;
            byte[] toSignBytes = getBytes(toSign);
            Mac signer = Mac.getInstance("HmacSHA256");
            SecretKeySpec keySpec = new SecretKeySpec(secretBytes, "HmacSHA256");
            signer.init(keySpec);
            signer.update(toSignBytes);
            byte[] signBytes = signer.doFinal();
            String signature = new String(Base64.encodeBase64(signBytes));
            return signature;
        }
        catch(Exception e) {
            throw new RuntimeException("NoSuchAlgorithmException thrown.", e);
        }
    }
    private String getTimestamp() {
        Calendar calendar = Calendar.getInstance();
        SimpleDateFormat dateFormat =
            new SimpleDateFormat("yyyy-MM-dd'T'HH:mm:ss'Z'");
        dateFormat.setTimeZone(TimeZone.getTimeZone("UTC"));
        return dateFormat.format(calendar.getTime());
    }
    private byte[ ] getBytes(String str) {
        try {
            return str.getBytes("UTF-8");
        }
        catch(Exception e) { throw new RuntimeException(e); }
    }
    private void generateFault(SOAPMessage msg, String reason) {
        try {
            SOAPBody body = msg.getSOAPBody();
            SOAPFault fault = body.addFault();
            fault.setFaultString(reason);
            throw new SOAPFaultException(fault);
        }
        catch(SOAPException e) { }
```

```
    }
}
```

## Signature Verification

The *predictionsSOAP* service does signature verification in basically the same way that Amazon does. To make a request against the *predictionsSOAP* service, a client needs a key. How this is distributed to the client is ignored in this example. In the Amazon case, the *secretKey* is provided when a user registers with Amazon, and, of course, Amazon maintains a copy of the *secretKey*. In the *predictionsSOAP* example, the service-side DataStore has a map whose lookup keys are usernames (for instance, *Moe*) and whose values are the users' secret keys (in this case, *MoeMoeMoe*). On an incoming message, the ServiceHashHandler recomputes the hash value—generated on the client side with the user's key—and then does a byte-by-byte comparison of the sent signature and the signature computed on the service side. The code is in the verify utility method:

```
private boolean verify(String sig1, String sig2) {
    return Arrays.equals(sig1.getBytes(), sig2.getBytes());
}
```

The argument sig1 is the sent signature, and the argument sig2 is the signature computed on the service side.

## Faults from the Application and Handler Levels

The API for generating a SOAP fault at the handler level differs significantly from the API for generating a SOAP fault at the application level. At the application level, the regular Java syntax of:

```
throw new VerbosityException(...);
```

suffices; at the handler level, by contrast, the SOAP fault needs to be constructed and then thrown. Here again is the generateFault method in the ServiceHashHandler:

```
private void generateFault(SOAPMessage msg, String reason) {
    try {
        SOAPBody body = msg.getSOAPBody();          ❶
        SOAPFault fault = body.addFault();          ❷
        fault.setFaultString(reason);               ❸
        throw new SOAPFaultException(fault);        ❹
    }
    catch(SOAPException e) { }
}
```

The generateFault method uses the incoming SOAP message (msg is the reference) to get the SOAP body (line 1). A SOAP fault is then added to body (line 2); the reason for the fault is given; and a SOAPFaultException, initialized with the fault information (line 3), is thrown—which in turn causes a SOAP fault message to be sent back to the requester (line 4). If desired, additional `Detail` could be added to the `SOAPFault`, which has an `addDetail` method.

## Linking the Service-Side Handler to the Service

The service-side handler `ServiceHashHandler` needs to be linked to the service itself, whose `@WebService`-annotated class is `PredictionsSOAP`. On the client side, the linking is dynamic. Here, for review, are the two critical lines of code in the `PredictionsClient`:

```
PredictionsSOAPService service = new PredictionsSOAPService();       ❶
service.setHandlerResolver(new ClientHandlerResolver(name, key));     ❷
```

Line 2 in the listing performs the dynamic linking. With Tomcat deployment, this option is not available. Instead, the *predictionsSOAP* service and the `ServiceHashHandler` are linked through an XML configuration file encapsulated in the deployed WAR file:

```
<handler-chains xmlns="http://java.sun.com/xml/ns/javaee">
  <handler-chain>                                                    ❶
    <handler>
      <handler-name>predictions.ServiceHashHandler</handler-name>    ❷
      <handler-class>predictions.ServiceHashHandler</handler-class>
    </handler>
  </handler-chain>
</handler-chains>
```

The name of the configuration file is arbitrary. A `handler-chain` (line 1) can include arbitrarily many `handler` instances but, in this case, there is but one `handler` in the `handler-chain`, the handler `ServiceHashHandler` (line 2). This configuration file then is referenced with a `@HandlerChain` annotation in the `PredictionsSOAP` class:

```
@WebService
@HandlerChain(file = "../../../WEB-INF/serviceHandler.xml")
public class PredictionsSOAP {
  ...
```

The *serviceHandler.xml* file winds up in the *WEB-INF* directory of the deployed WAR file because the usual Ant script is used to deploy the *predictionsSOAP* service to Tomcat.

The configuration document *serviceHandler.xml* shown above indicates, with its `handler-chain` tag, that multiple handlers might be in play on either the service or the client side. Figure 5-6 depicts the structure of such a chain. For an outgoing message, logical handlers come into play first. This is appropriate because such handlers have limited scope; that is, they have access only to the payload in the SOAP body. The (SOAP) message handlers then come into play and these handlers, as noted earlier, have access to the entire SOAP message. For an incoming message, the order is reversed: the (SOAP) message handlers have first access and the logical handlers have last access. Message handlers are sufficient for any handler logic precisely because they have access to the entire SOAP message, but logical handlers are convenient in that the runtime makes available only the SOAP body's payload.

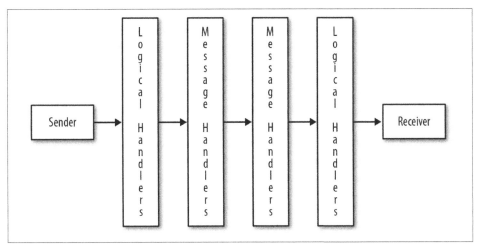

*Figure 5-6. The handler-chain structure*

The next section adds a second handler, in this case a LogicalHandler, to the client side of the *predictionsSOAP* service. The result is a true chain of handlers.

# A Handler Chain with Two Handlers

In the *predictionsSOAP* service, three of the operations require the id of a Predic tion: the *getOne*, *edit*, and *delete* operations. The id is a positive integer. What happens if the client, through oversight or mischief, submits a negative integer or zero as the id? The service throws a SOAP fault. A SOAP request with a bad id is a waste of time and bandwidth, and avoiding such a request would be a gain in efficiency.

To guard against an invalid id, a client-side handler could inspect every outgoing SOAP message to determine if it has an id and, if so, whether the id is a positive integer. If the id is negative, the handler could substitute the absolute value and let the request con tinue on its way to the service; if the id is zero, the handler could throw an exception immediately and thereby short-circuit a request that is doomed to fail on the service side. The client-side SOAPHandler already in place could be amended to do this work, as the SOAP handler has access to the entire SOAP message; however, a LogicalHan dler is better suited to the proposed task because the id is part of the payload in the SOAP request's body. The existing SOAPHandler can be left as is and a LogicalHan dler can be added to the handler chain. Modular design recommends this approach, which is also an opportunity to show a two-member handler chain in action.

There are two ways in which the LogicalHandler can access the payload of a SOAP message: as a native Java object generated with JAX-B or as an XML document. This example uses a Java object so that the id property can be inspected and perhaps changed using the familiar *get/set* idiom. If the id in the client request message is negative, a *set*-method then can be used to change the id value. If the id is zero, the handler can disable any further client-side handling and throw a fault to signal that the message cannot be fixed. With JAX-B in support, the processing is straightforward.

The IdHandler class (see Example 5-10) implements the LogicalHandler rather than the SOAPHandler interface (line 1). To implement this interface, the IdHandler needs to define close, handleFault, and handleMessage, but a LogicalHandler implementation, unlike a SOAPHandler implementation, does not define the getHeaders method precisely because a logical handler has no access to the SOAP headers. In this example, the close and handleFault methods are minimally defined.

*Example 5-10. The client-side IdLogicalHandler*

```
class IdHandler implements LogicalHandler<LogicalMessageContext> {        ❶
    public void close(MessageContext mctx) { }
    public boolean handleFault(LogicalMessageContext lmctx) {
        return true;
    }
    public boolean handleMessage(LogicalMessageContext lmctx) {
        Boolean outbound =
            (Boolean) lmctx.get(MessageContext.MESSAGE_OUTBOUND_PROPERTY);
        if (outbound) { // request?
            LogicalMessage msg = lmctx.getMessage();
            try {
                JAXBContext jaxbCtx = JAXBContext.newInstance("clientSOAP");  ❷
                Object payload = msg.getPayload(jaxbCtx);                     ❸
                // Check payload to be sure it's what we want.
                if (payload instanceof JAXBElement) {
                    Object value = ((JAXBElement) payload).getValue();
                    // Three possibilities of interest: GetOne, Edit, or Delete
                    int id = 0;
                    boolean getOne, edit, delete;
                    getOne = edit = delete = false;
                    if (value.toString().contains("GetOne")) {               ❹
                        id = ((GetOne) value).getArg0();
                        getOne = true;
                    }
                    else if (value.toString().contains("Edit")) {
                        id = ((Edit) value).getArg0();
                        edit = true;
                    }
                    else if (value.toString().contains("Delete")) {
                        id = ((Delete) value).getArg0();
                        delete = true;
                    }
                    else
```

```
                return true; // GetAll or Create
            // If id > 0, there is no problem to fix on the client side.
            if (id > 0) return true;                                          ❺
            // If the request is GetOne, Edit, or Delete and the id is zero,
            // there is a problem that cannot be fixed.
            if (getOne || edit || delete) {
                if (id == 0) // can't fix
                    throw new RuntimeException("ID cannot be zero!");         ❻
                // id < 0 and operation is GetOne, Edit, or Delete
                int newId = Math.abs(id);
                // Update argument.
                if (getOne) ((GetOne) value).setArg0(newId);                  ❼
                else if (edit) ((Edit) value).setArg0(newId);
                else if (delete) ((Delete) value).setArg0(newId);
                // Update payload.
                ((JAXBElement) payload).setValue(value);                      ❽
                // Update message
                msg.setPayload(payload, jaxbCtx);                             ❾
            }
        }
    }
    catch(Exception e) { throw new RuntimeException(e); }
}
return true;
    }
}
```

The logic in the handleMessage method is a bit tricky. Like the ClientHashHandler, the IdHandler needs to work only on outgoing (that is, request) messages; hence, the IdHandler first checks on the direction of the SOAP message. The logical handler then extracts the payload from an outgoing message. The payload is available in two formats:

- If the getPayload method is invoked with no arguments (line 3), the payload would be returned as an XML document. This document then could be parsed and edited, as required; the corresponding setPayload method would then be used to update the message payload.

- If the getPayload method is invoked with a JAXBContext as the argument, a reference to an Object is returned (line 3). In this example, the JAXBContext is created from the soapClient package (line 2) because three classes in this package are of interest: GetOne, Edit, and Delete. These *wsimport*-generated classes are the Java data types that represent SOAP request messages against the service's *getOne, edit,* and *delete* operations, respectively. If only a single SOAP request type were of interest, then the JAXBContext could be created for a single class instead of for the entire package of classes.

The extracted payload could be from any request. The next task, therefore, is to exclude requests that do not include an id. There are two such requests, one against the *getAll* operation and another against the *create* operation. The requests of interest are against the *getOne*, *edit*, and *delete* operations; an `if` construct, which starts on line 4, then determines whether the request is against one of these three operations. In summary, requests against the *create* and *getAll* operations are filtered out, and the remaining requests are inspected to determine if the outgoing id is a bad value.

If the outgoing message has an id, the handler extracts the id from the payload with a statement such as:

```
id = ((GetOne) value).getArg0();
```

There is one such statement for each of the three types: `GetOne`, `Edit`, and `Delete`. If the outgoing SOAP message is none of these, then `true` is returned from the `else` clause to signal that the `IdHandler` has finished its work and other handlers in the chain, if any, can begin theirs. Here is the code segment for review:

```
if (value.toString().contains("GetOne")) {
    id = ((GetOne) value).getArg0();
    getOne = true;
}
else if (value.toString().contains("Edit")) {
    id = ((Edit) value).getArg0();
    edit = true;
}
...
else
    return true; // GetAll or Create: no id
```

Once the payload's id value has been extracted, there are three possible outcomes:

- If the extracted id is a positive value, there is nothing more for the `IdHandler` to do and, therefore, the handler returns `true` (line 5), thereby indicating that other handlers in the chain, in any, can begin their processing. In fact, there is now another handler in the chain: the `ClientHashHandler`, which executes *after* the logical `IdHandler`. By the way, the id still may be out of bounds in the sense that no `Prediction` has such an id, but this is a problem that must be detected and managed on the service side, not the client side.

- If the extracted id is zero, a `RuntimeException` is thrown (line 6) to terminate the entire request process because zero is not a legitimate value for an id. It makes no sense to send an id of zero to the *predictionsSOAP* service.

- If the extracted id is negative (for instance, -31), then its absolute value (in this case, 31) is treated as the intended value. A *set*-method is invoked with the new id value (line 7), which updates the payload's value. The payload itself is updated (line 8) and, finally, this newly edited payload is inserted as a replacement in the outgoing SOAP message (line 9).

This handler logic is clearly lower level than is the application logic of invoking service operations such as *edit* or *getAll*. JAX-WS is designed under the *separation of concerns* principle: low-level message inspection and tweaking occur at the handler level, whereas high-level operation invocations occur at the application level.

The `IdHandler`, like the `ClientHashHandler`, is a nonpublic class in the same file as the `ClientHandlerResolver`, a `public` class. The reason is convenience: one file holds all of the low-level artifacts. The handlers and the resolver all could be `public` classes and, accordingly, in their own files. The `IdHandler`, again like the `ClientHashHandler`, needs to be registered with the runtime. Here is the revised `getHandlerChain` method in the `ClientHandlerResolver` class:

```
public List<Handler> getHandlerChain(PortInfo portInfo) {
    List<Handler> handlerChain = new ArrayList<Handler>();
    handlerChain.add(new IdHandler());                           ❶
    handlerChain.add(new ClientHashHandler(this.name, this.key)); ❷
    return handlerChain;
}
```

The logical handler `IdHandler` is added to the chain (line 1) in front of the message handler `ClientHashHandler` (line 2) because, on an outgoing message, logical handlers execute before message handlers. Yet even if the order were reversed in this code, the runtime still would ensure that the logical `IdHandler` executed before the message handler `ClientHashHandler`. For handlers in the same group (e.g., logical handlers), the specified order in the `getHandlerChain` method matters; for handlers in different groups, as in this example, the runtime orders the execution so that all logical handlers execute before any message handlers do.

The handler examples illustrate the various ways in which SOAP messages can be inspected and manipulated. The client-side `AwsSoapHandler`, a message handler, adds elements to the body of a SOAP request, and the client-side `ClientHashHandler`, also a message handler, adds blocks to the header of a SOAP request. The logical handler `IdHandler` inspects the payload of a SOAP request and, under the right circumstances, edits this payload so that the request has a chance of succeeding with the service. The code in all three handlers is appropriately low-level, as befits code designed to be close to the SOAP metal.

There are three possible parts to a SOAP message: the header blocks, the body, and attachments. The first and the last are optional. The examples so far have examined the SOAP header and the SOAP body through code examples. The next section does the same for SOAP attachments.

# SOAP-Based Web Services and Binary Data

In the examples so far, the SOAP messages contain text that is converted to service-appropriate types such as `List<Prediction>`. The type conversion is typically automatic, occurring in the JAX-WS infrastructure without application intervention, but handlers could use JAX-B and related technologies for converting text to and from Java types. Even a very simple example illustrates the power of this underlying, automatic conversion. Here is a SOAP response from the `RandService`, in particular a call to the *next1* operation, which returns a randomly generated integer:

```
<S:Envelope xmlns:S="http://schemas.xmlsoap.org/soap/envelope/">
   <S:Body>
      <ns2:next1Response xmlns:ns2="http://rand/">
         <return>-1691660782</return>
      </ns2:next1Response>
   </S:Body>
</S:Envelope>
```

The returned value `-1691660782` occurs as text in the SOAP message but is converted automatically to an `int` for a Java client, which does not need to do any explicit type conversion.

Type conversions come to the forefront in the issue of how binary data such as images, movies, and the like can be arguments passed to or values returned from SOAP-based service operations. SOAP-based services can deal with binary payloads but such payloads raise issues of efficiency. There are two general approaches to dealing with binary data in SOAP-based services:

- The binary data can be encoded using a scheme such as base64 encoding and then transmitted as the payload of the SOAP body—in other words, as text. The downside is that base64 and similar encoding schemes result in payloads that may be significantly larger in size than the original, unencoded binary data. Encoding binary data as text results in data bloat.
- The binary data be can transmitted as attachments, which minimizes data bloat.

In the course of SOAP development, there have been three options for attachments. *SwA* (SOAP with Attachments) is the original specification but does not work well with document-style services, which are the default. Moreover, some frameworks such as DotNet do not support *SwA* out of the box. *DIME* (Direct Internet Message Encapsulation) is a lightweight but proprietary encoding scheme, which has received little play outside of Windows. MTOM (Message Transmission Optimization Mechanism), which is based on XOP (XML-Binary Optimized Packaging), has the W3C seal of approval and enjoys widespread support. In short, MTOM is a modern, efficient, and interoperable way to share binary data through SOAP-based services.

---

To underscore the efficiency of MTOM, the first example uses base64 encoding. The SkiImageService class (see Example 5-11) has two @WebMethod operations: *getImage* returns a specified image about skiing, for instance, a picture of a nordic skier; *GetImageList* returns a list of the available skiing images.

*Example 5-11. The SkiImageService, which delivers images encoded as base64 text*

```
package images;

import javax.jws.WebService;
import javax.jws.WebMethod;
import java.util.Map;
import java.util.HashMap;
import java.util.Set;
import java.util.List;
import java.util.ArrayList;
import java.util.Iterator;
import java.awt.Image;
import java.io.FileInputStream;
import java.io.ByteArrayOutputStream;
import java.io.ByteArrayInputStream;
import javax.imageio.ImageIO;
import javax.imageio.stream.ImageInputStream;
import javax.imageio.ImageReader;

@WebService
public class SkiImageService {
    private Map<String, String> photos;

    @WebMethod
    public Image getImage(String name) { return createImage(name);  }
    @WebMethod
    public List<Image> getImages() { return createImageList(); }
    public SkiImageService() {
        photos = new HashMap<String, String>();
        photos.put("nordic", "nordic.jpg");
        photos.put("alpine", "alpine.jpg");
        photos.put("telemk", "telemk.jpg");
    }
    private Image createImage(String name) {
        String fileName = photos.get(name);
        byte[ ] bytes = getRawBytes(fileName);
        ByteArrayInputStream in = new ByteArrayInputStream(bytes);
        Iterator iterators = ImageIO.getImageReadersByFormatName("jpeg");
        ImageReader iterator = (ImageReader) iterators.next();
        Image image = null;
        try {
            ImageInputStream iis = ImageIO.createImageInputStream(in);
            iterator.setInput(iis, true);
            image = iterator.read(0);
        }
        catch(Exception e) { throw new RuntimeException(e); }
```

```
            return image;
    }
    private List<Image> createImageList() {
        List<Image> list = new ArrayList<Image>();
        for (String key : photos.keySet()) {
            Image image = createImage(key);
            if (image != null) list.add(image);
        }
        return list;
    }
    private byte[ ] getRawBytes(String fileName) {
        if (fileName == null) fileName = "nordic.jpg";
        ByteArrayOutputStream out = new ByteArrayOutputStream();
        try {
            FileInputStream in = new FileInputStream(fileName);
            if (in == null) in = new FileInputStream("nordic.jpg");
            byte[ ] buffer = new byte[2048];
            int n = 0;
            while ((n = in.read(buffer)) != -1)
                out.write(buffer, 0, n); // append to array
            in.close();
        }
        catch(Exception e) { throw new RuntimeException(e); }
        return out.toByteArray();
    }
}
}
```

Most of the code consists of utility methods that read bytes from a file and transform these into a Java Image. This service can be published straightforwardly with Endpoint:

```
package images;
import javax.xml.ws.Endpoint;
public class SkiImagePublisherBase64 {
    public static void main(String[ ] args) {
        System.out.println("URL: http://localhost:9876/ski");
        Endpoint.publish("http://localhost:9876/ski", new SkiImageService());
    }
}
```

Here is a Perl client against the service—a client that explicitly consumes the service WSDL before making a request:

```
#!/usr/bin/perl -w
use SOAP::Lite +trace => 'debug';
use strict;

my $url = 'http://localhost:9876/ski?wsdl';
my $service = SOAP::Lite->service($url);
print $service->getImage("nordic"), "\n"; # base64 string
```

There is nothing unusual in either the service or the client: a client request results in a SOAP response whose body is text, but in this case it is text that is potentially huge in size because of the base64 encoding. The XML Schema in the service WSDL points to the problem. Here is a slice:

```
<xs:complexType name="getImageResponse">
 <xs:sequence>
  <xs:element name="return" type="xs:base64Binary" minOccurs="0"></xs:element> ❶
 </xs:sequence>
</xs:complexType>
```

Line 1 shows that the XML Schema type of the response message getImageResponse is, indeed, xs:base64Binary. For dramatic effect, here is a slice of the more than 30K-byte response to a getImage request:

```
<?xml version="1.0" ?>
<S:Envelope xmlns:S="http://schemas.xmlsoap.org/soap/envelope/">
  <S:Body>
    <ns2:getImageResponse xmlns:ns2="http://images/">
      <return>iVBORw0KGgoAAAANSUhEUgAAAHwAAABWCAIAAACCS2W5AABY...</return> ❶
    </ns2:getImageResponse>
  </S:Body>
</S:Envelope>
```

The element tagged return (line 1) contains the base64 encoding of the image. The image itself, *nordic.jpg*, is just under 3K bytes—and the SOAP response is just over 30K bytes. In this case, the data bloat is ten-fold.

To avoid the data bloat associated with base64 or equivalent encoding, the service can be revised to take advantage of MTOM optimizations. Here are the steps to the revision:

- The SkiImageService class can be annotated to signal that MTOM is in play. The revision is line 1:

    ```
    @WebService(wsdlLocation = "mtom.wsdl")
    @BindingType(value = SOAPBinding.SOAP11HTTP_MTOM_BINDING) // optional ❶
    public class SkiImageService {
    ```

    There is also a SOAP 1.2 binding for MTOM.

- The XML Schema for the service WSDL needs to be edited in two places, as indicated in lines 1 and 2:

    ```
    <xsd:complexType name="getImagesResponse">
      <xsd:sequence>
        <xsd:element name="return" type="xsd:base64Binary"
                     minOccurs="0" maxOccurs="unbounded"
                     xmime:expectedContentTypes="application/octet-stream"  ❶
                     xmlns:xmime="http://www.w3.org/2005/05/xmlmime">
        </xsd:element>
      </xsd:sequence>
    </xsd:complexType>
    ...
    <xsd:complexType name="getImageResponse">
      <xsd:sequence>
    ```

```
<xsd:element name="return" type="xsd:base64Binary" minOccurs="0"
             xmime:expectedContentTypes="application/octet-stream"     ❷
             xmlns:xmime="http://www.w3.org/2005/05/xmlmime">
    ...
```

The MIME type `application/octet-stream` indicates that the images are to be
sent from the service to the client as a byte stream. For simplicity and for proof of
concept, the revised XML Schema can be inserted into the WSDL directly (line 1):

```
<definitions xmlns:soap="http://schemas.xmlsoap.org/wsdl/soap/"
             xmlns:tns="http://images/"
             xmlns:xsd="http://www.w3.org/2001/XMLSchema"
             xmlns="http://schemas.xmlsoap.org/wsdl/"
             targetNamespace="http://images/" name="SkiImageServiceService">
  <types>
    <xsd:schema xmlns:tns="http://images/"                              ❶
                xmlns:xsd="http://www.w3.org/2001/XMLSchema"
    ...
```

Assume that the revised WSDL file, with the XML Schema inserted into it, is
*mtom.wsdl*.

- The `@WebService` annotation for the `SkiImageService` needs to be parametrized
  with the location of the revised WSDL (line 1):

```
@WebService(wsdlLocation = "mtom.wsdl")     ❶
@BindingType(value = SOAPBinding.SOAP11HTTP_MTOM_BINDING) // optional
public class SkiImageService {
```

- If `Endpoint` is used to publish the revised service, then the publisher can be revised
  to indicate MTOM optimization (line 1), although this step is optional. Here is the
  revised `SkiImagePublisherMTOM` in full:

```
package images;
import javax.xml.ws.Endpoint;
import javax.xml.ws.soap.SOAPBinding;
public class SkiImagePublisherMTOM {
    private Endpoint endpoint;
    public static void main(String[ ] args) {
        SkiImagePublisherMTOM me = new SkiImagePublisherMTOM();
        me.createEndpoint();
        me.configureEndpoint();
        me.publish();
    }
    private void createEndpoint() {
        endpoint = Endpoint.create(new SkiImageService());
    }
    private void configureEndpoint() {
        SOAPBinding binding = (SOAPBinding) endpoint.getBinding();
        binding.setMTOMEnabled(true);      ❶
    }
    private void publish() {
        int port = 9876;
```

```
            String url = "http://localhost:" + port + "/ski";
            endpoint.publish(url);
            System.out.println(url);
        }
    }
```

The revised publisher shows that the `Endpoint` API is rich and flexible.

With these changes in place, an efficient Java client against the revised MTOM-based `SkiImageService` can be built upon the usual *wsimport* artifacts. The by now familiar command:

```
% wsimport -p clientMTOM -keep http://localhost:9876/ski?wsdl
```

generates the support classes for the revised `SkiImageClient` (see Example 5-12).

*Example 5-12. A Java client against the MTOM-based SkiImageService*

```
import clientMTOM.SkiImageServiceService;
import clientMTOM.SkiImageService;
import java.util.List;
import javax.activation.DataHandler;

public class SkiImageClient {
    public static void main(String[ ] args) {
        SkiImageService port = new SkiImageServiceService().getSkiImageServicePort();
        DataHandler image = port.getImage("nordic");                    ❶
        dump(image);
        List<DataHandler> images = port.getImages();                    ❷
        for (DataHandler dh : images) dump(dh);
    }
    private static void dump(DataHandler dh) {
        try {
            System.out.println("MIME type: " + dh.getContentType());    ❸
            System.out.println("Content:   " + dh.getContent());        ❹
        }
        catch(Exception e) { throw new RuntimeException(e); }
    }
}
```

The Java `DataHandler` type (lines 1 and 2) binds to the type `application/octet-stream`. Each image from the service is a `DataHandler` instance whose properties (for instance, the `contentType` and `content` properties shown in lines 3 and 4) are accessible with the familiar *get*-methods. The output from a sample client run is:

```
MIME type: application/octet-stream
Content:   java.io.ByteArrayInputStream@3f3e10ce
...
MIME type: application/octet-stream
Content:   java.io.ByteArrayInputStream@ca753f7
```

The `ByteArrayInputSteam` instances contain the bytes sent from the MTOM-enabled `SkiImageService`. Although the transmission is relatively efficient, the client now must deal with these bytes in some application-appropriate way—for instance, by reconstructing the JPG images from the bytes.

In JAX-WS a client, too, can use MTOM to send media attachments to a service. Here is a revision of the `SkiImageClient` that shows the setup (lines 1 through 3):

```
SkiImageService port = new SkiImageServiceService().getSkiImageServicePort();
BindingProvider bp = (BindingProvider) port;              ❶
SOAPBinding binding = (SOAPBinding) bp.getBinding();       ❷
binding.setMTOMEnabled(true);                             ❸
```

SOAP-based web services are at their best when dealing with text payloads, as the SOAP infrastructure then assumes the burden of converting between native language types (for instance, a Java `List<Prediction>`), on the one side, and XML Schema types, on the other side. This advantage goes away once the SOAP payloads are binary, regardless of whether the payload is base64 encoded text in the SOAP body or SOAP attachments. Can SOAP-based services handle binary payloads? The answer is a firm *yes*, but this answer invites the further question of whether SOAP-based services are ideally suited for binary payloads. The answer to this second question is *no*.

# The Transport Level

So far this chapter has focused on the distinction, within JAX-WS, between the application and handler levels. JAX-WS also provides access, on either the client side or the service side, to the transport level, which is usually HTTP(S). Such access has been used but not studied in earlier examples. This section focuses on the transport level with the deliberately minimalist `Echo` service and a sample `EchoClient`. Access to the transport level will be especially useful in the next chapter on security.

The `Echo` service (see Example 5-13) relies upon *dependency injection* through the `@Resource` annotation to get a non-`null` reference to the `WebServiceContext` (line 1). The `WebServiceContext`, in turn, can be used to access the `MessageContext` (line 2), which provides information about the transport level. To illustrate such access, the `echo` method gets the HTTP request headers as a `Map` (line 3) and then prints the map's contents to the standard output (line 4).

*Example 5-13. The Echo service, which accesses the transport level*

```
package mctx;

import java.util.Map;
import java.util.Set;
import javax.annotation.Resource;
import javax.jws.WebService;
import javax.jws.WebMethod;
```

```
import javax.xml.ws.WebServiceContext;
import javax.xml.ws.handler.MessageContext;


@WebService
public class Echo {
    @Resource
    WebServiceContext wctx;                                                   ❶
    @WebMethod
    public String echo(String in) {
        String out = "Echoing: " + in;
        // Hit the transport level to extract the HTTP headers.
        MessageContext mctx = wctx.getMessageContext();                        ❷
        Map requestHeaders = (Map) mctx.get(MessageContext.HTTP_REQUEST_HEADERS); ❸
        dump(requestHeaders, "");                                              ❹
        return out;
    }
    private void dump(Map map, String indent) {
        Set keys = map.keySet();
        for (Object key : keys) {
            System.out.println(indent + key + " : " + map.get(key));
            if (map.get(key) instanceof Map)
                dump((Map) map.get(key), indent += "   ");
        }
    }
}
```

On a sample run of the EchoClient, to be studied shortly, the output of the dump method was:

```
Host : [localhost:7777]
Content-type : [text/xml; charset=utf-8]
Accept-encoding : [gzip]                         ❶
Content-length : [193]
Connection : [keep-alive]
Greeting : [Hello, world!]                        ❷
User-agent : [JAX-WS RI 2.2.4-b01]
Soapaction : ["http://mctx/Echo/echoRequest"]
Accept : [text/xml, multipart/related]
```

Most of the lines in the HTTP header are standard (e.g., the blocks with Content-type and Accept as their keys). By contrast, the EchoClient manually inserts lines 1 and 2 into the HTTP headers. HTTP 1.1 allows arbitrary header blocks to be added to an HTTP message. In a security context, a username and a supporting credential could be inserted into an HTTPS header.

The EchoClient class (see Example 5-14) is a sample client against the Echo service. The client, too, accesses the transport level by casting the port reference to a Binding Provider. As the name suggests, a BindingProvider binds a SOAP message to a transport message, in this case an HTTP request message.

*Example 5-14. The EchoClient against the EchoService*

```java
import java.util.Map;
import java.util.Set;
import java.util.List;
import java.util.Collections;
import java.util.HashMap;
import javax.xml.ws.BindingProvider;
import javax.xml.ws.handler.MessageContext;
import echoClient.EchoService;
import echoClient.Echo;

public class EchoClient {
    private static final String defaultUrl = "http://localhost:7777/echo";
    public static void main(String[ ] args) {
        Echo port = new EchoService().getEchoPort();
        Map<String, Object> requestContext =
          ((BindingProvider) port).getRequestContext();                     ❶

        /* Sample invocation:
           java EchoClient http://localhost:7777/ echo  */
        String url = (args.length >= 2) ? (args[0] + args[1]) : defaultUrl;
        requestContext.put(BindingProvider.ENDPOINT_ADDRESS_PROPERTY, url);  ❷
        // Add application-specific HTTP header blocks.
        Map<String, Object> myHeaders = new HashMap<String, Object>();
        myHeaders.put("Accept-Encoding", Collections.singletonList("gzip")); ❸
        myHeaders.put("Greeting", Collections.singletonList("Hello, world!")); ❹
        requestContext.put(MessageContext.HTTP_REQUEST_HEADERS, myHeaders);  ❺
        String response = port.echo("Have a nice day :)");
        Map<String, Object> responseContext =
          ((BindingProvider) port).getResponseContext();                    ❻
        dump(responseContext, "");
    }
    private static void dump(Map map, String indent) {
        Set keys = map.keySet();
        for (Object key : keys) {
            System.out.println(indent + key + " : " + map.get(key));
            if (map.get(key) instanceof Map)
                dump((Map) map.get(key), indent += "   ");
        }
    }
}
```

The `BindingProvider` reference is used to invoke `getRequestContext` (line 1), which is a `Map` of the key/value pairs in the HTTP request. As proof of concept, the `Echo Client` shows how the *endpoint address* of the request can be set at the transport level (line 2). In lines 3 and 4, the class `EchoClient` adds two key/value pairs to a `Map` and then, in line 5, appends this `Map` to the HTTP headers that the underlying Java libraries produce.

The EchoClient prints the responseContext (line 6) to the standard output. On a sample run, the HTTP message from the *Echo* service was:

```
javax.xml.ws.wsdl.port : {http://mctx/}EchoPort
javax.xml.ws.soap.http.soapaction.uri : null
com.sun.xml.internal.ws.server.OneWayOperation : true
javax.xml.ws.wsdl.service : {http://mctx/}EchoService
com.sun.xml.internal.ws.client.handle : JAX-WS RI 2.2.4-b01:
                                  Stub for http://localhost:7777/echo
javax.xml.ws.reference.parameters : []
com.sun.xml.internal.ws.api.server.WSEndpoint : null
javax.xml.ws.http.response.code : 200
javax.xml.ws.wsdl.interface : {http://mctx/}Echo
javax.xml.ws.wsdl.operation : {http://mctx/}echo
com.sun.xml.internal.ws.handler.config :
            com.sun.xml.internal.ws.client.HandlerConfiguration@6c3a6465
javax.xml.ws.http.response.headers : {null=[HTTP/1.1 200 OK],
                              Content-type=[text/xml; charset=utf-8],
                              Transfer-encoding=[chunked]}
  null : [HTTP/1.1 200 OK]                                        ❶
  Content-type : [text/xml; charset=utf-8]                       ❷
  Transfer-encoding : [chunked]
  javax.xml.ws.service.endpoint.address : http://localhost:7777/echo  ❸
  com.sun.xml.internal.ws.api.message.HeaderList : []
  com.sun.xml.internal.ws.client.ContentNegotiation : none
```

The format here is Java's own rather than standard HTTP. Nonetheless, the details are readily recognized. Line 1 is the start line in the actual HTTP response, line 3 contains the endpoint address of the Echo service, and line 2 is the standard key/value pair for the key Content-type.

In summary, JAX-WS is more than just an application-level API. There is a powerful handler-level API and even a transport-level API. In the coming chapters, the transport-level API will be put to further use.

# Axis2

Axis2 (*http://bit.ly/12jbYqA*), which implements but also extends JAX-WS, is an alternative to the Metro implementation. The current version is 1.6.x. Axis2 can be downloaded in various formats, including as a self-contained WAR file, *axis2.war*, which can be copied to *TOMCAT_HOME/webapps*. An Axis2 service does not require annotations if the proper configuration file is used. This section introduces Axis2 using a deliberately simple service so that the focus is on the deployment steps.

The HiService class (see Example 5-15) is a POJO class, free of annotations, that implements the SOAP-based HiService in Axis2. Any public instance method in the class is thereby a service operation; in this case, there is a single operation: *echo*.

*Example 5-15. The HiService in Axis2*

```
package hello;

public class HiService {           // service
  public String echo(String name) { // service operation
    String msg =
      (name == null || name.length() < 1) ? "Hello, world!" : "Hello, " + name + "!";
    return msg;
  }
}
```

The configuration file *services.xml* (see Example 5-16) specifies that an instance of the Axis2 class `RPCMessageReceiver` will act as the interceptor for requests against the operation named *echo*. The configuration document *services.xml* must be deployed in the JAR file's *META-INF* directory.

*Example 5-16. The services.xml configuration file for the Axis2 HiService*

```
<service>
  <parameter name = "ServiceClass" locked = "false">hello.HiService</parameter>
  <operation name = "echo">
    <messageReceiver class = "org.apache.axis2.rpc.receivers.RPCMessageReceiver"/>
  </operation>
</service>
```

Here are the steps for deploying this Axis2 service:

1. The downloaded Axis2 implementation file, *axis2.war*, should be copied to *webapps* directory under *TOMCAT_HOME*. Tomcat *unwars* this WAR file, creating the directory *webapps/axis2*, which in turn has a subdirectory named *WEB-INF/services*. An Axis2 service is deployed as a JAR file copied to the *services* subdirectory.

2. The compiled service class, in this case `hello.HiService`, together with the configuration file *META-INF/services.xml*, should be put in a JAR file with an *.aar* extension, for example, *hi.aar*. Here is a snapshot of the contents of *hi.aar*:

   ```
   hello/HiService.java
   hello/HiService.class
   META-INF/services.xml
   ```

   The source code, *HiService.java*, is included in the JAR file for convenience.

3. The deployable JAR file, *hi.aar*, is then copied to *webapps/axis2/WEB-INF/services*.

Once the Axis2 service is deployed, *wsimport* can be used to generate client-side artifacts. The command is the usual one:

```
% wsimport -p clientAxis2 -keep http://localhost:8080/axis2/services/hi?wsdl
```

The *wsimport* utility outputs a warning that the portType in the WSDL is not standard and that, accordingly, there may be problems with the generated JAX-WS artifacts. This issue is addressed next.

The AxisClient class (see Example 5-17) is code for a sample client against the Axis2 HiService. The client is built on the familiar *wsimport*-generated classes in the package/ directory clientAxis2. These *wsimport*-generated classes are close but not identical to the classes that would be generated from a Metro service. In any case, the Axis2 versions do not set the service endpoint according to JAX-WS standards, which explains lines 2 and 3 in the code: these two lines change the endpoint address to the correct one, in this case to the endpoint given in line 1. Lines 2 and 3 represent transport-level code. With this small change using the JAX-WS transport-level API, the service operation can be invoked in the usual way (lines 4 and 5).

*Example 5-17. The AxisClient against the HiService*

```
import clientAxis2.HiPortType;
import clientAxis2.Hi;
import javax.xml.ws.BindingProvider;

public class AxisClient {
    public static void main(String[ ] args) {
        final String endpoint = "http://localhost:8080/axis2/services/hi";      ❶

        HiPortType port = new Hi().getHiHttpEndpoint();
        // Override the endpoint in the wsimport-derived classes.
        BindingProvider bp = (BindingProvider) port;                            ❷
        bp.getRequestContext().put(BindingProvider.ENDPOINT_ADDRESS_PROPERTY,   ❸
                                   endpoint);
        System.out.println(port.echo(null));                                    ❹
        System.out.println(port.echo("Fred"));                                  ❺
    }
}
```

The output is

```
Hello, world!
Hello, Fred!
```

Axis2 is a popular alternative to the Metro implementation of JAX-WS. Axis2 and Metro are close enough that the transition from one to the other should be mostly trouble-free.

# What's Next?

This chapter rounded out the coverage of SOAP-based services by focusing on the JAX-WS handler APIs, which provide fine-grained control, on either the client side or the service side, over incoming and outgoing SOAP messages. Such control is required in the SOAP message architecture, with its distinctions among sender, receiver, and intermediary nodes; this control allows any SOAP message to be inspected and manipulated as needed along the route from the message sender to the ultimate receiver. The chapter also examined SOAP faults at the handler and the application level. SOAP attachments are yet another relatively low-level part of JAX-WS. Although SOAP is not ideally suited for dealing with binary payloads, SOAP can do so efficiently with MTOM. The chapter also covered the JAX-WS transport-level API, which provides access to the (usually) HTTP messages that carry SOAP messages. Finally, this chapter introduced Axis2, a JAX-WS implementation that is an alternative to Metro.

Web services, whether REST-style or SOAP-based, typically require security. The term *security* is vague. In general, however, there are two broad security challenges. One challenge involves *wire-level* security; technologies such as HTTPS address this multifaceted challenge. A second challenge involves *users/roles* security—user authentication and authorization. Java has various ways to address this challenge. The next chapter clarifies various security challenges through a series of examples, thereby highlighting the technologies available for securing web services.

# CHAPTER 6

# Web Services Security

Security for web services covers a lot of territory, which cannot be explored all at once. To make the exploration more manageable, it seems best to analyze small chunks, one at a time, before pulling the exploration results together. Here is a sketch of how this chapter breaks up the broad topic of security into smaller pieces:

*Wire-level security*

Security begins at the transport or wire level with basic protocols that govern communications between a web service, whether SOAP-based or REST-style, and its clients. Security at this level typically provides three services. First, the client and service need transport-level assurance that each is communicating with the other rather than with some impostor. Second, the data sent from one side to the other need to be encrypted strongly enough so that an interceptor cannot decrypt the data and thus gain access to the confidential information carried therein. Third, each side needs assurance that the received message is the same as the sent message. This chapter covers the basics of wire-level security with code examples, most of which focus on HTTPS as a provider of wire-level security.

*User authentication and authorization*

Web services provide clients with access to resources. If a resource is secured, then a client needs the appropriate credentials to gain access. The credentials are presented and verified through a process that usually has two phases. In the first phase, a client (user) presents information such as a username together with a credential such as a password. If the credential is not accepted, access to the requested resource is denied. The first phase is known as *user authentication*. The second phase, which is optional, consists of fine-tuning the authenticated subject's access rights. For example, a stock-picking web service might provide all paying customers with a username and password, but the service might divide the customers into categories such as *regular* and *premier*. Access to certain resources might be restricted to *premier* clients. The second phase is known as *role authorization*. This chapter introduces users/roles security, a common name for the two-phase process.

*WS-Security*

WS-Security, or WSS for short, is a collection of protocols that specify how different levels of security can be enforced within the SOAP-messaging infrastructure rather than through a particular transport (for instance, HTTPS) or through a particular service container (for instance, Tomcat). For example, WSS specifies how digital signatures and encryption information can be inserted into SOAP headers. If SOAP-based services are to be transport-neutral, then various security features must be built into SOAP itself. Accordingly, WSS is meant to provide comprehensive end-to-end security regardless of the underlying transport and the container that hosts the service. This chapter introduces WS-Security with an example.

# Wire-Level Security

Consider a pay-for web service such as Amazon's S3 storage service. This service needs to authenticate requests to store and retrieve data so that only the paying clients have access to the service and that, moreover, a particular client has privileged access to its paid-for storage. In the RESTful version of S3, Amazon uses a customization of keyed HMAC to authenticate client requests. Amazon allows the authentication credential to be in either the query string (which is part of the HTTP headers) or in another header key/value pair with `Authorization` as the key. In either case, the basic approach is the same:

- Parts of the request data are concatenated together to form a single string, which becomes the input value for a hash computation. This string is the *input message*.

- The AWS (Amazon Web Services) *secretKey*, a unique bit string that Amazon provides to each client and which has been discussed with respect to clients against the Amazon E-Commerce service, is used to compute the hash value of the input message (see Figure 6-1). A hash value is also called a *message digest*, which is a fixed-length digest of arbitrarily many input bits. For the S3 service, Amazon uses the SHA-1 (Secure Hash Algorithm-1) version of HMAC, which produces a 160-bit digest no matter what the bit length of the input may be. Amazon calls this hash value the signature because the value functions like a digital signature, although technically a digital signature is an *encrypted* message digest. What Amazon calls the signature is not encrypted but is encoded in base64.

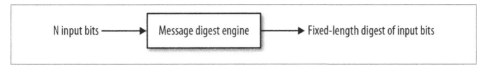

*Figure 6-1. A message digest*

- The Amazon signature is added to the request in the HTTP 1.1 `Authorization` header (or the query string).
- Upon receipt of the request, the Amazon S3 first validates the Amazon signature and then honors the request only if the validation succeeds. Essentially this is the same validation process used in the *predictionsSOAP* example of Chapter 5.

What prevents a client's request to Amazon S3 from being intercepted and the value of its `Authorization` header, the Amazon authentication signature, from being pirated? Amazon assumes that the request is sent over the secure communications channel that HTTPS (HyperText Transport Protocol Secure) provides. HTTPS is HTTP with an added security layer. Netscape did the original work in the design and implementation of this security layer and called it SSL. The IETF (International Engineering Task Force) has taken over SSL and renamed it TLS (Transport Layer Security). Although SSL and TLS differ in version numbers and in some technical details, they will be treated as basically the same here. In any case, it is common to use SSL, TLS, and SSL/TLS interchangeably.

Java has various packages that support SSL/TLS in general and HTTPS in particular. The JSSE (Java Secure Sockets Extension) API, which covers the packages `javax.net` and `javax.net.ssl`, has been part of core Java since JDK 1.4. Of interest here is that higher levels of security, such as user authentication, usually require wire-level security of the kind that HTTPS provides. Accordingly, the discussion of web services security begins with HTTPS and the wire-level security that this protocol provides.

## HTTPS Basics

HTTPS is easily the most popular among the secure versions of HTTP. HTTPS provides three critical security services over and above the transport services that HTTP provides. The following is a summary of the three (see Figure 6-2). In the figure, Alice needs to send a secret message to Bob. Eve, however, may be eavesdropping. Eve may try to dupe Alice and Bob into believing that they are communicating with one another when, in fact, each is communicating instead with Eve. This scenario is known as the MITM (Man in the Middle) attack. For secure communications, Alice and Bob need these three services:

*Peer authentication*

Alice needs Bob to authenticate himself so that she is sure about who is on the receiving end before she sends the secret message. Bob, too, needs Alice to authenticate herself so that he knows that the secret message is from her rather than an impostor such as Eve. This step also is described as *mutual authentication* or *mutual challenge*.

*Confidentiality*

Once Alice and Bob have authenticated each other, Alice needs to encrypt the secret message in such a way that only Bob can decrypt it. Even if Eve intercepts the encrypted message, Eve should not be able to decrypt the message, because doing so requires enormous computational power or incredibly good luck.

*Integrity*

The message that Alice sends should be identical to the one that Bob receives. If not, an error condition should be raised. The received message might differ from the sent one for various reasons; for instance, noise in the communications channel or deliberate tampering on Eve's part. Any difference between the sent and the received message should be detected.

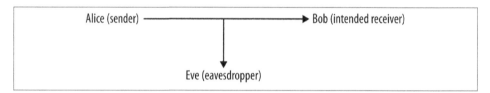

*Figure 6-2. A secret message from Bob to Alice despite Eve*

These features can be implemented in different ways. Before considering how HTTPS implements the three features, it will be useful to look briefly at data encryption and decryption because *confidentiality* is among the three services that HTTPS provides.

## Symmetric and Asymmetric Encryption/Decryption

Modern approaches to encryption follow two different approaches: symmetric and asymmetric. Under either approach, the bits to be encrypted (*plain bits*) are one input to an encryption engine. An encryption key is the other input (see Figure 6-3).

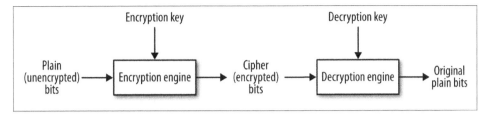

*Figure 6-3. Basic encryption and decryption*

The encrypted bits are the *cipher bits*. If the input bits represent text, then they are the *plaintext* and the output bits are the *ciphertext*. The cipher bits are one input to the decryption engine; a decryption key is the other input. The decryption produces the original plain bits. In the symmetric approach, the *same* key—called the *secret* or *single* key—is used to encrypt and decrypt (see Figure 6-4). The symmetric approach has the advantage of being relatively fast but the disadvantage of what is known as the *key distribution problem*. How is the secret key itself to be distributed to the sender and the receiver?

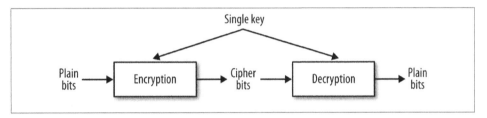

*Figure 6-4. Single key encryption and decryption*

In the asymmetric approach, the starting point is a *key pair*, which consists of a *private key* and a *public key*. As the names suggest, the private key should not be distributed but, rather, safeguarded by whoever generated the key pair. The public key can be distributed freely and publicly. If message bits are encrypted with the public key, they can be decrypted only with the private key—and vice versa. Figure 6-5 illustrates. The asymmetric approach solves the key distribution problem, but asymmetric encryption and decryption are roughly a thousand times slower than their symmetric counterparts.

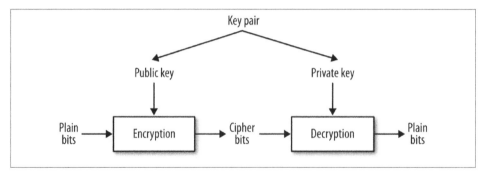

*Figure 6-5. Public key encryption and decryption*

The public key approach solves the confidentiality problem for Alice and Bob. If Alice encrypts the message with the public key from Bob's key pair, and Bob has the only copy of the private key from this pair, then only Bob can decrypt the message. Even if Eve intercepts Alice's message, she cannot decrypt the message with Bob's public key.

## How HTTPS Provides the Three Security Services

Of the three required security services—peer authentication, confidentiality, and integrity—the last is the least complicated. The message sent over HTTPS includes a digest value, which the receiver recomputes. If the sent digest value differs from the digest value that the receiver computes, then the message was altered during transmission, either by accident or design. If the sent digest value itself is altered during transmission, this likewise counts as integrity failure.

HTTPS handles peer authentication through the exchange of digital certificates. In many cases, however, it is only the client that challenges the server. Consider a typical website application in which a shopper finalizes an order for the contents of his shopping cart by submitting a credit card number to the vendor. Here is a summary of what typically happens when the client-side browser and the web server negotiate to set up an HTTPS connection:

- The customer's browser challenges the vendor's web server to authenticate itself, and the server responds by sending one or more digital certificates to the browser.

- The browser checks the web server's digital certificates against the browser's *truststore*, which is a database of digital certificates that the browser trusts. The browser's validation of an incoming certificate can be and, for practical reasons, typically is indirect. For example, suppose that the browser receives a certificate from Amazon but does not have an Amazon certificate in its truststore. Suppose further that the Amazon certificate contains a vouching signature from VeriSign, a well-known certificate authority (CA). If the browser's truststore has a VeriSign certificate, then the browser can use the VeriSign certificate to validate the VeriSign signature on the Amazon certificate.

How is the VeriSign certificate to be verified? For the verification process to terminate, at least one certificate in the chain must be taken as verified. For now, the point of interest is that the browser's truststore is its repository of certificates that are used to verify incoming certificates. If the browser cannot validate an incoming certificate against its truststore, then the browser typically asks the human user whether the certificate should be trusted this time only or permanently. If the user selects *permanently*, the browser adds the certificate to its truststore.

- The web server typically does *not* challenge the browser. For one thing, the website is interested in the shopper's credit card rather than in the identity of the user agent (in this case, the browser) that the shopper happens to be using. In web services as opposed to websites, two-way or peer authentication is common.

The usually one-sided authentication challenge at play in websites, with the client challenging the server but not the other way around, shows up in Tomcat's configuration file, *TOMCAT_HOME/conf/server.xml*. Here is the entry for HTTPS:

```
<Connector port="8443" protocol="HTTP/1.1" SSLEnabled="true"
           maxThreads="150" scheme="https" secure="true"
           clientAuth="false"    ❶
           sslProtocol="TLS"/>
```

The `clientAuth` attribute is set to `false` (line 1), thereby indicating that Tomcat does not challenge the client. If the `clientAuth` attribute were set to `true`, then Tomcat would challenge the client's user agent; a setting of `true` might be of interest for web services in particular. In this configuration file, there is no setting for a `serverAuth` because the default client behavior is to challenge the server.

## The HTTPS Handshake

For authentication and confidentiality, HTTPS relies on digital certificates, which are widely used in public key cryptography precisely because the exchange of secret keys is so difficult among many users. Here is a summary of how HTTPS authentication is intertwined with HTTPS confidentiality. The process is sometimes described as the *handshake* between client and server that culminates in a secure network connection. In this scenario, the client might be a browser or an application functioning as a web service client. For convenience, the term *web server* covers both a standard website server such as Tomcat or a full-bodied Java Application Server such as Oracle WebLogic, GlassFish, JBoss, or WebSphere:

- The client challenges the web server, which sends one or more digital certificates as authentication. Modern digital certificates usually have the X.509 format. The current X.509 version is named v3.

- An X.509 certificate is a *public key certificate* that serves as an *identity certificate* by binding the public key from a key pair to an identity such as a person (for instance, Alice) or an organization (for instance, Bob's employer). The certificate contains the digital signature of a CA such as VeriSign, although certificates can be self-signed for testing purposes. In signing a digital certificate, a CA endorses the certificate and thereby verifies that the certificate's public key is bound to a particular identity. For instance, VeriSign signs Alice's certificate and thereby verifies that the certificate's public key belongs to Alice's key pair.

- The client can determine whether to accept the server's digital certificates by checking these against its truststore. The check can be direct or indirect. In a direct check, the received digital certificate is checked against a copy in the truststore. In an indirect check, the CA's digital signature, which occurs as part of the certificate and vouches for its legitimacy, needs to be verified; this verification, in turn, requires a digital certificate from the CA.

- The server has the option of challenging the client. For a website, such a challenge is unusual; for a web service, such a challenge can serve as a way of identifying and authenticating the web service client.

- Once the challenge phase is over, the client begins the process of generating a secret key. The process begins with the client's generation of a *pre-master secret*, a string that is shared with the server. The pre-master is then used on each side to generate the same *master* secret key, which is used to encrypt and decrypt the traffic between the client and the server. At issue here is how the pre-master secret is sent securely from the client to the server.

- In a common scenario, the client encrypts a 48-bit pre-master secret with the server's public key, available on the server's digital certificate downloaded during the peer authentication phase. The encrypted pre-master secret is sent to the server, which decrypts the secret. If everything is still in order, each side confirms that encryption of traffic between them is to begin. The *public key/private key* pair is thus critical in solving the key distribution problem for secret keys.

- At any point, either the client or the server may insist on starting the entire process all over again. For example, if either Alice or Bob suspects that Eve is up to no good, either Alice or Bob can restart the handshake process.

A secret key is used to encrypt and decrypt traffic for several reasons. First, symmetric encryption has relatively high performance. Second, if the server does not challenge the client, then the server does not have the client's public key to encrypt messages to the client. The server cannot encrypt messages with its own private key, as any receiver (for instance, Eve) with access to the server's public key then could decrypt the message. Finally, encrypting and decrypting with two separate key pairs is inherently trickier—and significantly slower—than using a shared secret key.

The primary challenge is to get the pre-master secret securely from the client to the server, and the server's public key, available to the client in the server's digital certificate after the mutual challenge phase, fits the bill perfectly. The master secret key is generated only after the client and the server have agreed upon which *cipher suite*, or set of cryptographic algorithms, should be used. A cipher suite, including a key-pair algorithm and a hash algorithm, will be examined through a code example shortly.

Although digital certificates now play a dominant role in mutual challenge scenarios, they are not the only game in town. For example, SRP (Secure Remote Protocol) implements mutual challenge but without digital certificates. For more on SRP, see *srp.stanford.edu*.

## The HttpsURLConnection Class

It is time to flesh out these architectural sketches with a code example. The class HttpsURLConnection, which extends the HttpURLConnection class, supports HTTPS connections. The GoogleClient application (see Example 6-1) uses this class to issue a GET request under HTTPS against Google's home site. Note that the port number in the URL is 443 (line 1), the standard port for HTTPS connections.

*Example 6-1. A client that makes an HTTPS connection to Google*

```java
import java.net.URL;
import javax.net.ssl.HttpsURLConnection;
import java.net.MalformedURLException;
import java.security.cert.Certificate;
import java.io.IOException;
import java.io.BufferedReader;
import java.io.InputStreamReader;

public class GoogleClient {
    private static final String endpoint = "https://www.google.com:443/";        ❶

    // Send a GET request and print the response status code.
    public static void main(String[ ] args) {
        new GoogleClient().doIt();
    }
    private void doIt() {
        try {
            URL url = new URL(endpoint);
            HttpsURLConnection conn = (HttpsURLConnection) url.openConnection();   ❷
            conn.setDoInput(true);
            conn.setRequestMethod("GET");                                          ❸
            conn.connect();
            dumpDetails(conn);
        }
        catch(MalformedURLException e) { System.err.println(e); }
        catch(IOException e) { System.err.println(e); }
    }
```

```java
private void dumpDetails(HttpsURLConnection conn) {
    try {
        print("Status code:  " + conn.getResponseCode());              ❹
        print("Cipher suite: " + conn.getCipherSuite());               ❺
        Certificate[ ] certs = conn.getServerCertificates();           ❻
        for (Certificate cert : certs) {
            print("\tCert. type: " + cert.getType());
            print("\tHash code:  " + cert.hashCode());                 ❼
            print("\tAlgorithm:  " + cert.getPublicKey().getAlgorithm()); ❽
            print("\tFormat:     " + cert.getPublicKey().getFormat());  ❾
            print("");
        }
    }
    catch(Exception e) { System.err.println(e); }
}
private void print(Object s) { System.out.println(s); }
}
```

The endpoint URL for an HTTPS connection to Google begins with https (known in HTTP as the *scheme*), and the port number, 443, is the standard one for HTTPS connections. Modern web servers typically accept HTTP connections on port 80 and HTTPS connections on port 443, although these numbers are configurable. For example, Tomcat by default listens on port 8080 for HTTP connections and on port 8443 for HTTPS connections. The HTTPS URL for Google is line 1 in the code listing.

The GoogleClient next opens an HTTPS connection (line 2) and prepares for a GET request against Google (line 3). Once the connection is made, the application invokes dumpDetails to print information about the secure connection: the type of certificates returned from Google during the challenge, the *hash code* or *fingerprint* that identifies each certificate, the algorithm used to generate the key pair, and the format of the certificate (lines 5 through 9 in the code listing). The dumpDetails method also prints the response code, the by now familiar 200 that signals a successful GET request. On a sample run, the output from dumpDetails was:

```
Status code:  200
Cipher suite: TLS_ECDHE_RSA_WITH_RC4_128_SHA ❶
        Cert. type: X.509
        Hash code:  12584213
        Algorithm:  RSA
        Format:     X.509

        Cert. type: X.509
        Hash code:  2815543
        Algorithm:  RSA
        Format:     X.509
```

Line 1 in the listing gives the cipher suite, a collection of information about the algorithms used in the initial handshake and in the encryption/decryption of messages exchanged after a successful handshake. Underscore characters separate the parts of the cipher suite. Here is a summary of the parts:

*TLS*

The Transport Layer Security, added to HTTP, yields HTTPS and thus accounts for the **S** in HTTPS.

*ECDHE*

The acronym stands for Elliptic Curve Diffie-Hellman Key Exchange, which is the algorithm that governs the handshake.

*RSA*

This is the *public key cryptography algorithm*, named after Rivest, Shamir, and Adleman, the former MIT professors who designed it. RSA is the most commonly used public key algorithm. It is used to encrypt the pre-master that is sent from the client to the server. Also, the public key on exchanged digital certificates comes from an RSA-generated key pair.

*RC4_128*

The *stream cipher algorithm*, which is used to encrypt and decrypt the bit traffic between client and server, has a key length of 128 bits. The R is for Rivest in RSA, and the C is for cipher. (Sometimes RC is said to be shorthand for *Ron's Code*, as Rivest's first name is Ron.) RC4 is the most commonly used stream cipher. RC4_128 is used to encrypt the data traffic once the handshake is completed.

*SHA*

The certificate's 160-bit identifying hash, also called its fingerprint, is generated with the Secure Hash Algorithm, officially officially known as a *cryptographic hash function*. There is a family of SHA algorithms but SHA-1, used here, is probably still the most widely used member of this family.

The Google web server sent two digital certificates during the mutual challenge phase. Each is an X.509 certificate generated with the RSA algorithm, and each of the SHA fingerprints is 160 bits in length. The format of each certificate follows the X.509 specification.

How does the `GoogleClient` verify the two X.509 certificates the Google web server sends? There is nothing in the `GoogleClient` code to suggest certificate verification. The core Java JDK ships with a default truststore (*JAVA_HOME/jre/lib/security/ cacerts*). Because the `GoogleClient` opens an HTTPS connection to the Google web server, the Java runtime intervenes to handle the certificate verification, and because Google is such a standard website, the *cacerts* truststore has entries to verify the Google certificates. What about HTTPS connections to less popular and prominent sites? Java's security API makes it possible to disable peer authentication so that a client such as the `GoogleClient` can take over certificate verification and make its own decisions about what to accept and reject. The `GoogleTrustingClient` (see Example 6-2) revises the

GoogleClient and shows how programmatic verification can be done—or bypassed altogether.

*Example 6-2. The GoogleTrustingClient, which turns off certificate verification*

```
import java.net.URL;
import java.security.SecureRandom;
import java.security.cert.X509Certificate;
import javax.net.ssl.SSLContext;
import javax.net.ssl.HttpsURLConnection;
import javax.net.ssl.TrustManager;
import javax.net.ssl.X509TrustManager;
import java.net.MalformedURLException;
import java.security.cert.Certificate;
import java.io.IOException;
import java.io.BufferedReader;
import java.io.InputStreamReader;

class GoogleTrustingClient {
    private static final String endpoint = "https://www.google.com:443/";

    public static void main(String[ ] args) {
        new GoogleTrustingClient().doIt();
    }
    private void doIt() {
        try {
            // Configure the HttpsURLConnection so that it does not
            // check certificates.
            SSLContext sslCtx = SSLContext.getInstance("TLS");            ❶
            TrustManager[ ] trustMgr = getTrustMgr();                     ❷
            sslCtx.init(null,                // key manager               ❸
                    trustMgr,                // trust manager             ❹
                    new SecureRandom()); // random number generator       ❺
            HttpsURLConnection.setDefaultSSLSocketFactory(
                            sslCtx.getSocketFactory());                  ❻

            URL url = new URL(endpoint);
            HttpsURLConnection conn = (HttpsURLConnection) url.openConnection();
            conn.setDoInput(true);
            conn.setRequestMethod("GET");
            conn.connect();
            dumpDetails(conn);
        }
        catch(MalformedURLException e) { System.err.println(e); }
        catch(IOException e) { System.err.println(e); }
        catch(Exception e) { System.err.println(e); }
    }
    private TrustManager[ ] getTrustMgr() {                               ❼
        // No exceptions thrown in any of the methods.
        TrustManager[ ] certs = new TrustManager[ ] {
            new X509TrustManager() {
                public X509Certificate[ ] getAcceptedIssuers() {         ❽
```

```
                return null;
            }
            public void checkClientTrusted(X509Certificate[ ] certs,      ❾
                                            String type) { }
            public void checkServerTrusted(X509Certificate[ ] certs,      ❿
                                            String type) { }
        }
    };
    return certs;
}
private void dumpDetails(HttpsURLConnection conn) {
    try {
        print("Status code:  " + conn.getResponseCode());
        print("Cipher suite: " + conn.getCipherSuite());
        Certificate[ ] certs = conn.getServerCertificates();
        for (Certificate cert : certs) {
            print("\tCert. type: " + cert.getType());
            print("\tHash code:  " + cert.hashCode());
            print("\tAlgorithm:  " + cert.getPublicKey().getAlgorithm());
            print("\tFormat:     " + cert.getPublicKey().getFormat());
            print("");
        }
    }
    catch(Exception e) { System.err.println(e); }
}
private void print(String s) { System.out.println(s); }
}
```

The GoogleTrustingClient first gets an instance of an SSLContext (line 1) and then invokes getTrustManager (line 2) to get a TrustManager[ ], an array of managers for the in-memory truststore. A TrustManager defines three methods:

getAcceptedIssuers
> This method (line 8) returns an array of X509Certificate instances. In this case, null is returned, which is explained shortly.

checkClientTrusted
> This method (line 9) expects, as one argument, an array of X509Certificate instances and, as a second argument, a String that describes the certificate's type (for instance, X509). The method has void as the return type.

checkServerTrusted
> This method (line 10) expects the same arguments as checkClientTrusted.

Each method is minimally defined but—and this is the critical point—no method throws a CertificateException, which means that the TrustManager effectively accepts *all* certificates. The TrustManager array returned from the getTrustManager method (line 7) has a single member, and this member is all-trusting. The result is that GoogleTrustingClient effectively turns off certificate verification, a move that can be useful during development. In production, the `TrustManager` could implement whatever certificate-inspection logic is appropriate.

The security details about HTTPS can be examined concretely with a lightweight HTTPS server, introduced in the next section. The `Endpoint` utility class, used in earlier chapters to publish both REST-style and SOAP-based services, does not support HTTPS connections. The `Endpoint` publisher is built with the `HttpServer` class, which ships with core Java. The next section uses the related class `HttpsServer` to clarify, with code, how HTTPS works.

# A Very Lightweight HTTPS Server and Client

An HTTPS server needs two stores for digital certificates:

*keystore*
> A *keystore* contains digital certificates, including the certificates that an HTTPS server sends to clients during the *peer authentication* phase of the HTTPS handshake. When the server is challenged to establish its identity, the server can send one or more certificates for its keystore to the challenger. If peer authentication is truly mutual, then a client needs a keystore with the client's own digital certificates, which can be sent to the server for verification.

*truststore*
> A truststore is a keystore with a specified function: the truststore stores trusted certificates used to verify other certificates. When a host, server or client, receives a certificate to be verified, this received certificate can be compared against truststore entries. If the truststore does not contain such a certificate, the truststore may contain at least a certificate from a CA such as VeriSign, whose digital signature is on the received certificate.

Although the keystore and the truststore differ in core purpose (see Figure 6-6), one and the same file can function as both keystore and truststore, and, in development, this option is attractively simple.

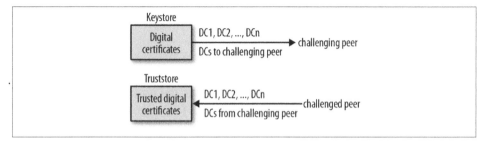

*Figure 6-6. A depiction of how a keystore and a truststore function*

In fleshing out these and related details about HTTPS security, the HttpsPublisher (see Example 6-3) code may be useful.

*Example 6-3. The lightweight HttpsPublisher*

```
import java.net.InetSocketAddress;
import javax.net.ssl.SSLContext;
import javax.net.ssl.SSLParameters;
import javax.net.ssl.SSLEngine;
import javax.net.ssl.TrustManager;
import javax.net.ssl.X509TrustManager;
import java.security.cert.X509Certificate;
import java.security.KeyStore;
import javax.net.ssl.KeyManagerFactory;
import javax.net.ssl.TrustManagerFactory;
import java.io.FileInputStream;
import javax.xml.ws.http.HTTPException;
import java.io.OutputStream;
import java.io.InputStream;
import java.security.SecureRandom;
import com.sun.net.httpserver.HttpHandler;
import com.sun.net.httpserver.HttpsServer;
import com.sun.net.httpserver.HttpsConfigurator;
import com.sun.net.httpserver.HttpExchange;
import com.sun.net.httpserver.HttpsParameters;
import service.IService;

public class HttpsPublisher {
    private static final int defaultPort = 3443;
    private static final int backlog = 12;
    private static final String keystore = "test.keystore";
    private IService serviceInstance;                                       ❶

    public static void main(String[ ] args) {
        if (args.length < 2) {
            System.err.println("Usage: java HttpsPublisher <service> <path>");
            return;
        }
        // % java HttpsPublisher myService.Service /service
        new HttpsPublisher().init(args[0],  // service name
                                  args[1]); // URI
    }
    private void init(String serviceName, String uri) {
        try {
            Class serviceClass = Class.forName(serviceName);                ❷
            serviceInstance = (IService) serviceClass.newInstance();        ❸
        }
        catch(Exception e) { throw new RuntimeException(e); }
        HttpsServer server = getHttpsServer(uri, defaultPort);
        if (server != null) {
            server.createContext(uri);                                      ❹
            System.out.println("Server listening on port " + defaultPort);
```

```
                    server.start();                                                ⑤
                }
                else
                    throw new RuntimeException("Cannot create server instance.");
            }
            private HttpsServer getHttpsServer(String uri, int port) {
                HttpsServer server = null;
                try {
                    InetSocketAddress inet = new InetSocketAddress(port);
                    server = HttpsServer.create(inet, backlog);
                    SSLContext sslCtx = SSLContext.getInstance("TLS");
                    // password for keystore
                    char[ ] password = "qubits".toCharArray();
                    KeyStore ks = KeyStore.getInstance("JKS");
                    FileInputStream fis = new FileInputStream(keystore);
                    ks.load(fis, password);
                    KeyManagerFactory kmf = KeyManagerFactory.getInstance("SunX509");
                    kmf.init(ks, password);
                    TrustManagerFactory tmf = TrustManagerFactory.getInstance("SunX509");
                    tmf.init(ks); // same as keystore
                    sslCtx.init(kmf.getKeyManagers(),
                                tmf.getTrustManagers(),
                                new SecureRandom());
                    // Create SSL engine and configure HTTPS to use it.
                    final SSLEngine eng = sslCtx.createSSLEngine();
                    server.setHttpsConfigurator(new HttpsConfigurator(sslCtx) {
                            public void configure(HttpsParameters parms) {
                                parms.setCipherSuites(eng.getEnabledCipherSuites());
                                parms.setProtocols(eng.getEnabledProtocols());
                            }
                        });
                    server.setExecutor(null); // use default, hence single-threaded
                    server.createContext(uri, new MyHttpsHandler(this.serviceInstance));
                }
                catch(Exception e) { throw new RuntimeException(e); }
                return server;
            }
        }
}
// The handle method is called on a particular request context,
// in this case on any request to the server that ends with /<uri>.
class MyHttpsHandler implements HttpHandler {
    private IService service;

    public MyHttpsHandler(IService service) {
        this.service = service;
    }
    public void handle(HttpExchange ex) {
        // Implement a simple routing table.
        String verb = ex.getRequestMethod().toUpperCase();
        if (verb.equals("GET"))         service.doGet(ex);
        else if (verb.equals("POST"))   service.doPost(ex);
        else if (verb.equals("PUT"))    service.doPut(ex);
```

```
        else if (verb.equals("DELETE")) service.doDelete(ex);
        else throw new HTTPException(405);
    }
}
```

The HttpsPublisher can be started with a command such as:

```
% java HttpsPublisher service.TestService /test
```

The first command-line argument, service.TestService (see Example 6-4), is the fully qualified name of a RESTful service's implementation class; the second command-line argument, in this case /test, is the URI that identifies the service. Any service deployed with the HttpsPublisher must implement the IService interface (see Example 6-5), which means that the four CRUD methods doGet, doPost, doPut, and doDelete must be defined. The HttpsPublisher declares a reference of data type IService (line 1 in the listing) and then uses the Class.forName utility to load a service class such as TestService from the filesystem (line 2) and create an instance (line 3). The IServ ice interface thus allows the HttpPublisher to publish any service that implements the RESTful CRUD operations with the designated method names.

The HttpsPublisher sets the context for requests (line 4), which in this example means that a client must use the URI /test to hit the TestService. The publisher maintains a queue of up to backlog requests, currently set to 16, on the specified HTTPS port 3443. Finally, the start method is invoked on the HttpsServer instance (line 5), which starts the server for an indefinitely long run.

*Example 6-4. The TestService published with the HttpsPublisher*

```
package service;

import java.io.OutputStream;
import com.sun.net.httpserver.HttpExchange;

public class TestService implements IService {
    public void doGet(HttpExchange e) { respond2Client(e, "doGet"); }
    public void doPost(HttpExchange e) { respond2Client(e, "doPost"); }
    public void doPut(HttpExchange e) { respond2Client(e, "doPut"); }
    public void doDelete(HttpExchange e) { respond2Client(e, "doDelete"); }

    private void respond2Client(HttpExchange ex, String response) {
        try {
            ex.sendResponseHeaders(200, 0); // 0 == as many bytes as there are
            OutputStream out = ex.getResponseBody();
            out.write(response.getBytes());
            out.close(); // effectively ends session
        }
        catch(Exception e) { throw new RuntimeException(e); }
    }
}
```

*Example 6-5. The IService interface*

```
package service;
import com.sun.net.httpserver.HttpExchange;

public interface IService {
    public void doGet(HttpExchange e);
    public void doPost(HttpExchange e);
    public void doPut(HttpExchange e);
    public void doDelete(HttpExchange e);
}
```

Once the RESTful service class has been loaded, the HttpsServer begins the tricky security configuration. A client that opens an HTTPS connection to the HttpsServer is going to challenge this server to verify its identity, and the HttpsServer responds with a digital certificate. The core Java JDK comes with a *keytool* utility that can be used to create a *self-signed* rather than a CA-certified digital certificate. For development, the self-signed digital certificate is good enough; for production, a CA-certified digital certificate would be needed. The command:

```
% keytool -genkey -keyalg RSA -keystore test.keystore
```

eventually creates the file *test.keystore*, which contains an X.509 digital certificate generated using the RSA algorithm. This file is the keystore. The *keytool* utility is interactive, prompting the user with questions that must be answered. The first such question is about a password to protect access to the keystore. In this case, the password is *qubits*. For the current example, the keystore file *test.keystore* (the name is arbitrary) performs various functions:

- The file acts as a regular keystore that contains the digital certificate that the HttpsPublisher sends to any challenger, in this case the HttpsClient, which is introduced shortly.

- The file doubles as the HttpsPublisher truststore and as the HttpsClient truststore. Accordingly, the fix is in. When the HttpsPublisher sends the one and only digital certificate in the keystore *test.keystore*, the HttpsClient verifies this digital certificate by checking it against the very same keystore—but a keystore now functioning as a truststore. Were the HttpsPublisher to challenge the HttpsClient, the client would send the same digital certificate as its identity voucher—and the HttpsPublisher would verify this digital certificate against itself, in effect.

Using the keystore for multiple purposes simplifies the setup and keeps the focus on the technical coding details. In a production environment, of course, there would be four keystores involved in this scenario: the HttpsPublisher would have a keystore with its certificates and a truststore with the certificates that it trusts; the same would hold for the HttpsClient.

The `HttpsPublisher` reads into memory the digital certificate stored in the file named *test.keystore*. Here is a block of initialization code:

```
SSLContext sslCtx = SSLContext.getInstance("TLS");                    ❶
char[ ] password = "qubits".toCharArray();                           ❷
KeyStore ks = KeyStore.getInstance("JKS");
FileInputStream fis = new FileInputStream(keystore);
ks.load(fis, password);                                              ❸
KeyManagerFactory kmf = KeyManagerFactory.getInstance("SunX509");
kmf.init(ks, password);                                              ❹
TrustManagerFactory tmf = TrustManagerFactory.getInstance("SunX509");
tmf.init(ks); // same as keystore
sslCtx.init(kmf.getKeyManagers(),                                    ❺
            tmf.getTrustManagers(),
            new SecureRandom());
final SSLEngine eng = sslCtx.createSSLEngine();
server.setHttpsConfigurator(new HttpsConfigurator(sslCtx) {
    public void configure(HttpsParameters parms) {
        parms.setCipherSuites(eng.getEnabledCipherSuites());        ❻
        parms.setProtocols(eng.getEnabledProtocols());              ❼
    }});
server.setExecutor(null); // use default, hence single-threaded     ❽
server.createContext(uri, new MyHttpsHandler(this.serviceInstance)); ❾
```

The `SSLContext` (line 1) is the central data structure, and this context supports secure (that is, TLS-based) communications from clients to the `HttpsPublisher`. After the password bytes are stored in an array (line 2), the contents of the keystore file, *test.keystore*, are loaded into memory (line 3) and a `KeyManagerFactory` is initialized with the contents of this keystore file (line 4). There is now an in-memory version of the file *test.keystore*. The `TrustStoreFactory` (line 5) is initialized with the contents of the very same keystore file. At this point, the `SSLContext` is initialized with the *key managers* of the keystore file and the *trust managers* of the truststore file, which are the same file.

The next security initialization steps involve setting the appropriate cipher suites (line 6), which are used during the handshake negotiations with a client. The security protocols that are available to the server are likewise part of the initialization (line 7). For demonstration purposes, the `HttpsPublisher` remains single-threaded, which explains the `null` in line 8. To make the publisher multithreaded, a non-`null` value for the `Executor` (that is, the thread manager) would be used. Finally, the HTTPS server specifies a *handler* to handle requests against the URI, in this case `/test` (line 9).

The setup code is tricky, but its gist can be summarized as follows:

- An `SSLContext` data structure is populated with security information, in particular the keystore and truststore contents that the `HttpsPublisher` needs to conduct the handshake with a prospective client.

- The HttpsPublisher also uses the SSLContext to create an SSLEngine, which manages the cipher suites and related security protocols.

When the setup is complete, the HttpsPublisher is ready to accept HTTPS connections from potential clients. Client requests are dispatched to an instance of the class My HttpsHandler:

```
server.createContext(uri, new MyHttpsHandler(this.serviceInstance));
```

The constructor call to MyHttpsHandler has, as its single argument, a reference to the IService instance so that GET requests can be forwarded to the serviceInstance method doGet, POST requests to doPost, and so on. The MyHttpsHandler class implements the HttpHandler interface, which has a single method: handle. Here is the implementation:

```
public void handle(HttpExchange ex) {
    String verb = ex.getRequestMethod().toUpperCase();
    if (verb.equals("GET"))        service.doGet(ex);
    else if (verb.equals("POST"))  service.doPost(ex);
    else if (verb.equals("PUT"))   service.doPut(ex);
    else if (verb.equals("DELETE")) service.doDelete(ex);
    else throw new HTTPException(405); // bad verb
}
```

The flow of control (see Figure 6-7) is straightforward: a request targeted at the URI /test goes to the MyHttpsHandler instance, which implements the handle method. The handle method dispatches GET requests to the service's doGet method, POST requests to the service's doPost method, and so on. The critical point is that the communications between the HttpsPublisher and the client are over a secure HTTPS channel.

*Figure 6-7. The routing in the HttpsPublisher*

In the current implementation, the TestService instance encapsulates minimalist versions of *doGet*, *doPost*, *doPut*, and *doDelete* operations. The point of interest is the security configuration, not the actual behavior of the RESTful service. Each CRUD operation returns a string confirming that the operation has been invoked. For HTTPS requests with bodies (that is, POST and PUT), the HttpsClient (see Example 6-6) sends a short string that the service operations ignore.

*Example 6-6. The sample* `HttpsClient` *against the* `TestService`

```java
import java.net.URL;
import javax.net.ssl.HttpsURLConnection;
import javax.net.ssl.SSLContext;
import java.security.KeyStore;
import javax.net.ssl.TrustManagerFactory;
import javax.net.ssl.X509TrustManager;
import javax.net.ssl.HostnameVerifier;
import javax.net.ssl.SSLSession;
import java.security.cert.X509Certificate;
import java.io.FileInputStream;
import java.io.InputStream;
import java.io.OutputStream;
import java.security.SecureRandom;

public class HttpsClient {
    private static final String endpoint = "https://localhost:3443/test/";
    private static final String truststore = "test.keystore";

    public static void main(String[ ] args) {
        new HttpsClient().runTests();
    }
    private void runTests() {
        try {
            SSLContext sslCtx = SSLContext.getInstance("TLS");
            // password for truststore (same as server's keystore)
            char[ ] password = "qubits".toCharArray();
            KeyStore ks = KeyStore.getInstance("JKS");
            FileInputStream fis = new FileInputStream(truststore);
            ks.load(fis, password);
            TrustManagerFactory tmf = TrustManagerFactory.getInstance("SunX509");
            tmf.init(ks); // same as keystore
            sslCtx.init(null,                     // not needed, not challenged
                        tmf.getTrustManagers(),
                        null);                    // use default: SecureRandom
            HttpsURLConnection.setDefaultSSLSocketFactory(sslCtx.getSocketFactory());
            URL url = new URL(endpoint);
            HttpsURLConnection conn = getConnection(url, "GET");
            getTest(conn);
            conn = getConnection(url, "POST");
            postTest(conn);
            conn = getConnection(url, "PUT");
            putTest(conn);
            conn = getConnection(url, "DELETE");
            deleteTest(conn);
        }
        catch(Exception e) { throw new RuntimeException(e); }
    }
    private HttpsURLConnection getConnection(URL url, String verb) {
        try {
            HttpsURLConnection conn = (HttpsURLConnection) url.openConnection();
            conn.setDoInput(true);
```

```
        conn.setDoOutput(true);
        conn.setRequestMethod(verb);
        // Guard against "bad hostname" errors during handshake.
        conn.setHostnameVerifier(new HostnameVerifier() {
                public boolean verify(String host, SSLSession session) {
                    return host.equals("localhost"); // for development
                }
            });
        return conn;
    }
    catch(Exception e) { throw new RuntimeException(e); }
}
private void getTest(HttpsURLConnection conn) {              ❶
    try {
        conn.connect();
        readResponse("GET request: ", conn);
        conn.disconnect();
    }
    catch(Exception e) { throw new RuntimeException(e); }
}
private void postTest(HttpsURLConnection conn) {            ❷
    try {
        conn.connect();
        writeBody(conn);
        readResponse("POST request: ", conn);
        conn.disconnect();
    }
    catch(Exception e) { throw new RuntimeException(e); }
}
private void putTest(HttpsURLConnection conn) {             ❸
    try {
        conn.connect();
        writeBody(conn);
        readResponse("PUT request: ", conn);
        conn.disconnect();
    }
    catch(Exception e) { throw new RuntimeException(e); }
}
private void deleteTest(HttpsURLConnection conn) {          ❹
    try {
        conn.connect();
        readResponse("PUT request: ", conn);
        conn.disconnect();
    }
    catch(Exception e) { throw new RuntimeException(e); }
}
private void writeBody(HttpsURLConnection conn) {
    try {
        OutputStream out = conn.getOutputStream();
        out.write("foo bar baz".getBytes()); // anything will do
        out.flush();
    }
```

```
        catch(Exception e) { throw new RuntimeException(e); }
    }
    private void readResponse(String msg, HttpsURLConnection conn) {
        try {
            byte[ ] buffer = new byte[512]; // plenty for testing
            InputStream in = conn.getInputStream();
            in.read(buffer);
            System.out.println(msg + new String(buffer));
        }
        catch(Exception e) { throw new RuntimeException(e); }
    }
}
```

The HttpsClient (see Example 6-6) makes requests against the four CRUD operations (lines 1, 2, 3, and 4) in the TestService published with the HttpsPublisher. This client is similar in structure to the GoogleTrustingClient examined earlier except that the HttpsClient does demand a digital certificate from the HttpsPublisher and does verify this certificate against a truststore. As noted earlier, the client's truststore is the same file, *test.keystore*, as the server's keystore; hence, the verification is guaranteed to succeed. The HttpsClient reads the truststore data into memory and uses these data to initialize the all-important SSLContext. Here is the relevant code:

```
FileInputStream fis = new FileInputStream(truststore);
ks.load(fis, password);
TrustManagerFactory tmf = TrustManagerFactory.getInstance("SunX509");
tmf.init(ks); // same as keystore
sslCtx.init(null, // not needed, not challenged   ❶
            tmf.getTrustManagers(),
            new SecureRandom());
```

In the call to init (line 1), the first argument is null, which represents the keystore managers. The assumption is that the HttpsPublisher will not challenge the HttpsClient, which therefore does not need a keystore for the handshake. Were mutual challenge in operation, then the HttpsClient setup would be the same, with respect to the keystore and the truststore, as in the HttpsPublisher.

Of course, a non-Java client also can connect over HTTPS to the HttpsPublisher. As proof of concept, here is a very short Perl client that connects but does not bother to verify the digital certificates that the HttpsPublisher sends to the client:

```
use Net::SSLeay qw(get_https);
my ($type, $start_line, $misc, $extra) = get_https('localhost', 3443, '/test');
print "Type/value:  $type\n";
print "Start line:  $start_line\n";
print "Misc:        $misc => $extra\n";
```

The output from a sample run was:

```
Type/value:   doGet
Start line:   HTTP/1.1 200 OK
Misc:         CONNECTION => close
```

Changing from HTTP to HTTPS transport does not imperil the language neutrality and interoperability of web services—assuming, of course, that the languages used on client side and the service side include HTTPS libraries, as modern languages usually do.

# HTTPS in a Production-Grade Web Server

The HttpsPublisher is simple enough in structure to illustrate the basics of wire-level security. Among the several reasons for going with a production-grade web server such as Tomcat or Jetty is that these servers provide such good support for HTTPS, at the application and at the administrative level. Although these web servers provide first-rate HTTPS support, they do require setup comparable to that illustrated with the HttpsPublisher. This section focuses on Tomcat.

Tomcat does not ship with a keystore of digital certificates and, accordingly, does not enable HTTPS by default. The service must be turned on by editing the configuration file *TOMCAT_HOME/conf/server.xml*, with details provided shortly. The same keystore file used in the HttpsPublisher example, *test.keystore*, could be re-used for Tomcat. A modern browser connecting over HTTPS to Tomcat should complain that the digital certificate in *test.keystore* is self-signed and, therefore, worthless as a security credential. In production, a keystore with commercial-grade keystore digital certificates would be needed. Yet the point of immediate interest is that Tomcat does require the programmer to jump through a few hoops in order to switch from an HTTP-accessible to an HTTPS-accessible service. There are only three such hoops:

- HTTPS connections must be enabled in Tomcat by editing the *server.xml* file. Details follow shortly.

- A keystore must be made available so that Tomcat can perform the handshake with potential clients and afterwards support the encryption and decryption of exchanged messages.

- The configuration file *web.xml* must turn on HTTPS support for the website or web service. No change is required to the site or service code, however.

The first two changes are covered in "Setting Up Tomcat for HTTPS Support" on page 255.

---

# Setting Up Tomcat for HTTPS Support

The primary configuration file for Tomcat is *TOMCAT_HOME/conf/server.xml*. If this file is edited, Tomcat must be restarted in order for the changes to take effect. The file contains several elements tagged `Connector`. For example, here is the entry for the HTTP connector:

```
<Connector executor="tomcatThreadPool"
           port="8080" protocol="HTTP/1.1"
           connectionTimeout="20000"
           redirectPort="8443" />
```

The Tomcat port of HTTP connection is 8080 but this could be changed to, for instance, port 80. The last attribute in this XML element has `redirectPort` as its key and 8433 as its value. Suppose that a website or web service requires HTTPS access but that a client tries to hit the site or service using HTTP. Tomcat then counters with an *HTTP redirect*, instructing the client (for instance, a browser in the case of a website) to redirect to port 8443, the port at which Tomcat awaits HTTPS connections. Tomcat, however, is not yet configured for HTTPS.

The `Connector` element for HTTPS is commented out in *server.xml*:

```
<!--
<Connector port="8443" protocol="HTTP/1.1" SSLEnabled="true"
           maxThreads="150" scheme="https" secure="true"
           clientAuth="false" sslProtocol="TLS" />
-->
```

After removing the comment delimiters and restarting Tomcat, HTTPS should be enabled.

One further change is in order. Tomcat needs access to a keystore. The *test.keystore* from the `HttpsPublisher` example could be used, of course, or a fresh keystore could be created. In any case, the recommended change is to have the HTTPS `Connector` element point explicitly to this file:

```
<Connector port="8443" protocol="HTTP/1.1" SSLEnabled="true"
           maxThreads="150" scheme="https" secure="true"
           clientAuth="false" sslProtocol="TLS"
           keystoreFile="${user.home}/tcKeystore.keystore"    ❶
           keystorePass="qubits"/>                            ❷
```

Line 1 is the change, with the keystore file *tcKeystore.keystore* stored in my home directory with the password *qubits* (line 2). The keystore file can be located anywhere on the local filesystem. Recall that Tomcat now must be restarted for these changes to take effect.

---

With these changes in place, entering the URL:

```
https://localhost:8443/
```

in a browser or as an argument to the *curl* utility results in the fetch of Tomcat's familiar welcome page, the same page accessible through the HTTP URL:

```
http://localhost:8080/
```

The attributes in the HTTPS Connector element are intuitive. The maxThreads value of 150 signals that Tomcat will queue up to 150 requests against an HTTPS service before issuing a *connection refused* response to a client attempting to connect. The SSL protocol is the current standard, TLS; the HTTP scheme used to connect over HTTPS is, as expected, *https*.

## Enforcing HTTPS Access to a Web Service

A website or a web service can instruct Tomcat to enforce HTTPS access to either the entire resource (for instance, all of the HTML pages in the website and all of the operations in the web service) or only parts thereof (for instance, to administrative HTML pages in the site or to selected operations in the service). The instructions to Tomcat occur in a security-constraint section of the *web.xml* deployment file. To illustrate, the RESTful *predictions2* service of Chapter 2, originally deployed with HTTP access only, can be redeployed with HTTPS access only. This requires no change whatsoever in the code. The revised *web.xml* is Example 6-7.

*Example 6-7. The web.xml revised for security*

```
<?xml version = "1.0" encoding = "UTF-8"?>
<web-app>
  <servlet>
    <servlet-name>predictor</servlet-name>
    <servlet-class>predictions2.PredictionsServlet</servlet-class>
  </servlet>
  <security-constraint>                                          ❶
    <web-resource-collection>
      <url-pattern>/*</url-pattern>                              ❷
    </web-resource-collection>
    <user-data-constraint>
      <transport-guarantee>CONFIDENTIAL</transport-guarantee>    ❸
    </user-data-constraint>
  </security-constraint>
  <servlet-mapping>
    <servlet-name>predictor</servlet-name>
    <url-pattern>/*</url-pattern>
  </servlet-mapping>
</web-app>
```

The changes are limited to the security-constraint section (line 1). In this example, the security constraint is enforced on the entire resource because the url-pattern (line 2) has /* as its value. The deployed WAR file *predictions2.war* (created, as usual, with the Ant script) could be partitioned in subdirectories, for example:

```
/admin    ;; contains administrative operations
/public   ;; contains publicly accessible operations
```

Under this partition, the service operations in the /admin directory might require HTTPS but not the ones in the /public directory. To enforce this policy, the url-pattern in line 2 would change to /admin/*. The transport-guarantee element, with a value of CONFIDENTIAL (line 3), instructs Tomcat to enforce HTTPS access on the specified resource, in this example on the entire *predictions2* WAR file. If a client tried to access the *predictions2* service under HTTP, Tomcat would respond with an HTTP status code of 302 and the appropriate *https* URL, thereby signaling to the client that a new request with an HTTPS connection should be attempted.

Within the web-resource-collection element of *web.xml*, access constraints can be specified that depend on the HTTP verb of the client request. For example, the *web.xml* segment:

```
<web-resource-collection>
  <url-pattern>/*</url-pattern>
  <http-method>POST</http-method>  ❶
  <http-method>PUT</http-method>   ❷
</web-resource-collection>
```

specifies that access to the resource, in this case the entire *predictions2* service, is con-strained only on POST and PUT requests (lines 1 and 2). If no specific HTTP verbs are specified, then the constraint covers them all.

## An HTTPS Client Against the predictions2 Service

Example 6-8 shows the HttpsPredictionsClient against the *predictions2* service.

*Example 6-8. The HttpsPredictionsClient against the predictions2 service*

```
import java.net.URL;
import javax.net.ssl.HttpsURLConnection;
import javax.net.ssl.SSLContext;
import java.security.KeyStore;
import javax.net.ssl.TrustManagerFactory;
import javax.net.ssl.X509TrustManager;
import javax.net.ssl.HostnameVerifier;
import javax.net.ssl.SSLSession;
import java.security.cert.X509Certificate;
import java.security.SecureRandom;
import java.io.FileInputStream;
import java.io.InputStream;
import java.io.OutputStream;
```

```java
import java.io.ByteArrayOutputStream;

public class PredictionsHttpsClient {
    private static final String endpoint = "https://localhost:8443/predictions2";
    private static final String truststore = "test.keystore";

    public static void main(String[ ] args) {
        new PredictionsHttpsClient().runTests();
    }
    private void runTests() {
        try {
            SSLContext sslCtx = SSLContext.getInstance("TLS");
            char[ ] password = "qubits".toCharArray();
            KeyStore ks = KeyStore.getInstance("JKS");
            FileInputStream fis = new FileInputStream(truststore);
            ks.load(fis, password);
            TrustManagerFactory tmf = TrustManagerFactory.getInstance("SunX509");
            tmf.init(ks); // same as keystore
            sslCtx.init(null,                    // not needed, not challenged
                        tmf.getTrustManagers(),
                        new SecureRandom());
            HttpsURLConnection.setDefaultSSLSocketFactory(sslCtx.getSocketFactory());
            getTest();
            postTest();
            getTestAll();      // confirm POST test
            deleteTest("31");
            getTestAll();      // confirm DELETE test
        }
        catch(Exception e) { throw new RuntimeException(e); }
    }
    private HttpsURLConnection getConnection(URL url, String verb) {
        try {
            HttpsURLConnection conn = (HttpsURLConnection) url.openConnection();
            conn.setDoInput(true);
            conn.setDoOutput(true);
            conn.setRequestMethod(verb);
            conn.setHostnameVerifier(new HostnameVerifier() {
                    public boolean verify(String host, SSLSession session) {
                        return host.equals("localhost"); // for development
                    }
                });
            return conn;
        }
        catch(Exception e) { throw new RuntimeException(e); }
    }
    private void getTest() {
        getTestAll();
        getTestOne("31");
    }
    private void getTestAll() {
        try {
            URL url = new URL(endpoint);
```

```java
            HttpsURLConnection conn = getConnection(url, "GET");
            conn.connect();
            readResponse("GET all request:\n", conn);
            conn.disconnect();
        }
        catch(Exception e) { throw new RuntimeException(e); }
    }
    private void getTestOne(String id) {
        try {
            URL url = new URL(endpoint + "?id=" + id);
            HttpsURLConnection conn = getConnection(url, "GET");
            conn.connect();
            readResponse("GET request for " + id + ":\n", conn);
            conn.disconnect();
        }
        catch(Exception e) { throw new RuntimeException(e); }
    }
    private void postTest() {
        try {
            URL url = new URL(endpoint);
            HttpsURLConnection conn = getConnection(url, "POST");
            conn.connect();
            writeBody(conn);
            readResponse("POST request:\n", conn);
            conn.disconnect();
        }
        catch(Exception e) { throw new RuntimeException(e); }
    }
    private void deleteTest(String id) {
        try {
            URL url = new URL(endpoint + "?id=" + id);
            HttpsURLConnection conn = getConnection(url, "DELETE");
            conn.connect();
            readResponse("DELETE request:\n", conn);
            conn.disconnect();
        }
        catch(Exception e) { throw new RuntimeException(e); }
    }
    private void writeBody(HttpsURLConnection conn) {
        try {
            String pairs = "who=Freddy&what=Avoid Friday nights if possible.";
            OutputStream out = conn.getOutputStream();
            out.write(pairs.getBytes());
            out.flush();
        }
        catch(Exception e) { throw new RuntimeException(e); }
    }
    private void readResponse(String msg, HttpsURLConnection conn) {
        try {
            byte[ ] buffer = new byte[4096];
            InputStream in = conn.getInputStream();
            ByteArrayOutputStream out = new ByteArrayOutputStream();
```

```
            int n = 0;
            while ((n = in.read(buffer)) != -1) out.write(buffer, 0, n);
            in.close();
            System.out.println(new String(out.toByteArray())); // stringify and print
        }
        catch(Exception e) { throw new RuntimeException(e); }
    }
}
```

The PredictionsHttpsClient (see Example 6-8) is a test client against the HTTPS-deployed version of the *predictions2* service. This client is roughly similar to the HttpsClient (Example 6-6) but methods such as readResponse and writeBody now are beefed up in order to make realistic CRUD requests against the service. For example, the postTest adds new Prediction to the collection, which requires that writeBody insert the key/value pairs for the key who (the predictor) and the key what (the prediction); the getTestAll must read all of the bytes returned from the service in order to display the Prediction list.

Tomcat's approach to HTTPS exemplifies the separation-of-concerns principle. A web service (or a website) need not be changed at the code level to move from HTTP to HTTPS access. It bears repeating that no code in the original *predictions2* service had to be changed; instead, only the deployment descriptor *web.xml* needed to change, and then only a little. Tomcat also assumes responsibility for enforcing HTTPS access in accordance with the policy given in the *web.xml* document: a client that now tries to hit the *predictions2* service with an HTTP-based request is signaled that an HTTPS-based request should be used instead.

# Container-Managed Security

Wire-level security and users/roles security are related as follows. Under users/roles security, a client furnishes an identification such as a *username* or even a digital certificate together with a security credential that vouches for the identification (for instance, a *password* or a signature on the digital certificate from a certificate authority). To avoid hijacking, the identification and the credential should be sent from the client to the server through a secure channel, for instance, over an HTTPS connection. Wire-level security is thus the foundation upon which users/roles security should be implemented, and HTTPS is an ideal way to provide wire-level security for *web*-based systems such as web services.

Users/roles security is a two-phase process (see Figure 6-8). In the first and required phase, the user provides an identification and a credential that vouches for the identification. A successful user authentication phase results in an *authenticated subject*. In the optional second phase, role authorization, the access permissions of the authenticated subject can be refined as needed. For example, in a software development organization there might be a distinction between a *senior engineer* and a *starting programmer*, in that the former can access resources (for instance, sensitive records in a database) that the latter cannot access. This distinction could be implemented with different authorization roles.

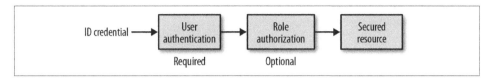

*Figure 6-8. Users/roles security*

At what level should users/roles security be enforced? Enforcement at the application level does not scale easily, in that every web service (or website) would require code, perhaps consolidated into a library, dedicated to security; a web service still would need to link to such library code. The preferred approach is to hand over the security concerns to the service container—to Tomcat or Jetty. This is *container-managed security*, which is considered best practice. Tomcat's implementation of container-managed security, like its management of wire-level security, is unobtrusive at the service level: no changes are required in the web service code to enable users/roles security. Once again, the configuration document *web.xml* is the key.

The RESTful *predictions2* service once again can be augmented with container-managed security—and without any change to the code. The revised *web.xml* document is displayed in Example 6-9.

*Example 6-9. The revised web.xml to support both HTTPS and users/roles security*

```
<?xml version = "1.0" encoding = "UTF-8"?>
<web-app>
  <servlet>
    <servlet-name>predictor</servlet-name>
    <servlet-class>predictions2.PredictionsServlet</servlet-class>
  </servlet>
  <security-role>                                              ❶
    <role-name>bigshot</role-name>                             ❷
    <!-- other roles as needed -->
  </security-role>
  <security-constraint>
    <web-resource-collection>
      <url-pattern>/*</url-pattern>
    </web-resource-collection>
    <auth-constraint>                                          ❸
      <role-name>bigshot</role-name>
    </auth-constraint>
    <user-data-constraint>
      <transport-guarantee>CONFIDENTIAL</transport-guarantee>
    </user-data-constraint>
  </security-constraint>
```

```
<login-config>                                           ❹
  <auth-method>BASIC</auth-method>                       ❺
</login-config>
<servlet-mapping>
  <servlet-name>predictor</servlet-name>
  <url-pattern>/*</url-pattern>
</servlet-mapping>
</web-app>
```

The numbered lines in the revised *web.xml* need clarification.

*Security role declaration*

Line 1 declares a `security-role`, which is an *authorization* role, and line 2 sets the role's name to `bigshot`. On the Tomcat side, a data store must contain the same role name, with details to follow.

*Authorization constraint*

The `security-constraint` element, introduced earlier, now contains two specific constraints: the `user-data-constraint`, which enforces HTTPS transport, from the earlier example; and the new `auth-constraint` (line 3), which is an authorization rather than an authentication constraint in the context of users/roles security. The authorization constraint specifies that access to the *predictions2* resource, the service and its operations, is restricted to a client authorized as a `bigshot`.

*User authentication method*

The `login-config` element (line 4) designates `BASIC` as the user authentication method (line 5). HTTP 1.1 supports four *authentication types*: BASIC, FORM, DIGEST, and CLIENT-CERT. These four types were designed with websites in mind but are adaptable to web services as well. Here is a summary of the differences:

- The BASIC type, a holdover from HTTP 1.0, centers on a username and a password, each passed from the client to the server for authentication. The username/password pair is encoded in base64 but not encrypted unless, of course, HTTPS is also in play.

- The FORM type refines the BASIC type by providing a form-based authentication mechanism, with specified names for the input fields in the form. This type also requires an error form to handle authentication failures. Further, the authentication procedure is laid out in detail for the FORM variant, unlike the BASIC variant. For modern websites, FORM-based authentication is best practice. The FORM type, like the BASIC type, requires HTTPS or equivalent transport-level support to provide data encryption.

- The BASIC and FORM types require that the username and the password be stored on the server side because the server needs to compare the submitted username/password pair against the server's own copies of these. A modern user, who is aware of the threat that security breaches represent, may be understandably wary of having a password stored on devices that the user does not control. The DIGEST type meets this challenge by sending a digest (hash value) of the password rather than the password itself. Accordingly, only a digest of the password needs to be stored on the server. The server-side login process computes the digest, compares the computed digest against the stored digest, and grants access only if these match. In general, digest or hash functions are *one-way secure*: given the digest and even the algorithm used to compute the digest, it is still computationally intractable to recover the original password. Indeed, message digests are fixed-length; hence, from the digest itself it is a daunting task to recover even the *length* of the original password. The DIGEST type as well requires HTTPS or the equivalent transport-level support to provide data encryption.

- The CLIENT-CERT type uses a digital certificate instead of a username/password or username/password-digest pair for authentication. For user access to websites, this approach may be impractical because a user may wish to hit a website from a device that does not have a copy of the user's digital certificate. Also, such certificates have expiration dates and so must be refreshed periodically. For web service clients, by contrast, the CLIENT-CERT type may have more appeal. For example, the client application might access the digital certificate from a database or similar data store that is managed automatically to ensure up-to-date digital certificates.

The very simplicity of the BASIC type is attractive for clients against RESTful services, especially if BASIC authentication is combined with HTTPS transport, which then provides the required username/password encryption.

## Linking the Service web.xml with a Tomcat Security Realm

The revised *web.xml* document specifies the type of HTTP authentication in use, BASIC, as well as the authorization role, `bigshot`, required of the client that accesses the *predictions2* service. The next question is how Tomcat puts this security information to use, in other words, how Tomcat's container-managed security works under the hood. Tomcat implements container-managed security with *realms*, which are akin to *groups* in Unix-type operating systems. In simplest form, a realm is a collection of usernames and passwords together the authorization roles, if any, associated with the usernames. The purpose of a realm is to coordinate various security resources in support of a single policy on access control. On the service side, security information needs to be saved in a data store such as a relational database system; Tomcat realms provide the details about how the security information is to be saved and accessed.

Tomcat7 comes with six standard plug-ins, all of which have `Realm` in their names. Developers are free to develop additional `Realm` plug-ins. Here are the six native Tomcat plug-ins with a short description of each:

*JDBCRealm*

The authentication information is stored in a relational database accessible through a JDBC driver.

*DataSourceRealm*

The authentication information again is stored in a relational database and accessible through a Java JDBC `DataSource`, which in turn is available through a JNDI (Java Naming and Directory Interface) lookup service.

*JNDIRealm*

The authentication information is stored in an LDAP-based (Lightweight Directory Access Protocol) directory service, which is available through a JNDI provider.

*UserDatabaseRealm*

The authentication information is stored in a JNDI resource coordinated by default with the file *TOMCAT_HOME/conf/tomcat-users.xml*. This is the default realm in Tomcat7.

*MemoryRealm*

The authentication information is read into memory, at Tomcat startup, from the file *tomcat-users.xml*. This is an earlier version of the `UserDatabaseRealm` and remains as an option for backward compatibility.

*JAASRealm*

The authentication information is available through a JAAS (Java Authentication and Authorization Service) framework. This is the most powerful but also the most complicated realm. Java Application Servers such as WebSphere and JBoss rely upon JAAS providers for users/roles security, and this option is available in Tomcat as well.

Under any of these choices, it is the Tomcat container rather than the application that becomes the security provider. With respect to the options, the path of least resistance leads to the default, the `UserDatabaseRealm`. Here is the data store, the XML file *tomcat-users.xml*. The five elements commented out act as Tomcat's tutorial about how the file is to be used. My additions are lines 1 and 2. Line 1 declares the security role used in line 2, which specifies a username and an associated password:

```
<tomcat-users>
  <role rolename="bigshot"/>                                    ❶
  <user username="moe" password="MoeMoeMoe" roles="bigshot"/>   ❷
</tomcat-users>
```

With the UserDatabaseRealm now configured, the security process can be summarized as follows:

- The revised deployment file *web.xml* requires not only HTTPS transport but also users/roles authentication and authorization.

- To access the secured *predictions2* service, a client must provide a username and a password that match an entry in *tomcat-users.xml*.

- For the authorization phase to succeed, a matching user entry in the file *tomcat-users.xml* must include bigshot among the roles.

## The Client Side in Users/Roles Security

On the service side, Tomcat is responsible for conducting the user authentication and role authorization. The burden now shifts to the client, which must properly format, within an HTTPS request, the username and password information. On the service side, the required changes are limited to the web service's configuration file, *web.xml*, and to the Tomcat UserDatabaseRealm file, *tomcat-users.xml*. No code in the *predictions2* service needs to change.

The PredictionsHttpsClientAA (see Example 6-10) adds users/roles security on the client side to the earlier HTTPS client against the *predictions2* service. The changes are quite small.

*Example 6-10. The PredictionsHttpsClientAA client against the predictions2 service*

```
import java.net.URL;
import javax.net.ssl.HttpsURLConnection;
import javax.net.ssl.SSLContext;
import java.security.KeyStore;
import javax.net.ssl.TrustManagerFactory;
import javax.net.ssl.X509TrustManager;
import javax.net.ssl.HostnameVerifier;
import javax.net.ssl.SSLSession;
import java.security.cert.X509Certificate;
import java.security.SecureRandom;
import java.io.FileInputStream;
import java.io.InputStream;
import java.io.OutputStream;
import java.io.ByteArrayOutputStream;
import org.apache.commons.codec.binary.Base64;

public class PredictionsHttpsClientAA {
    private static final String endpoint = "https://localhost:8443/predictions2";
    private static final String truststore = "test.keystore";

    public static void main(String[ ] args) {
        new PredictionsHttpsClientAA().runTests();
```

```
    }
    private void runTests() {
        try {
            SSLContext sslCtx = SSLContext.getInstance("TLS");
            char[ ] password = "qubits".toCharArray();
            KeyStore ks = KeyStore.getInstance("JKS");
            FileInputStream fis = new FileInputStream(truststore);
            ks.load(fis, password);
            TrustManagerFactory tmf = TrustManagerFactory.getInstance("SunX509");
            tmf.init(ks); // same as keystore
            sslCtx.init(null,                    // not needed, not challenged
                        tmf.getTrustManagers(),
                        new SecureRandom());
            HttpsURLConnection.setDefaultSSLSocketFactory(sslCtx.getSocketFactory());
            // Proof of concept tests.
            String uname = "moe";
            String passwd = "MoeMoeMoe";
            getTest(uname, passwd);
            postTest(uname, passwd);
            getTestAll(uname, passwd);       // confirm POST test
            deleteTest(uname, passwd, "31");
            getTestAll(uname, passwd);       // confirm DELETE test
        }
        catch(Exception e) { throw new RuntimeException(e); }
    }
    private HttpsURLConnection getConnection(URL url,
                                             String verb,
                                             String uname,
                                             String passwd) {
        try {
            HttpsURLConnection conn = (HttpsURLConnection) url.openConnection();
            conn.setDoInput(true);
            conn.setDoOutput(true);
            conn.setRequestMethod(verb);
            // authentication (although header name is Authorization)
            String userpass = uname + ":" + passwd;
            String basicAuth = "Basic " +
                new String(new Base64().encode(userpass.getBytes()));
            conn.setRequestProperty ("Authorization", basicAuth);
            conn.setHostnameVerifier(new HostnameVerifier() {
                    public boolean verify(String host, SSLSession session) {
                        return host.equals("localhost"); // for development
                    }
                });
            return conn;
        }
        catch(Exception e) { throw new RuntimeException(e); }
    }
    private void getTest(String uname, String passwd) {
        getTestAll(uname, passwd);
        getTestOne(uname, passwd, "31");
    }
```

```
private void getTestAll(String uname, String passwd) {
    try {
        URL url = new URL(endpoint);
        HttpsURLConnection conn = getConnection(url, "GET", uname, passwd);
        conn.connect();
        readResponse("GET all request:\n", conn);
        conn.disconnect();
    }
    catch(Exception e) { throw new RuntimeException(e); }
}
private void getTestOne(String uname, String passwd, String id) {
    try {
        URL url = new URL(endpoint + "?id=" + id);
        HttpsURLConnection conn = getConnection(url, "GET", uname, passwd);
        conn.connect();
        readResponse("GET request for " + id + ":\n", conn);
        conn.disconnect();
    }
    catch(Exception e) { throw new RuntimeException(e); }
}
private void postTest(String uname, String passwd) {
    try {
        URL url = new URL(endpoint);
        HttpsURLConnection conn = getConnection(url, "POST", uname, passwd);
        conn.connect();
        writeBody(conn);
        readResponse("POST request:\n", conn);
        conn.disconnect();
    }
    catch(Exception e) { throw new RuntimeException(e); }
}
private void deleteTest(String uname, String passwd, String id) {
    try {
        URL url = new URL(endpoint + "?id=" + id);
        HttpsURLConnection conn = getConnection(url, "DELETE", uname, passwd);
        conn.connect();
        readResponse("DELETE request:\n", conn);
        conn.disconnect();
    }
    catch(Exception e) { throw new RuntimeException(e); }
}
private void writeBody(HttpsURLConnection conn) {
    try {
        String pairs = "who=Freddy&what=Avoid Friday nights if possible.";
        OutputStream out = conn.getOutputStream();
        out.write(pairs.getBytes());
        out.flush();
    }
    catch(Exception e) { throw new RuntimeException(e); }
}
private void readResponse(String msg, HttpsURLConnection conn) {
    try {
```

```
        byte[ ] buffer = new byte[4096];
        InputStream in = conn.getInputStream();
        ByteArrayOutputStream out = new ByteArrayOutputStream();
        int n = 0;
        while ((n = in.read(buffer)) != -1) out.write(buffer, 0, n);
        in.close();
        System.out.println(new String(out.toByteArray())); // stringify and print
    }
    catch(Exception e) { throw new RuntimeException(e); }
  }
}
```

The `getConnection` method has three newlines:

```
String userpass = uname + ":" + passwd;                                      ❶
String basicAuth = "Basic " +
                  new String(new Base64().encode(userpass.getBytes())); ❷
conn.setRequestProperty ("Authorization", basicAuth);                        ❸
```

A `userpass` string is created as a key/value pair, with the colon, :, as the separator, from the parameters `uname` and `passwd` (line 1). The `userpass` is then encoded in base64 and has `Basic` prepended (line 2). The result is inserted into the HTTPS headers, with `Authorization` as the key. For `moe` as the username and `MoeMoeMoe` as the password, the resulting header is:

```
Authorization: Basic bW9lOk1vZU1vZU1vZQ==
```

This setup follows HTTP 1.1 guidelines and meets Tomcat expectations about how the authentication/authorization information is to be formatted in the HTTPS request. As usual, a client against a RESTful service needs to stay close to the HTTP/HTTPS metal.

## Using the curl Utility for HTTPS Testing

The *curl* utility is an alternative to a full-blown RESTful client written in Java or some other language. For the *predictions2* service accessible through HTTPS and with user-authentication/role authorization in play, this *curl* command sends a GET request:

```
% curl --verbose --insecure --user moe:MoeMoeMoe \
     https://localhost:8443/predictions2
```

The `--insecure` flag means that *curl* goes through handshake process but does not verify the digital certificates sent from the server; the verification would require that *curl* be pointed to the appropriate truststore file. In any case, the output from a sample run, edited slightly for readability, is shown in Example 6-11.

*Example 6-11. The output from a curl request over HTTPS*

```
* About to connect() to localhost port 8443 (#0)
*   Trying ::1... connected
* Connected to localhost (::1) port 8443 (#0)
* successfully set certificate verify locations:
```

```
*   CAfile: none
  CApath: /etc/ssl/certs
* SSLv3, TLS handshake, Client hello (1):
* SSLv3, TLS handshake, Server hello (2):
* SSLv3, TLS handshake, CERT (11):
* SSLv3, TLS handshake, Server key exchange (12):
* SSLv3, TLS handshake, Server finished (14):
* SSLv3, TLS handshake, Client key exchange (16):
* SSLv3, TLS change cipher, Client hello (1):
* SSLv3, TLS handshake, Finished (20):
* SSLv3, TLS change cipher, Client hello (1):
* SSLv3, TLS handshake, Finished (20):
* SSL connection using EDH-RSA-DES-CBC3-SHA
* Server certificate:
  ...
*   SSL certificate verify result: self signed certificate (18), ❶
  continuing anyway.
* Server auth using Basic with user 'moe'
> GET /predictions2 HTTP/1.1
> Authorization: Basic bW9lOk1vZU1vZU1vZQ==
> User-Agent: curl/7.19.7 (x86_64-pc-linux-gnu) libcurl/7.19.7
            OpenSSL/0.9.8k zlib/1.2.3.3 libidn/1.15
> Host: localhost:8443
> Accept: */*
>
< HTTP/1.1 200 OK
< Server: Apache-Coyote/1.1
< Cache-Control: private
< Expires: Wed, 31 Dec 1969 18:00:00 CST
< Transfer-Encoding: chunked
...
<
<?xml version="1.0" encoding="UTF-8"?>
<java version="1.6.0_21" class="java.beans.XMLDecoder">
...
```

In the *curl* output, the character > introduces text lines sent from *curl* to the server, whereas the character < introduces text lines from from the server to *curl*. The lines that begin with a star, *, trace the TLS handshake process. Although *curl* recognizes (line 1) that the self-signed certificate from the server is worthless as a security credential, *curl* continues the process, again because of the --insecure flag, by sending a GET request over HTTPS to the *predictions2* service; the service responds with a list of the predictions.

# A @WebService Under HTTPS with Users/Roles Security

Tomcat supports HTTPS transport and users/roles security for SOAP-based services as well. A SOAP-based client built atop *wsimport*-generated artifacts can use a slightly higher level API than its REST-style counterpart to insert the required security credentials into an HTTPS request. This section uses a minimal SOAP-based service to focus on security in the client against the service.

The SOAP-based *TempConvert* service (see Example 6-12) has two operations: *f2c* converts temperatures from fahrenheit to centigrade and *c2f* converts them from centigrade to fahrenheit. With respect to security, the *web.xml* for this service is essentially the same as for the RESTful and secure *predictions2* service.

*Example 6-12. The SOAP-based TempConvert service*

```java
package tc;
import javax.jws.WebService;
import javax.jws.WebMethod;

@WebService
public class TempConvert {
    @WebMethod
    public float c2f(float t) { return 32.0f + (t * 9.0f / 5.0f); }
    @WebMethod
    public float f2c(float t) { return (5.0f / 9.0f) * (t - 32.0f); }
}
```

However, the *web.xml* for the SOAP-based service needs to reference the Metro WSServ let (line 2), which acts as the intermediary between the servlet container and the service (see Example 6-13); the additional configuration file, *sun-jaxws.xml*, is likewise required.

*Example 6-13. The web.xml document for the SOAP-based TempConvert service*

```xml
<?xml version = "1.0" encoding = "UTF-8"?>
<web-app>
  <listener>
    <listener-class>
      com.sun.xml.ws.transport.http.servlet.WSServletContextListener    ❶
    </listener-class>
  </listener>
  <servlet>
    <servlet-name>wsservlet</servlet-name>
    <servlet-class>
      com.sun.xml.ws.transport.http.servlet.WSServlet                   ❷
    </servlet-class>
  </servlet>
  <security-role>
    <role-name>bigshot</role-name>
    <!-- other roles as needed -->
  </security-role>
  <security-constraint>
    <web-resource-collection>
      <url-pattern>/*</url-pattern>
    </web-resource-collection>
    <auth-constraint>
```

```
      <role-name>bigshot</role-name>
    </auth-constraint>
    <user-data-constraint>
      <transport-guarantee>CONFIDENTIAL</transport-guarantee>
    </user-data-constraint>
  </security-constraint>
  <login-config>
    <auth-method>BASIC</auth-method>
  </login-config>
  <servlet-mapping>
    <servlet-name>wsservlet</servlet-name>
    <url-pattern>/*</url-pattern>
  </servlet-mapping>
</web-app>
```

Lines 1 and 2 are the only changes to the *web.xml* used in the earlier *predictions2* service. With the *web.xml* and *sun-jaxws.xml* in place, the TempConvert service can be deployed in the usual way:

```
% ant deploy -Dwar.name=tc
```

How should the *wsimport*-generated artifacts be generated for a service accessible only through HTTPS? The attempt:

```
% wsimport -p tcClient -keep https://localhost:8443/tc?wsdl
```

generates a sun.security.validator.ValidatorException precisely because *wsimport* is unable to conduct the HTTPS handshake: the utility does not have access to a truststore against which the server's digital certificate(s) can be verified. The service is HTTPS-secured and, therefore, so is the service's dynamically generated WSDL. The *wsgen* utility provides a workaround. The command:

```
% wsgen -cp . tc.TempConvert -wsdl
```

generates the *TempConvertService.wsdl* file and the *TempConvertService_schema1.xsd* file. The *wsimport* utility can now be targeted at the WSDL:

```
% wsmport -p tcClient -keep TempConvertService.wsdl
```

The only drawback is that the service's URL is not in the class TempConvertService because the WSDL used is not generated dynamically. The TempConvertClient (see Example 6-14) shows how to overcome this drawback.

*Example 6-14. The TempConvertClient against the SOAP-based TempConvert service*

```
import tcClient.TempConvertService;
import tcClient.TempConvert;
import javax.xml.ws.BindingProvider;
import java.util.Map;
import javax.net.ssl.HostnameVerifier;
import javax.net.ssl.SSLSession;
import javax.net.ssl.SSLContext;
```

```java
import javax.net.ssl.TrustManager;
import javax.net.ssl.X509TrustManager;
import javax.net.ssl.HttpsURLConnection;
import java.security.cert.Certificate;
import java.security.cert.X509Certificate;

public class TempConvertClient {
    private static final String endpoint = "https://localhost:8443/tc";
    // Make the client "trusting" and handle the hostname verification.
    static {                                                              ❶
        HttpsURLConnection.setDefaultHostnameVerifier(new HostnameVerifier() {
                public boolean verify(String name, SSLSession session) {
                    return true; // allow everything
                }
            });
        try {
            TrustManager[ ] trustMgr = new TrustManager[ ] {
                new X509TrustManager() {
                    public X509Certificate[ ] getAcceptedIssuers() { return null; }
                    public void checkClientTrusted(X509Certificate[ ] cs, String t)
                        { }
                    public void checkServerTrusted(X509Certificate[ ] cs, String t)
                        { }
                }
            };
            SSLContext sslCtx = SSLContext.getInstance("TLS");
            sslCtx.init(null, trustMgr, null);
            HttpsURLConnection.setDefaultSSLSocketFactory(sslCtx.getSocketFactory());
        }
        catch(Exception e) { throw new RuntimeException(e); }
    }
    public static void main(String args[ ]) {
        if (args.length < 2) {
            System.err.println("Usage: TempConvertClient <uname> <passwd>");
            return;
        }
        String uname = args[0];
        String passwd = args[1];
        TempConvertService service = new TempConvertService();
        TempConvert port = service.getTempConvertPort();
        BindingProvider prov = (BindingProvider) port;                    ❷
        prov.getRequestContext().put(BindingProvider.ENDPOINT_ADDRESS_PROPERTY,
                                     endpoint);                           ❸
        prov.getRequestContext().put(BindingProvider.USERNAME_PROPERTY,
                                     uname);                              ❹
        prov.getRequestContext().put(BindingProvider.PASSWORD_PROPERTY,
                                     passwd);                             ❺
        System.out.println("f2c(-40.1) = " + port.f2C(-40.1f));
        System.out.println("c2f(-40.1) = " + port.c2F(-40.1f));
        System.out.println("f2c(+98.7) = " + port.f2C(+98.7f));
    }
}
```

The `TempConvertClient` uses a `static` block (line 1) to make itself into a *trusting* client that does not check the server's digital certificate during the HTTPS handshake; the `static` block also instructs the `HostnameVerifier` to allow client access to any host, including *localhost*. The `static` block isolates the transport-level security so that the focus can be kept on the users/roles security. By the way, the `static` block exploits the fact that a JAX-WS client uses, under the hood, the `HttpsURLConnection` of earlier RESTful examples.

To gain access to the transport level, in particular to the headers in the HTTPS request, the `TempConvertClient` casts the `port` reference to a `BindingProvider` (line 2). The endpoint then is set (line 3) to the correct URL because the *wsimport*-generated classes do not have a usable URL. The username and password, entered as command-line arguments, are likewise placed in the HTTPS headers (lines 4 and 5). This SOAP-based client need not bother with creating a single string out of the username and password or with encoding these in base64. Instead, the client uses the intuitive:

```
BindingProvider.USERNAME_PROPERTY
BindingProvider.PASSWORD_PROPERTY
```

keys and sets the value for each. After the setup, the client makes three calls against the SOAP-based service. The output is:

```
f2c(-40.1) = -40.055557
c2f(-40.1) = -40.18
f2c(+98.7) = 37.055557
```

## Using a Digested Password Instead of a Password

A downside of BASIC authentication is that a client's password must be stored, as is, on the server side so that the received password can be compared against the stored password. The DIGEST option requires only that the *hash value* of the password be stored on the server. The setup for the DIGEST option is trickier than for the BASIC option, however. Yet the BASIC option can be tweaked so that it behaves just like the DIGEST option. This section illustrates.

Tomcat comes with a *digest* utility: *digest.sh* for Unixy systems and *digest.bat* for Windows. The command:

```
% digest.sh -a SHA MoeMoeMoe
```

generates a 20-byte hash value, in hex, using the SHA-1 algorithm. Here is the value:

```
0f9e52090a322d7f788db2ae6b603e8efbd7fbd1
```

In the *TOMCAT_HOME/conf/tomcat-users.xml* file, this value replaces the password for moe (line 1):

```
<?xml version='1.0' encoding='utf-8'?>
<tomcat-users>
```

---

```
        <role rolename="bigshot"/>
        <user username="moe"
              password="0f9e52090a322d7f788db2ae6b603e8efbd7fbd1"  ❶
              roles="bigshot"/>
    </tomcat-users>
```

The file is otherwise unchanged.

The *digest* utility is implemented with the `RealmBase.Digest` method, which can be used in a Java client. The revised client against the `TempConvertService`, named `Temp ConvertClient2` (see Example 6-15), illustrates.

*Example 6-15. The revised `TempConvertClient2`*

```
import tcClient.TempConvertService;
import tcClient.TempConvert;
...
import org.apache.catalina.realm.RealmBase;                                       ❶

public class TempConvertClient2 {
    private static final String endpoint = "https://localhost:8443/tc";

    static {
        ...
    }
    public static void main(String args[ ]) {
        if (args.length < 2) {
            System.err.println("Usage: TempConvertClient <uname> <passwd>");
            return;
        }
        String uname = args[0];
        String passwd = args[1];
        String passwdHash = RealmBase.Digest(passwd,  // password              ❷
                                     "SHA",   // algorithm
                                     null);   // default encoding: utf-8
        TempConvertService service = new TempConvertService();
        TempConvert port = service.getTempConvertPort();
        BindingProvider prov = (BindingProvider) port;
        prov.getRequestContext().put(BindingProvider.ENDPOINT_ADDRESS_PROPERTY,
                                     endpoint);
        prov.getRequestContext().put(BindingProvider.USERNAME_PROPERTY,
                                     uname);
        prov.getRequestContext().put(BindingProvider.PASSWORD_PROPERTY,
                                     passwdHash);                               ❸
        ...
    }
}
```

Most of the code in the `TempConvertClient2` client is the same as that in the original. The `import` in line 1 is the first difference: the Tomcat libraries include the `RealmBase` class whose `Digest` method is of interest (line 2). The `Digest` method generates the hash

---

value for the sample password, in this case MoeMoeMoe, which is given as a command-line argument. The hash value instead of the actual password then is placed in the HTTPS headers (line 3). On the service side, the send hash value is compared against the hash value stored in the revised *tomcat-users.xml*. The ZIP with the sample code includes *runClient.xml*, an Ant script to compile and execute the TempConvert Client2. A sample invocation with output is:

```
% ant -f runClient.xml -Darg1=moe -Darg2=MoeMoeMoe

Buildfile: run.xml
compile:
run:
     [java] f2c(-40.1) = -40.055557
     [java] c2f(-40.1) = -40.18
     [java] f2c(+98.7) = 37.055557
```

# WS-Security

WS-Security is a family of specifications (see Figure 6-9) designed to augment wire-level security (e.g., HTTPS) and container-managed security (e.g., Tomcat) by providing a unified, transport-neutral, container-neutral, end-to-end framework for higher levels of security such as message confidentiality and authentication/authorization.

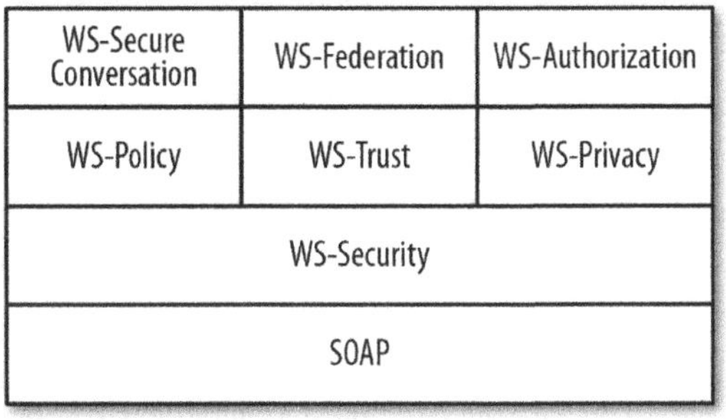

*Figure 6-9. The WS-Security specifications*

The layered blocks above WS-Security in Figure 6-9 can be clarified briefly as follows. The first layer consists of WS-Policy, WS-Trust, and WS-Privacy. The second layer of WS-SecureConversation, WS-Federation, and WS-Authorization builds upon this first layer. The architecture is thus modular but also complicated. Here is a short description of each specification, starting with the first layer:

*WS-Policy*

This specification describes general security capabilities, constraints, and policies. For example, a WS-Policy assertion could stipulate that a message requires security tokens or that a particular encryption algorithm be used.

*WS-Trust*

This specification deals primarily with how security tokens are to be issued, renewed, and validated. In general, the specification covers brokered trust relationships.

*WS-Privacy*

This specification explains how services can state and enforce privacy policies. The specification also covers how a service can determine whether a requester intends to follow such policies.

*WS-SecureConversation*

This specification covers, as the name indicates, secure web service conversations across different sites and, therefore, across different security contexts and trust domains. The specification focuses on how a security context is created and how security keys are derived and exchanged.

*WS-Federation*

This specification addresses the challenge of managing security identities across different platforms and organizations. At the heart of the challenge is how to maintain a single, authenticated identity (for example, Alice's security identity) in a heterogeneous security environment.

*WS-Authorization*

This specification covers the management of authorization data such as security tokens and underlying policies for granting access to secured resources.

WS-Security is often associated with federated security in the broad sense, which has the goal of cleanly separating web service logic from the high-level security concerns, in particular authentication/authorization, that challenge web service deployment. This separation of concerns is meant to ease collaboration across computer systems and trust realms.

Recall that SOAP-based web services are meant to be transport-neutral. Accordingly, SOAP-based services cannot depend simply on the reliable transport that HTTP and HTTPS provide, although most SOAP messages are transported over HTTP. HTTP and HTTPS rest on TCP/IP (Transmission Control Protocol/Internet Protocol), which supports reliable messaging. What if TCP/IP infrastructure is not available? The WS-ReliableMessaging specification addresses precisely the issue of delivering SOAP-based services over unreliable infrastructure.

A SOAP-based service can rely on the authentication/authorization support that a web container such as Tomcat or an application server such as Oracle WebLogic, JBoss, GlassFish, or WebSphere may provide. In this case, the service outsources users/roles security to the service container. The WS-Security specifications are a guide to how security in general can be handled from *within* SOAP messaging. Accordingly, the WS-Security specifications address security issues as part of SOAP itself rather than as the part of the infrastructure that happens to be in place for a particular SOAP-based service. The goals of WS-Security are often summarized with the phrase *end-to-end* security, which means that security matters are not delegated to either the transport level (e.g., HTTPS) or a particular service container (e.g., Tomcat) but, rather, handled directly through an appropriate security API. A framework for end-to-end security needs to cover the situation in which a message is routed through intermediaries, each of which may have to process the message, before reaching the ultimate receiver; thus, end-to-end security focuses on message content rather than on the underlying transport or the service container. As a result, SOAP messaging becomes considerably more complicated.

## Securing a @WebService with WS-Security

In order to focus squarely on WS-Security, the sample web service (see Example 6-16) is deliberately bare bones. Further, the Endpoint publisher is used to host the service despite the fact that Endpoint supports neither wire-level security nor users/roles authentication and authorization. The very point of WS-Security is to provide security *within* SOAP messaging. The Echo service focuses on how WS-Security supports user authentication in particular.

The publisher (see Example 6-17) first sets an Echo instance as the service endpoint (line 1) and then gets the Binding (line 2) in order to register a service-side handler (lines 3, 4, and 5). The publisher finishes its work by publishing the service at the specified URL (line 6).

*Example 6-16. The bare-bones Echo service*

```
package echoService;
import javax.jws.WebService;
import javax.jws.WebMethod;

@WebService
public class Echo {
    @WebMethod
    public String echo(String msg) { return "Echoing: " + msg; }
}
```

The Echo class gives no hint of WS-Security, which is delegated to the handler level, in this case to the message handler ServiceHandler. This separation of concerns means that, at the application level, the *Echo* service looks like any other @WebService: the service is a collection of operations, in this case only the echo method.

*Example 6-17. The EchoPublisher, which publishes the Echo service*

```
package echoService;

import javax.xml.ws.Endpoint;
import javax.xml.ws.Binding;
import java.util.List;
import java.util.LinkedList;
import javax.xml.ws.handler.Handler;

public class EchoPublisher {
    public static void main(String[ ] args) {
        Endpoint endpoint = Endpoint.create(new Echo());        ❶
        Binding binding = endpoint.getBinding();                 ❷
        List<Handler> hchain = new LinkedList<Handler>();        ❸
        hchain.add(new ServiceHandler());                        ❹
        binding.setHandlerChain(hchain);                         ❺
        endpoint.publish("http://localhost:7777/echo");          ❻
        System.out.println("http://localhost:7777/echo");
    }
}
```

At this point, a shift to the client side may be helpful because the client, too, has a handler; the service-side handler validates the information that the client-side handler puts into the SOAP request message. The client-side handler inserts a username and a password into the header of every SOAP request from the client. The service-side handler then verifies the identity of the user by using the password as the credential that vouches for the identity. The client's request hits the Echo service only if the service-side handler is successful in its verification.

On the client side and on the service side, the labor is divided in similar ways. The client-side message handler inserts the username and password into the outgoing SOAP message but relies upon the Prompter, which in turn is a CallbackHandler, to prompt for and read in the username and password; this CallbackHandler obscures but, in this example, does not encrypt the password. The client-side message handler also inserts other security information into the SOAP request message (see Figure 6-10).

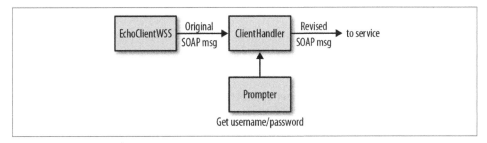

*Figure 6-10. The client-side architecture in the Echo service*

On the service side, the message handler delegates verification to a CallbackHandler of its own, the Verifier (see Figure 6-11). The Verifier, in turn, relies on other CallbackHandler instances to extract the authentication information and to verify the sent username/password against service-side copies of these. The architecture on the service side thereby complements the architecture on the client side.

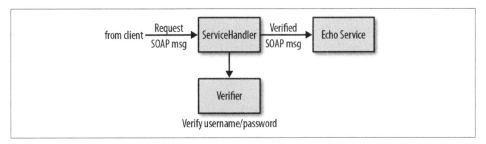

*Figure 6-11. The service-side architecture in the Echo service*

An examination of a familiar request/response exchange, starting from a client request through the service response, should cast light on the implementation details. The EchoClientWSS client (see Example 6-18) relies on the usual *wsimport*-generated artifacts (lines 1 and 2) to get a port reference (line 3), which is cast to the data type BindingProvider (line 4) so that the client-side SOAPHandler, an instance of the ClientHandler class, can be linked dynamically with the client (line 5). With this setup in place, the EchoClientWSS then makes a call against the *Echo* service (line 6) and prints the response for confirmation (line 7). All of the WS-Security code is relegated to the ClientHandler.

*Example 6-18. The sample EchoClientWSS against the Echo service*

```
import java.util.List;
import java.util.LinkedList;
import javax.xml.ws.handler.Handler;
import javax.xml.ws.BindingProvider;
import javax.xml.ws.Binding;
```

```
import echoClient.EchoService;                                              ❶
import echoClient.Echo;                                                     ❷

public class EchoClientWSS {
    public static void main(String[ ] args) {
        try {
            List<Handler> hchain = new LinkedList<Handler>();
            hchain.add(new ClientHandler());
            EchoService service = new EchoService();
            Echo port = service.getEchoPort();                             ❸
            Binding binding = ((BindingProvider) port).getBinding();       ❹
            binding.setHandlerChain(hchain);                               ❺
            String response = port.echo("Goodbye, cruel world!");          ❻
            System.out.println("From Echo service: " + response);          ❼
        }
        catch (Exception e) { throw new RuntimeExceptione(e); }
    }
}
```

The ClientHandler receives, from the underlying SOAP libraries on the client side, a SOAP message that represents a call to the *echo* operation in the *Echo* service. This message is passed to the ClientHandler (see Example 6-19), which does the WS-Security work. The result of this work impacts only the SOAP header, not the SOAP body; hence, the ClientHandler must be a SOAPHandler in order to access the SOAP header.

*Example 6-19. The client-side ClientHandler, which uses the Prompter*
```
import java.util.Set;
import java.util.HashSet;
import javax.xml.namespace.QName;
import javax.xml.soap.SOAPMessage;
import javax.xml.ws.handler.MessageContext;
import javax.xml.ws.handler.soap.SOAPHandler;
import javax.xml.ws.handler.soap.SOAPMessageContext;
import java.io.FileInputStream;
import java.io.File;
import com.sun.xml.wss.ProcessingContext;
import com.sun.xml.wss.SubjectAccessor;
import com.sun.xml.wss.XWSSProcessorFactory;
import com.sun.xml.wss.XWSSProcessor;

public class ClientHandler implements SOAPHandler<SOAPMessageContext> {
    private XWSSProcessor xwssClient;
    private boolean trace;

    public ClientHandler() {
        XWSSProcessorFactory fact = null;
        try {
            fact = XWSSProcessorFactory.newInstance();                                      ❶
            FileInputStream config = new FileInputStream(new File("client.xml"));           ❷
```

```
        xwssClient =                                                    ❸
            fact.createProcessorForSecurityConfiguration(config, new Prompter());
        config.close();
    }
    catch (Exception e) { throw new RuntimeException(e); }
    trace = true; // set to true to enable message dumps
}
// Add a security header block
public Set<QName> getHeaders() {                                        ❹
    String uri = "http://docs.oasis-open.org/wss/2004/01/" +
                 "oasis-200401-wss-wssecurity-secext-1.0.xsd";
    QName securityHdr = new QName(uri, "Security", "wsse");
    HashSet<QName> headers = new HashSet<QName>();
    headers.add(securityHdr);
    return headers;
}
public boolean handleMessage(SOAPMessageContext msgCtx) {
    Boolean outbound = (Boolean)
        msgCtx.get (MessageContext.MESSAGE_OUTBOUND_PROPERTY);
    SOAPMessage msg = msgCtx.getMessage();
    if (outbound.booleanValue()) {
        ProcessingContext pCtx = null;
        try {
            pCtx = xwssClient.createProcessingContext(msg);            ❺
            pCtx.setSOAPMessage(msg);                                  ❻
            SOAPMessage secureMsg = xwssClient.secureOutboundMessage(pCtx);  ❼
            msgCtx.setMessage(secureMsg);                              ❽

            if (trace) dump("Outgoing message:", secureMsg);
        }
        catch (Exception e) { throw new RuntimeException(e); }
    }
    return true;
}
public boolean handleFault(SOAPMessageContext msgCtx) { return true; }
public void close(MessageContext msgCtx) { }
private void dump(String msg, SOAPMessage soapMsg) {
    try {
        System.out.println(msg);
        soapMsg.writeTo(System.out);
        System.out.println();
    }
    catch(Exception e) { throw new RuntimeException(e); }
}
}
```

The ClientHandler no-argument constructor creates an XWSSProcessor (lines 1
through 3), which generates the WS-Security artifacts that go into the revised SOAP
message. Two arguments are required for the creation of the XWSSProcessor: a file from
which configuration information can be read and a CallbackHandler, in this case the

Prompter, that provides the username and password. The configuration file is minimalist:

```
<xwss:SecurityConfiguration
    xmlns:xwss="http://java.sun.com/xml/ns/xwss/config"
    dumpMessages="true" >
    <xwss:UsernameToken digestPassword="false"/>
</xwss:SecurityConfiguration>
```

The code for the Prompter is examined shortly.

A SOAP message handler must define four methods: getHeaders, handleMessage, handleFault, and close. Of the four methods, getHeaders executes first. Earlier examples of SOAP handlers defined the getHeaders method but never put this method to work. In this case, the getHeaders method (line 4) is put to work—the method adds an empty header block in the SOAP message:

```
<S:Header>
    <wsse:Security
        xmlns:wsse="http://docs.oasis-open.org/ \
                    wss/2004/01/oasis-200401-wss-wssecurity-secext-1.0.xsd"
        S:mustUnderstand="1">
    </wsse:Security>
</S:Header>
```

Although this header block is empty, it does contain the mustUnderstand attribute, with a value of 1 for *true*; WS-Security requires the attribute. Once the getHeaders method has done its part, the handleMessage method takes over to complete the work. This method creates a WS-Security *processing context* (line 5) that is used to transform the current SOAP message (line 6), with its newly added wsse:Security header block, into a *secured SOAP message* whose header contains the username and password (lines 7 and 8). Behind the scenes, the Prompter instance works with the XWSSProcessor to provide the required username and password. When the handleMessage method exits, the SOAP message has been transformed into something much larger. The client-side SOAP message before the handler operates is small (see Example 6-20), but this message becomes significantly larger after the handler has done its work (see Example 6-21).

*Example 6-20. The SOAP request before the ClientHandler transforms the message*

```
<?xml version="1.0" encoding="UTF-8"?>
<S:Envelope xmlns:S="http://schemas.xmlsoap.org/soap/envelope/">
    <S:Body>
        <ns2:echo xmlns:ns2="http://echoService/">
            <arg0>Goodbye, cruel world!</arg0>
        </ns2:echo>
    </S:Body>
</S:Envelope>
```

*Example 6-21. The SOAP request after the `ClientHandler` transforms the message*

```
<?xml version="1.0" encoding="UTF-8"?>
<S:Envelope xmlns:S="http://schemas.xmlsoap.org/soap/envelope/">
  <S:Header>
    <wsse:Security
       xmlns:wsse="http://docs.oasis-open.org/wss/2004/01/\
                   oasis-200401-wss-wssecurity-secext-1.0.xsd"
       S:mustUnderstand="1">
      <wsse:UsernameToken
         xmlns:wsu="http://docs.oasis-open.org/wss/2004/01/\
                    oasis-200401-wss-wssecurity-utility-1.0.xsd"
         wsu:Id="XWSSGID-1365549760320-535388749">
        <wsse:Username>fred</wsse:Username>                            ❶
        <wsse:Password                                                 ❷
           Type="http://docs.oasis-open.org/wss/2004/01/\
                 oasis-200401-wss-username-token-profile-1.0#PasswordText">
          ****
        </wsse:Password>
        <wsse:Nonce                                                    ❸
           EncodingType="http://docs.oasis-open.org/wss/2004/01/\
                         oasis-200401-wss-soap-message-security-1.0#Base64Binary">
          Q945eYMcu3NWuq90IjmNXjDy
        </wsse:Nonce>
        <wsu:Created>...</wsu:Created>
      </wsse:UsernameToken>
    </wsse:Security>
  </S:Header>
  <S:Body>
    <ns2:echo xmlns:ns2="http://echoService/">
      <arg0>Goodbye, cruel world!</arg0>
    </ns2:echo>
  </S:Body>
</S:Envelope>
```

The outgoing SOAP request now has, in the header, three items of security interest:

- The username, which is the client's identity (line 1).

- The obscured but not encrypted password, which is the credential that vouches for the username (line 2).

- A *cryptographic nonce*, a randomly generated value that is used just once in order to thwart so-called *replay attacks* (line 3). Each time that the EchoClientWSS sends a request to the *Echo* service, the username and password might be the same but the nonce differs from preceding ones; the WSS libraries on the service side validate the nonce.

The low-level work on the client side falls to the Prompter class (see Example 6-22), which implements the CallbackHandler interface by defining the handle method. The details are tedious but the gist is clear: the Prompter, in a production environment, would prompt for a username and password by using a UsernameCallback (line 1) and a PasswordCallback, respectively. The XWSSProcessor, which has access to the two callbacks through the processing context, extracts the username and password so that these can be inserted into the outgoing SOAP message.

*Example 6-22. The Prompter callback handler, which helps the ClientHandler*

```
import javax.security.auth.callback.Callback;
import javax.security.auth.callback.CallbackHandler;
import com.sun.xml.wss.impl.callback.PasswordCallback;
import com.sun.xml.wss.impl.callback.PasswordValidationCallback;
import com.sun.xml.wss.impl.callback.UsernameCallback;
import java.io.BufferedReader;
import java.io.InputStreamReader;

// For ease of testing, the username and password are
// hard-wired in the handle method with local variables
// username and password. For production, the hard wirings
// would be removed.
public class Prompter implements CallbackHandler {
    private String readLine() {
        String line = null;
        try {
            line = new BufferedReader(new InputStreamReader(System.in)).readLine();
        }
        catch(Exception e) { throw new RuntimeException(e); }
        return line;
    }
    // Prompt for and read the username and the password.
    public void handle(Callback[ ] callbacks) {
        try {
            for (int i = 0; i < callbacks.length; i++) {
                if (callbacks[i] instanceof UsernameCallback) {
                    UsernameCallback cb = (UsernameCallback) callbacks[i];    ❶
                    /* Disable for testing.
                    System.out.print("Username: ");
                    String username = readLine();
                    */
                    String username = "fred"; // hard-wire for testing
                    if (username != null) cb.setUsername(username);
                }
                else if (callbacks[i] instanceof PasswordCallback) {
                    PasswordCallback cb = (PasswordCallback) callbacks[i];    ❷
                    /* Disable for testing
                    System.out.print("Password: ");
                    String password = readLine();
                    */
                    String password = "rockbed"; // hard-wire for testing
                    if (password != null) cb.setPassword(password);
                }
            }
        }
    }
```

```
        catch(Exception e) { throw new RuntimeException(e); }
    }
}
```

On the client side, the XWSSProcessor could do more than it does in this example. For instance, the security processor could encrypt the blocks in the SOAP header, particularly the one with the password, and encrypt even the payload in the SOAP body. However, this first look at WS-Security is focused on the architecture and flow of control, and these additional steps would distract from that focus. It is now time to move over to the service side.

On the service side, the incoming SOAP message goes to the ServiceHandler (see Example 6-23), which verifies the security header blocks that the ClientHandler injects into the SOAP request. This handler also pares down the incoming message (see Example 6-21) to an ordinary-looking SOAP request:

```
<S:Envelope xmlns:S="http://schemas.xmlsoap.org/soap/envelope/">
  <S:Header/>
  <S:Body>
    <ns2:echo xmlns:ns2="http://echoService/">
      <arg0>Goodbye, cruel world!</arg0>
    </ns2:echo>
  </S:Body>
</S:Envelope>
```

This is almost the very request that the EchoClientWSS generates *before* the client-side handler goes into action. The one difference is that the pared-down, incoming message has a SOAP header—but an empty one.

*Example 6-23. The service-side* ServiceHandler

```
package echoService;

import java.util.Set;
import java.util.HashSet;
import javax.xml.namespace.QName;
import javax.xml.soap.SOAPMessage;
import javax.xml.ws.handler.MessageContext;
import javax.xml.ws.handler.soap.SOAPHandler;
import javax.xml.ws.handler.soap.SOAPMessageContext;
import java.io.ByteArrayInputStream;
import com.sun.xml.wss.ProcessingContext;
import com.sun.xml.wss.SubjectAccessor;
import com.sun.xml.wss.XWSSProcessorFactory;
import com.sun.xml.wss.XWSSProcessor;

public class ServiceHandler implements SOAPHandler<SOAPMessageContext> {
    private XWSSProcessor xwssServer = null;
    private boolean trace;

    public ServiceHandler() {
```

```
        XWSSProcessorFactory fact = null;
        try {
            fact = XWSSProcessorFactory.newInstance();              ❶
            ByteArrayInputStream config = getConfig();             ❷
            xwssServer =                                           ❸
                fact.createProcessorForSecurityConfiguration(config,
                                                    new Verifier());
        }
        catch (Exception e) { throw new RuntimeException(e); }
        trace = true; // set to true to enable message dumps
    }
    public Set<QName> getHeaders() {                              ❹
        String uri = "http://docs.oasis-open.org/wss/2004/01/" +
                    "oasis-200401-wss-wssecurity-secext-1.0.xsd";
        QName securityHdr = new QName(uri, "Security", "wsse");   ❺
        HashSet<QName> headers = new HashSet<QName>();
        headers.add(securityHdr);
        return headers;                                          ❻
    }
    public boolean handleMessage(SOAPMessageContext msgCtx) {
        Boolean outbound = (Boolean)
            msgCtx.get (MessageContext.MESSAGE_OUTBOUND_PROPERTY);
        SOAPMessage msg = msgCtx.getMessage();
        if (!outbound.booleanValue()) {
            // Validate the message.
            try{
                ProcessingContext pCtx =
                    xwssServer.createProcessingContext(msg);
                pCtx.setSOAPMessage(msg);
                SOAPMessage verifiedMsg =
                    xwssServer.verifyInboundMessage(pCtx);         ❼
                msgCtx.setMessage(verifiedMsg);                    ❽
                if (trace) dump("Incoming message:", verifiedMsg);
            }
            catch(Exception e) { throw new RuntimeException(e); }
        }
        return true;
    }
    public boolean handleFault(SOAPMessageContext msgCtx) { return true; }
    public void close(MessageContext msgCtx) { }
    private void dump(String msg, SOAPMessage soapMsg) {
        try {
            System.out.println(msg);
            soapMsg.writeTo(System.out);
            System.out.println();
        }
        catch(Exception e) { throw new RuntimeException(e); }
    }
    private ByteArrayInputStream getConfig() {                    ❾
        String config =
            "<xwss:SecurityConfiguration " +
            "xmlns:xwss=\"http://java.sun.com/xml/ns/xwss/config\" " +
```

```
            "dumpMessages=\"true\"><xwss:RequireUsernameToken " +
            "passwordDigestRequired=\"false\"/> " +
            "</xwss:SecurityConfiguration>";
        return new ByteArrayInputStream(config.getBytes());
    }
}
```

The structure of the ServiceHandler is very close to that of the ClientHandler. In the ServiceHandler, the handleMessage method is interested only in incoming SOAP messages, that is, requests. This handler has a XWSSProcessor (lines 1 through 3) created from a hard-wired configuration document (line 9) and associated with a Verifier instance, a Callbackhandler that extracts the security information—the nonce, the username, and the password—from the SOAP header for verification. Once the SOAP request has been validated, the newly verified and simplified SOAP message is passed on to the usual SOAP libraries, which transform the XML document into the appropriate Java objects so that the *Echo* service can do its thing.

The ServiceHandler also makes use of the getHeaders method, which is particularly important with respect to the SOAP response from the EchoService. Recall that the ServiceHandler, like every handler, is inherently bidirectional. The handleMessage method is coded so that this method ignores outgoing messages, but the getHeaders method injects, into the SOAP response from the *Echo* service, a WS-Security header with the mustUnderstand attribute set to *true* (line 5). In effect, the ServiceHandler is demanding that any receiver of the SOAP response, including the EchoClientWSS, stick by the WS-Security rules. If the getHeaders method simply returned null, a client-side exception would be thrown because the incoming message would not be formatted according to WS-Security standards.

The service-side Verifier, like the client-side Prompter, is a CallbackHandler delegated to do grunt work. In a production environment, the Verifier might check the username and password against a database record, but here, for simplicity, these are hard-wired in the code. The Verifier also uses a PlainTextPasswordVerifier because the password itself rather than a hash value of the password is sent in the message (Example 6-24).

*Example 6-24. The service-side* Verifier, *a callback handler that helps the* Service Handler

```
package echoService;

import javax.security.auth.callback.Callback;
import javax.security.auth.callback.CallbackHandler;
import javax.security.auth.callback.UnsupportedCallbackException;
import com.sun.xml.wss.impl.callback.PasswordCallback;
import com.sun.xml.wss.impl.callback.PasswordValidationCallback;
import com.sun.xml.wss.impl.callback.UsernameCallback;
```

```
// Verifier handles service-side callbacks for password validation.
public class Verifier implements CallbackHandler {
    // Username/password hardcoded for simplicity and clarity.
    private static final String _username = "fred";
    private static final String _password = "rockbed";

    // For password validation, set the validator to the inner class below.
    public void handle(Callback[ ] callbacks) throws UnsupportedCallbackException {
        for (int i = 0; i < callbacks.length; i++) {
            if (callbacks[i] instanceof PasswordValidationCallback) {
                PasswordValidationCallback cb =
                    (PasswordValidationCallback) callbacks[i];
                if (cb.getRequest() instanceof
                    PasswordValidationCallback.PlainTextPasswordRequest)
                    cb.setValidator(new PlainTextPasswordVerifier());
            }
            else
                throw new UnsupportedCallbackException(null, "Not needed");
        }
    }
    // Encapsulated validate method verifies the username/password.
    private class PlainTextPasswordVerifier
        implements PasswordValidationCallback.PasswordValidator {
        public boolean validate(PasswordValidationCallback.Request req)
            throws PasswordValidationCallback.PasswordValidationException {
            PasswordValidationCallback.PlainTextPasswordRequest plain_pwd =
                (PasswordValidationCallback.PlainTextPasswordRequest) req;
            return_username.equals(plain_pwd.getUsername()) &&
                _password.equals(plain_pwd.getPassword());
        }
    }
}
```

On a successful verification, the Verifier validates fred (the username) as an authenticated subject whose *public credential* is the name fred and whose *private credential* is the password that vouches for Fred's identity.

The security illustrated in this sample could be ratcheted up to Mutual Challenge Security (MCS) with digital certificates used on both sides for peer authentication. Further, the contents of SOAP messages could be encrypted at the SOAP level, which would result in significantly larger SOAP headers that specified all of the cryptographic information: encryption and message digest algorithms, digital certificate formats, policies on confidentiality, encoding practices, specification of which parts of the SOAP message are to be encrypted and even digitally signed, and so on.

# Compiling and Running the Echo Service and the EchoClientWSS

The WS-Security packages do not ship with core Java but can be downloaded (*http://bit.ly/13zIOGy*) in a single JAR file. The current version, *xws-security-3.0.jar*, is included in the ZIP file with the sample code. The ZIP file also includes an executable JAR for the service and an Ant script to compile and execute the client.

- The *EchoPublisher.jar* file can be used to launch the publisher:

    ```
    % java -jar EchoPublisher.jar
    ```

- The script *runClient.xml* can be used to compile and execute the EchoClientWSS:

    ```
    % ant -f runClient.xml
    ```

    The client-side message handler, like its service-side counterpart, has a *dump* utility that can be turned on or off in the code. With the dump turned off, the output should be similar to:

    ```
    Buildfile: runClient.xml
    compile:
        [javac] Compiling 4 source files to /home/mkalin/jwsur2/ch6/wss
    run:
        [java] com.sun.xml.wss.impl.filter.DumpFilter process
        [java] From Echo service: Echoing: Goodbye, cruel world!
    ```

The client uses *wsimport*-generated artifacts, which are created in the usual way:

```
% wsimport -p echoClient -keep http://localhost:777/echo?wsdl
```

In a production environment, the Prompter on the client side would read the username and password either from a data store or interactively, with the latter as the default. It is easier to execute the client from the Ant script *runClient.xml* without any interaction; hence, for testing purposes, the username and password are hard-wired in the code. For a more realistic experience, the Prompter sections currently commented out can be uncommented. In this case, the Prompter awaits client input. At the command-prompt, the input should be:

```
fred
rockbed
```

These are the username and password that the ServiceHandler will verify.

Also in a production environment, the Verifier on the service side would verify a received username/password pair against a data store such as a database. Again for simplicity, the Verifier has the data hard-wired in the code.

# What's Next?

The examples so far have published RESTful and SOAP-based services with command-line utilities such as `Endpoint` and production-grade web servers such as Tomcat and Jetty. At the production level, Tomcat or Jetty represent a lightweight option; a JAS such as IBM WebSphere, JBoss, GlassFish (the reference implementation), or Oracle Web-Logic (formerly BEA WebLogic) represents a heavier-weight option. In the early 2000s, the *lightweight Java movement*, often associated with the Spring (*http://www.spring source.org*) framework, emerged as a reaction against the complexities of J2EE and the JASes used to deliver J2EE applications. In the meantime, the move from J2EE to Java EE 5 and 6 has meant significant weight loss for JASes because Java EE 5/6 offers a lightweight alternative to the earlier J2EE. The popular JASes now support the updated Java EE specifications.

Packaging and configuration have become significantly easier with the new JAS versions, which have administrative and other utilities that make the JAS an attractive option for deploying web services. For example, Java EE applications now can express configuration information with annotations instead of with complicated XML documents; indeed, a Java EE application, including a web service, officially can be deployed without any configuration document, although the *web.xml* remains the rule rather than the exception for both websites and web services. The next chapter considers the publication of REST-style and SOAP-based services under GlassFish and TomcatEE, emphasizing the nuts and bolts details of such software but also the trade-offs involved in using a JAS for deployment.

# CHAPTER 7

# Web Services and Java Application Servers

This chapter examines how web services can be deployed using a JAS, the software centerpiece of enterprise Java. The current version of enterprise Java is Java EE 6, which includes EJB 3.x. Yet if web services, REST-style and SOAP-based alike, can be published straightforwardly using the production-grade web servers such as Tomcat and Jetty, why bother with a JAS at all? The chapter also delves into the reasons why a JAS might be preferred over a standalone web server such as Tomcat or Jetty. To begin, an overview of available JASes might be useful.

*Apache Geronimo (http://geronimo.apache.org)*
> This is an open source project.

*Apache TomEE (http://tomee.apache.org)*
> This is essentially the Tomcat7 web server with OpenEJB extensions. This chapter includes a code example of a SOAP-based service deployed as a `@Stateless` Session EJB and using JPA to persist data in an HSQLDB database. The service is deployed under TomEE as a standard WAR file—indeed, as a WAR file that requires no *web.xml* document.

*IBM WebSphere (http://ibm.com/products)*
> This is a JAS with various extensions. There is a free version for developers.

*JBoss (http://jboss.org)*
> This JAS has been a community-based project and a JAS innovator from the start. It is currently under Red Hat.

*GlassFish (http://glassfish.java.net)*
> This JAS is part of the community-based GlassFish Metro project, which includes the Metro implementation of JAX-WS. GlassFish is the reference implementation. This chapter includes a pair of examples that involve GlassFish, including a SOAP-based service deployed as a `@Stateless` Session EJB and using JPA to persist data in a backend Apache Derby database.

*Oracle WebLogic (http://www.oracle.com/weblogicserver)*
> This JAS originated as BEA WebLogic, another pioneering innovator. There is a free version for developers available, as well as more information about this JAS (which is also known as Fusion).

The complexity of a JAS results from its combining, into a single software application, a variety of APIs and their implementations. The following subsections describe the different architectural pieces that together make up a JAS. Even this overview of a JAS may seem overwhelming because there are so many details to cover. It is worth keeping in mind that a JAS is a very powerful, but likewise complicated, software system.

# The Web Container

A web container hosts websites and web services, both of which are deployed as WAR files. Tomcat Catalina is the RI for a web container. A website in Java is a mix of static HTML pages; servlets; higher level servlet generators and HTML-templating constructs such as JSP and JSF (Java Server Faces) scripts; backend JavaBeans dedicated specifically to servlets and the equivalent; utility classes of all kinds; and, of course, JavaScript embedded in the HTML pages. There are many JVM-centric frameworks for web development, including Netty, Seam, Sitemesh, Tapestry, Wicket, Struts, Spring MVC, VRaptor, Grails, and even Rails on JRuby.

Tomcat, like other web containers such as Jetty, can be embedded in an application server as the JAS web container. JBoss, for example, once bundled Tomcat into one JAR file (with a *.sar* extension for *service archive*) and Jetty into another, leaving it up to the JAS administrator about which of these to use as the JBoss web container. Some JASes still use embedded Tomcat for the community edition but roll their own for the production edition. Whatever the implementation choice, a JAS has a web container for deploying websites and, increasingly, web services. The deployed WAR files typically contain the standard configuration document *web.xml* and may contain vendor-specific configuration documents as well. To host web services, a web container usually relies upon a servlet interceptor that mediates between the client and the web service.

In contemporary websites, the model-view-controller (MVC) pattern has become popular, even dominant. A *model* maintains state information about the site and is responsible for persistence through a data store such as a database system; a *view* provides an appropriate representation of a model; and a *controller* is a request endpoint that implements the business logic that coordinates interaction between models on the one side and views on the other side. Java EE has the `@Entity` annotation to signal that instances of the annotated class are to be persisted, typically in a relational database system. An `@Entity` class is thus a natural way to build a model with persistence. (The section below on the EJB container goes into more detail on the `@Entity` annotation.) In interactive web applications, JSP, JSF, or even higher level templating constructs can generate an

HTML view of a model; either a servlet or a servlet coordinated with a Session EJB, discussed shortly, is a natural way to implement a controller.

For Java-based web services deployed in an application server such as GlassFish, `@En tity` instances are likewise a natural way to implement models. The web service itself is the controller that exposes business logic in `@WebMethod` or RESTful code and interacts, as appropriate, with models. Views in web services are basically response documents, with XML and JSON as the usual formats.

## The Message-Oriented Middleware

The message-oriented middleware in a JAS requires a *JMS* (Java Message Service) provider, which furnishes the store-and-forward technologies lumped together under the term *messaging*. JMS supports synchronous and asynchronous messaging styles and two types of message repository: topics, which are akin to bulletin boards in that a *read* operation does not automatically remove a posted message; and queues, which are FIFO (First In, First Out) lists in which a *read* operation, by default, removes the read item from a queue. Under JMS, a *publisher* publishes messages to a topic and a sender sends messages to a queue. A *subscriber* to a topic or a receiver on a queue receives such messages either synchronously through a blocking *read* operation or asynchronously through either a nonblocking read or the JMS event-driven notification mechanism. JMS topics implement the publisher/subscriber model of messaging, whereas JMS queues implement the point-to-point model.

## The Enterprise Java Bean Container

The EJB container holds EJB instances, which are of three types: Session, Entity, and Message-Driven. Session and traditional Entity EJBs are built on a Java RMI foundation, whereas Message-Driven EJBs are built on a JMS foundation. A Message-Driven EJB is a JMS `MessageListener` implemented as an EJB. A listener receives an event notification whenever a new message arrives at a topic or a queue at which the listener has registered interest.

A Session EJB typically implements an enterprise application's business logic and interacts as needed with other application components, either local (for instance, other EJBs in the same container) or remote (for instance, clients on a different host). As the name suggests, a Session EJB is designed to maintain a client session. A Session EJB is either stateless or stateful. A stateless Session EJB is, in effect, a collection of mutually independent instance methods that should operate only on data passed in as arguments. The EJB container assumes that a stateless Session EJB instance does not maintain state information in instance fields. Suppose, for example, that a Session EJB encapsulates two instance methods, $m_1$ and $m_2$. If this EJB were deployed as stateless, then the EJB container would assume that a particular client, $C$, could invoke $m_1$ in one EJB instance and $m_2$ in another EJB instance because the two methods do not share state. If the same

Session EJB were deployed as stateful, then the EJB container would have to ensure that the *C* invocation of $m_1$ and $m_2$ involved the *same* EJB instance because the two methods presumably share state. As this summary implies, an EJB container automatically manages a pool of EJB instances for all types of EJB. A @Stateless Session EJB automatically becomes a SOAP-based web service by adding the @WebService annotation; hence, legacy stateless session EJBs become SOAP-based web services through a single additional annotation.

In J2EE, the precursor to Java EE 5, EJBs in general and Entity EJBs in particular were tricky to code and even trickier to configure, as the configuration required a complicated XML document, the notorious *ejb-jar.xml* document—the DD (Deployment Descriptor). A case could be made that J2EE is too much work for too little reward. Things are much better with Java EE. For example, Java EE 5 and greater allow the programmer to configure an EJB with in-code annotations such as @Stateless instead of with a separate XML document; hence, the DD is now optional. Prior to Java EE 5, an Entity EJB instance was the preferred way to provide an enterprise application with an in-memory cache of a database object such as a table row. The Entity EJB was the persistence construct that brought ORM capabilities to the application. A traditional Entity EJB could be deployed with either BMP (Bean Managed Persistence) or CMP (Container Managed Persistence). At issue was whether the programmer or the EJB container maintained coherence between the data source (for instance, a table row) and the EJB instance. In the early days of EJB containers, the case could be made that BMP was more efficient. Yet the EJB containers quickly improved to the point that CMP became the obvious choice. Indeed, CMP emerged as a major inducement for and benefit of using traditional Entity EJBs. An EJB deployed with CMP also had to deploy with CMT (Container Managed Transactions). All of this changed with Java EE 5, which extended the capabilities of the original Entity EJB to POJO classes annotated with @Entity. In effect, the @Entity annotation let Java programmers enjoy many benefits of the traditional Entity EJB without enduring the pain of configuring and programming this kind of EJB. Although the legacy Entity EJB remains a powerful programming construct, it has given way to the @Entity annotation at the center of the JPA. JPA integrates features from related technologies such as Hibernate, Oracle's TopLink, Java Data Objects, and traditional Entity EJBs. The @Entity is now the preferred way to handle persistence. This chapter has two examples that illustrate JPA.

EJBs, unlike servlets, are thread-safe: the EJB container assumes responsibility for thread synchronization. As in the case of requests against servlets, each request against an EJB executes as a separate thread. Even in a traditional browser-based web application, EJBs are thus well suited as backend support for servlets. For instance, a servlet might pass a request along to a Session EJB, which in turn might use instances of various classes, annotated with @Entity, as persisted data sources (see Figure 7-1).

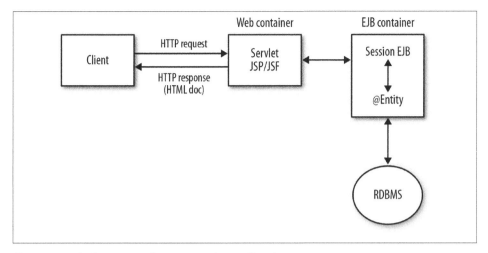

*Figure 7-1. Architecture of an enterprise application*

## The Naming and Lookup Service

The web container, message-oriented-middleware provider, and the EJB container expose different APIs, and components in each container may require security and persistence services (e.g., with a relational database management system handling the persistence). A challenge is for components in one container or service to find those in another. The JNDI provider in a JAS handles the registering-by-name and finding-by-name of components across containers and services. In a JAS, the JNDI provider maintains, at the least, a *naming service* in which names (for instance, the deployed name of an EJB or a message queue) are bound to entities (in this case, the deployed EJB or the queue). If the JNDI provider supports *directory services* as well, then the name of an entity binds to the entity and its attributes. In the simple case, a JNDI provider maintains a hierarchical database of name/entity pairs. Any component dropped into a JAS container is automatically registered with the naming service and thereafter available for lookup. In Java EE 5 and later, the JNDI provider is largely unseen infrastructure; the naming conventions are simpler than they once were.

## The Security Provider

The security provider brings to the JAS high-level security services for components deployed in any of the containers. Among these services are, of course, authentication and authorization. The security provider has to be JAAS compliant. Nowadays a security provider typically has plug-ins for providers such as an LDAP provider. The security in an application server is usually integrated. For instance, the container-managed security that the web container provides is integrated into the default JAAS-based security that the EJB container provides. It is common, moreover, for a JAS such as GlassFish to deploy, by default, a web service with both an HTTP and an HTTPS endpoint.

## The Client Container

The client container consists of the software libraries that a client requires to interact with deployed components such as message topics or EJBs and to use services such as JNDI and security. In the case of web service clients, however, there is essentially no change if the service is deployed under the lightweight `Endpoint` publisher, a web server such as Tomcat or Jetty, or a JAS. Even in the JAS environment, web services represent a simplified approach to distributed systems.

## The Database System

A JAS typically comes with a RDBMS, which serves as the persistence store. In a modern JAS, the JPA provider manages connections between in-memory objects such as `@Entity` instances and database entities such as table rows or join views. A modern JAS also allows an RDBMS to be plugged in so that the administrator has a range of choices. GlassFish, for example, comes with Apache Derby but it is uncomplicated to use a different system such as MySQL or PostgreSQL. This chapter has examples that involve Derby (*http://db.apache.org/derby*) and HSQLDB (*http://www.hsqldb.org*), both of which are implemented in Java. HSQLDB supports in-memory as well as disk-based tables, and both database systems support transactions.

# Toward a Lightweight JAS

As a bundle of so many components, features, containers, and services, a JAS is unavoidably complicated software. At issue among Java programmers is whether the benefits that come with a JAS offset the complexity of using a JAS. This complexity stems, in large part, from the fact that so many APIs come into play. For example, a deployed application that incorporates servlets, JSP scripts, JSF scripts, messaging, and EJBs must deal with at least five distinct APIs. This state of affairs accounts for recent efforts among vendors to provide seamless integration of Java EE components, which presumably would result in a lighter-weight, more programmer-friendly framework for doing enterprise Java. JBoss Seam and TomEE OpenEJB are examples. It should be emphasized, however, that Java EE 5 is significantly easier to use than its predecessor, J2EE 1.4. Java EE is definitely moving down the road that lighter frameworks such as Spring cut out for enterprise Java. As a result, the JASes that deliver Java EE applications are more nimble and manageable.

The GlassFish (*http://glassfish.java.net*) application server is open source and the reference implementation of a JAS. (To be legalistic, a particular *snapshot* of GlassFish is the RI.) It is available either separately or integrated with the NetBeans IDE. TomEE likewise represents a deliberately lightweight approach to Java EE. This chapter has examples deployed under both GlassFish and TomEE.

---

# GlassFish Basics

GlassFish can be installed in various ways, including via installers for the standard operating systems. The entire download is also available as a ZIP file. However GlassFish is installed, the installation process includes prompts for an administrator username (the default is `admin`) and a password. GlassFish has a web console (*localhost:4848* by default) and a command-line utility named *asadmin* (in Windows, *asadmin.bat*) that can be used to administer the JAS. The web console (see Figure 7-2) can be used only if GlassFish is already running.

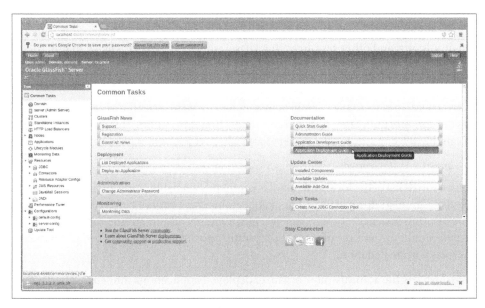

*Figure 7-2. The GlassFish web console home page*

During installation, it is possible to have GlassFish made into a system service so that GlassFish starts automatically whenever the system reboots. At startup, GlassFish checks for available ports on which to listen for connections. For example, if Tomcat or some other application is running and listening already on port 8080 for client connections, GlassFish notes this and asks for an alternative port to receive HTTP connections. (On my system, Tomcat listens on port 8080 for HTTP connections and GlassFish listens on port 8081.) By default, GlassFish listens for HTTPS connections on port 8181. GlassFish allows administrative overrides of all defaults.

The GlassFish web console is well organized and informative. GlassFish groups together, under the tab *Applications*, websites, web services, EJBs, and other deployed artifacts. This tab gives pertinent information about each deployed item and supports operations such as *undeploy*. The web console is particularly helpful because it lists, in the case of

SOAP-based web services, the URLs for the WSDL; in the case of EJB-based services, GlassFish also provides a web-based test client. The use of plural URLs also deserves clarification: by default, GlassFish publishes a site or a service under HTTP and HTTPS. GlassFish comes with a keystore, although the self-signed certificates therein would need to be upgraded for production-level use.

The GlassFish *Applications* tab makes it easy to check whether a service has deployed. This tab also can be used to upload WAR files and deploy them. For that reason, my sample deployments under GlassFish use the web console rather than the Ant script familiar from earlier examples of Tomcat deployment.

In the web console, there is also a *Resources* tab in the same left panel as the *Applications* tab. The *Resources* tab lists database connections, JMS message topics and queues, email sessions, and other resources that GlassFish applications are likely to use. In this chapter, the section on EJB-based services illustrates a database connection with two `@Entity` examples, one involving GlassFish and the other involving TomEE.

If *AS_HOME* points to the GlassFish install directory, the *AS_HOME/bin* subdirectory has the *asadmin* utility that runs as a command-line application. This utility can be used, as can the web console, to administer GlassFish. At the *asadmin* prompt, the command:

```
asadmin>list-commands
```

gives a sorted list of the local and remote commands available. Some of these commands require administrator privilege. For example, the *stop-instance* command, which stops an executing instance of the GlassFish JAS, requires administrator status; hence, the *asadmin* utility would prompt for the administrator name and password given during the GlassFish installation.

GlassFish lets the administrator organize deployed applications into *domains*. At start-up, for example, it is common to have GlassFish create a domain named *domain1*; the domain names are arbitrary but, of course, each must be unique. A domain can be stopped:

```
% asadmin stop-domain domain1
```

and started again:

```
% asadmin start-domain domain1
```

A domain also can be restarted with the *restart-domain* command.

GlassFish domains are implemented as subdirectories of the *domains* directory, and each domain, in turn, has an *autodeploy* subdirectory. Deploying an application is straightforward. Consider the *predictions.war* file RESTful service from Chapter 1, which is created using the Ant script. This file, with no changes, can be deployed to the GlassFish *domain1* by copying the WAR file to:

```
AS_HOME/glassfish/domains/domain1/autodeploy
```

The copying can be done at the command line or through the GlassFish web console. To confirm a successful deployment, GlassFish creates an empty marker file:

```
AS_HOME/glassfish/domains/domain1/autodeploy/predictions.war_deployed
```

If the deployment fails, GlassFish indicates so with a marker file:

```
AS_HOME/glassfish/domains/domain1/autodeploy/predictions.war_deployedFailed
```

If the *predictions* service is undeployed by removing the file *predictions.war* from the *autodeploy* subdirectory, GlassFish likewise confirms with another marker file:

```
AS_HOME/glassfish/domains/domain1/autodeploy/predictions.war_undeployed
```

As noted earlier, the GlassFish web console is an easy way to deploy applications, including web services, to a specified domain. The deployed file (for instance, a WAR file or a web service) can be uploaded from a remote machine to the GlassFish server.

The Derby database system, which ships with GlassFish3, is not started automatically when a domain is activated. The database system can be started with the command:

```
% asadmin start-database
```

An EJB example in this chapter accesses Derby with JPA.

# Servlet-Based Web Services Under GlassFish

GlassFish distinguishes between *servlet-based* and *EJB-based* web services. Servlet-based services include REST-style and SOAP-based services of the sort published earlier with Tomcat, Jetty, or a command-line publisher. EJB-based services also may be REST-style or SOAP-based services implemented as Session EJBs. For example, a JAX-RS service might be implemented as a Session EJB. Yet GlassFish and other JASes make it especially attractive to implement legacy @Stateless EJBs as SOAP-based web services because this requires only an additional annotation, @WebService. For servlet-based services under the JAX-WS umbrella, @WebService and @WebServiceProvider instances, the deployment under GlassFish is simpler than the deployment under Tomcat because GlassFish includes, among its libraries, the full Metro implementation of JAX-WS; hence, the Metro JAR files need not be (indeed, should not be) packaged in the deployed WAR file. GlassFish can handle JAX-WS out of the box.

Among the services in the previous chapters deployed with Tomcat or Jetty, all would count as servlet-based in GlassFish terms. They can be deployed, as is, to GlassFish as servlet-based services. Here is a sample selection of services from Chapters 2 and 5. This review focuses on what needs to be included in a WAR file for GlassFish deployment of servlet-based services.

*predictions2*

This is the *predictions* RESTful service implemented as an HttpServlet. Here, for review, are the contents of the deployed WAR file under GlassFish:

```
WEB-INF/web.xml
WEB-INF/classes/predictions2/Prediction.class
WEB-INF/classes/predictions2/Predictions.class
WEB-INF/classes/predictions2/PredictionsServlet.class
WEB-INF/data/predictions.db
WEB-INF/lib/json.jar
```

None of the source code needs to change; indeed, this WAR file can be deployed, as is, under Tomcat, Jetty, or GlassFish. For review, the service supports all of the CRUD operations and responds with either XML (the default) or JSON (if the HTTP header includes the key/value pair `Accept: application/json`). The *json.jar* file in the deployed WAR generates the JSON.

There is a subtle difference between the URLs used in calls against the Tomcat or Jetty deployment, on the one side, and the GlassFish deployment, on the other side. For example, for Tomcat/Jetty, the *curl* call:

```
% curl localhost:8080/predictions2?id=31
```

returns in XML format the `Prediction` with an `id` value of 31. Against the GlassFish deployment, the URL becomes:

```
% curl localhost:8081/predictions2/?id=31   ;; /?id=31 instead of ?id=31
```

Under GlassFish deployment, a slash, /, occurs after the WAR filename. In this example, the port number for Tomcat is 8080 as usual. For the sample runs in this section, the assumption is that GlassFish is started after Tomcat was already running; hence, GlassFish awaits HTTP connections on port 8081.

The *predictions2* service does not require an *interceptor* servlet that acts as the intermediary between client requests and the web service. In the case of the *predictions2* service, the implementation class is `PredictionsServlet`, a subclass of `HttpServlet`. In short, the service instance is itself a servlet. In this sense, the *predictions2* service is the least complicated implementation among the REST-style and SOAP-based implementations of the *predictions* and *adages* services in Chapter 2. The SOAP-based *predictionsSOAP* implementation uses the Metro `WSServlet` as the interceptor. The JAX-RS implementation, *predictions3*, uses the Jersey `ServletContainer` as the interceptor, and the Restlet implementation of the *adages* RESTful service relies upon the `ServerServlet` as the interceptor.

## predictions3

This a RESTful version of the service using JAX-RS. The WAR file can be deployed, as is, under Tomcat, Jetty, or GlassFish. Here, for review, are the contents of the deployed WAR file:

```
WEB-INF/web.xml
WEB-INF/classes/predictions3/Prediction.class
WEB-INF/classes/predictions3/PredictionsList.class
WEB-INF/classes/predictions3/PredictionsRS.class
```

```
WEB-INF/classes/predictions3/RestfulPrediction.class
WEB-INF/data/predictions.db
WEB-INF/lib/asm.jar
WEB-INF/lib/jackson-annotations.jar
WEB-INF/lib/jackson-core.jar
WEB-INF/lib/jackson-databind.jar
WEB-INF/lib/jersey-core.jar
WEB-INF/lib/jersey-server.jar
WEB-INF/lib/jersey-servlet.jar
```

The various *jackson* JAR files provide the JSON support and the *jersey* JARs are the RI implementation of JAX-RS. The *predictions3* service also supports all of the CRUD operations. The syntax of the CRUD calls changes deliberately in order to highlight the JAX-WS @Path annotation. For example, the *curl* call:

```
% curl http://localhost:8081/predictions3/resourcesP/json/31
```

would return, in JSON format, the Prediction with the id value 31.

*adages2*

This is a Restlet implementation of the RESTful *adages* service. Nothing in the WAR file changes from the Tomcat or Jetty deployments. The service supports all of the CRUD operations with intuitive URIs such as /create to create a new Adage or /delete/9 to delete the Adage with the id value of 9. For review, here are the contents of the deployed WAR file:

```
WEB-INF/web.xml
WEB-INF/classes/aphorism2/Adage.class
WEB-INF/classes/aphorism2/Adages.class
WEB-INF/classes/aphorism2/AdagesApplication$1.class
WEB-INF/classes/aphorism2/AdagesApplication.class
WEB-INF/classes/aphorism2/CreateResource.class
WEB-INF/classes/aphorism2/JsonAllResource.class
WEB-INF/classes/aphorism2/PlainResource.class
WEB-INF/classes/aphorism2/UpdateResource.class
WEB-INF/classes/aphorism2/XmlAllResource.class
WEB-INF/classes/aphorism2/XmlOneResource.class
WEB-INF/lib/org.json.jar
WEB-INF/lib/org.restlet.ext.json.jar
WEB-INF/lib/org.restlet.ext.servlet.jar
WEB-INF/lib/org.restlet.ext.xml.jar
WEB-INF/lib/org.restlet.jar
```

This service, like the others, deploys straightforwardly to GlassFish.

*predictionsSOAP*

This is the SOAP-based implementation of the *predictions* service, which also supports all of the CRUD operations but in this case with four methods annotated with @WebMethod. The implementation includes a service-side handler that verifies a security credential sent with a request. For the GlassFish deployment, the interceptor servlet is the Metro `WSServlet`, but the Metro JAR files are not in the deployed WAR file because GlassFish comes with the Metro libraries. Here, for review, are the contents of the deployed WAR file:

```
WEB-INF/web.xml
WEB-INF/classes/predictions/DataStore.class
WEB-INF/classes/predictions/Prediction.class
WEB-INF/classes/predictions/Predictions.class
WEB-INF/classes/predictions/PredictionsSOAP.class
WEB-INF/classes/predictions/ServiceHashHandler.class
WEB-INF/classes/predictions/VerbosityException.class
WEB-INF/data/predictions.db
WEB-INF/lib/commons-codec.jar
WEB-INF/serviceHandler.xml
WEB-INF/sun-jaxws.xml
```

The upshot of this review is that services deployed under `Endpoint`, Tomcat, or Jetty should deploy either as is or with very small changes (for instance, removing Metro JARs from the WAR file) to GlassFish.

The next section picks up a theme from Chapter 3, which focused on clients against REST-style services. The idea is to illustrate how a service-side API (in this case, Restlet) can be combined with a different client-side API (in this case, the JAX-WS `Dispatch` interface). In the world of JASes, mixed APIs are more the rule than the exception. The Restlet/JAX-WS combination is not without complication, however; the section is thus an opportunity to review, in the context of GlassFish deployment, the challenges of RESTful services before moving on to SOAP-based services under GlassFish.

## An Example with Mixed APIs

JAX-RS, Restlet, and JAX-WS with `@WebServiceProvider` have service-side and client-side APIs. Chapter 3 includes an example of the JAX-RS client-side API. This section introduces a client-side API designed specifically for `@WebServiceProvider` services, but this API will be used, as an illustration, against the Restlet *adages2* service deployed with GlassFish. In summary, the service-side API is Restlet and the client-side API is JAX-WS, in particular the `Dispatch` client-side API targeted at `@WebServiceProvider` services.

"A RESTful Service as a @WebServiceProvider" on page 85 of Chapter 2 covers the REST-style *adages3* service, which is implemented as a `@WebServiceProvider`. The implementation class begins as follows:

```
public class AdagesProvider implements Provider<Source> {
```

The `Provider<Source>` provides XML documents: a `Source` is a source of XML specifically. To implement the `Provider` interface, the `AdagesProvider` class defines the method:

```
public Source invoke(Source request); // declaration
```

The `invoke` method on the service side expects an XML `Source`, perhaps `null`, and returns an XML `Source`, which also could be `null`. In the usual case, the response `Source` is not `null`; the request `Source` would be `null` on HTTP bodyless requests such as GETs and DELETEs. A `Source` can serve as the source of a transformation, which yields a `Result`. For example, a `Source` of XML might be transformed into an HTML, plain text, or some other MIME type of document. The standard JAX-P `Transformer` class encapsulates a `transform` method that takes two arguments: the first is a `Source` of XML and the second is a `Result` (see Figure 7-3).

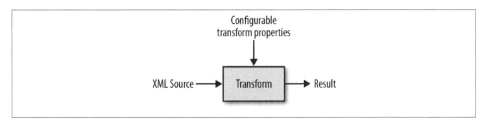

*Figure 7-3. A transformation from a Source to a Result*

The `Provider` interface used on the service side has, as a client-side counterpart, the `Dispatch` interface. A `Dispatch` object, which serves as *dynamic service-proxy*, likewise encapsulates an `invoke` method that expects a `Source` (perhaps `null`) and returns a `Source` (perhaps `null` but typically not). The details of a `Dispatch` and `Provider` interaction can be summed up as follows (see Figure 7-4):

- A client calls the `Dispatch` method `invoke` with an XML document as the `Source`. If the request does not require such a document as an argument, the `Source` can be `null`.

- The client request is dispatched, on the service side, to the `invoke` method in a `Provider`. The `Source` argument passed to the service-side `invoke` corresponds to the `Source` argument passed to the client-side `invoke`.

- The service transforms the `Source` into an appropriate `Result`—for instance, a DOM tree that can be searched for content of interest or an HTML document suitable for display in a browser.

- The service returns an XML `Source` as a response; the response is typically not `null`.

- The client receives the `Source` from the service as the return value of the `Dispatch` method `invoke`. The client then transforms this `Source`, as needed, into an appropriate `Result` for client-side processing.

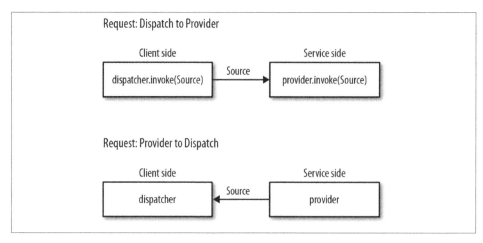

*Figure 7-4. The interaction between the* `Dispatch` *and* `Provider` *invoke methods*

The `DispatchClient` (see Example 7-1) uses the `invoke` method in a `Dispatch` service-proxy to make CRUD calls against the Restlet *adages2* service. This client creates a `Service` instance (line 1), whose identity is a `QName`, in this case `uri:restlet`. The name is arbitrary but should be unique. The Restlet service, written with an altogether different API, has no `invoke` method to pair up with the `Dispatch` method named `in voke`. Nonetheless, the communication between the two is mostly trouble-free. The trouble spot is clarified next.

*Example 7-1. The* `DispatchClient` *against the Restlet adages2 service*

```
import javax.xml.ws.Service;
import javax.xml.namespace.QName;
import javax.xml.ws.http.HTTPBinding;
import javax.xml.ws.ServiceMode;
import javax.xml.ws.Dispatch;
import javax.xml.transform.Source;
import javax.xml.transform.stream.StreamSource;
import javax.xml.transform.stream.StreamResult;
import javax.xml.ws.handler.MessageContext;
import java.util.Map;
import java.io.StringReader;

public class DispatchClient {
    private static final String baseUrl = "http://localhost:8081/aphorisms2/";

    public static void main(String[ ] args) {
        new DispatchClient().callRestlet();
    }
    private void callRestlet() {
        QName qname = getQName("uri", "restlet"); // service's name
        Service service = Service.create(qname);                          ❶
```

```
        runTests(service);
    }
    private void runTests(Service service) {
        // get all -- plain text
        Dispatch<Source> dispatch = getDispatch(service, getQName("get", "All"),   ❷
                                                baseUrl);
        setRequestMethod(dispatch, "GET");                                          ❸
        Source result = dispatch.invoke(null);                                      ❹
        stringifyAndPrintResponse("Result (plaintext):", result);
        // get all -- xml
        dispatch = getDispatch(service, getQName("get", "AllXml"), baseUrl + "xml");
        setRequestMethod(dispatch, "GET");
        result = dispatch.invoke(null);
        stringifyAndPrintResponse("Result (xml):", result);
        // get all -- json
        dispatch =
            getDispatch(service, getQName("get", "AllJson"), baseUrl + "json");
        setRequestMethod(dispatch, "GET");
        result = dispatch.invoke(null);
        stringifyAndPrintResponse("Result (json):", result);
        // get one -- xml
        dispatch =
            getDispatch(service, getQName("get", "OneXml"), baseUrl + "xml/2");
        setRequestMethod(dispatch, "GET");
        result = dispatch.invoke(null);
        stringifyAndPrintResponse("Result (one--xml):", result);
        // delete
        dispatch =
            getDispatch(service, getQName("delete", "One"), baseUrl + "delete/3");
        setRequestMethod(dispatch, "DELETE");
        result = dispatch.invoke(null);
        stringifyAndPrintResponse("Result (delete):", result);
        // post -- failure
        dispatch =
            getDispatch(service, getQName("post", "Create"), baseUrl + "create");
        setRequestMethod(dispatch, "POST");
        String cargo = "<a>words=This test will not work!</a>"; // minimal XML     ❺
        StringReader reader = new StringReader(cargo);
        result = dispatch.invoke(new StreamSource(reader));
        stringifyAndPrintResponse("Result (post):", result);
    }
    private Dispatch<Source> getDispatch(Service service, QName portName,
        String url) {
        service.addPort(portName, HTTPBinding.HTTP_BINDING, url);
        return service.createDispatch(portName,
                                      Source.class,
                                      javax.xml.ws.Service.Mode.MESSAGE);
    }
    private void setRequestMethod(Dispatch<Source> dispatcher, String method) {
        Map<String, Object> rc = dispatcher.getRequestContext();
        rc.put(MessageContext.HTTP_REQUEST_METHOD, method);
    }
```

```
        private QName getQName(String ns, String ln) {
            return new QName(ns, ln);
        }
        private void stringifyAndPrintResponse(String msg, Source result) {
            String str = null;
            if (result instanceof StreamSource) {
                try {
                    StreamSource source = (StreamSource) result;
                    byte[ ] buff = new byte[1024]; // adages are short
                    source.getInputStream().read(buff);
                    str = new String(buff);
                }
                catch(Exception e) { throw new RuntimeException(e); }
            }
            System.out.println("\n" + msg + "\n" + str);
        }
    }
}
```

After the setup, the DispatchClient makes six calls against the Restlet service (lines 2 through 4 illustrate), which can be summarized as follows:

getAllPT

The first call gets all of the Adages in plain text. The response, extracted from the Source, is:

```
1: What can be shown cannot be said. -- 7 words
2: If a lion could talk, we could not understand him. -- 10 words
...
```

This call uses a GET request with the default URI /, the slash.

For all of the calls against the Restlet service, the Source of XML returned as a response is sent to the stringifyAndPrintResponse method. This method first checks whether the Source is, in fact, a StreamSource and, if so, extracts the bytes from the InputStream encapsulated in the StreamSource. These bytes then are fed to a String constructor, which produces a string. The resulting string may be plain text, as in this first sample call, or XML and JSON, as in later sample calls.

getAllXml

This call becomes another GET request but the URI is now /xml. The response has the same informational content as getAllPT but the format is XML.

getAllJson

This call also results in a GET request but with a URI of /json. The response is in JSON format.

getOne

This call results in yet another GET request with the URI /xml/2, which specifies the Adage with an id of 2. The response is an XML document.

deleteOne

This call becomes a DELETE request with the URI /delete/3, which specifies the Adage with an id of 3 as the one to remove from the list of Adages. The response is a plain text confirmation of the deletion.

create

This call fails. The response is an error message:

```
No words were given for the adage.
```

The problem arises because, with a POST request against the URI /create, the Source argument to the invoke method cannot be null but, rather, must contain the words in the Adage to be created. The Restlet service expects a simple HTML-like form in the body of the POST request, and this form has key/value pairs such as:

```
words=This is the way the world ends
```

The Restlet service searches on the key words to get the value, in this case the line from the T. S. Eliot poem "The Hollow Men." On the client side, however, the call to the *create* operation uses a POST request against the URI /create, and the contents of the POST body are given as a Source instance—of XML. When the underlying XML libraries parse the non-XML string above, the parser throws an exception. The fix is to turn the string into XML, for example, the minimalist XML document (line 5):

```
<a>words=This is the way the world ends</a>
```

When this document is turned into a StreamSource argument to the Dispatch method invoke, the XML parser is satisfied. The problem now shifts to the service side because the Restlet service expects a simple key/value pair, not a key/value pair embedded as text in an XML element. As a result, the Restlet service complains that it cannot find the lookup key words in the body of the POST request.

The example reinforces a hard lesson in programming and many other activities: the devil is in the details. The fix to the problem would be relatively straightforward; perhaps the easiest fix would be to make the Restlet service flexible enough to handle POST requests whose cargo is either plain text or XML. The example also underscores that the JAX-WS @WebServiceProvider API is XML-centric. In this API, a Dispatch client against a Provider service such as the *adages3* service (see Section 2.5 in Chapter 2) would be natural because each side would be dealing with XML Source arguments and return values.

# An Interactive Website and a SOAP-Based Web Service

This section has an example that uses GlassFish to host a website and Tomcat to host a SOAP-based web service that the website accesses. Chapter 3, on RESTful clients, has examples in which jQuery clients make calls against REST-style services that respond with JSON payloads; the JavaScript embedded in the web page puts the JSON to good use. The website in the current example is old school in that the HTML page contains no JavaScript. Instead, the page has a familiar *submit* button that, when pressed, causes an HTML form to be POSTed to a JSP script, which then calls upon a SOAP-based service to perform simple computations. The results of these computations are displayed on the web page. The interaction is among an HTML page, a JSP script with access to *wsimport*-generated artifacts, and a SOAP-based service (see Figure 7-5). This distributed application performs temperature conversions. To make the example realistic and to set up a comparison between deployment details, the web service is published with standalone Tomcat and the website is published with GlassFish.

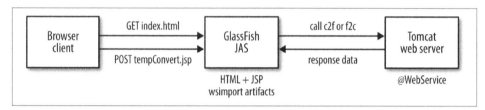

*Figure 7-5. An architectural sketch of the tcSiteAndService*

The HTML page *index.html* (see Example 7-2) contains a simple form with a text box into which a user enters temperatures to be converted into fahrenheit and centigrade. To keep matters simple, the CSS styling is embedded in the HTML. When the HTML form is submitted with a button push, a POST request is sent to the JSP script named *tempConvert.jsp*. There is also an error script, *error.jsp*, to handle errors that result from trying to convert non-numeric input (e.g., the string *foo*) into a decimal number. The two JSP scripts and the HTML page, together with some other artifacts discussed shortly, are deployed in the WAR file *tcWeb.war*. GlassFish hosts the website.

*Example 7-2. The HTML document index.html*

```
<!DOCTYPE html>
<html>
  <head>
    <style type = "text/css">
      input {background-color: white; font-weight: bold; font-size: medium}
      legend {color:#990000; font-size: large;}
      fieldset {width: 600px; background-color: rgb(225, 225, 225);}
    </style>
  </head>
  <body>
```

```
<form method = 'post' action = 'tempConvert.jsp'>          ❶
  <fieldset>
    <legend>Temperature conversion</legend>
    <table>
      <tr>
        <td>Temperature:</td>
        <td><input type = 'text' name = 'temperature'/></td>  ❷
      </tr>
    </table>
    <input type = 'submit' value = ' Convert '/>           ❸
  </fieldset>
</form>
</body>
</html>
```

For context, the main contents of the website WAR file are:

```
WEB-INF/web.xml
WEB-INF/classes/tempConvertClient/C2F.class
WEB-INF/classes/tempConvertClient/C2FResponse.class
WEB-INF/classes/tempConvertClient/F2C.class
WEB-INF/classes/tempConvertClient/F2CResponse.class
WEB-INF/classes/tempConvertClient/ObjectFactory.class
WEB-INF/classes/tempConvertClient/TempConvert.class
WEB-INF/classes/tempConvertClient/TempConvertService.class
error.jsp
index.html
tempConvert.jsp
```

The HTML page *index.html* provides a text field (line 2) into which a user can enter input. When the form (line 1) is submitted by clicking the *submit* button (line 3), the targeted action is the JSP script *tempConvert.jsp*, which receives the contents of the text field as request data.

The code of JSP script *tempConvert.jsp* (see Example 7-3) has two **page** directives (lines 1 and 2), which import *wsimport*-generated classes for the web service. These classes reside in the package/directory *tempConvertClient*, which is included in the deployed WAR file *tcWeb.war*. The JSP script extracts the user input from the HTTP POST request (line 3) and then tries to convert the input to a floating-point number. If there are any errors, control immediately goes via an automatic redirect, which GlassFish manages, to the error page *error.jsp* (see Example 7-4); the HTTP status code is 400 for *bad request* (see line 1 in the displayed error page). The error page announces an input error and, through a hyperlink back to *index.html*, gives the user the option of trying again.

*Example 7-3. The JSP script tempConvert.jsp, deployed in the tcWeb.war file*

```
<!DOCTYPE html>
<%@ page errorPage = "error.jsp" %>
<!-- wsimport-generated artifacts -->
<%@ page import = "tempConvertClient.TempConvertService" %>     ❶
<%@ page import = "tempConvertClient.TempConvert" %>            ❷
```

```html
<html>
  <head>
  <style type = 'text/css'>
    a {color: #151b8d; text-decoration:none;}
    a:visited {color: #151b8d;}
    a:hover {color: #fff; background-color: #666;}
    .p {color: blue; font-size: large;}
    legend {color:#990000; font-size: large;}
    fieldset {width: 600px; background-color: rgb(225, 225, 225);}
  </style>
  <%! private float f2c, c2f, temp; %>
  <%
    String tempStr = request.getParameter("temperature"); // text field ❸
    if (tempStr != null) this.temp = Float.parseFloat(tempStr.trim());
    this.f2c = this.c2f = this.temp;
    TempConvert port = new TempConvertService().getTempConvertPort();
    c2f = port.c2F(temp);                                                    ❹
    f2c = port.f2C(temp);                                                    ❺
  %>
  <body>
    <fieldset>
      <legend>Temperature conversions</legend>
      <p><%= this.temp %>F = <%= this.c2f %>C</p>                           ❻
      <p><%= this.temp %>C = <%= this.f2c %>F</p>                           ❼
    </fieldset>
    <hr/>
    <a href = 'index.html'>Try another</a>                                  ❽
  </body>
</html>
```

If the conversion of the input data to a floating-point number succeeds, the JSP script calls the SOAP-based *tcService*, running on Tomcat, to convert the number into centigrade (line 4) and fahrenheit (line 5). The values returned from the *tcService* then are displayed (lines 6 and 7). A hyperlink at the bottom of the page (line 8) gives the user the option to try again.

*Example 7-4. The error page error.jsp*

```jsp
<%@ page isErrorPage = "true" %>
<!DOCTYPE html>
<html>
  <head>
    <style type = 'text/css'>
      a {color: #151b8d; text-decoration:none;}
      a:visited {color: #151b8d;}
      a:hover {color: #fff; background-color: #666;}
      .p {color: red; font-size: large;}
    </style>
  </head>
  <body>
    <% response.setStatus(400); %> <!-- bad request -->    ❶
    <p class = 'p'>Numbers only, please.</p>
```

```
    <hr/>
    <a href = 'index.html'>Try again.</a>
  </body>
</html>
```

The *tcService.war* file, which contains the SOAP-based web service, has these contents:

```
WEB-INF/web.xml                                    ❶
WEB-INF/classes/tempConvert/TempConvert.class
WEB-INF/lib/webservices-api.jar                    ❷
WEB-INF/lib/webservices-rt.jar                     ❸
WEB-INF/sun-jaxws.xml                              ❹
```

Two deployment files are needed (lines 1 and 4) because the Metro JWSServlet acts as the intermediary between the client request and the TempConvert service. The *web.xml* (see Example 7-5) specifies the Metro servlet (line 1) as the request handler, and the *sun-jaxws.xml* then routes the request from the Metro servlet to a TempConvert instance (see Example 7-5). Further, the two Metro JAR files (lines 2 and 3) are needed because Tomcat does not come with the Metro implementation of JAX-WS.

*Example 7-5. The web.xml for the TempConvert service deployed under Tomcat*

```
<?xml version="1.0" encoding="UTF-8"?>
<web-app>
  <listener>
    <listener-class>
      com.sun.xml.ws.transport.http.servlet.WSServletContextListener
    </listener-class>
  </listener>
  <servlet>
    <servlet-name>jaxws</servlet-name>
    <servlet-class>
      com.sun.xml.ws.transport.http.servlet.WSServlet       ❶
    </servlet-class>
    <load-on-startup>1</load-on-startup>
  </servlet>
  <servlet-mapping>
    <servlet-name>jaxws</servlet-name>
    <url-pattern>/*</url-pattern>
  </servlet-mapping>
</web-app>
```

The JSP script *tempConvert.jsp* makes calls against the *tcService* by using the *wsimport*-generated classes in the package/directory *tempConvertClient*. This JSP script together with the HTML page, the error page, and the contents of the *tempConvert-Client* directory are encapsulated in the WAR file *tcWeb.war*, which is deployed with GlassFish instead of Tomcat. The point of interest is that the Metro JAR files are *not* included in the deployed *tcWeb.war* precisely because GlassFish itself comes with the full Metro implementation. Accordingly, if the *tcService* were deployed under GlassFish instead of standalone Tomcat, the two JAR files in *tcService.war* could be removed—

indeed, these JAR files would have to be removed in order to avoid a conflict with the Metro library that comes installed with GlassFish. The *tcService* still would use the JWSServlet as the intermediary, which in turn means that the *web.xml* and the *sun-jaxws.xml* configuration files would be needed as well.

It is hardly surprising that GlassFish includes the Metro libraries. Metro is the reference implementation of JAX-WS; the GlassFish JAS includes this implementation as one of the JAS components. The GlassFish JAS officially comes under the *GlassFish Metro Project*, which in turn includes the full web service stack that implements JAX-WS. As earlier examples with Tomcat and Jetty illustrate, the web service stack can be used independently of the GlassFish JAS. Among JASes, Oracle WebLogic also includes the Metro web service stack.

# A @WebService as a @Stateless Session EJB

Why should SOAP-based web services be deployed as EJBs instead of as POJOs? One answer is quite practical. If an organization already has stateless Session EJBs in place, these can become SOAP-based services as well by adding the @WebService annotation to the EJB code; no other change to the EJB code is needed. At a more technical but still practical level, the EJB container is programmer-friendly in handling issues such as thread safety. A web container such as Tomcat's Catalina or Jetty does not provide thread safety for web sites and web services, but an EJB container does provide such safety. Concurrency issues are formidable challenges in Java, and it is appealing to offload such challenges from the programmer to the container. GlassFish and other JASes also offer first-rate development support for web services deployed as @Stateless Session EJBs. Upon successful deployment of the service, for example, GlassFish generates a web page that can be used to test all of the service operations; another page to inspect the WSDL; another page to inspect performance; and so on. In any event, the good news is that Java programmers have options about how to implement SOAP-based as well as REST-style web services. This section explores one such option for SOAP-based services: the @Stateless Session EJB. The EJB example also uses a database for persistence, which is an opportunity to illustrate how the @Entity annotation works. For reference, this version of the service is *predictionsEJB*.

In the *predictionsEJB* service, instances of the Prediction class, which is annotated as an @Entity (line 1 in Example 7-6), are persisted in the database, in this case the Derby database that comes with GlassFish. A configuration document, clarified shortly, instructs the GlassFish JPA provider to generate a table that stores Prediction instances. Because a Prediction has three properties (who, what, and id), the table will have three fields. By default, the field names are the property names and the table name is the class name.

*Example 7-6. The Prediction class, annotated as an @Entity*

```
package predEJB;

import javax.persistence.Entity;
import javax.persistence.NamedQuery;
import javax.persistence.NamedQueries;
import javax.persistence.Id;
import javax.persistence.GeneratedValue;
import java.io.Serializable;

@Entity                                                          ❶
@NamedQueries({                                                  ❷
  @NamedQuery(name = "pred.list", query = "select p from Prediction p")
})
public class Prediction implements Serializable {
    private String who;    // person
    private String what;   // his/her prediction
    private int    id;     // identifier used as lookup key

    public Prediction() { }
    public String getWho() { return this.who; }
    public void setWho(String who) { this.who = who; }
    public String getWhat() { return this.what; }
    public void setWhat(String what) { this.what = what; }
    @Id                                                          ❸
    @GeneratedValue                                              ❹
    public int getId() { return this.id; }
    public void setId(int id) { this.id = id; }
}
```

The Prediction class uses four annotations but JPA has others that might be of interest. Immediately after the @Entity annotation (line 1) come two additional annotations: @NamedQueries and @NamedQuery (line 2). For convenience, the Prediction class includes a named query in the JPA QL (Query Language), which is close to but not identical with SQL. QL acts as a uniformly structured alternative to the various SQL dialects; hence, QL promotes portability across database systems. In the select query the letter p, short for *prediction*, is arbitrary but serves as a placeholder for each Prediction row to be selected. The query is used in the PredictionEJB class, which is clarified shortly.

In the Prediction class, the id property is annotated as an @Id (line 3), which means that the id of a Prediction becomes the primary key for a record in the database table. The id also is annotated as a @GeneratedValue (line 4), which means that the database system will generate unique primary keys for each Prediction; the keys are ascending integers, starting with 1. Other annotations are available. For example, the who property might be annotated with:

```
@Column(name = "predictor", nullable = false, length = 64)
```

In this case, the database field would be named *predictor*; the database would ensure that the content of the field could not be NULL; and the database would enforce a maximum length of 64 characters on the who value.

The JPA details for the *predictionsEJB* service could be provided programmatically, but the best practice is to isolate such details in a configuration document named *persistence.xml* (see Example 7-7). Under this approach, the database configuration could be changed without changing any code. The *persistence.xml* file in this example is deliberately minimalist to show that database configuration need not be complicated. The persistence-unit (line 1) has a name that is referenced in the EJB, which is examined shortly, and the persistence unit also has a transaction-type, in this case JTA (Java Transaction API, the default). Three properties are set in the document (lines 2, 3, and 4). The first property (line 1) automates the creation of the database table and also causes the table to be dropped whenever the application is redeployed; in production, create-tables might be used instead. The second property (line 2) ensures that the table generation impacts the database resource associated with the *predictionsEJB* service; in this example, the database is the default, Apache Derby. The third and last property (line 3) specifies the JDBC driver that connects the service to the database system; this driver, as its name indicates, targets the Derby database system.

*Example 7-7. The persistence.xml JPA configuration document*

```
<?xml version = "1.0" encoding = "UTF-8"?>
<persistence>
  <persistence-unit name = "predictionsDB" transaction-type = "JTA">   ❶
    <properties>
      <property name  = "eclipselink.ddl-generation"                    ❷
                value = "drop-and-create-tables"/>
      <property name  = "eclipselink.ddl-generation.output-mode"        ❸
                value = "database"/>
      <property name  = "javax.persistence.jdbc.driver"                 ❹
                value = "org.apache.derby.jdbc.ClientDriver"/>
    </properties>
  </persistence-unit>
</persistence>
```

The *persistence.xml* document does not specify what, in GlassFish terminology, is the JDBC Resource. Each Resource has a JNDI name for identification in lookup operations. Neither does the *persistence.xml* document specify a table name in the database. As a result, the defaults kick in. The default JDBC Resource, which is a DataSource, is named:

```
jdbc/__default
```

The default table name derives from the name of class annotated as an @Entity, in this case Prediction. Accordingly, the *Prediction* table is accessible through a data source named *jdbc/__default*. Of course, GlassFish allows an administrator to create and name other data sources.

The `PredictionEJB` class (see Example 7-8) is the service implementation. The class is annotated with both `@Stateless` (line 1) and `@WebService` (line 2), although this order is arbitrary. Line 3 is the all-important `@PersistenceContext` annotation on the `Enti tyManager` reference `em`. In the `@PersistenceContext` annotation, the `name` attribute has `predictionsDB` as its value, which is likewise the value of the `name` attribute in the `persistence-unit` element of the *persistence.xml* document. Accordingly, the `@Persis tenceContext` annotation links the `PredictionEJB` service to the configuration file *persistence.xml*. The `@PersistenceContext` annotation also causes dependency injection on the `em` reference: the runtime ensures that `em` refers to a suitable `EntityManag er` instance, which manages the connection between the `PredictionEJB` and the back-end database.

The *predictionsEJB* service implements the CRUD operations, all of which now reference the database using the `EntityManager` methods, which can include JPA QL constructs. The `EntityManager` operations, which are implemented under the hood as transactions, are the four CRUD operations with intuitive method names: for example, the *create* operation in the *predictionsEJB* service occurs in the `create` method (line 4).

*Example 7-8. The `PredictionEJB` class, annotated as a `@Stateless @WebService`*

```
package predEJB;

import javax.ejb.Stateless;
import javax.jws.WebService;
import javax.jws.WebMethod;
import java.util.List;
import java.util.Arrays;
import javax.persistence.PersistenceContext;
import javax.persistence.EntityManager;

@Stateless                                                      ❶
@WebService                                                     ❷
public class PredictionEJB {
    @PersistenceContext(name = "predictionsDB")                ❸
    private EntityManager em;

    @WebMethod
    public Prediction create(String who, String what) {
        if (who == null || what == null) return null;
        if (who.length() < 1 || what.length() < 1) return null;
        Prediction prediction = new Prediction();
        prediction.setWho(who);
        prediction.setWhat(what);
        try {
            em.persist(prediction);                            ❹
        }
```

```
        catch(Exception e) {
            throw new RuntimeException("create:persist -- " + e);
        }
        return prediction;
    }
    @WebMethod
    public Prediction edit(int id, String who, String what) {
        if (id < 1 || who == null || what == null) return null;
        if (who.length() < 1 || what.length() < 1) return null;
        Prediction prediction = em.find(Prediction.class, id);
        if (prediction == null) return null;

        prediction.setWho(who);
        prediction.setWhat(what);
        return prediction;
    }
    @WebMethod
    public String delete(int id) {
        String msg = "Could not remove prediction with ID " + id;
        if (id < 1) return msg;
        Prediction prediction = em.find(Prediction.class, id);       ❺
        if (prediction == null) return msg;
        em.remove(prediction); // delete from database              ❻

        return prediction.toString() + " -- deleted";
    }
    @WebMethod
    public Prediction getOne(int id) {
        if (id < 1) return null;
        Prediction prediction = em.find(Prediction.class, id);       ❼
        if (prediction == null) return null;
        return prediction;
    }
    @WebMethod
    public List<Prediction> getAll() {
        List<Prediction> predList =                                  ❽
            em.createNamedQuery("pred.list", Prediction.class).getResultList();
        return predList;
    }
}
```

After a new Prediction is constructed and its who and what properties are set, the
EntityManager method persist is invoked with the new Prediction as its argument:

```
em.persist(prediction);
```

This statement saves the Prediction to the database.

The *delete* operation (line 6) first requires a *read* operation (line 5). The Prediction
has to be found before it can be removed:

```
Prediction prediction = em.find(Prediction.class, id);
```

If the `find` succeeds, the `Prediction` then can be removed from the database:

```
em.remove(prediction);
```

The same call to `find` is used in the *getOne* operation (line 7).

Updating a `Prediction` in the *edit* operation requires no explicit JPA call. Instead, the `who` and `what` properties are *set* in the usual way. The JPA infrastructure manages the coherence between an in-memory `Prediction` instance and the corresponding database record. After the `find` call fetches the `Prediction` to be updated, its properties are *set* in the usual way—and that is the end of the *update* operation.

The *getAll* operation in the *predictionsEJB* service uses the `@NamedQuery` from the `Prediction` class to select all of the `Prediction` rows from the table (line 8). For review, the statement is:

```
List<Prediction> predList =
    em.createNamedQuery("pred.list", Prediction.class).getResultList();
```

The string `pred.list` is the `@Query` name and the result list includes all of the rows selected. The `getAll` method returns the `predList` reference. The `EntityManager` encapsulates several methods besides `createNamedQuery` for creating queries against a database.

All of the methods in the `PredictionEJB` class are annotated with `@WebMethod`. In the *predictionsEJB* service, these annotations are mandatory in order for a `public` method to count as a `@WebService` operation. The EJB container takes seriously the distinction between the SEI and the SIB, the latter of which is now the `@Stateless` Session EJB. In a standalone SEI, the `@WebService` annotation is required; hence, the EJB container insists that this annotation be present in a case such as the `PredictionEJB`, the single class that serves as both the SEI and the SIB. In the servlet-based implementations seen so far, the annotation `@WebService` is recommended but technically optional. The *predictionsEJB* service could have a separate SEI and SIB but, for convenience, these have been combined into one class, `PredictionEJB`.

## Packaging and Deploying the predictionsEJB Service

Packaging and deploying a `@WebService` as a `@Stateless` Session EJB is simpler overall than deploying its servlet-based counterpart. It bears repeating that the EJB-based deployment enjoys complete thread safety. Here is a summary of the steps:

- The *.java* classes obviously need to be compiled, but packages such as `javax.ejb` and `javax.persistence` are not included among the core Java libraries. GlassFish provides these packages in the JAR file *AS_HOME/glassfish/lib/javaee.jar*. This JAR file thus needs to be on the classpath for compilation.

- The compiled *.class* files can be placed, as is, in a JAR file with any name. In this example, the JAR file is *ejbWS.jar* and its main contents are:

```
META-INF/persistence.xml      ❶
predEJB/PredictionEJB.class
predEJB/Prediction.class
```

  The critical requirement is that the *persistence.xml* document (line 1) be in the *META-INF* subdirectory.

- The JAR file with the EJB (in this case, `PredictionEJB`) and any supporting classes (in this case, `Prediction`) is then placed inside another JAR file, preferably with an *ear* (Enterprise ARchive) extension. The name is arbitrary. In this example, the EAR file is *predService.ear* and its contents are:

```
ejbWS.jar
```

- The EAR file is copied to *AS_HOME/glassfish/domains/domain1/autodeploy*. The GlassFish web console is an easy way, under the *Applications* tab, to confirm that the deployment succeeded.

- The GlassFish domain *domain1* must be up and running. To ensure that the domain is active, the command is:

```
% asadmin start-domain domain1
```

  Also, the database must be started. The command is:

```
% asadmin start-database
```

Neither the JAR file *ejbWS.jar* nor the EAR file *predService.ear* requires any configuration document other than the *persistence.xml* file in *ejbWS.jar*. GlassFish generates the traditional *ejb-jar.xml* document for the JAR file and the traditional *application.xml* document for the EAR file if these are not provided.

Once the *predictionsEJB* service is deployed, there is no need to write a test client because GlassFish generates such a client automatically. In the GlassFish web console, under the *Applications* tab, is a list of all deployed applications; for web services, the list includes servlet-based and EJB-based instances. In the *Applications* tab, the name given for the *predictionsEJB* service is the name of the EAR file: `predService` without the *.ear* extension. Clicking on this name makes the service endpoints available. There are two:

- Endpoints for the WSDL, one for HTTP and another for HTTPS. The URI for each is:

```
/PredictionEJBService/PredictionEJB?wsdl
```

  The naming convention used in this URI is:

  — the name of the `@WebService` class, in this case `PredictionEJB`, with `Service` appended

— a slash (/)

— the name of the @WebService class again

— the query string ?wsdl

> The WSDL can be used with the *wsimport* utility to generate the by now familiar client-support classes.

- The endpoint is */PredictionEJBService/PredictionEJB?Tester*, which is the GlassFish-generated test client as a web page (see Figure 7-6). The test page covers all of the operations and displays, including the request and the response SOAP message for each. Operations carried out on the test page impact the database. This test page obviates the need to write the kind of test client familiar in the servlet-based examples.

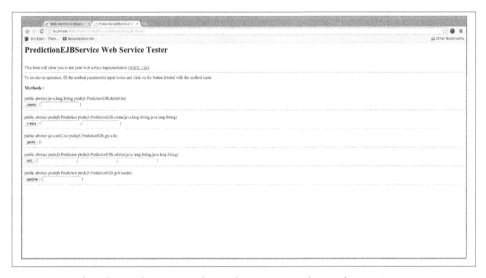

*Figure 7-6. The GlassFish-generated test client against the predictionsEJB service*

## A Client Against the predictionsEJB Service

Although the test page in the GlassFish web console is excellent for round one of testing, a Java client can be built in the usual way with *wsimport*:

```
% wsimport -p clientEJB -keep \
  http://localhost:8081/PredictionEJBService/PredictionEJB?wsdl
```

The ClientEJB (see Example 7-9) uses the *wsimport*-generated artifacts.

*Example 7-9. The sample ClientEJB built with wsimport-generated classes*

```
import clientEJB.PredictionEJBService;
import clientEJB.PredictionEJB;
import clientEJB.Prediction;
import java.util.List;

public class ClientEJB {
    public static void main(String[ ] args) {
        new ClientEJB().runTests();
    }
    private void runTests() {
        PredictionEJB port =
            new PredictionEJBService().getPredictionEJBPort();
        create(port);                       ❶
        getAll(port);                       ❷
        edit(port);      // id == 2         ❸
        getOne(port);    // id == 2         ❹
        delete(port);    // id == 2         ❺
        getAll(port);                       ❻
    }
    private void getAll(PredictionEJB port) {
        System.out.println("\n### getAll:");
        List<Prediction> predictions = port.getAll();
        for (Prediction pred : predictions) stringify(pred);
    }
    private void getOne(PredictionEJB port) {
        System.out.println("\n### getOne:");
        Prediction pred = port.getOne(2);
        stringify(pred);
    }
    private void create(PredictionEJB port) {
        System.out.println("\n### create:");
        String who = "River Friesen";
        String what = "Decentralized 24/7 hub will target robust web-readiness.";
        Prediction pred = port.create(who, what);
        stringify(pred);

        who = "Kaden Crona";
        what = "Optional static definition will unleash dynamic e-tailers.";
        pred = port.create(who, what);
        stringify(pred);
    }
    private void edit(PredictionEJB port) {
        System.out.println("\n### edit:");
        Prediction pred = port.edit(2, "Testing! New who", "Testing! New what");
        stringify(pred);
    }
    private void delete(PredictionEJB port) {
        System.out.println("\n### delete:");
        String msg = port.delete(2);
```

```
        System.out.println(msg);
    }
    private void stringify(Prediction pred) {
        if (pred == null) return;
        String s = String.format("%2d ", pred.getId()) +
            pred.getWho() + ": " + pred.getWhat();
        System.out.println(s);
    }
}
```

The `ClientEJB` runs preliminary tests against the service's CRUD operations (lines 1 through 6): predictions are created, fetched all at once and one at a time, edited, and deleted. Here is the output from a sample run right after the *predictionsEJB* had been deployed:

```
### create:
 1 River Friesen: Decentralized 24/7 hub will target robust web-readiness.
 2 Kaden Crona: Optional static definition will unleash dynamic e-tailers.
### getAll:
 1 River Friesen: Decentralized 24/7 hub will target robust web-readiness.
 2 Kaden Crona: Optional static definition will unleash dynamic e-tailers.
### edit:
 2 Testing! New who: Testing! New what
### getOne:
 2 Testing! New who: Testing! New what
### delete:
predEJB.Prediction@dbb5965 -- deleted
### getAll:
 1 River Friesen: Decentralized 24/7 hub will target robust web-readiness.
```

It should be noted that this sample run occurred immediately after deploying the service for the first time. The Derby database system maintains the primary keys—the integers that identify the `Prediction` records in the database table. Subsequent test runs of the `ClientEJB` will result in different primary keys, which means that the tests for editing and deleting need to be modified. At present, each of these tests uses 2 as the key.

# TomEE: Tomcat with Java EE Extensions

Apache TomEE (*http://tomee.apache.org*) can be downloaded in various ways, including as a standalone Java EE application server or as a bundled WAR file that can be published with Tomcat7. TomEE adds the OpenEJB container to Tomcat7 but also includes, for example, the Apache CXF implementation of the JAX-RS API and a JMS provider. TomEE, like Tomcat, can be installed anywhere on the filesystem, and the TomEE directory structure is almost identical to that of Tomcat7. TomEE is designed with simplicity in mind. The Java world is awash with options and, with respect to JASes, TomEE is one worth considering.

---

## Managing the TomEE Web Server and EJB Container

In a TomEE installation, the web server can be started and stopped independently of the EJB components, which includes the EJB container. A typical startup scenario would be:

- In *TomEE_HOME/bin*, run the startup script:

    ```
    % shartup.sh  ;; startup.bat under Windows
    ```

- In the same directory, run the startup script for the EE components:

    ```
    % tomee.sh start
    ```

The TomEE web server would be stopped in the usual way:

```
% shutdown.sh ;; shutdown.bat under Windows
```

The TomEE EE components are stopped with this command:

```
% tomee.sh stop
```

The TomEE web server furnishes the usual Tomcat7 web console (*localhost:8080*), which also includes a TomEE web console (*localhost:8080/tomee*) for the distinctly EE components.

---

## Porting the predictionsEJB Web Service to TomEE

The two *.java* files in the *predictionsEJB* service, *Prediction.java* (see Example 7-6) and *PredictionEJB.java* (see Example 7-8), are completely unchanged in the port from GlassFish to TomEE. The configuration files, however, are different. The TomEE configuration files are the *persistence.xml* file (see Example 7-10), the same name as in GlassFish, and the *openejb.xml* file (see Example 7-11).

*Example 7-10. The persistence.xml document for the TomEE port of the predictionsEJB service*

```
<persistence>
  <persistence-unit name = "predictionsDB">
    <jta-data-source>predictionsDB</jta-data-source>
    <class>predEJB.Prediction</class>                          ❶
    <properties>
      <property name  = "openjpa.jdbc.SynchronizeMappings"    ❷
                value = "buildSchema(ForeignKeys=true)"/>      ❸
    </properties>
  </persistence-unit>
</persistence>
```

---

In the *persistence.xml* document, lines 2 and 3 ensure that the OpenJPA provider automatically generates whatever database tables are required to persist `Prediction` instances. The configuration document also names the `@Entity` class `Prediction` (line 1) whose instances are mapped to table rows.

*Example 7-11. The openejb.xml for the TomEE port of the predictionsEJB service*

```
<Resource id = "predictionsDB" type = "DataSource">    ❶
  JdbcDriver = org.hsqldb.jdbcDriver                    ❷
  JdbcUrl = jdbc:hsqldb:mem:predictionsDB               ❸
</Resource>
```

The second configuration document, *openejb.xml*, names the `DataSource` (line 1); specifies the JDBC driver (line 2), in this case the driver for the HSQLDB database, a convenient RDBMS with, by default, in-memory tables; and ends with the JNDI name (line 3) of the database system. The HSQLDB system comes with TomEE. TomEE documentation covers sample `Resource` configuration for various other popular database systems such as Derby, MySQL, and PostgreSQL. The two configuration files shown here must occur in the *META-INF* subdirectory of the deployed JAR file. The deployment options and details are laid out in the next section.

TomEE, like GlassFish, provides a JAR file with the required Java EE packages such as `javax.persistence`. All of the TomEE libraries come as JAR files and most of these are in the *TomEE_HOME/lib* directory, which contains more than 100 JAR files, including the files for the Apache CXF implementation of JAX-RS. There is also the directory *TomEE_HOME/endorsed*, which holds a few additional JAR files. The TomEE JAR for the core Java EE packages is named *javaee-api-N-tomcat.jar*, with a version number where the *N* occurs. This JAR, roughly the TomEE counterpart of the GlassFish file *javaee.jar*, can be used for compilation.

## Deploying an EJB in a WAR File

TomEE comes with the familiar *TomEE_HOME/webapps* subdirectory already in place. The subdirectory *TomEE_HOME/apps* is not present but can be created manually, and the *TomEE_HOME/bin/tomee.sh* command has *deploy* and *undeploy* options that can be used to deploy EAR files whose contents are one or more JAR files, each with its own EJB. The deploy and undeploy options target the *apps* subdirectory, which TomEE supports for backwards compatibility with versions of Java EE earlier than 6. Under Java EE 6, the same Java class loader can load the contents of servlets and EJBs; hence, the Java EE 6 specification enables EJB deployment in a WAR file. This style of deployment is preferred practice in TomEE. The deployment details for the *predictionsEJB* service under TomEE can be summarized as follows:

- A standard WAR can be built using the (perhaps slightly modified) Ant script from earlier chapters. A *web.xml* document is not required. Suppose that the name of this file is *pred.war*. The two configuration files can be inserted into the WAR file subdirectory *META-INF*:

```
% jar uf pred.war META-INF/*.xml  ;; persistence.xml and openejb.xml
```

The resulting WAR structure is:

```
META-INF/MANIFEST.MF
META-INF/openejb.xml
META-INF/persistence.xml
WEB-INF/classes/predEJB/PredictionEJB.class
WEB-INF/classes/predEJB/Prediction.class
```

- The WAR file is copied to *TomEE_HOME/webapps* for deployment. A website or a servlet-based service would be deployed in exactly the same way.

- The usual client-side artifacts can be constructed with the *wsimport* utility:

```
% wsimport -p clientEJB -keep \
   http://localhost:8080/pred/webservices/PredictionEJB?wsdl
```

The TomEE endpoint URL for an EJB service differs slightly from the GlassFish endpoint. In particular, the TomEE URI in this example is */pred/webservices/PredictionEJB*: the URI begins with the slash and the name of the WAR file (*/pred*), the term *webservices* is appended (*/pred/webservices*), and then the name of the `@WebService` class is appended to yield */pred/webservices/PredictionEJB*. The very same `ClientEJB` used for the GlassFish deployment of *predictionsEJB* (see Example 7-9) can be used, once recompiled against the *wsimport*-generated artifacts to get the correct endpoint URL, against the TomEE deployment. It is a nice TomEE touch to support conventional WAR deployment of even EJBs, including EJB-based web services.

# Where Is the Best Place to Be in Java Web Services?

This book is a code-centric tour through the APIs and implementation technologies that support web services under Java. The tour has taken seven chapters. To set up an answer to the question posed in this section's title, it may be useful to review the stops along the way.

*Chapter 1*

This chapter opens the tour with a broad look at REST-style and SOAP-based services. This overview includes a short history of alternatives to distributed software systems, such as systems based on the DOA that predate and still compete with deliberately lightweight web services. The chapter sketches the relationship between web services and SOA, which can be viewed as a reaction against DOA. Chapter 1 likewise clarifies the core meaning and especially the spirit of REST as an approach to the design of distributed software systems, especially systems built on in-place, widely available, and free protocols and technologies such as HTTP and XML/JSON. A dominant theme in this overview of web services is *interoperability*, which in turn requires language and platform neutrality. Chapter 1 ends with the implementation of a small RESTful service that consists of a JSP script and two backend POJO classes. The *predictions* RESTful service is published with the Tomcat web server, and the sample client calls are done with the *curl* utility.

*Chapter 2*

This chapter narrows the focus to the various APIs and API implementations available for programming and delivering REST-style services in Java. The main APIs are:

- `HttpServlet` classes along with JSP and other scripts that become, at runtime, instances of `HttpServlet`.

- JAX-RS and Restlet classes with high-level annotations for HTTP verbs, URIs (paths), MIME types, and status codes together with support for automatically generating XML and JSON payloads.

- JAX-WS with its relatively low-level `@WebServiceProvider` and XML-centric API that gets the programmer close to the metal.

This chapter looks at various ways of generating both XML and JSON payloads, particularly given the rising popularity of JSON as a data-interchange format. Java offers a range of options for XML generation, from the `XMLEncoder` class to the rich assortment of classes in the JAX-B packages. The code samples adhere to RESTful principles such as honoring the intended meaning of each CRUD verb, using intuitive URIs to name resources, and taking full advantage of HTTP status codes to signal the fate of a request against a REST-style service. Chapter 2 and later chapters also explore, for publishing these RESTful services, production-grade web servers such as Tomcat and Jetty together with development-level publishers such as `Endpoint`, `HttpsServer`, and the Restlet `Component`. All of the APIs are quite good, on the service side and on the client side, at adhering to the separation-of-concerns principle: the programming of a web service is one thing and its publication is another—and independent— thing.

*Chapter 3*

This chapter turns from the service side to the client side. There are clients based upon the grizzled but trusty `URLConnection` class and upon REST-specific client-side APIs such as JAX-RS. As proof of concept for interoperability, clients are written in different languages. For instance, there are Perl and jQuery clients against Java services and Java clients against services whose implementation language is unknown. The code samples explore the various possibilities for dealing with XML and JSON payloads, in particular with the standard JAX-B and the third-party utilities such as `XStream` for automating the transformation of XML documents in particular into native Java objects. Most modern RESTful services furnish at least an XML Schema for the service, and Java has utilities such as *xjc* that covert an XML Schema or comparable XML-based grammar into Java types. The chapter has clients against real-world services. For instance, there are two sample clients against Amazon's E-Commerce service as well as clients against the Twitter and Chicago Transit Authority RESTful services.

The chapter pays special attention to the growing importance of JavaScript clients against RESTful services, in particular JavaScript clients embedded in HTML documents. The JavaScript clients are written in the widely used jQuery dialect, and these clients highlight ways in which JSON payloads can be treated as native JavaScript objects. This chapter also illustrates how web services can be composed or orchestrated, that is, built out of other web services.

*Chapters 4 and 5*

These chapters turn from REST-style to SOAP-based web services, in particular to the JAX-WS API and its `@WebService` annotation. Chapter 4 focuses on the application level in SOAP-based services, a level at which SOAP, an XML dialect, remains transparent. Chapter 5 studies the handler level at which the entire SOAP message or the payload in the SOAP body are exposed for inspection and manipulation. This chapter also looks at the transport level, which provides access to HTTP(S) transport in particular. The handler level and the transport level are especially important for security, the topic of Chapter 6.

In terms of popularity, SOAP-based services have lost ground in recent years to REST-style ones; indeed, REST-style services can be seen as a reaction against the creeping complexity of SOAP-based frameworks and services. Yet if SOAP-based services are delivered over HTTP(S), then such services can be seen as a programmer-friendly variant of REST-style services. The programmer-friendliness comes from the fact that SOAP hides the XML payloads, allowing programmers on either the service side or the client side to deal with familiar native data types.

SOAP effectively and fully automates the transformation between native language types and XML types: there is no reason, at the application level, ever to create manually or to parse an XML document. The basic profile of SOAP remains uncomplicated, and this profile promotes interoperability through its powerful, high-level API. Furthermore, dynamically generated service contracts—the WSDL documents—are ubiquitous in the SOAP world. Major SOAP frameworks such as Java and DotNet furnish utilities (in Java, *wsimport*) that can generate client-support code from the document. Although WSDLs could be used in the RESTful world, they typically are not; nothing in the RESTful world quite matches the ease of writing a client against a SOAP-based service. In short, SOAP-based services still deserve serious consideration.

Chapters 4 and 5 also include clients against real-world services such as the Amazon's E-Commerce service, and the chapters explore both synchronous and asynchronous clients. SOAP-based web services, like their REST-style cousins, usually work with text payloads—XML or JSON documents. Yet SOAP messages can include arbitrarily many binary attachments, which Chapter 5 shows with code examples. For the most part, the examples in Chapters 4 and 5 use the Metro implementation of JAX-WS. However, there is also an example of an Axis2 service and an Axis2 client. Axis2 remains a popular, alternative implementation of JAX-WS.

*Chapter 6*

This chapter covers security, a core issue that cuts across SOAP and REST. The chapter opens with a study of wire-level security and services that a transport protocol such as HTTPS offers: peer authentication, message confidentiality, and message integrity. Underlying technologies like message digest, *message encryption and decryption, digital certificate, certificate authority*, and cipher suite are clarified in due course. The concepts are fleshed out in a series of examples, starting with a simple Java HTTPS client against the Google home site. Another example builds a very lightweight HTTPS server and an HTTPS client against a RESTful service published with this server. Wire-level security is, for services delivered over HTTP, required infrastructure for the next security level, commonly known as users/roles security. The relevant concepts are user authentication (that is, establishing a user's true identity) and role authorization (that is, fine-tuning the access permissions for an authenticated user).

Managing users/roles security at the service level is tricky; for one thing, this approach does not scale well. The recommended approach is container-managed security: the user authentication and role authorization are handed off from the web service to the (servlet) container. The configuration is relatively easy and the responsibility then shifts from the web service to the publisher such as Tomcat or Jetty. Indeed, a chief benefit of using a production-grade web server is that it can handle both wire-level security (typically in the form of HTTPS) and users/roles security.

For users/roles security, client access to the transport level is critical because an identity such as username and a credential such as a password typically are expected, on the service side, to be inside the HTTP request header. Various ways of injecting header blocks in an HTTP request are thus covered with examples. Wire-level and users/roles security are equally pertinent in REST-style and SOAP-based services. By contrast, WS-Security is a relevant only in SOAP-based services and represents an effort to provide end-to-end security at the SOAP level rather than at the transport (that is, HTTPS) or container (that is, Tomcat or Jetty) level. The WS-* initiatives, which promote the goals of transport-neutral and container-neutral messaging, are what make SOAP complicated. The chapter ends with a WS-Security example, which provides a first look at SOAP beyond the basic profile.

*Chapter 7*

The current chapter considers the trade-offs in deploying web services with a JAS rather than with a standalone web server such as Tomcat or Jetty. Various JASes are available: IBM WebSphere, Oracle WebLogic, Red Hat JBoss, Apache Geronimo, GlassFish, and Apache TomEE. This chapter begins with an overview of the components and resources that are bundled into a JAS. Among these are a web container, an EJB container, a message-oriented middleware provider, a naming service, a security service, and usually a database management system. A web service, REST-style or SOAP-based, that can be published with a standalone web server such as Tomcat can be published, essentially as is, with a JAS. Such services are described as servlet-based because the service itself either executes as an `HttpServ` `let` instance or relies upon such an instance (e.g., the `WSServlet` that comes with Metro) as an intermediary between the client and web service. A JAS offers, as an alternative, an EJB-based service, which could be REST-style or SOAP-based.

Of particular interest is that a `@Stateless` Session EJB becomes a SOAP-based web service if annotated as a `@WebService`. The EJB's `public` methods become service operations if annotated with `@WebMethod`. An EJB-based service, unlike a servlet-based one, is thread-safe because the EJB container bestows thread safety on the components therein. This chapter also covers some miscellaneous topics such as the interaction of a GlassFish-hosted website and a Tomcat-hosted web service; the chapter revisits the JAX-WS client-side API with a sample client against a Restlet service. The main example is a SOAP-based service that uses JPA to persist data in a backend database. GlassFish and TomEE are contrasted as two modern JASes.

# Back to the Question at Hand

In summary, the book explores Java-based web services with code examples that cover a range of APIs and implementations. The code examples themselves are meant to highlight the pluses and minuses. Nonetheless, this code-driven exploration invites an obvious question: Where is the best place to be with respect to Java web services? Which API is superior to the rest? Which implementation should be preferred over the others? These questions, natural as they are, overlook a principal reason for using Java in the first place. To be sure, the Java language and the JVM runtime are major players in the world of software development and deployment, and the runtime is best-in-breed among production-grade virtual machines. From the start, however, Java has been renowned for its options. There is no single IDE for Java or even a single library for, say, parsing XML, making network connections, or implementing users/roles security. There is now growing variety among the languages that compile to JVM byte-codes and are able to reference the huge number of runtime libraries, standard and third party, available in the JVM. There is even choice about which Java runtime to use.

A sensible principle in software development is to pick the least complicated toolset that is up to the task at hand. The toolkit for Java web services is rich in tools. It makes no sense to declare a winner among, for example, the `HttpServlet`, JAX-RS/Restlet, and `@WebServiceProvider` APIs for REST-style services. These APIs differ and in this difference are to be found choices for addressing specific programming and deployment challenges. For SOAP-based services, even the JAX-WS API has at least two excellent implementations, Metro and Axis2; Axis2 adds features to JAX-WS for those who require such extensions. For publishing web services, the choices are likewise varied, from development and testing environments through staging and up to production-level publishing. Tomcat and Jetty are excellent standalone web servers that include first-rate servlet containers. It is hard to make a bad choice here. The next step up, in complexity but also in features, is where the Java Application Servers are. Even here there are choices. WebSphere and Oracle WebLogic have been in the game for a long time, and their for-free counterparts such as Geronimo, GlassFish, JBoss, and TomEE are likewise fine pieces of software. Over the past decade, the Java EE API has become simpler and, therefore, more attractive. JPA is an API that deserves a special pat on the back. At the implementation level, the thread safety that comes with an EJB container is enticing.

Where is the best place to be in Java web services? The answer depends on the challenges in place and resources at hand. Java comes with first-rate options for programming and publishing web services, REST-style and SOAP-based. This means that the question has more than one good answer. Let the task at hand and the resources in place decide the matter.

# Index

## Symbols

@Entity, 293, 294, 296, 298, 312–315
@GET operations, 72
@Stateless, 291, 294, 299, 312–319
@WebService, 145, 270, 277, 317
@WebServiceProviders
    basics of, 37
    in mixed API example, 302–307
    refinement for SOAP-based services, 145
    RESTful service as, 85–94

## A

access key id (accessId), 101, 104, 106
access rights, 232
ActiveX controls, 10
Adages class, 54, 59
adages web service, 56
addPrediction method, 44
Ajax polling, 140
Amazon E-Commerce site
    choosing a client for, 122
    clients against, 101–109, 119–123, 173–182
    multiple operations in, 123
    query string formatting, 101
    request message restrictions, 194
    search-and-shop automation, 5
    SOAP fault messages, 186
    website vs. web service, 105

Ant scripts, 24, 31, 56
Apache Axis2, 145, 227
Apache Geronimo, 291
Apache Software Foundation, 14
Apache TomEE, 291
asymmetric encryption/decryption, 234
asynchronous clients, 179
authentication/authorization
    basics of, 232
    constraints on, 262
    one-sided, 237
    user authentication methods, 262
AwsHandlerResolver class, 189
AwsSoapHandler class, 189, 192
Axis 2, 145, 227

## B

bare parameter style, 175
base64 encoding, 218
BASIC type authentication, 262, 273
binary data, 218–224
    approaches to dealing with, 218
    attachment options, 218
    base64 encoding of, 218
    MTOM (Message Transmission Optimization Mechanism) for, 219
    transmission as attachments, 218

*We'd like to hear your suggestions for improving our indexes. Send email to index@oreilly.com.*

# C

C# clients, 156
c2f operation, 171, 270
cacerts truststore, 242
centigrade conversion, 171
certificate authorities (CA), 237
cipher bits, 235
cipher suites, 239, 241
ciphertext, 235
CLIENT-CERT type authentication, 263
ClientHandlerResolver class, 204
ClientHashHandler class, 204
code vs. contract first, 167
confidentiality, 234
container-managed security
 @WebService under HTTPS, 270
 client-side users/roles security, 265
 digested passwords, 273
 testing with curl utility, 268
 user/roles security, 260
 web.xml service with Tomcat, 263
controllers, 293
conversion, automation of, 114
CORBA (Common Object Request Broker Architecture), 9
create, 307
CRUD (Create, Read, Update, Delete), 16, 40, 44, 74, 96
cryptographic algorithms, 239
cryptographic nonce, 283
CTA (Chicago Transit Authority) bus-tracking service, 123–126
curl utility, 33, 52, 83, 268

# D

data bloat, 218, 221
data sources, web services as, 6
data storage, 74, 296
data types, binding of, 166
DataSourceRealm, 264
DCE (Distributed Computing Environment), 9
deleteOne, 307
dependency injection, 225
deserializing/serializing, 114
DIGEST type authentication, 263, 273
digital certificates, 236, 242, 244
digital signatures, 232

# E

e-commerce web services (see Amazon E-Commerce site)
ECDHE (Elliptic Curve Diffie-Hellman Key Exchange), 241
echo function, 10
Echo service, 224, 277
EchoClient example, 224
EchoClientWSS, 289
EJB (Enterprise Java Bean) web containers, 293, 323
encoding, 165
encryption/decryption, 234
end-to-end security, 277
Entity EJBs (Enterprise Java Bean), 9
error messages, SOAP faults, 186

# F

Fahrenheit conversion, 171
federated security, 276
Fielding, Roy, 14
fingerprints, 241
FORM type authentication, 262
405 status code, 51
function calls, 8

# G

Geronimo, 291
GET requests, 16, 19, 21
getAll, 317

DIME (Direct Internet Message Encapsulation), 218
distributed computing
 benefits of, 13
 definition of, 9
distributed software systems, 2, 7
DLL (Dynamic Link Library), 10
DOA (Distributed Object Architecture)
 challenges in, 11
 evolution of, 9
document parsing, 95, 100–101
documents, wrapped vs. unwrapped, 168
doDelete method, 90
doGet method, 48, 90, 99
doPost, 50
DotNet, 126

MTOM (Message Transmission Optimization Mechanism), 218
multithreading, 51
mutual authentication, 234
mutual challenge, 234
MVC (model-view-controller) pattern, 293

# N

naming/lookup service, 295
nextN vs. next1, 159
nodes, in messaging architecture, 185
notifications, 2
nouns, 17

# O

one-sided authentication, 237
one-way patterns, 2
opaque nouns, 17
open infrastructure, 4
Oracle WebLogic, 292

# P

parameter styles, 174
parseXml function, 99
parsing, 95
password authentication, 263, 273
peer authentication, 234
Perl clients
    against Java RandService, 157
    against Java RESTful web service, 96
    binary data and, 220
    CRUD calls in, 96
    scalar variables in, 99
persistent data stores, 74
plain bits, 234
platform transparency, 4, 6
POJO classes, 54, 58, 312
polling, 140
POST requests, 16, 19, 100
pre-master secrets, 238
Prediction class, 41
predictions web service example
    Ant script in, 31
    as stateless Session EJB, 317
    backend prediction code, 26
    client against, 33
    getPredictions method, 28

HTTPS client against, 257
HttpServlet implementation, 40–53
JSP script in, 25
organization of, 24
porting to TomEE, 322
SOAP backend support classes, 199
SOAP credential injection, 202–208
SOAP service-side handler, 212
SOAP signature verification in, 211
SOAP-based handlers/faults in, 194–198, 211
SOAP-based implementation of, 302
Tomcat web server, 30
WADL document for, 127
XML response from, 25
PredictionsClient, 202
PredictionServlet, 44
private keys, 235
programmatic verification, 242
provider/consumer pair, 8
public key encryption/decryption, 235, 238, 241
PUT requests, 100

# Q

query string formatting, 101

# R

Rails routing style, 21
RandService
    asynchronous clients against, 179
    clients against, 153–160
    in SOAP-based web services, 146
    in two files, 151
    WSDL for, 161
RC4_128 stream cipher algorithm, 241
read requests, 15
relational database management systems (RDMS)
    web containers and, 296
    web services integration, 6
request/response pattern, 2, 10, 18–20, 185
RequestHelper class, 101, 106
resource, concept of, 14, 54
response-document parsing, 101
REST (REpresentational State Transfer), 14
RESTful web service clients
    against Amazon E-Commerce site, 101–109, 119–123
    avoiding document parsing, 95

## About the Author

**Martin Kalin** has a PhD from Northwestern University and is a professor in the College of Computing and Digital Media at DePaul University. He has cowritten a series of books on C and C++ and written a book on Java for programmers. He enjoys commercial programming and has codeveloped large distributed systems in process scheduling and product configuration.

## Colophon

The animal on the cover of *Java Web Services: Up and Running*, Second Edition, is a great cormorant (*Phalacrocorax carbo*). This bird is a member of the Phalacrocoracidae family, which consists of about 40 species of cormorants and shags—large seabirds with hooked bills, colored throats, and stiff tail feathers. The name "cormorant" is derived from the Latin *corvus marinus*, or sea raven, because of its black plumage.

An adult cormorant is about 30 inches long and has a wingspan of 60 inches. It has a long neck, a yellow throat, and a white chin patch. The cormorant has a distinctive way of spreading its wings as it perches, which many naturalists believe is a way of drying its feathers, although this explanation is disputed. The cormorant lives mainly near Atlantic waters, on western European and eastern North American coasts, and particularly in the Canadian maritime provinces. It breeds on cliffs or in trees, building nests out of twigs and seaweed.

The cormorant is an excellent fisher, able to dive to great depths. In China and Japan, other species of cormorants are trained to fish using a centuries-old method, in which they tie cords around the throats of the birds—to prevent them from swallowing—and send them out from boats. The cormorants then catch fish in their mouths, return to the boats, and the fishermen retrieve their catch. Although once a successful industry, today cormorant fishing is primarily used for tourism.

The cover image is from Cassell's *Popular Natural History, Vol. III: Birds*. The cover font is Adobe ITC Garamond. The text font is Adobe Minion Pro; the heading font is Adobe Myriad Condensed; and the code font is Dalton Maag's Ubuntu Mono.

# Have it your way.

# Get even more for your money.

**Join the O'Reilly Community, and register the O'Reilly books you own. It's free, and you'll get:**

- $4.99 ebook upgrade offer
- 40% upgrade offer on O'Reilly print books
- Membership discounts on books and events
- Free lifetime updates to ebooks and videos
- Multiple ebook formats, DRM FREE
- Participation in the O'Reilly community
- Newsletters
- Account management
- 100% Satisfaction Guarantee

### Signing up is easy:

1. **Go to: oreilly.com/go/register**
2. **Create an O'Reilly login.**
3. **Provide your address.**
4. **Register your books.**

Note: English-language books only

**To order books online:**
oreilly.com/store

**For questions about products or an order:**
orders@oreilly.com

**To sign up to get topic-specific email announcements and/or news about upcoming books, conferences, special offers, and new technologies:**
elists@oreilly.com

**For technical questions about book content:**
booktech@oreilly.com

**To submit new book proposals to our editors:**
proposals@oreilly.com

**O'Reilly books are available in multiple DRM-free ebook formats. For more information:**
oreilly.com/ebooks

O'REILLY®

Spreading the knowledge of innovators                    oreilly.com

Lightning Source UK Ltd.
Milton Keynes UK
UKOW07f1211290316

271092UK00015B/114/P